FORCE
AND
STATECRAFT

Diplomatic Challenges of Our Time

FIFTH EDITION

Paul Gordon Lauren
University of Montana

Gordon A. Craig
Stanford University

Alexander L. George
Stanford University

New York   Oxford
OXFORD UNIVERSITY PRESS

3-19-14
ww
$57.95

To Gordon and Alex
teachers, colleagues, collaborators, friends, and exemplars

Oxford University Press is a department of the University of Oxford.
It furthers the University's objective of excellence in research,
scholarship, and education by publishing worldwide.

Oxford   New York
Auckland   Cape Town   Dar es Salaam   Hong Kong   Karachi
Kuala Lumpur   Madrid   Melbourne   Mexico City   Nairobi
New Delhi   Shanghai   Taipei   Toronto

With offices in
Argentina   Austria   Brazil   Chile   Czech Republic   France   Greece
Guatemala   Hungary   Italy   Japan   Poland   Portugal   Singapore
South Korea   Switzerland   Thailand   Turkey   Ukraine   Vietnam

For titles covered by Section 112 of the US Higher Education Opportunity
Act, please visit www.oup.com/us/he for the latest information about
pricing and alternate formats.

Published by Oxford University Press
198 Madison Avenue, New York, NY 10016
www.oup.com

Oxford is a registered trademark of Oxford University Press.

Library of Congress Cataloging-in-Publication Data

Lauren, Paul Gordon.
Force and statecraft : diplomatic challenges of our time / Paul Gordon Lauren
University of Montana, Gordon A. Craig, Stanford University (Emeritus),
Alexander L. George, Stanford University (Emeritus).—Fifth edition.
pages cm
Includes index.
ISBN 978-0-19-539546-4
1. World politics—19th century.   2. World politics—20th century.
3. World politics—21st century.   4. Diplomacy.   I. Craig, Gordon Alexander,
1913–   II. George, Alexander L.   III. Title.
D363.L34 2013
909.81—dc23
2013003849

Printing number: 9 8 7 6 5 4 3 2 1

Printed in the United States of America
on acid-free paper

CONTENTS

PART TWO: HISTORY, THEORY, AND PRACTICE

PART THREE: RESTRAINTS AND REFLECTIONS

PREFACE

TO THE

FIFTH EDITION

This book grew out of the authors' long-standing concern over international peace and security and their conviction that it would be extremely valuable to examine the kinds of challenges involving force and statecraft that confront policy makers from the combined perspectives of history and strategy. We have enjoyed the great pleasure and the privilege of working together as valued colleagues, collaborators, and friends for nearly forty years in this interdisciplinary endeavor. The process began when the three of us first developed a course with these objectives in mind at Stanford University, selecting for focused comparison a variety of historical cases from the past in order to help us understand the diplomatic challenges of our own time. The success of that original course and many others subsequently modeled after it, both in the United States and abroad, the enthusiastic responses of readers to previous editions of the book, and the momentous developments in global politics and war in recent years all encouraged the writing of this thoroughly revised and updated edition.

New to This Edition

Significant changes to the fifth edition include:

- Up-to-date discussion and analysis of recent global developments and American foreign policy;
- More recent and revealing cases with their up-to-date challenges;
- New illustrations, improved maps, and a very helpful comprehensive index;
- New discussion of the powerful impact of technology on the "digital revolution," weapons and the revolution in military affairs (RMA), eDiplomacy and the "information revolution," command and control, surveillance and reconnaissance, and social networking sites;
- More analysis of the meaning of security, the "invisibility of security," "hard" and "soft" power, human rights, and international law;
- New scholarship and interpretation that has appeared, as well as official documentary evidence released by declassification.

Part One focuses on the historical context of force and statecraft. It ranges all the way from a discussion of the early techniques, instruments, and ideas of diplomacy to the profoundly dangerous changes brought about by contemporary terrorism, violent extremism, and weapons of mass destruction (WMD). Chapters cover the emergence of the Great Powers, the classical system of diplomacy and its balance of power, the upheavals of the diplomatic revolution, the creation of the United Nations and its search for collective security, and the rise and then demise of the Cold War. The last chapter in this section adds significant new material on several critical current and ongoing developments: globalization, the impact of modern technology, the "global war on terror" and the wars in Afghanistan and Iraq, nuclear proliferation, cyber security, and the emergence of "Responsibility to Protect" (R2P). Assessments also are made of the recent global financial crisis, the diplomacy of the G-20, the foreign policies of the Obama administration, the appearance of WikiLeaks, the ongoing ramifications of the "Arab Spring," the unprecedented power of the United States, and the persistent rise of China.

Part Two on History, Theory, and Practice begins with a pivotal chapter on the intriguing subject of "Lessons of History and Knowledge for Statecraft" and then proceeds to systematically examine four particularly critical subjects by combining theory with specific historical cases. Particular care has been taken in this edition to include a number of revealing new cases, including the Mumbai Crisis resulting from a major terrorist attack against India in 2008 and the current news-breaking threats of weapons of mass destruction in North Korea and Iranian nuclear enrichment. These cases range from Europe and the United States to the Middle East and Asia in order to demonstrate the truly global dimensions of the diplomatic challenges of our time.

Part Three opens with a revised and expanded chapter entitled "Ethics and Other Restraints on Force and Statecraft." It explores practical, structural, and political restraints upon policy makers and then moves into debates over the nature of ethics and international politics, paying particular attention to the difficult matter of observing ethical restraints on the use of force in warfare from conventional battlefields to current insurgencies and terrorism. Significant new material is added to this edition on the concept of legitimacy, international law, the just war tradition (JWT), and the pivotal subject of human rights and its relationship to international peace and security. A completely rewritten and updated Conclusion brings together the major themes of the book and offers a number of reflections about the use of "hard" and "soft" power, the appropriate relationship between ends and means, the Nuclear Security Project, the role of values and self-imposed restraints, and insights from history, theory, and policy for the challenges ahead.

Every chapter concludes with a section called "Suggestions for Further Exploration" to assist readers in finding references to citations within the text, bibliographical entries ranging from the most updated scholarship on the topic at hand as well as classical works that have stood the test of time, and valuable Web sites. Each of the analytical chapters now provides suggestions of other historical cases for those who wish to explore specific topics in more detail. In addition, maps are included in this edition to help readers understand the impact of geographical location, and illustrations are provided to assist in appreciating the human element of force and statecraft.

Many thoughtful comments and suggestions have been made over the years from readers, professional colleagues, and experts from diplomatic, military, political, business, and intelligence communities around the world who have helped to improve each successive edition of this book. Among others, these include Dan Caldwell, and reviewers Joseph Becelia, George Mason University; David Edelstein, Georgetown University; Erik Goldstein, Boston University; Francine McKenzie, University of Western Ontario; Nicholas J. Steneck, Ohio State University; Steven Weber, University of California, Berkeley. We are grateful for them all.

May this book continue to stimulate serious thought, discussion, and reflection about how force and statecraft are used in the world and how peace and security might be found.

PAUL GORDON LAUREN

INTRODUCTION

I t is likely that there is no issue on earth more elemental than that of survival. From the beginning of time to the present, individuals and societies have struggled with how they and their descendants might find peace and security in a world where war, violence, and insecurity are always possible or present. Primitive petroglyph drawings in caves, ancient Sanskrit texts and Chinese strategist Sun Tzu's *Art of War*, accounts in the Torah and Qu'ran, and traditional literary epics from highly diverse cultures around the world all record early and frequent recourse to threats and the use of armed force when people are unable or unwilling to resolve their disputes by peaceful means. The famous Greek historian Thucydides, writing in his *History of the Peloponnesian War* 400 years before the birth of Jesus, tells us how force was threatened by the powerful Athenians to intimidate the much weaker Melians. Failure to comply with their demands, they declared, would result in devastation:

> You, by giving in, would save yourselves from disaster...[for] your actual resources are too scanty to give you a chance of survival against the forces that are opposed to you at this moment. You will therefore be showing an extraordinary lack of common sense if...you still fail to reach a conclusion wiser than anything you have mentioned so far....Think it over again...and let this be a point that constantly recurs to your minds—that you are discussing the fate of your country, that you have only one country, and its future for good or ill depends upon this one single decision which you are going to make.

The Athenians brutally summarized their approach with the often-quoted statement that "the strong do what they have the power to do and the weak accept what they have to accept." Similar expressions have been heard throughout history, as well as today, from those wanting to take full advantage of their unrivaled power, weapons of mass destruction, sheer numbers of troops, highly sophisticated military technology, or willingness to kill innocent civilians in terrorist acts—all to gain advantage over their adversaries. The persistence of war and violence in our own time bears all too ample and painful evidence that the dangers continue.

When confronted with this human experience, for better or for worse, most leaders responsible for the survival of their people have concluded that in a world with an absence of any central governing authority and ever possible anarchy, there are times when armed force is an absolute necessity. They have not eagerly embraced or enthusiastically endorsed force—but have reluctantly acknowledged its existence and recognized its impact. If peaceful means and rational persuasion do not always succeed in resolving conflicts and competition, and if adversaries exist who engage in aggression and who seem to understand only the language of force, they have reasoned, then sheer prudence requires that force be one of the essential instruments of statecraft.

Even those who have no aggressive designs at all and genuinely desire peace have acknowledged this. Drawing on his desire to learn lessons from history, the Chinese sage Confucius observed centuries ago:

> The superior man, when resting in safety, does not forget that danger may come. When in a state of security, he does not forget the possibility of ruin. When all is orderly, he does not forget that disorder may come. Thus, his person is not endangered; his states and all his clans are preserved.

Many, many others have reached the same conclusion. Watching the violence around him, the ancient Roman writer Vegetius with reluctance observed, *Si vis pacem, para bellum*: "If you want peace, prepare for war." In the wake of the devastating revolutionary and Napoleonic wars of the late eighteenth and early nineteenth centuries, peacemakers recognized the necessity of creating a balance of power to deter any new aggressor. Following the destruction of the First World War, President Woodrow Wilson reluctantly concluded, "In the last analysis the peace of society is obtained by force.... If you say 'We shall not have any war,' you have to have the force to make that 'shall' bite." In the aftermath of the even more ruinous Second World War, President Franklin Roosevelt envisioned creating the United Nations and similarly concluded: "The problem of security rests with the powers who have the military force to uphold it."

But herein lies the fundamental dilemma for force and statecraft. Although armed force may be necessary in certain circumstances, it also can be extraordinarily dangerous. It may be used to maintain peace and security, defend vital interests, protect innocents from egregious human rights abuses and atrocities, provide collective security, and enforce international law. Yet, at the same time, it can be used for aggression, territorial conquest, genocide, to inflict pain against innocent civilians, subjugation, and intimidation. Armed force is a blunt and dangerous instrument that is not always effective, cannot always be controlled, and sometimes even triggers unwanted wars that might otherwise have been avoided. Indeed, its very existence threatens others, increases the risk of escalation in crises, and carries a seductive appeal to those who believe that military might will enable them to act as they wish and get what they want.

The enormous tension between the necessities of armed force and the dangers of armed force thus long has challenged those deeply concerned about survival. Indeed, it has posed some of the most central and difficult challenges in the entire theory and the practice of statecraft: If, when, how, and/or under what conditions can force be used legitimately and most effectively as an instrument to achieve peace and security?

Countless numbers of people have struggled with this problem throughout history. They understandably have feared the wanton chaos, destruction, pain, and taking of human lives made possible by the use of raw armed force.

But, instead of passively resigning themselves to brutalist notions of a world characterized as no more than inevitable, perpetual, and unbridled anarchy, they actively have searched for ways in which they might prevent or tame war and violent conflict. Some have attempted to do this by relying on military doctrines or strategies designed to match the level of violence to political objectives and thus avoid unnecessary devastation or death. Some have used other forms of power such as economic strength, industrial capacity, technological sophistication, culture, or political ideas to moderate the behavior of others. Some have placed their hopes on normative values of self-imposed ethical restraints or religious codes teaching compassion and forbidding the resort to war. Others have turned to legal agreements or negotiated treaties to restrict or abolish the use of certain kinds of weapons or to limit the use of military force.

Still others have attempted to combine these various elements and approaches in such a way that they might use force and statecraft together as a means of regulating and controlling the behavior of highly competitive states that are capable of launching wars and causing great harm to others. They have turned to diplomacy and the creation of international systems with an accepted body of normative rules and values, along with sufficient force in a balance of power to keep rivalries within certain bounds and to make wars unprofitable or dangerous to aggressors. The Portuguese sculptor Maximiano Alves captures some sense of this in his evocative and perceptive allegorical statue entitled *Diplomacy* that appears on the cover of this book. The central figure conveys a deep sense of purpose and a realization of the seriousness of the decisions confronting her. She holds an olive branch in her right hand. It is suspended above several instruments of statecraft: collections of rules and understandings, books of ethical norms, legal documents, peace treaties, and agreements. Should these tools prove to be insufficient, her left hand grips another instrument of statecraft to use if necessary: the sword of armed force.

As long historical experience reveals, considerable skills are necessary to wisely use and wield the tools in each of these hands. It is not at all easy to use diplomacy to resolve disputes or to establish some order out of chaos and anarchy. Indeed, as we shall see, it took centuries of war and competition, the threat of domination by a single power, and the long development of a rational theory of statecraft before the major states could agree to even attempt to form some kind of international system capable of maintaining peace and security. They did so only after they all had reached one critical conclusion: the reality that in a world of incessant rivalry their own resources alone were woefully insufficient to protect them, and thus that their very survival depended on creating some measure of shared interests and partnership with others.

They came to discover, as did those who would follow them, that the success of any collective efforts to create and maintain a viable international system by means of diplomacy depends on meeting several requirements. In the first instance, there must be agreement among the principal states with the most power concerning shared goals and objectives that they are seeking to achieve. To do this, the actors must be able to recognize that they share common interests as well as issues of conflict, and thus at the same time are both partners as well as rivals within the system. Second, there must be a structure appropriate to the number of states interacting with each other, the geographical boundaries or scope of the system, the relative distribution of power or capabilities among the actors, and the stratification and status hierarchy among them. Third, there must be commonly accepted normative values and procedures in the form of norms, methods, rules, practices, institutions, and expectations for the achievement of the aims and objectives of the system as a whole. These are designed to provide restraints that help members of the system to deal with the challenges that they share in common and must include shared conceptions about when and how armed force can be legitimately threatened or used. They are purposefully created by states because it is in their mutual interests to do so.

Finally, the effectiveness of any international system depends on its ability to adapt and adjust to new developments and to internal changes within its membership that affect its performance and its ability to maintain itself. Throughout most of history, and certainly at the time of the classical system of diplomacy, the rate of these changes was relatively slow. During our own modern period, however, the speed and extent of transformation has been rapid, profound, and persistent in military technology, transportation and Internet communication, a globalized market economy, the growing influence of non-state actors, and the evolution of norms governing international human rights and international criminal law, to say nothing of those mutations in the internal political structure of states resulting from the rise of public opinion, the emergence of organized interest groups, and the increasing scope and complexity of governmental organization itself. It has also been an age of intense nationalism, enhanced by the breakup of the old colonial empires and the multiplication of new sovereign states, and of political and religious ideological conflict on a global scale. All of these forces, singly and in combination, have had an impact on international politics that results in nothing short of a diplomatic revolution. This has made it increasingly difficult to revive and maintain old structures or to devise new ones. Indeed, adapting to accelerated change has become one of the major challenges of modern statecraft, testing the ingenuity and the fortitude of those charged with the responsibility for devising means of controlling international violence and maintaining survival.

To explore the meaning and ramifications of these issues, we begin in Part One by establishing a broad historical context, focusing on the richness of history, the ways that leaders have wrestled with challenges before them, the range of attempts through time to create international systems, and the dynamics of change and continuity from the past to the present. A transition from history to policy is then provided by Part Two, by examining how "lessons of history" can be learned for statecraft and how some of these are manifest in four particularly important and challenging subjects: negotiation, deterrence, coercive diplomacy, and crisis management. This is done through the methodology of a structured, focused comparison delineating theoretical principles, followed by a description and analysis of three specific historical cases. These are presented chronologically, with the first drawn from the classical system of the nineteenth century, the second from the twentieth century, and the last from recent international events. Particular effort is made to analyze why certain strategies succeeded and why others failed.

Part Three addresses restraints and reflections on force and statecraft. At a time when increasing numbers of citizens have deep and conscientious concerns about the tendencies, methods, and dangers of contemporary global politics, we believe that it is only appropriate to include a chapter on the difficult and thought-provoking problem of the role of self-restraint and ethical norms in international affairs, especially during times of war. This leads us, finally and naturally, to several concluding reflections about the relationship of the past to the present, of theory to practice, and the continuing diplomatic challenges of force and statecraft in our time.

PART ONE

FROM THE PAST
TO THE PRESENT

— 1 —

The Emergence of Diplomacy and the Great Powers

The origins of diplomacy go back to the beginnings of recorded history itself. When organized groups of men and women came into contact with others different from themselves, they realized their desperate need to develop techniques that might facilitate interaction beyond merely resorting to violence and war. Their survival depended on it. No negotiations could possibly take place in creating an alliance, distributing territory, or establishing the terms of a truce, for example, unless messengers from both sides received certain protections that enabled them to communicate and reach agreements. Consequently, various oral traditions, inscriptions on stone monuments, images on clay tablets, the classic epics of poetry and literature, and even religious texts frequently depict or describe the use of emissaries to represent and to convey messages from one ruler to another. This explains why the Greek writer Homer discussed the value of heralds in the *Iliad*, the Hindu leader Kautilya devoted an entire chapter in his classic treatise on statecraft entitled *The Arthashastra* to the duties of envoys, and the Christian apostle Paul in his second letter to the Corinthians described himself as an ambassador. City-states, empires, kingdoms, tribes, clans, and dynastic states, among others, each in its own way and often by experimental trial and error over centuries, developed various practices and methods to advance their interests by facilitating the conduct of relations among themselves and with others. These emerged by necessity wherever political entities found themselves forced to interact with others, beginning where civilizations first arose in the ancient Near East, Asia, and the Indian subcontinent. Through time, contributions increasingly came from the West, thereby creating what historian M. S. Anderson describes as "the system of regulated and organized contacts between states which Europe had evolved...and which, with all its faults, was one of her more important gifts to the world."

The Early Practices, Techniques, and Ideas of Diplomacy

A number of the practices and techniques of diplomacy emerged during the height of Greek civilization when the emergence of several city-states increased the level of competition among them and thereby raised issues of force and statecraft to the fore. As Thucydides reveals so brilliantly in his *Peloponnesian War*, this required that they carefully consider the advantages and disadvantages of remaining isolated or of working in partnership with others. When the representatives of Corcyra approached Athens, he records, they spoke candidly:

> We used to think that our neutrality was a wise thing, since it prevented us being dragged into danger by other people's policy; now we see it clearly as a lack of foresight and as a source of weakness....We recognize that, if we have nothing but our own resources, it is impossible for us to survive, and we can imagine what lies in store for us if they overpower us. We are therefore forced to ask for assistance, both from you and from everyone else; and it should not be held against us that now we have faced the facts and are reversing our old policy of keeping ourselves to ourselves.

In this setting, Thucydides tells us, there were those who argued that "the strong do what they have the power to do and the weak accept what they have to accept." But there were many others who understood that this approach, as discussed in our introduction, represented no more than a recipe for international anarchy that would produce only more tumult and warfare. They sought instead to develop ways that would reduce the level of friction, facilitate their interactions, and develop restraints that might keep their competition within certain bounds.

For this reason, the Greeks began to create some of the diplomatic practices still used today. Indeed, their emphasis upon communication is revealed in the fact that diplomacy itself takes its name from the Greek word for an official folded letter, *diploma*. From the sixth century B.C. onward, they developed the practice of selecting ambassadors, or those who would represent them, from among their finest public speakers and most plausible forensic advocates to plead eloquently the cause of their city-state before the assemblies of foreign leagues or other city-states. This was extremely important, for as the statesman and orator Demosthenes observed, "Ambassadors have no battleships at their disposal, or heavy infantry, or fortresses; their only weapons are words and opportunities." Over time these ambassadors received special privileges and diplomatic immunity in order that they might be able to fulfill their missions. In addition, the Greeks established procedures for the exchange of ambassadors, diplomatic credentials, the functions of consuls, the status of neutrality, diplomatic conferences, the ratification of treaties, the right of asylum, extradition, the responsibilities of partners in alliances or leagues, and techniques of arbitration. Thucydides provides an example:

> When the Corcyreans heard of these preparations they sent an embassy to Corinth, accomplished by some envoys from Sparta and Sicyon to support them. There they demanded that Corinth should withdraw her troops and colonists from Epidamnus....They were prepared, however, if Corinth wished to put in a counter claim, to accept arbitration. Cities in the Peloponnese should be chosen by mutual agreement to act as arbitrators, and the colony should go to whichever side the arbitrators awarded it.

These practices helped to establish some of the first rules for the conduct of diplomacy.

Statesmen of Rome, on the other hand, were interested more in empire than in negotiation among equals. Like those of ancient Egypt, China, or other imperial systems, they focused on keeping their vast holdings together through superior organization whenever possible. Their contribution to diplomacy, therefore, can be found in the area of administrative rules, legal contracts, and the early foundations of what would become international law. They extended immunity to visiting ambassadors as well as to their staffs. They established the profession of trained archivists as specialists in diplomatic precedents and procedure and created normative rules and laws dealing with declarations of war, the conclusion of peace, and the handling of hostages. In addition, the Romans gave great attention to the development of legal concepts such as *jus gentium* (the customary law of nations), *jus naturale* (the law common to all mankind), and *pacta sunt servanda*, or the importance of respecting legal obligations and of honoring the sanctity of treaties. As the great statesman and philosopher Marcus Tullius Cicero argued, this law cannot be violated and must be seen as "valid for all nations and all times."

Practical survival continued to require that external relations and statecraft be taken seriously. This became apparent when Constantine the Great became the emperor of Rome and decided in the fourth century to move the capital of his far-flung empire to the strategically located and powerful city of Byzantium (now Istanbul), situated at the crossroads of the major land and sea routes of the time and at the point where Europe and Asia meet. He and his successors in the Eastern Roman Empire and then the Byzantine Empire throughout late antiquity and the medieval era became the first to organize a permanent governmental department to provide specialization and institutional continuity in foreign affairs. They understood that diplomatic communication often required dealing with those who spoke and wrote different languages, and thus they employed a staff of interpreters and translators. Moreover, they made considerable effort to train professional negotiators to serve as their ambassadors, providing them with written instructions for precise missions and expecting them to furnish full reports about foreign governments and the relations of those governments to each other. These tasks demanded more than the qualities of the herald or orator. Instead, they required experience and the trained powers of observation, reporting, and sound judgment.

These various practices, techniques, and ideas developed over several centuries were eventually passed on to the Italian city-states of the Renaissance, which made their own contributions and created the origins of modern diplomacy as we know it. With intense and incessant rivalry among them, as well as vulnerability to external threats, they realized that their survival required unceasing vigilance and acute attention to foreign affairs. To accomplish this, Venetian leaders of the fifteenth century came to understand that they could no longer rely on sending out ambassadors for special missions on an ad hoc basis only after a crisis already had arisen. Constant insecurity and danger required that they establish missions staffed by resident diplomats. Venice therefore developed a sophisticated network of permanent representatives who pursued the interests of the republic by providing accurate information, realistic appraisals of opportunities and risks, and skillful negotiations, all with an unusual freedom from sentimentality and illusion.

This model came to be followed by other city-states on the Italian peninsula of approximately equal power, such as Florence, Milan, Mantua, and Tuscany. Together they established a network of permanent embassies with resident ambassadors, seeking to use diplomacy rather than warfare as the basis of their security, and in the process developed a multipolar system in miniature. Through time, they also began to write early diplomatic manuals describing the characteristics and skills that diplomats should possess and providing clear advice about how diplomats should act. Not surprisingly, this produced differing opinions, as it does in our own time. Some, like Bernard du Rosier, the provost and later archbishop of Toulouse, wrote a treatise based on his religious beliefs in which he argued that the mission of an ambassador must always be peace, that diplomats must labor not only for their particular employer but for the common good, and that they should never be sent to stir up wars or internal dissensions. Others, like Venetian politician and diplomat Ermolao Barbaro, argued in 1490, in sharp contrast, that "the first duty of an ambassador is exactly the same as that of any other servant of government: that is, to do, say, advise, and think whatever may best serve the preservation and aggrandizement of his own state." Regardless of the disagreements over what diplomats actually ought to do, however, all sides understood the importance of accurate information. For this reason, the Italian city-states became the first to systematically preserve their diplomatic archives. They realized that in issues of force and statecraft, facts need to be scrutinized closely and dispassionately before any action can be undertaken. This placed a premium on collecting, registering, and indexing all relevant information and making it readily accessible to policy makers whenever needed.

The necessity of establishing such techniques and norms of diplomacy became all the more evident by the persistence of unremitting competition and nearly continuous warfare. As Philippe de Commynes, a Flemish solider-diplomat of the fifteenth century, argued, there was nothing at all glorious about war and violence. He feared the consequences of unrestrained rivalries and saw clearly that states shared certain common interests and were dependent on each other, whether they liked it or not. This line of thinking became more pronounced by the next century with the writings of the Dominican theologian and law professor Francisco de Vitoria, his Jesuit successor Francisco Suarez, and professor of law Alberico Gentili, who stressed the need to establish commonly held, international legal principles and norms for just war theory focused on justice of war and justice in war.

All these developments contributed to a larger movement that sought to approach challenges of force and statecraft in a systematic and rational manner. Some observers thus began to construct theories about the nature of government and the conduct of policy itself, thereby creating the modern discipline of political science. The most noted of these was Niccolò Machiavelli, a man who had been in the diplomatic service of Florence, but then was forced to watch in horror and humiliation as French invaders completely defeated and overthrew his ruler. He himself was dismissed from office, imprisoned and tortured, and then condemned to exile. It is not surprising that these hard and bitter experiences would be reflected in his *Discourses, Art of War*, and his most famous, or infamous, 1513 treatise entitled *The Prince*. Here he expressed his determination to learn lessons from history, to focus on "how things are in real life," to warn of the dangers of ignorance or weakness, and to acknowledge that "when princes think more of luxury than of arms, they lose their state." This led him directly into a discussion of the relationship between force and statecraft:

> You must know that there are two methods of fighting, one by law, the other by force; the first method is that of men, the second of beasts; but as the first method is often insufficient, one must have recourse to the second. It is therefore necessary for a prince to know well how to use both the beast and the man.

Machiavelli stressed the importance for leaders "to keep good faith and live with integrity" in their relations with others, but when it came to advancing the interests of their state, he brutally concluded, in language that has haunted his work ever since: "the end justifies the means."

Such thinking produced both condemnation by many for its dismissal of Christian ethics and praise among others for its advocacy of power politics. For those who sought to amass greater political power, Machiavelli's writings provided justification for their objectives and their methods. They believed that the small Italian city-states of the past, especially at a time of diminishing influence of the Papacy and its claims of universality under the impact of the Reformation, soon would be irrevocably dwarfed in magnitude and strength by those monarchies capable of forging powerful, secular nation-states. The French political philosopher Jean Bodin encouraged this new development by enunciating the principle of sovereignty in his 1576 book *Les Six livres de la république*. The future belonged to states, he asserted, that possessed sovereignty, which he defiantly described as "power absolute and perpetual," "supreme," and "subject to no law." Indeed, claimed Bodin, such sovereign power provided "the distinguishing mark of a state," giving it the sole authority to decide how it would treat its own people, how it would behave in the world, and how it would use armed force in the world.

War, States, and *Raison d'état* in the Seventeenth Century

When the seventeenth century began, therefore, emerging states in Europe possessed certain customs and practices of diplomacy as well as growing assertions about the prerogatives of their sovereignty. But what would eventually be called the Great Powers still did not exist. In 1600, for instance, Russia was a remote and ineffectual land, separated from the west by the large territory that was called Poland-Lithuania with whose rulers it waged periodic territorial conflicts, as it did with the Ottoman Turks to the south. Prussia, as the Electorate of Brandenburg, lived a purely German existence, like Bavaria or Württemberg, with no wider significance. England, a country of considerable commercial strength, was not accorded much geopolitical importance. As a result of internal anarchy and strife, France seemed destined to play a minor role in European politics. The strongest political center in Europe was the old Holy Roman Empire with its capital in Vienna and its alliance with Spain, which still possessed a vast empire and formidable military power.

Why did this situation not persist? Or, to put it another way, why was the European system transformed so radically that the Holy Roman Empire became an insignificant political force and the continent came in the eighteenth century to be dominated by Britain, France, Austria, Prussia, and Russia? The answer is war. War shaped the formation, the character, and the development of modern states.

From 1618 until 1721, a long series of raging wars changed the rank order of European states by exhausting some and exalting others. Virtually all of the major dynastic rivalries, religious differences, drawing of borders, possession of cities and fortresses, control of trade routes and colonies, and ultimately the destinies of kingdoms and empires were decided by the use of armed force. At the beginning of the century, a European battle might involve as few as 25,000 troops on both sides. Within a few decades, France alone created an army of 400,000. As if bent on supplying evidence for the later nineteenth-century Darwinians, those states that became the Great Powers proved themselves in the grinding struggle of the age to be the fittest—the ones far better organized and more efficient—to meet the demands of protracted competition in warfare. Only they could marshal the resources to destroy another state. Only they could defend themselves from external attack. Only they could negotiate treaties of peace and security.

The process of transformation began with the Thirty Years' War, which stretched from 1618 to 1648. It is sometimes called the last of the religious wars, a description that is justified by the fact that it was motivated originally by the desire of the Catholic House of Habsburg to restore the Protestant parts of the empire and because, in years of fighting, the religious motive gave way to political and material considerations. For the states that initiated this wasting conflict, the war was an unmitigated disaster. The Hapsburgs became so debilitated by it that they lost their former control over the German states, and their empire became a mere adjunct of the Austrian crown lands. Austria, moreover, emerged so weakened by the exertions and losses of the war that after 1648 it barely could protect its eastern possessions and watched in horror when in 1683 the Turkish army threatened to capture Vienna itself. At the same time, its strongest ally, Spain, squandered an infantry once judged to be the best in the world with terrible losses suffered in German territory and the Netherlands, thereby leading to Spain's long and irreversible decline.

In sharp contrast, some states profited from the Thirty Years' War. One of these was the Netherlands, which, under leaders like Maurice of Nassau and

Jan de Witt, won its independence from Spain and became a commercial and financial center of major importance. Sweden, led by the "Lion of the North" Gustavus Adolphus and his use of the combined arms of infantry, cavalry, and artillery, emerged as the strongest power in the Baltic region. And, of particular importance, there was France, which emerged at the end of the war as the most powerful state in all of Europe.

It is no accident that these particular states were so successful, for they represented excellent examples of the process that historians describe as the rise of the modern state as *the* political unit to be admired, feared, and ultimately copied by others. Each of these developed effective armed forces, a well-established diplomatic corps, an able bureaucracy, and a theory to support the state that restrained dynastic exuberance by defining political interest in rational, practical terms. Indeed, the seventeenth century saw the emergence of what came to be called *raison d'état* or *ragione di stato*—the idea that the state was more than its ruler and more than the expression of his or her wishes; that it transcended crown and land, prince and people; that objectives should never be sought in excess of capabilities; that it had its particular set of interests and a particular set of necessities based on them; and that the art of government lay in recognizing those interests and necessities and acting in accordance with them, even if this might violate ethical standards based on religious belief. The effective state, argued its supporters, must have the kinds of servants who would interpret *raison d'état* wisely and would be willing to use the kinds of material and physical resources necessary to advance it.

One of the foremost spokesmen for, and practitioners of, this approach was Armand Jean du Plessis, Cardinal Richelieu, who served as the chief minister of France from 1624 to 1642. In this capacity, he relentlessly promulgated and ruthlessly pursued the concept of *raison d'état* for the benefit of his state. He began by creating a centralized Ministry of External Affairs to manage the rational and continuous pursuit of foreign policy. He also wisely stressed the importance of carefully selecting skilled ambassadors, of calculating risks and opportunities, of giving continuous attention to foreign affairs, and of honoring treaty commitments. These valuable contributions, however, often were overshadowed by Richelieu's extremes; for, like others who sometimes fancy themselves as unusually shrewd practitioners of statecraft, he seemed to recognize few limits or restraints. He placed French political goals above everything else, including the religious values that he supposedly represented as an official of the church. Upon learning of his death, for example, the pope allegedly responded, "If there is a God, then Cardinal de Richelieu will have much to answer for. If not ... well, he had a successful life." In order to advance what he regarded as the interests of France, he aggressively crushed domestic adversaries, employed a vast network of spies and agents, launched and deliberately prolonged foreign wars, subsidized Protestants to wage war against Catholics, bribed, manipulated, and fomented insurrections. As he stated in his *Political Testament*, "In matters of state it is necessary to profit from everything possible; whatever is useful is never to be despised." The end to be achieved, he declared directly, was simple: "power."

Such a maxim of statecraft hardly went uncontested. In fact, the views and practices of Richelieu often provoked outrage among those who viewed them as deeply offensive to legal and ethical values. One of the most devastating critiques came from the renowned theologian Cornelius Jansenius, who wrote:

> Do they believe that a secular, perishable state should outweigh religion and the Church?...Should not the Most Christian King believe that in the guidance and administration of his realm there is nothing that obliges him to extend and protect that of Jesus Christ, his Lord?...Would he dare say to God: Let your power and glory and the religion which teaches men to adore You be lost and destroyed, provided my state is protected and free of risks?

The brilliant Dutch jurist and diplomat, Hugo Grotius, similarly argued that if leaders behaved exclusively on narrow definitions of *raison d'état* and expediency, they would only perpetuate uncontrolled international violence and anarchy. He feared a world, according to his monumental 1625 book, *On the Law of War and Peace*, in which

> a license in making war of which even barbarous nations would have been ashamed; recourse was had to arms for slight reasons, or for no reason; and when arms were taken up, all reverence for divine and human law was thrown away; just as if men were henceforth authorized to commit all crimes without restraint.

The only way to break this vicious pattern, Grotius insisted, could be found in creating a broader system based on norms that respected the "laws of nations," the "natural rights" of human beings, and specific criteria for "just war" placing limits on the use of force in statecraft. Others went even further in protesting prevailing practices, including the Quakers, who issued their famous testimony of pacifism, opposing all war as a matter of ethical principle.

Despite these arguments, the exercise of power in the seventeenth century was such that Grotius was imprisoned and the protestors largely silenced, while Richelieu continued to rise in prominence. His successes, those of his even more ruthless and less popular successor Cardinal Mazarin, and the capacity of modern states to create and mobilize armed forces, were not only demonstrated in the Thirty Years' War but confirmed by the landmark 1648 Peace of Westphalia. This settlement provided legal recognition of an emerging new order, composed not of feudal, imperial, or ecclesiastical actors, but rather of several powerful, roughly equivalent, juridically independent, autonomous, but coexisting, secular states.

The publication of the influential and uncompromising *Leviathan* by English political philosopher Thomas Hobbes only three years later described the condition of the world as "a perpetual and restless desire of power after power" with "war of every man against every man" and argued that there should be no authority above that of the sovereign state. Armed with such theoretical justification, kings and other government leaders increasingly argued that they could act in the name of their state largely as they wished or were able, safe in the knowledge that they were shielded from individual responsibility for their actions, including the abuse of human rights or the conduct of war.

The newfound power of these states, and the prerogative of sovereignty that they so vociferously claimed, could be seen in a number of cases. When Frederick William inherited the leadership of Brandenburg-Prussia, for example, he held only a loose collection of territories surrounded by adversaries, overrun with foreign troops, and a population depleted by famine and pestilence. He calculated that a close, reciprocal relationship existed between military and political institutions, and believed that he could never survive without an efficient bureaucracy and a strong army. The last was the key to the whole. As he wrote in his political testament, "A ruler is treated with no consideration if he does not have troops of his own. It is these, thank God!, that have made me *considerable* since the time I began to have them." Thus, in the course of his reign from 1640 to 1688, he organized one of the first departments of war to oversee the details of creating a large and efficient military force. To administer this army and to collect taxes to pay for it, Frederick William laid the foundations of the famous Prussian bureaucracy, which, in turn, helped him to further build and centralize state power. All this inspired a young, energetic, and determined czar (who would eventually earn the name of Peter the Great) to believe that similar efforts could transform his own fragmented state and who thereby set about to make an emerging Russia parallel an emerging Prussia.

No state proved better at harnessing resources and accelerating this process of centralizing power than France. Over time, some of the victors of the Thirty Years' War lost their strength: Sweden threw its gains away under a less rational ruler, and the Netherlands yielded its commercial and naval supremacy to England, which, among other victories, had conquered the Dutch colonial possession of New Netherland in North America and renamed it New York. But this was not the case in France. Under Louis XIV, who ruled from 1643 to 1715, its ascendancy prevailed in European politics, culture, architecture, science, art, administration, warfare, and diplomacy. In fact, the extraordinary influence of France itself seemed to be embodied in its best resident ambassadors, who linked the capitals and courts of Europe and whose instructions, reports, and skills served as a model of diplomatic practice for years to come and made the French language the *lingua franca* of diplomacy itself.

Confirmation of this serious attention to diplomatic method also appeared with the publication in 1681 of a book by Abram de Wicquefort entitled *L'Ambassadeur et ses fonctions.* Based on his own observations about force and statecraft, well-seasoned by his checkered career as a diplomat, this work provided both a commentary on the political ethics of the seventeenth century and an incisive analysis of the art and practice of diplomacy. Wicquefort was not abashed by the peccadilloes of his colleagues, which varied from financial peculation and sins of the flesh to crimes of violence. He believed that in a corrupt age, one could not expect that embassies would be oases of virtue. A state could afford to be served by bad men, but not by incompetent ones. Competence, in his mind, began with a clear understanding on the diplomat's part of the nature of their job, which "consisted in maintaining effective communication between the two Princes, in delivering letters that his master writes to the Prince at whose court he resides, in soliciting answers to them,...in protecting his Master's subjects and conserving his interests." In this pursuit, Wicquefort stressed that prudence and moderation were the qualities that should be cultivated most assiduously. The former he equated with caution and reflection, and the latter with the ability to curb one's temper and remain cool and collected in moments of tension. "Those spirits who are compounded of sulphur and saltpeter, whom the slightest spark can set afire, are easily capable of compromising affairs by their excitability, because it is so easy to put them in a rage or drive them to a fury, so that they do not know what they are doing."

The means of diplomacy, however, are not the same as the ends to which they are employed. As the French writer Jean de la Bruyère wrote mockingly, the diplomats of the age "spoke only of peace, alliance, and public tranquility...and thought only of their special interest." This became perfectly clear as Louis XIV continued to amass power and wealth and to grow in strength. Through time, the skill, style, and sophistication of his diplomats could not mask the fact that he wanted them used to secure the ends of greater glory and influence, dreaming that both domestic and foreign affairs might revolve around him as the planets revolve around the sun. He used diplomacy when he could, but when he wanted more, he quickly turned to warfare as the means of overturning the territorial settlements of Westphalia. His armies were the most powerful and most feared in Europe. It was no accident that in his luxurious palace of Versailles, built in part to impress and intimidate foreign envoys, decorations commemorated military victories and his throne was located adjacent to his *Salon de Guerre*, or War Room. He maintained alliances with the Swedes in the north and the Turks in the south to prevent Russian interference while he placed his own candidate on the throne of Poland. He also used his Turkish connection to distract Austria on its eastern frontiers so that he could simultaneously dabble in German politics. Bavaria and the Palatinate were bound to the French court by marriage, and almost all of the other German princes accepted subsidies at one time or another from France. He employed the same methods of infiltration in Italy, Portugal, and Spain, where the young king married a French princess and his ambassadors exerted considerable influence in internal affairs. In addition, Louis sought to undermine the independence of the Netherlands and to bribe Charles II with a pension in order to reduce the possibility of English interference as he did so. When his army invaded the Low Countries, they quickly crushed their opponents. Only flooding caused by the opening of the dikes prevented the French from entering the province of Holland itself.

This growing French dominance became so great in the second half of the seventeenth century, in fact, that it seriously threatened not only other states, but European peace and security as a whole. As such, the overpowering influence and hegemony of France invited resistance in the form of combinations and alliances on the part of others. This is exactly what happened, and due to calculations of their own *raison d'état*, they began to formulate a new appreciation for a partnership and a balance of power. That is, they began to understand that if any state or combination of states became too powerful, the peace and security of all the others would be seriously threatened. The only way to prevent this, they believed, would be to create a balance of countervailing power through collective security. In the words of the German historian Leopold von Ranke, "The concept of the European balance of power was developed in order that a union of many other states might resist the pretensions of the 'exorbitant' court, as it was called." This is a statement worth noting. A type of balance of power, of course, had been practiced in Machiavelli's time in the intermittent warfare between the city-states of the Italian peninsula, but now it was being deliberately invoked as a principle and an instrument of statecraft within a multipolar system as a safeguard against domination. As we shall see, this concept evolved further in the eighteenth century, and during the nineteenth century it became one of the basic principles of the international system itself.

Such thinking played a significant role as the powers attempted to respond to France's continued and dangerous expansion. They worried as Louis XIV sent his troops into Alsace and captured the vital bridgehead of Strasbourg. Their fears intensified as he then moved into northern Italy. When he attempted to seize Cologne, they finally took action and launched what came to be the Nine Years' War, which raged from 1688 to 1697. This resulted in the formation of the first of the great balance-of-power coalitions. It included the forces of Austria, which a short time before had repulsed the Turks at the gates of Vienna; the Dutch, who were threatened most directly; and England, which had just overcome the debilitating effects of a civil war. The contending forces were so evenly matched that the war dragged on and settled little, but it demonstrated that a coalition could be formed when necessary to counter a common threat.

WAR AND COMPETITION IN THE EIGHTEENTH CENTURY

The eighteenth century opened, continued, and closed with warfare. One of the great paradoxes of the age is that the century that produced an articulation of the principles of democracy and human rights from the Enlightenment philosophers, the ethical restraints proposed by Immanuel Kant, the exquisite music of Mozart and Handel, enormous advances in the sciences, and that called itself "The Age of Reason" also witnessed ruthless competition, an anarchy of all against all, aggression and violence, preparations for war, and war. Virtually all of the alliances of the period were calculated to expand capabilities and to aggrandize territory. It was a century encompassing three systemic wars involving all or most of the Great Powers and seven wars involving at least two of them, resulting in battlefield deaths estimated to be seven or eight times greater than those that would occur in the following century.

All this began with the Great Northern War of 1700–1721, fought for supremacy in the Baltic area. Denmark and Saxony began by invading Sweden but, to their considerable dismay, were routed by armed forces led by the eighteen-year-old and daring ruler, Charles XII. The Danes capitulated at once, and

Charles without pause threw his troops against a much larger Russian force advancing on Narva and quickly defeated them. But brilliant military victories sometimes create the foundation of greater defeats, for they often lead to an exaggerated sense of strength and ability and a corresponding lack of perspective and restraint. Now overconfident, Charles determined to punish the Saxons and to exert control over Poland. It proved to be his undoing, for it distracted him from the more serious threat from the east under the leadership of Peter the Great. If anyone was forced to acknowledge the constant presence of warfare during this time, it surely was Peter. Indeed, during his entire reign of 1689–1725 he experienced only eighteen consecutive months of peace. Survival required that he bring Russia into the modern world. He had carefully observed that those states emerging in the West all had done so because of their ability to create a centralized bureaucracy, build a standing army and navy, and practice *raison d'état*. He used this as a model for his own country, and when his armed forces were ready, he sent them into action. Charles responded with an invasion; and this, like other later invasions of Russia, was defeated by winter and famine. He ultimately suffered a monumental military loss at the Battle of Poltava in 1709. The new Russian fleet then defeated the Swedish navy. These events broke the power of Sweden, eventually enabling Peter to gain possessions, build his new capital of St. Petersburg, and establish a foreign ministry and permanent diplomatic service, thereby confirming the dramatic emergence of Russia as a Great Power and shifting the political axis of Europe.

Warfare raged simultaneously in the west with the War of Spanish Succession fought between 1702 and 1714. When the elaborate efforts to find an heir to the throne of Spain failed, the rivalries and ambitions of the Bourbon and the Hapsburg dynasties exploded into open war. Louis XIV again sent his troops smashing into the Netherlands. This threatened the others, and, in response, William III of England formed the Grand Alliance, the largest coalition of forces aligned against a single power that modern Europe had ever seen. The allied objectives were to prevent any unification of the thrones of France and Spain and thereby thwart domination by Louis XIV. In this campaign, the resources of the Netherlands, Austria, and Prussia were all brought to bear, in addition to England's significant contributions of finances, naval forces, and a land army of nearly 70,000 troops. The brilliant military partnership of John Churchill, the Duke of Marlborough, from England and Prince Eugene of Savoy from Austria defeated a supposedly invulnerable French army on several occasions, including the famous Battle of Blenheim in 1704 and the Battle of Ramillies in 1706.

These and other victories laid the basis for two agreements of 1713 and 1714, collectively known as the Treaty of Utrecht. According to its terms, France was forced to renounce any union of the French and Spanish thrones, give up the Spanish Netherlands to Austria, relinquish all territorial gains east of the Rhine River, raze the fortifications at Dunkirk, and surrender important territories in North America to Great Britain (as England became known after its union with Scotland in 1707). Britain also acquired the strategically valuable base of Gibraltar from Spain. In addition, the treaty elevated the status of Prussia. The broader significance of the Utrecht settlement is that it marked the first treaty that explicitly referenced a balance of power. In letters accompanying the treaty between Queen Anne and Louis XIV, the French ruler noted that the purpose of "obtaining a general Peace and securing the Tranquility of *Europe* by a Ballance of Power." The Spanish king similarly acknowledged the importance of "the Maxim of securing forever the universal Good and Quiet of Europe, by an equal Weight of Power, so that many being united in one, the Ballance of the Equality desired might not turn to the Advantage of one, and the Danger and Hazard of the Rest."

Some of the most serious and profound thinking about force and statecraft, as we shall see, occurs at the end of prolonged wars or in the wake of dangerous crises. These are the times when issues of survival are most acute, when the futility of violence alone becomes apparent, and when leaders and peoples alike become vitally interested in finding ways of avoiding future strife. The end of the War of Spanish Succession, for example, brought Louis XIV himself to the point of reflection on the exercise of power in the world, and he said to his great grandson with great solemnity, "My child, you will one day be a great king. Do not imitate me in my taste for war. Always relate your actions to God and make your subjects honor Him." The same war also motivated one of Louis XIV's most gifted diplomats, François de Callières, to write his famous *De la manière de négocier avec les souverains* (*On the Manner of Negotiating with Princes*) in 1716. It has been called "a mine of political wisdom" and described by no less an authority than diplomat and historian Sir Harold Nicolson as a book that "remains to this day the best manual of diplomatic method ever written."

Callières began by insisting that since statecraft was so "high, important, and difficult," it required extremely skilled people with very special knowledge and qualities. Among these he emphasized "an observant mind, a spirit of application which refuses to be distracted by pleasures or frivolous amusements, a sound judgment which takes the measure of things, as they are, and which goes straight to its goal by the shortest and most neutral paths without wandering into useless refinements and subtleties which as a rule only succeed in repelling those with whom one is dealing." Callières also stressed careful discernment, self-control, creativity, a patient temperament, agreeable manners, prudence, and a sense of moderation. Of particular interest, and in sharp contrast to those who callously argued that an ambassador was no more than "an honest man sent to lie abroad for the good of his country," Callières warned of those who tried to get what they wanted by dishonesty. The good diplomat, he wrote,

> will never rely for the success of his mission either on bad faith or on promises that he cannot execute. It is a fundamental error, and one widely held, that a clever negotiator must be a master of deceit. Deceit is indeed the measure of the smallness of mind of him who uses it; it proves that he does not possess sufficient intelligence to achieve results by just and reasonable means. Honesty is here and everywhere the best policy....Apart from the

fact that a lie is unworthy of a great Ambassador, it actually does more harm than good to negotiation, since though it may confer success today, it will create an atmosphere of suspicion which tomorrow will make further success impossible....The negotiator therefore must be a man of probity and one who loves truth; otherwise he will fail to inspire confidence.

Perhaps the most distinctive feature of Callières's treatise was the passion with which he wisely argued that a nation's foreign relations should be conducted by trained professionals rather than by politically connected amateurs. He complained bitterly of the grave damage done to state interests by those novices "appointed so to speak over-night to important embassies in countries of which they know neither the interests, the laws, the customs, the language, nor even the geographical situation." Governments should seriously reflect, he insisted, on the story of the Duke of Tuscany who, upon complaining to a visitor about the inadequate capacities of a Venetian resident at his court and receiving the answer, "I am not surprised. We have many fools in Venice,"

"A Mine of Political Wisdom": François de Callières, *On the Manner of Negotiating with Princes*

retorted with spirit: "We have many fools in Florence, but we take care not to export them." Extreme care, he insisted, should be taken in the selection of one's representatives, and they should be carefully educated in the lessons of history, trained in diplomatic skills and techniques, and know "exactly the state of the military forces both on land and sea" in order to understand force and statecraft. "Diplomacy," he declared,

> is a profession by itself which deserves the same preparation and assiduity of attention that men give to other recognized professions.... [T]here are many qualities which may be developed with practice, and the greatest part of the necessary knowledge can only be acquired, by constant application to the subject.... [T]hose who think to embark upon a diplomatic mission as a pleasant diversion from their common task only prepare disappointment for themselves and disaster for the cause which they serve.

These words of de Callières found reinforcement in Antoine Pecquet's *Discours sur l'art de négocier* in 1737. Together, they represented not only personal views but an acknowledgment of the requirements of the age. The states that emerged in the course of the seventeenth and eighteenth centuries were those that could modernize their governmental structure, mobilize their resources, build up effective and disciplined military establishments, and create a professional bureaucracy that administered state business in accordance with the principles of *raison d'état*. An indispensable part of that civil service was the establishment of a foreign ministry, led by a foreign minister or state secretary for foreign affairs, supervising a well-trained diplomatic corps and advancing the state's vital interests.

If any doubts remained about the effectiveness of this process of state-building, they would have been answered by the emergence of Prussia. When soldier-king Frederick William I assumed the throne during the wars against Louis XIV, he was determined to strengthen his state by whatever means necessary. To do this, he completed the centralization and modernization of the Prussian bureaucracy, built up the officer corps of the army, improved its weapons, wrote its first handbook of field regulations, and expanded its numbers. Indeed, during the course of his reign, he increased the size of his military establishment to 83,000 men, which made Prussia's army the fourth largest in Europe, although the state ranked only tenth in territory and thirteenth in population.

This is the Prussian army and state that he bequeathed to his son, Frederick II, who eventually came to be called Frederick the Great. Here was a man who seemed to combine so many of the paradoxes of the age in his own person. He prided himself on being a product of the Enlightenment and Age of Reason, corresponded with French philosophers like Voltaire whom he invited to his palace at Sans Souci, studied poetry, loved music, became an accomplished flutist and composer, and wrote a long treatise attacking the advice of Machiavelli. Yet, at exactly the same time, he single-mindedly pursued what he perceived as Prussia's *raison d'état*, or national interest, by further expanding and improving his armed forces. Indeed, as he explained it in one of his more famous statements: "Negotiations without arms produce as little impression as musical scores without instruments."

In 1740, Frederick secured the throne. The same year saw the death of the Austrian emperor, Charles VI, who had asked the European powers before he died to subscribe to a document called the Pragmatic Sanction, promising that they would observe the integrity of his possessions under the rule of his young and inexperienced daughter, Maria Theresa. Frederick signed this agreement along with most other rulers. Nevertheless, neither his signature nor the arguments against unethical behavior that he himself had used in his *Anti-Machiavel* treatise deterred him now from taking advantage of what seemed to him to be an ideal opportunity for aggrandizement. He consequently wrote a memorandum to his ministers that should be quoted in full for the glaring light that it throws on him and war and competition in the eighteenth century:

> Silesia is the portion of the Imperial heritage to which we have the strongest claim and which is most suitable to the House of Brandenburg. The superiority of our troops, the promptitude with which we can set them in motion, in a word, a clear advantage we have over our neighbors, gives us in this unexpected emergency an infinite superiority over all other powers in Europe. If we wait till Saxony and Bavaria start hostilities, we could not prevent the aggrandizement of the former which is wholly contrary to our interest.... [As for the other powers], England and France are our foes. If France should meddle in the affairs of the empire, England could not allow it, so I can always make a good alliance with one or the other. England could not be jealous of my getting Silesia, which would do her no harm, and she needs allies. Holland will not care, all the more since the loans of the Amsterdam business world secured on Silesia will be guaranteed. If we cannot arrange with England and Holland, we can certainly make a deal with France, who cannot frustrate our designs and will welcome the abasement of the imperial house. Russia alone might give us trouble. If the empress lives...we can bribe the leading counselors. If she dies, the Russians will be so occupied that they will have no time for foreign affairs....All this leads to the conclusion that we must occupy Silesia before the winter and then negotiate. When we are in possession we can negotiate with success. We should never get anything by negotiations alone except very onerous conditions in return for a few trifles.

This memorandum requires little comment. Here is a mind that is completely dominated by *raison d'état*, or (in German) *Staatsräson*, and one that admits no legal or ethical restraints to state ambition. With such calculations and without hesitation, he dismissed his treaty obligations and ordered his armies to invade and seize the rich Austrian province of Silesia. This patent act of aggression is still remembered as the "Rape of Silesia."

Frederick's attack began a complex series of interrelated power struggles and two wasting wars in which the original cause often dropped completely out of view. In the first of these, the so-called War of Austrian Succession, extending from 1740 to 1748, Prussia was joined by France, Spain, Bavaria, and Saxony (which changed sides in midcourse), who together resembled a pack of wolves stalking its injured and vulnerable prey, all hoping to gain something at Austrian expense. Britain supported Austria, but many of its troops were sent to attack French and Spanish possessions in the New World. The second was the Seven Years' War, which raged from 1756 to 1763. This began with Frederick's surprise attack on Saxony, which provided a temporary tactical military advantage but quickly produced the very strategic alliance of Austria, France, and Russia that he had hoped to prevent. Only Britain and Hanover supported Prussia. In both wars, the change of allies from one side to the other resulted not from any overriding principle of an international system or order, but rather from a lust for selfish gain, whether in Europe, India, or in North America, where the struggle was known as the French and Indian War. In fact, these eighteenth-century wars for empire further extended European power over much of the rest of the world.

It is difficult to read of these struggles in which the powers changed sides without the guidance of any but the meanest of principles without thinking of the eighteenth century as an age of anarchy and rapine. Promises and treaty commitments seemed to mean little, and enemies and allies changed with little warning. Frederick established Prussia's status as a Great Power, but at the cost of bleeding his country white in twenty-three years of almost continuous warfare. Moreover, the rapaciousness of the age, evidenced in so many ways, became even clearer with the blatant land grabs in 1772, 1793, and 1795, when Austria, Russia, and Prussia ruthlessly carved up Poland and distributed the booty between them in accordance with their own selfish interests. One contemporary statesman described this condition as no more than "a continuous quarrel between people without morals, intent on taking and perpetually hungry."

There were, to be sure, those who refused to fatalistically accept these practices, who spoke out against them, who sought to establish restraints on such rapacious behavior and to place limits on the expansive claims of state sovereignty. Some, like Emmerich de Vattel who wrote *Le Droit des gens* in 1758, Fortuné Barthélemy de Félice the author of *Code de l'humanité* in 1778, and Georg Friedrich von Martens in his *Précis du droit des gens* of 1789, looked to the rule of law and tried to enunciate certain norms that might govern force and statecraft. Others turned to philosophy, religious belief, ethics, or human reason to lay a foundation for some form of collective society, federation, institution, or international organization that might restrain war and competition, including such notable thinkers as Jean-Jacques Rousseau in his essay on *Projet de paix perpétuelle* in 1782, Jeremy Bentham in *A Plan for Universal and Perpetual Peace* in 1789, and Immanuel Kant in *Perpetual Peace* in 1795.

The hopeful also drew attention to the fact that although the powers frequently fought against each other, there were some restraints on the level of violence. It certainly helped, of course, to engage in wars of tactical maneuver on battlefields restricted to what one could see with the naked eye and to fight in neat line formations with weapons of such limited lethality that brightly colored uniforms could be worn. But there was more. Few statesmen were willing to run the risk of challenging the larger equilibrium as established at Utrecht. In addition, the fear of excessive casualties played a restraining role, as did seasonal weather, which annually sent troops into winter quarters. Theologians and philosophers developed theories of just war, and various leaders made tentative efforts to develop several laws of war that placed restrictions on military commanders concerning the destruction of crops, livestock, or civilian dwellings and the taking of hostages. No authority existed to enforce these rules, and they were often violated, but their very existence gave hope that some level of cooperation could be obtained to ameliorate civilian society from the horrors that accompanied warfare of the time.

But the broader ideas of cooperation, common interests, and mutual restraints often remained largely confined to philosophical discourse and visions of what might be rather than actual practice. During the eighteenth century, they rarely influenced the deliberations and actions of governments that were dominated by greed, envy, and fear, and going about their intrigue and violent ways without bothering themselves with such thoughts. As historian Friedrich Meinecke starkly concluded in his book *Die Idee der Staatsräson*: "Never was the isolation of the power-state carried so far...never, either before or since, did universally European ideas and interests form such a small part, as they did then, in European policy of the first rank." To make the Great Powers pay attention to such matters, something of sufficient magnitude was needed to seriously frighten them into genuine collaborative action, something that would force them to think beyond themselves alone and covert the dream of a European concert into a working reality.

That shock finally came in the form of the French Revolution and the wars of the Republic and the Napoleonic Empire. When the revolution broke out in 1789, however, so entrenched were the European powers in their customary, competitive ways that they believed France would become so paralyzed and incapable of conducting foreign policy that they could pick up the spoils. The idea that the domestic revolution might actually have threatening, external consequences hardly seems to have occurred to them. This attitude proved almost fatal, for it allowed the revolutionary forces in France to consolidate themselves before going on the offensive and then made the others highly vulnerable to being divided and conquered once those forces were unleashed. Once this occurred, in the notable words of historian R. R. Palmer, "The wars of kings were over; the wars of peoples had begun."

When France launched its first offensive war in 1792, it did so for a variety of reasons, not the least of which was the old ploy of distracting attention away from domestic problems by focusing on a foreign adversary. But even this did not unduly alarm the other powers. The Prussians and the Austrians responded in uncoordinated campaigns and seemed to be more nervous about each other than about their common enemy, France. Indeed, the Prussians sold out their Austrian ally by a secret treaty that promised the French territory if they received other lands as compensation elsewhere. Similar examples could be given, as each in turn seemed to be eager to strike their own deals, turning to appeasement, neutrality, alliance, or any other arrangement that might offer them temporary advantage. This kind of selfish, shortsighted, and unreliable behavior enabled the French armies, now made so much stronger by the huge numbers and patriotic zeal produced by the *levée en masse,* or general conscription, to conquer the Rhineland and then to penetrate into southern German lands, Switzerland, and Italy. Once Napoleon Bonaparte seized power in 1799, France was either at war or preparing for war for the next sixteen years, and its imperial ambitions and conquests gained in momentum and success. Napoleon's military victories defeated Austrian, Prussian, and Russian forces one after the other. He used diplomacy not to resolve conflicts or sustain mutually beneficial partnerships, but rather to find temporary client states that could be manipulated, frequently employing soldiers in diplomatic roles to thwart attempts to build effective coalitions against him. This enabled him to extend his empire and to become the dominating master of the continent. "Europe seemed about to be swallowed up by France," observed historian Leopold von Ranke. "The universal monarchy, that had hitherto seemed only a remote danger, was almost realized."

But like other military conquerors, Napoleon suffered from not knowing when to stop. He fatally overreached himself in 1812 when he decided to invade Russia. The vastness of the land, harsh winter weather, distant lines of communication, and the unrelenting "scorched earth" policy of the Russians that sought to deny him any semblance of victory all proved to be too much. They decimated his army and shattered the myth of his invincibility. Once this occurred, the other powers finally formed a coalition that would bring about his final demise.

Their successful collaboration produced defeat for French forces during the Battle of Nations at Leipzig in 1813. But their awareness that they had not yet fully escaped danger made them realize the necessity of keeping the coalition together and, at long last, induced them to take the first real step toward converting the aspiration of a concert into action. The agonies of the wars of the eighteenth century and those of Napoleon convinced them that peace and security could not simply be left to the ad hoc residue of the collision of each state narrowly defining and then asserting its own *raison d'état*. The disasters they experienced made them consider the possibility that their own national self-interest might be best served by considering their collective interests as a whole. Consequently, the governments of Austria, Prussia, Russia, and Britain signed the Treaty of Chaumont in 1814 in which they agreed not only to continue the war against Napoleon until a definitive victory had been gained, but also—as a conscious design—to continue their alliance well after their victory. As they significantly explained: "The present Treaty of Alliance having for its object the maintenance of the balance of Europe, to secure the repose and independence of the Powers, and to prevent the invasions which for so many years have devastated the world, the High Contracting Parties have agreed among themselves to extend its duration for twenty years from the date of signature." This held them together until Napoleon was finally and decisively defeated at the Battle of Waterloo in 1815 and then, remarkably, went on to serve as the basis for the first notable experiment in creating an international system based on the principles of balance and concert on behalf of peace and security.

Suggestions for Further Exploration

On the origins and development of diplomacy and its methods, see Keith Hamilton and Richard Longhorne, *The Practice of Diplomacy* (New York, 2011 ed.); Jeremy Black, *A History of Diplomacy* (London, 2010); Geoff Berridge et al. (eds.), *Diplomatic Theory from Machiavelli to Kissinger* (London, 2001); Raymond Cohen and Raymond Westbrook (eds.), *Amarna Diplomacy* (Baltimore, 2002); Linda and Marsha Frey, *The History of Diplomatic Immunity* (Columbus, OH, 1999); M. S. Anderson, *The Rise of Modern Diplomacy* (London, 1993); Torbjörn Knutsen, *A History of International Relations Theory* (Manchester, 1992); Garret Mattingly, *Renaissance Diplomacy* (New York, 1988 ed.); D. E. Queller, *The Office of the Ambassador in the Middle Ages* (Princeton, 1967); Heinrich Wildner, *Die Technik der Diplomatie* (Vienna, 1959); the readable Harold Nicolson, *The Evolution of Diplomatic Method* (London, 1954); and Leon van der Essen, *La Diplomatie* (Brussels, 1953). The classics remain Thucydides, *The Peloponnesian War*, and Niccolò Machiavelli, *The Prince*, which appear in many editions.

Force and statecraft during the seventeenth century are treated in Olaf Asbach and Peter Schröder (eds.), *War, the State, and International Law in the Seventeenth Century* (Farnham, UK, 2010); Madeleine Haehl, *Les Affaires étrangères au temps de Richelieu* (Brussels, 2006); Derek Croxton and Anuschka Tischer, *The Peace of Westphalia* (Westport, CT, 2001); Geoffrey Parker (ed.), *The Thirty Years' War* (London, 1997 ed.); Henry Kissinger, *Diplomacy* (New York, 1994), with his favorable interpretation of Richelieu; Derek McKay and H. M. Scott, *The Rise of the Great Powers, 1648–1815* (London, 1983); Robert Massie, *Peter the Great* (New York, 1980); William Roosen, *The Age of Louis XIV: The Rise of Modern Diplomacy* (Cambridge, MA, 1976); Cardinal Richelieu, *The Political Testament of Cardinal Richelieu*, Henry Bertram Hill (trans.) (Madison, WI, 1968); and John B. Wolf, *The Emergence of the Great Powers, 1685–1715* (New York, 1951). A modern reprint of Abram de Wicquefort's 1681 *L'ambassadeur et ses fonctions* (Whitefish, MT, 2010) now exists, and many editions of Thomas Hobbes, *The Leviathan*, and Hugo Grotius, *On the Law of War and Peace*, are available.

Thoughtful discussions of war and competition during the eighteenth century can be found in H. M. Scott, *The Birth of the Great Power System* (London, 2005 ed.); Armstrong Starkey, *War in the Age of the Enlightenment* (New York, 2003); Frederick II, *Frederick the Great on the Art of War*, Jay Luvaas (ed. and trans.) (New York, 1999); Paul Schroeder, *The Transformation of European Politics* (Oxford, 1996); Geoffrey Parker, *The Military Revolution: Military Innovation and the Rise of the West* (Cambridge, 1996 ed.); Christopher Duffy, *Frederick the Great* (New York, 1988 ed.); Friedrich Meinecke, *Die Idee der Staatsräson* (Munich, 1963 ed.); Gordon A. Craig, *The Politics of the Prussian Army* (New York, 1955); and Walter Dorn, *Competition for Empire* (New York, 1940). The classic by François de Callières, *De la manière de négocier avec les souverains*, can be found in translation as *On the Manner of Negotiating with Princes* in several editions, now supplemented with a recent biography by J.-C. Waquet, *François de Callières* (Paris, 2005).

For the revolutionary period, see R. R. Palmer, "Frederick the Great, Guibert, Bülow: From Dynastic to National War," in Peter Paret (ed.), *Makers of Modern Strategy* (Princeton, 1986 ed.); Jonathan Dull, *The French Navy and American Independence: A Study of Arms and Diplomacy, 1774–1787* (Princeton, 1976); and Felix Gilbert, *To the Farewell Address* (Princeton, 1970 ed.). On the Napoleonic era, see Paul Johnson, *Napoleon* (New York, 2002); Robert Asprey, *The Reign of Napoleon Bonaparte* (New York, 2002); Antoine d'Arjuzon, *Castlereagh, ou Le défi à l'Europe de Napoléon* (Paris, 1995); Henry Kissinger,

A World Restored (New York, 1973 ed.); and Enno Kraehe, *Metternich's German Policy* (Princeton, 1963).

Broad treatments can be found in Barry Buzan and Richard Little, *International Systems in World History* (Oxford, 2000); Andreas Osiander, *The States System of Europe* (Oxford, 1994); Paul Kennedy, *The Rise and Fall of the Great Powers* (New York, 1987); and Hedley Bull, *The Anarchical Society* (London, 1977).

2

The Classical System of Diplomacy, 1815–1914

The greatest challenge for force and statecraft during the nineteenth-century was the task of devising a system that would contain international violence and prevent convulsive wars like those that had just ripped their world apart. Leaders desperately wanted to avoid a repetition of the bloodshed caused by the brutal competition of the eighteenth century and by the more recent upheaval of revolution and Napoleonic domination. They concluded that only collective action would guarantee their survival, and thus began to speak explicitly and quite self-consciously of the necessity for a "system" and what was "best for the general interest of Europe *as a whole.*" Three generations of statesmen worked at this and their efforts found expression in three different approaches to the balance of power, each of which reflected the characteristic tendencies of its time. In doing so, they succeeded in producing what historian Hajo Holborn describes as a

> system whose foundations lasted for a full century. For a hundred years there occurred no wars of world-wide scope like those of the twenty-odd years after 1792. Europe experienced frightful wars, particularly between 1854 and 1878, but none of them was a war in which all the European states or even all the great European powers participated. The European wars of the nineteenth century produced shifts of power, but they were shifts within the European political system and did not upset that system as such.

Their efforts created a period of unprecedented peace and a system that, despite its imperfections, is still described as the "classical system" of diplomacy.

BUILDING A SYSTEM WITH A BALANCE OF POWER AND A CONCERT

This system began at the Congress of Vienna in 1814–1815 and those who participated in it were path-breakers. There had been diplomatic congresses and conferences before, but those meetings had been largely for the purpose of ending hostilities and dividing the spoils of war. The leaders gathered at Vienna set themselves another, more important task. Austrian foreign

minister Prince Clemens von Metternich, who served as host, made this clear
when he said:

> No great political insight is needed to see that this Congress could not be
> modeled on any which had taken place. Former assemblies which were
> called congresses met for the express purpose of settling a quarrel between
> two or more belligerent powers — the issue being a peace treaty. On this
> occasion, peace had already been made [he was referring to the First Peace
> of Paris, which had ended hostilities] and the parties meet as friends who,
> though differing in their interests, wish to work together towards the con-
> clusion and affirmation of the existing treaty.

What did he mean by "conclusion and affirmation"? He believed that their
major task was not to merely terminate a specific war, but to actually construct
a broad-ranging and viable international system of peace and security.

This did not mean that the statesmen gathered at Vienna utterly neglected
the kinds of things that usually preoccupy political and military leaders at the
end of hostilities. They made sure that they received compensation in accordance with the degree of their sacrifice and their contribution to the victory and
that titles and territories were restored to rulers who had been deprived of
them. But they did not allow these matters to obtrude upon their more important task of building a system. In this effort (and in sharp contrast with those
who would follow them at the Paris Peace Conference of 1919), these skilled
negotiators wisely refused to allow themselves to succumb to the temptation for revenge against the recently defeated. Wilhelm von Humboldt, the
Prussian ambassador to Vienna and classical scholar, who played a leading role in devising the agenda for the congress, had been in Paris when the
Silesian army entered the conquered city and became horrified when the soldiers wanted to blow up all the bridges over the Seine simply because they
were named for Napoleonic victories. He and his colleagues knew that this
kind of vindictiveness might satisfy temporary passions but would harm any
chance of consensus and thereby the long-term maintenance of a system. They
understood perfectly well that they would need France to play its appropriate
role as a Great Power in the postwar period, and thus they refused to exclude
her from the negotiations or to cripple her in any serious way that might sow
the seeds of future war and bloodshed. Most important, they believed that
their own interests were best served by recognizing the legitimate interests
of others.

Metternich and Robert Stewart, Viscount Castlereagh, the British foreign
secretary, served as the two principal architects of this new system. They
understood in a most impressive way that any international system requires
several critical components, one of which is an appropriate structure. In this
case, they agreed on a balance of power. They recognized the importance of
power rather than ignoring or deploring it, and therefore attempted to address
one of the most difficult yet most essential tasks of statecraft: how to put power
into the service of peace and security. They believed that those capable of using
force needed to be willing and able to maintain the principle of what they

called "a just equilibrium" and to resist any unilateral attempts at domination. The negotiators at Vienna consequently went through enormous efforts to adjust territory, resources, and population as equitably as possible and to distribute capabilities among the Great Powers—balancing off Russian gains in Poland and Finland with Austrian holdings in Italy, Prussian acquisitions in the Rhineland and Saxony with British possessions in the Mediterranean, and constructing buffer zones between them in the Low Countries and in the territories that lay between Prussia and Austria. Such a division of German-speaking lands, for example, as one delegate said later, was designed to serve as a kind of shock absorber and hence had to remain disunited in the interests of peace, preserving the "balance through an inherent force of gravity." These system builders believed that by investing these territorial arrangements with the sanction of legitimacy, they would create a structure that would balance their strengths against each other, deter aggression, and thereby afford the best guarantee for peace and security. They knew that no one would be completely satisfied, but, as Henry Kissinger observes, they wisely understood that this actually would assist in maintaining the system as a whole:

> Paradoxically, the generality of this dissatisfaction is a condition of stability, because were any one power *totally* satisfied, all others would have to be *totally* dissatisfied and a revolutionary situation would ensue. The foundation of a stable order is the *relative* security—and therefore the *relative* insecurity—of its members.

The men who had guided this work were not, however, so naive as to believe that they had created a utopia or insured themselves against future trouble simply by this elaborate exercise in cartography. They had learned the important lesson from the Utrecht experience that a purely mechanical balance of power could not operate automatically on its own. They had seen many arrangements come and go and were well aware that change would occur and that a new Frederick or a new Napoleon—or, for that matter, a new revolution—might arise to challenge their settlement. Consequently, they realized the necessity of adding another essential component for any system of peace and security: the acceptance of shared goals and objectives.

To do this, Metternich, Castlereagh, and their colleagues, including the Prussian king Frederick William III and the Russian czar Alexander I, realized that, despite their vastly different personalities, they would have to reach agreement not only on common goals and objectives, but on their joint responsibility to the system as a whole and their determination to maintain and defend it. They understood that those with greater power had to accept greater obligations. For this reason, they determined to build upon their earlier Treaty of Chaumont of 1814, which stressed a commitment to use their forces for collective security, by creating the more permanent Quadruple Alliance of 1815 (soon broadened to include France), tying themselves together by treaty requiring that they institute an executive body or directorate of their foreign ministers to jointly hold conferences "for the purpose of consulting upon their common interests, and for the consideration of measures which...shall be considered the most salutary for the repose and prosperity of Nations and for the maintenance of the Peace of Europe." In this way, the new system was constructed with a guiding document and a regulatory mechanism to continuously watch over and protect it should any threats emerge. This marked the establishment of what came to be called the Concert of Europe.

Only time and practice, of course, would reveal how this concert would actually work and whether by compromise and consent it could find solutions short of war. The Great Powers would have to decide what was and was not a threat, what was and was not legitimate, how their patterns of conflict and cooperation linked them together, and how far they were committed to go in taking common action to manage and defend their system. This might not be easy. When Metternich and Czar Alexander became concerned about the threat that liberalism and nationalism posed to the existing thrones of Europe, for example, they tried to turn the Quadruple Alliance into an agency that would intervene to suppress revolutionary or democratic movements. The British viewed such attempts as a subversion of the true purpose of the concert, and in a determined note of 1818, Castlereagh protested that "nothing would be more immoral or more prejudicial to the character of governments generally than the idea that their force was collectively to be prostituted to the support of established power without any consideration of the extent to which it was abused." He subsequently made it clear that, while Britain could not countenance a policy of joint meddling in the internal affairs of other states, its cooperation could always be counted on when there was a genuine threat to the peace of Europe, the balance of power, or the system as a whole. His successors periodically repeated this pledge, as did Lord John Russell in a 1852 House of Commons speech declaring:

> We are connected...with the general system of Europe, and any territorial increase of one Power, any aggrandizement which disturbs the general balance of power in Europe, although it might not immediately lead to war, could not be a matter of indifference to this country and would, no doubt, be the subject of conference, and might ultimately, if that balance was seriously threatened, lead to war.

These were not only words. The British and other members of the Concert of Europe were able to work together remarkably well to develop a political consensus on normative values and rules of restraint with certain procedures, mechanisms, and institutions to make them effective in practice. They held mutual consultations and made collective decisions, for example, in every crisis that threatened the peace between 1815 and 1854 by finding solutions that prevented the outbreak of any war between them. This was true in the Belgian crisis of 1830, the Near Eastern crisis of 1838, and the first Schleswig-Holstein crisis of 1850, to mention only some of the more challenging disputes. In all these cases—and in many others—statesmen demonstrated their ability to hold conferences and practice crisis management, as we shall discuss in Chapter 11, and in preserving the balance of power and the system created at the Congress of Vienna when it appeared to be threatened. Indeed, as Keith Hamilton and

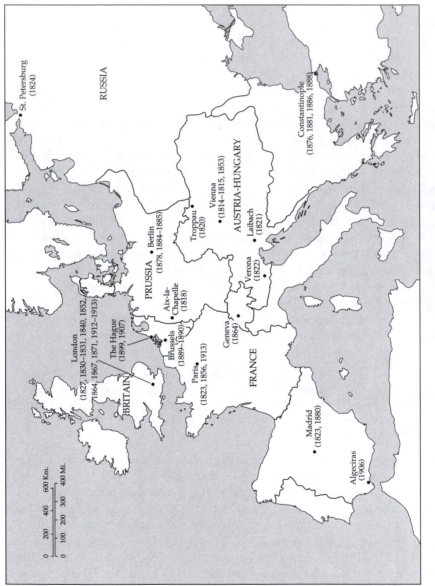

A Physical Balance and Sense of Responsibility: The Classical System's 1815 Settlement and Subsequent Conferences

RUSSIA

St. Petersburg
(1824)

Constantinople
(1876, 1881, 1886, 1888)

Vienna
(1814–1815, 1853)

AUSTRIA-HUNGARY

Troppau
(1820)

Laibach
(1821)

Berlin
(1878, 1884–1885)

PRUSSIA

Verona
(1822)

Aix-la-
Chapelle
(1818)

Geneva
(1864)

London
(1827, 1830–1831, 1840, 1852, 1864, 1867, 1871, 1912–1913)

The Hague
(1899, 1907)

BRITAIN

Brussels
(1889–1890)

Paris
(1823, 1856, 1913)

FRANCE

Madrid
(1823, 1880)

Algeciras
(1906)

0   200   400   600 Km.

0   100   200   300   400 Mi.

Richard Langhorne write in *The Practice of Diplomacy*, their designed peace-time conferences became "the master institution of classical diplomacy in the Concert of Europe."

There were less dramatic, but nevertheless effective, examples of other forms of management through cooperation and partnership as well. The participants in the Concert of Europe also worked to develop ways of regulating their competition by developing techniques of crisis prevention. That is, in order to help prevent crises and wars from breaking out between them in the first place, they created certain means to coordinate relations, minimize friction, avoid misperceptions and miscalculations, clarify respective interests, establish restraints, and make clear distinctions between legitimate and illegitimate ends and means in the pursuit of policy. Some of these rules of accommodation took the form of binding obligations in explicit treaty form with the force of international law, as when they established the neutrality of Belgium in 1831, in their words, "to prevent events from disturbing the general peace." Others were more implicit in nature, taking the form of tacit understandings, gentlemen's agreements, advanced consultations, or the offering of good offices for mediation, as occurred during the 1826 dispute between Greece and the Ottoman Empire and the 1842 conflict between Britain and France.

This system was not perfect, but there can be little doubt that the balance of power and the Concert of Europe worked particularly well in preventing major wars until 1854, in keeping the wars of the 1850s and 1860s within limits, and in ensuring that they ended with moderate rather than vindictive settlements. It is instructive to ask why this was so.

One explanation can be found in the fact that statecraft at this time was led by some unusually skilled individuals with a sense of responsibility and not subject to certain pressures that subsequently caused governments, often reluctantly, to do things that were bound to arouse the suspicion and fear of other powers and to invite violent retaliation. For the most part, statesmen of these years did not have to worry about public opinion as they set their course in foreign affairs. There were exceptions to this, of course. Early human rights advocates exerted pressure at the Congress of Vienna to end the international slave trade, and Turkish atrocities against Christians in the Balkans certainly provoked public outrage and demands for intervention to protect the victims of persecution. But in general, foreign ministers did not overly concern themselves about what might be in tomorrow's headlines. Governments were also free from massive pressure from organized economic interests, for at this stage of industrialization and capitalism, most businessmen were convinced that the best thing that governments could do for them was to simply leave them alone. The problem of reconciling foreign policy objectives with the desiderata of powerful private interests, which in our own time often makes the use of economic sanctions ineffective, did not plague foreign offices.

The maintenance of this system was also enormously enhanced by the limitations upon armed force. In order to avoid the dangerous excesses of the "nation in arms" produced by the French Revolution and used by Napoleon, armies in the first part of the century were deliberately and by mutual agreement scaled back and composed of professionals rather than mass, citizen-conscripted soldiers. There was an absence of any serious arms race, and no military pressure groups issued demands that complicated the policy-making process or disturbed international relations. The technological limits were even more striking. Simple, smooth-bore muskets firing solid lead balls represented the most sophisticated weapons, and their inaccuracy was such that combatants believed that they could stand upright in line formations wearing brightly colored uniforms.

This is precisely the context in which one of the most insightful books of the nineteenth century appeared in 1832: Carl von Clausewitz's famous *On War*. Based on his study of history and his own hard-won experiences in combat, he wrote not only about the essence of warfare, but about armed force as an instrument of statecraft. In this regard, his most-quoted sentence in the entire book is as simple as it is profound: "war is...a continuation of political activity by other means." "No one," he warned," starts a war—or rather no one in his senses...—without first being clear in his mind what he intends to achieve by that war and how he intends to conduct it." As such, war must never become an end in itself, and priority must always be given to political over military purposes. "The political object is the goal," he concluded, "war is the means of reaching it, and means can never be in isolation from their purpose." When this principle was ignored (as during the First World War when the insubordination of the German military chiefs destroyed the ability of civilian leaders to maintain control), the results could be disastrous. But when it was followed, as it was throughout so much of this period, limited ends and limited means significantly reinforced each other, thereby contributing toward the maintenance of the system as a whole.

Yet another reason why this system worked so well was the fact that whatever ideological differences existed, they were not sufficient to lead to war. There were moments, to be sure, when serious divisions surfaced. After the revolution of 1830, Europe seemed to be divided between liberal Britain and France and conservative Russia, Prussia, and Austria. The British foreign secretary, Lord Palmerston, acknowledged this fact when he said, "The three and the two think differently and therefore they act differently." But if one examines the record carefully, it is clear that the powers ignored their ideological differences more than they observed them. The British had no compunction about concluding agreements with the Eastern powers in moments in which they felt the French were threatening their interests; while on the French side, Louis Philippe sought an accommodation with the Eastern powers even at the expense of his entente with Britain. When Metternich became worried about the czar's policy in the Near East, he consulted the British about ways of restraining him; when the czar became annoyed with his Prussian ally's Baltic ambitions, he collaborated with the British to frustrate them. Interests rather than ideology brought them together. As Clausewitz observed:

> If we consider the community of states in Europe today, we...find major
> and minor interests of states and peoples interwoven in the most varied

and changeable manner. Each point of intersection binds and serves to balance one set of interests against the other. The broad effect of all these fixed points is obviously to give a certain amount of cohesion to the whole. Any change will necessarily weaken this cohesion to some degree. The sum total of relations between states thus serves to maintain the stability of the whole....

Finally, whatever differences existed between the Great Powers were largely subordinated to the high degree of consensus on shared values and a broad sense of responsibility among them. The leaders fundamentally accepted the balance of power created at Vienna, but they understood that whereas such a balance might inhibit the ability to overthrow the international system, agreement on shared values with their self-imposed restraints inhibits the actual desire to do so. They accepted the legitimacy of the system and were able to establish a high degree of restraint on the part of single powers (Czar Nicholas probably could have exacted a higher price for his aid to the Turks in 1833 but refused to do so because he feared that such unilateral action might lead to emulation), a willingness to accept the validity of existing treaties (in no age in modern times was there greater respect paid to the principle *pacta sunt servanda*), and, when a single power seemed on the point of seeking aggrandizement (as was true of France in 1840), a willingness to participate in concerted action to restrain it. This consensus provided an essential element in holding them together in what they often called the "Family of Nations" that preserved the major features of the Vienna settlement and maintained an equilibrium of forces from 1815 to 1854.

CHANGE AND AN EXPERIMENT WITH A DEFENSIVE ALLIANCE SYSTEM

The world never stands completely still, and no international system can sustain itself unless it is able to adjust and adapt to new circumstances. Over time, new forces, personalities, ideas, values, discoveries, and technological developments sooner or later challenge existing arrangements and bring about transformations. In this regard, the nineteenth century certainly provided no exception. After the revolutions of 1848, a new spirit began to emerge in Europe—one that found its strongest expression in the policies of a new generation of young men in a hurry, infused with nationalism for their own countries, and no longer willing to fully abide by the collaborative principles and practices invented and followed by the statesmen of Vienna. These newcomers included Felix zu Schwarzenberg of Austria, Camillo di Cavour of Piedmont, Otto von Bismarck of Prussia, and Louis Napoleon of France. The vent that opened the way to the fulfillment of the ambitions of these *Realpolitiker* (a term invented in the 1850s by the political activist and writer Ludwig von Rochow to describe those who defined statecraft solely in terms of the calculation and exercise of raw power) was the outbreak of war between Russia and Britain (supported by France and Piedmont) in 1854. The two powers whose collaboration had prevented the revolutions of 1848 from escalating into a major international conflict now slipped into the Crimean War,—a senseless struggle that resulted not from any deliberate threat to either one, but rather from imaginary dangers.

By the time the war was over, more soldiers had lost their lives from disease than in military combat and neither side had secured any appreciable gains. This explains in part why the negotiators at the Conference of Paris in 1856 made great strides in addressing certain norms limiting the operation of armed force by formulating rules for naval warfare, protecting the rights of noncombatants, and guaranteeing the rights of neutrals in times of war. But the war and the distrust that it caused also left a situation in which Russia, France, Prussia, and the rising power of Piedmont all wanted some territorial revisions of the balance of power. Britain, wearied by its exertions in the Crimea, emerged in a pronouncedly isolationist mood. After this, the concert could not always completely manage crises or exert effective restraints, as evidenced by four wars of unification: the Austro-Italian war of 1859, the Danish War of 1864, the Austro-Prussian War of 1866, and the Franco-Prussian War of 1870. These were all limited wars of short duration, and not one escalated into a European or system-wide conflict. Nevertheless, they caused the balance of power to be modified by the creation of the two new states of Italy and Germany.

With these changes, the tasks of statesmanship became increasingly more difficult. Psychologically, there was no longer the experience of a commonly shared invasion by an obvious aggressor like Napoleon to remind them of the necessity of working together, and the lessons of history learned by one generation are not always accepted by another. Moreover, tensions did not relax after 1871 as they had after 1815. The resentments and frustrations left by the wars of unification encouraged a combativeness that was fed by the widespread currency of Darwinism and by the sensationalism of newspapers that deliberately pandered to a gullible and excitable public and introduced the expression "jingoism." The emotional dimensions of French *revanchisme*, Pan Slavism, Pan Germanism, irredentism, and hypersensitive nationalism made this situation even worse. The French, unwilling to forget the annexation of Alsace and Lorraine by Germany; the Austrians, seeking to expand into the Balkans and arousing Russia's anger and distrust; and the Italians, dissatisfied with the extent of their new state and burning to despoil the Austrians of any remaining areas inhabited by Italian minorities, all posed serious problems for the maintenance of the system. Further tensions arose as the Industrial Revolution increasingly revealed inventions and weapons that would eventually transform armed force.

Friction between the powers also increased due to structural readjustments and political and economic developments. Italian and German unification, for example, managed to significantly reduce the number of buffer zones, or shock absorbers, created by those assembled earlier at Vienna. This meant that the Great Powers now possessed more contiguous borders, and these made them rub up against each other uncomfortably. At the same time, the age of free trade was coming to an end and the age of neomercantilism and imperialism dawning, so that tariff wars and colonial competition between powers would be more likely. Statesmen interested in following sensible partnerships in foreign policies were no longer as free of domestic pressures as Metternich had been. Groups with similar economic interests were becoming more organized and beginning to develop techniques for persuading governments to alter policies in order to assist them. Pressure groups from industry and agriculture, for example, increasingly began to push for tariffs, for colonies, and then for expanded armaments.

These developments were sources of deep concern to the diplomats of Europe, especially to the leading statesman of the period, Otto von Bismarck. His country, Germany, had been the principal beneficiary of the new balance of power that he had done so much to forge, and he was determined to keep the gains secure. Toward this end, he regarded Germany as a sated power and now wanted nothing but peace and stability. As he wrote to his ambassador in St. Petersburg, "we do not pursue power-politics, but safety-politics." But history shows few examples of sudden conversions, like the apostle Paul on the road to Damascus, whereby leaders who gained their reputations by launching wars suddenly became men of peace. Consequently, although Bismarck's objectives had genuinely changed, he continued to be haunted by his earlier reputation for "blood and iron" and *Realpolitik*, with the consequence that the other powers did not always trust him. He thus came to learn that it is often much easier to upset a diplomatic system than to maintain it. During the war scare crisis of 1875 and the possibility of an Austro-Russian conflict in the Balkans that would almost certainly involve Germany, for example, it became apparent to Bismarck that wishing for peace was not enough and that he would have to take a more active role. This explains why he worked so hard, as we shall see in Chapter 11, to serve as a crisis manager and act as an "honest broker" in 1878, inviting the contentious powers to the Congress of Berlin and successfully averting a war in the Near East. But at the end of the crisis the Russian government believed that the settlement marked a betrayal of past friendship and began to talk of an alliance with France. It was thus clear to Bismarck that times and conditions had changed and that the traditional friendship among Prussia, Austria, and Russia, forged in the war against Napoleon, could no longer be relied upon. If the existing balance of power, and Germany's place in it, was to be preserved, it would have to be by some new means.

Bismarck reluctantly concluded that the only way of achieving his objective would be to maintain a strong army for deterrence and to create defensive alliances. At a minimum, he hoped that these would relieve Germany of potential isolation and might, if things went well, give him some measure of control over the policies of enough of the other powers to prevent them from embarking upon actions that would threaten the general peace. To do this, he began by negotiating a series of general treaties in 1873 between the conservative governments of Germany, Austria, and Russia, tying them together in what became known as the Three Emperors' League for the purpose of preserving the international as well as the domestic status quo. His next step involved the creation of the more serious Dual Alliance of 1879 with Austria, specifically stipulating mutual defense in the event of an attack by Russia and benevolent neutrality if either ally were attacked by a power other than Russia. Although the details of the treaty with Austria were secret, the conclusion was not, and it startled the Russians into changing their tune and asking for a renewal and further elaboration of the Three Emperors' League in 1881, strengthening the ties between the signatories and seeking to reduce their level of friction. The Triple Alliance followed the next year between Germany, Austria, and Italy, providing for defense against France or against "two or more Great Powers not members of the alliance," in other words, any combination of France, Britain, or Russia. Bismarck hoped that these measures would greatly reduce the chance of a Russian attack on Germany, would block the possibility of a Franco-Russian alliance, and would minimize the possibility of a war between Austria and Russia in the Balkans or a conflict between rivals Austria and Italy.

Bismarck's elaborate defensive alliance system thus was much different from the earlier arrangements of the Vienna system. It tied most of the powers in one way or another to Berlin. Although Bismarck carefully cultivated the British and worked to avoid confrontations with them, they chose to remain apart. France, against its will, remained isolated. The Bismarckian way of maintaining this equilibrium of forces was a complicated one, and that was its chief weakness. It operated on the basis of insecurity and by means of secrecy, a high degree of disingenuousness, and constant maneuver. Indeed, the German Emperor William I looked at this alliance system and said to Bismarck, "I would not be in your shoes. You seem to me at times to be like a rider who juggles on horseback with five balls, never letting one fall." This became apparent during the tense Bulgarian crisis of 1886–1887, when a renewal of Austro-Russian antagonism in the Balkans dissolved the Three Emperors' League and a simultaneous wave of *revanchisme* in France made a Franco-Russian alliance seem possible, Bismarck was able to contain these dangers only by the most questionable means: a deliberately manufactured war-scare designed to intimidate the French and professed support of Russian objectives in the Balkans that was belied by covert connivance with third powers and stock market manipulations that rendered his promises meaningless. Bismarck's performance in this affair has often been described as a tour de force, but the course that he followed was so subterranean, devious, and manipulative that the other powers came to believe that he was lying to them. As their distrust increased, the days of the Bismarckian alliance system were numbered.

Despite these strains and problems, the fact remains that on many occasions the Great Powers demonstrated their capacity after the Crimean War to act together in concert with flexibility and moderation to reach mutual accommodation in order to maintain the system as a whole. The successes of their numerous diplomatic conferences revealed their sense of responsibility to participate in collective decisions and actions, respect treaties, and generally observe restraint in their international actions. They agreed, for example, to establish neutral, demilitarized zones in an attempt to prevent crises from occurring between them in the first place, as they did in their 1863 treaty on the Ionian Islands of Greece, pledging that "no armed force, either naval or military, shall at any time be assembled or stationed upon the territory or in the waters of those islands." The next year they broke dramatic new ground with the famous Geneva Convention, the first multilateral treaty in history designed to lay the foundations of humanitarian law and the creation of the International Committee of the Red Cross by protecting the rights of individuals wounded in times of war, irrespective of their nationality. Soldiers, they announced, did not surrender all of their basic human rights simply because their countries forced them to put on a military uniform. They also successfully worked to localize or contain certain regional and non-European conflicts in order to prevent larger confrontations among themselves, fearing that a minor or peripheral dispute might easily escalate out of control. When an insurrection broke out in Bosnia and Herzegovina in 1875, to illustrate, their negotiations resulted in a collective accord stating:

> The Powers have come to an agreement to make use of all the influence at their disposal in order to localize the conflict, and diminish its dangers and calamities by preventing Serbia and Montenegro from participating in the movement. Their language has been the more effectual from being identic, and has, consequently, testified the firm determination of Europe not to permit the general peace to be imperilled by rash impulses.

They practiced crisis-management techniques sufficient to avert general war, as demonstrated at the Congress of Berlin in 1878 when defusing danger in the Balkans. Moreover, the diplomats of this period also understood the importance of crisis prevention, and they worked to draw demarcation lines of interest, set limits, and establish restraints and ground rules for governing their interactions in order to avoid serious misunderstandings and disputes. This was the motivation for the well-known 1884–1885 Conference of Berlin, which, in the words of one authority, "had not been called as the result of a crisis, but rather in an attempt to forestall the possibility of one arising." Such achievements at a time of considerable tension and competition are indicative of what could be accomplished by diplomacy within this classical system.

FURTHER CHANGE AND AN EXPERIMENT WITH BIPOLAR ALIGNMENT

Given the nature of change and the need to adapt to evolving circumstances, it is not surprising that with time, other experiments would be tried as well. Thus, the third came in the years from 1907 to 1914, when all of the major European powers arranged themselves into a bipolar alignment. It was this particular manifestation of the politics of equilibrium that fastened itself upon the imagination of later generations and, because of its catastrophic end, made "balance of power" an opprobrious term in the postwar period, particularly in the United States.

It is possible—and not entirely unjustified—to place blame for the emergence of this other experiment, with all of its deplorable consequences, upon German policy after 1890. The abrupt dismissal of Bismarck from his post and the German government's decision to dismantle its alliance with Russia precipitated the shift. Whatever the weaknesses of the Bismarckian arrangement, the fact remains that it did not divide Europe into two confrontational camps of countervailing power. Instead, it brought most states into a defensive and interlocking network in which no single power, including Germany, could be assured of support in any unilateral aggressive action. Because the system would come into operation against any effort to upset the system as a whole, as historian Norman Rich observes, it was defensive by nature and thus served as a deterrent to chauvinistic agitators in every country. This critical feature began to change once the German-Russian alliance was severed, for it encouraged the Russians to look elsewhere for friends and left Europe in a much more unstable and fragile condition.

Perhaps things would have evolved differently with more able and restrained leaders, but German foreign policy was now directed by the often impulsive and bombastic Kaiser William II, his vain chancellor Bernhard von Bülow, and his assertive chief of the imperial naval office Admiral Alfred von Tirpitz, who together launched a new offensive policy, which they described as a "new course" of *Weltpolitik* designed to make Germany a global power. They were no longer interested in mere defense, but wanted more, and aggressively pushed to acquire colonial possessions and to build a huge new navy. This immediately brought them into conflict with the spheres of influence of the other Great Powers in Africa, the Pacific, and the Middle East. The Russians, for example, became deeply worried to find the Germans trying to move into the Persian Gulf, and began to reconsider their options. The British and the French, who competed in Africa after 1882 and came uncomfortably close to a war in the Sudan in 1898, discovered that Germany was becoming a potential threat to both of them and began to mend their fences. At the same time, an alliance of domestic conservative political parties and groups that derived their financial support from heavy industry and big agriculture steadily began to push the German government into launching an ambitious naval armaments program in 1898 and 1900, challenging others on the seas and imposing tariff barriers on trade. This could not help but alienate the British, French, and Russians, and in the end drive them toward each other. As one insightful British Foreign Office analyst concluded in a famous memorandum: "The union of the greatest military with the greatest naval power in one state would compel the world to combine for the riddance of such an incubus."

It would be a mistake, however, to think of this fateful course as having been caused solely by German clumsiness and impercipience. Even if William II, Bülow, and Tirpitz had been wiser, more responsible, and less provocative, it is difficult to believe that the apprehensiveness of others would have been any different. As historian Paul Kennedy observes, it was the transformation of Germany from a cluster of second-rate states under insignificant princelings to a united empire with a significant population, impressive industrial resources, and advanced technology that provided the root cause of concern. By the end of the nineteenth century, Germany was not only growing out of its European "skin" but acquiring the early attributes of a world power. To the British in particular, this change brought about new anxieties and tensions and made it easy for them to regard Germany not just as a competitor but as a future foe. Lord Esher was not alone in thinking "there is no doubt that within measurable distance there looms a titanic struggle between Germany and Europe for mastery. The years 1793–1815 will be repeated, only Germany, not France, will be trying for European domination." Such fears increasingly led the British to conclude that they could no longer maintain their security alone and that their cherished "splendid isolation" might no longer be so splendid. They consequently sought to contain this threat by entering into partnerships with Germany's other antagonists.

The resulting experiment did not suddenly occur overnight, but took seventeen years to unfold after the first precipitous events of 1890. Diplomats in Paris and St. Petersburg worked from 1891 to 1894 to transform an exchange of notes and a military convention into an alliance between republican France and czarist Russia. After considerable negotiation, Britain and France agreed to settle their major differences and signed the Entente Cordiale in 1904. The Anglo-Russian Agreement followed in 1907. These two bilateral accords initially sought simply to settle major differences, and both deliberately avoided using the word "alliance." Nevertheless, through time and as tensions increased, they evolved more into serious military partnerships. These various arrangements came to divide the powers into two groups: the Triple Alliance (Germany, Austria, and Italy) and the Triple Entente (Britain, France, and Russia), a fact confirmed in their strategic war plans predicated on two armed and hostile camps.

This new iteration of equilibrium possessed both similarities and differences with the other experiments of the nineteenth century. They all involved attempts to balance the power and the interests of the Great Powers of Europe. This latest effort, like the Bismarckian arrangement but unlike the Vienna settlement, relied less and less on general agreement and more on formal secret agreements among the selected parties themselves. In addition, this new variant created a bipolar alignment that came to be much more inflexible than the two previous experiments, causing it to last for a much shorter period of time. There was little interpenetration here as there had been after Vienna, and no control by a strong alliance leader as there had been at the time of Bismarck. As a consequence, the years from 1907 to 1914 often were characterized by accelerating armament races, inflexible war plans and arrangements made by military staffs on their own (sometimes without any regard for political implications), mutual suspicions, and fears of being encircled and destroyed.

Nevertheless, even in the midst of this intense bipolar competition, the Great Powers demonstrated that it was still possible to manage their relations through diplomacy. During the Hague Conferences of 1899 and 1907, they made pioneering efforts to establish not only the principle of international arbitration but also practical rules of procedure and a formal institution to settle conflicts, and did so by accepting the restraints of the Convention for the Pacific Settlement of International Disputes and creating the Permanent Court of Arbitration. During the Algeciras Conference of 1906, they managed to keep the highly combustible first Moroccan crisis from exploding into war. Similarly, in 1907 and 1908, the powers demonstrated mutual restraint by prohibiting weapons and armed forces from the strategically important Åland Islands astride both the Baltic Sea and the Gulf of Bothnia, as they said at the time, in order "to remove distrust and avoid conflict by means of international agreement rather than have recourse to the sword." The negotiators further pledged that if events threatened international stability in the area, they would "communicate with each other for concerting among themselves" on ways to take common measures to protect peace and security.

But, through time, it became increasingly difficult to reach these kinds of agreements. Crises in the Balkans, Morocco, and other parts of the decaying Ottoman Empire began to take their toll, as governments began to worry about how long they could continue to go to the brink and still keep their alignments together. Governments seemed to suffer from recurrent nightmares in which they saw themselves abandoned by their allies and encircled by a host of enemies. Since it seemed increasingly important to possess friends—and much more dangerous to lose them—they came to strengthen the loyalty of their allies, even when it was foolish to do so. Bismarck, for example, had prudently restrained Austria by making it clear that any commitment from Berlin would be limited to cases of self-defense if attacked. During a crisis in Bosnia, however, the German chief of general staff abandoned this policy by specifically telling his counterpart in Vienna that he now could rely upon the widespread support of Germany, regardless of the origins of the conflict. Such an assurance was patently dangerous. The British and the French began to have similar apprehensions about losing the Russians, and consequently tended to give them an unusual degree of latitude instead of warning them that, if they were foolhardy, they would have to stand alone. This not only reduced flexibility and the ability to respond to changing circumstances, but placed the stronger members of the respective alignments at the mercy of their junior and less-stable partners. The danger, of course, was that all of the participants of the Triple Entente and Triple Alliance might easily be pulled into a conflict precipitated by their most irresponsible members, thereby placing the system itself at great risk.

CHARACTERISTICS OF THE SYSTEM

Statesmen of the nineteenth century, as we have seen, worked to construct and then maintain a viable diplomatic system for peace and security. Their success left a remarkable record: not one war occurred between the Great Powers for forty years and, after the Crimean War, no general war for another sixty years. To accomplish this, they needed not only to confront their fear of repeating the nearly disastrous mistakes of the past, but to respond to the changes that occurred during their own times. They consequently developed three specific experiments or approaches. Although each of these had their differences, they all occurred within the system and shared certain features to a greater or lesser extent that reveal much about the nature of diplomacy and its challenges as well as the classical system as a whole.

This system was characterized in the first instance by its **composition, numbers, and types of actors**. The major participants were the Great Powers of Europe, or what Castlereagh called "the powers of the first order." This hierarchy included Britain, France, Prussia (then Germany), Austria, Russia, and, to a lesser extent after its unification, Italy. Their relative strength gave them power over much of the rest of the world, and they thus made and enforced the rules of behavior for everyone else. The only other states that showed any serious or sustained interest in international relations at the time also tended to be European. Two others, the United States and Japan, still stood in the wings, waiting but not yet called upon to play their parts. Indeed, when one foreign ministry official once suggested seeking more cordial relations with the United States, Bismarck dismissed the notion with contempt because, as he explained it, Americans "don't matter at all." Such a system, composed only of a very small number of actors that were all nation-states from a single continent, greatly simplified the tasks of statecraft.

The **structure** of this system took the form of a balance among these Great Powers. They believed that a countervailing balance of power, however arranged at any given point of time, was essential for deterring any one state from seeking hegemony against the others. This required that they—as the ones capable of using armed force and thereby doing the most damage to each other and to all other lesser states—each play a role and cooperate as necessary to preserve that balance or equilibrium. Even if one of them was defeated in a war, for example, they needed to be readmitted as participants in the balancing process. Such structural readjustments worked best when the powers maintained flexibility in making alliances and shifted partners as changing circumstances required; but at their worst when they tried to isolate one of the members or began to lose their ability to adjust, as they did in the dangerous years from 1907 to 1914. They also understood that this structure would contribute to the maintenance of the system only if the major actors remained of roughly comparable power vis-à-vis one another. Toward this end, they tried to avoid cases of unilateral aggrandizement by a number of means, sometimes by applying the principle of compensation: when one of the Great Powers acquired—or wished to acquire—additional territory, population, or resources, it was understood that the others had to receive payoffs in kind, usually at the expense of weaker neighbors or imperial possessions.

In addition, this structure was designed to support a decentralized, self-regulating system of sovereign nation-states. Power and responsibility remained solely in the hands of the constituent state actors. This obviously marked a significant difference from the structure of other systems (such as that of Manchu China during roughly the same period), proposals for world government that have emerged from time to time, or broad-based international organizations. There was, in other words, no single hegemonic power or supranational political authority at the apex of the system to regulate their quarrels, to ensure that international politics did not become anarchic, or to enforce the rules. These requirements must be met for the maintenance of any system, but in this case the Great Powers achieved them by coordinating and regulating their own behavior.

The classical system of diplomacy also possessed the characteristic of **shared goals and objectives**. Statesmen realistically understood that no system can possibly survive unless there is an essential consensus on fundamental assumptions and aims by all the major participants, especially among those necessary to maintain the system. A balance of power inhibits the *capacity* to overthrow a diplomatic system, but—of critical importance—agreement on shared values inhibits the *desire* to do so. There could be no major actor so dissatisfied that it questioned the legitimacy of the entire order and therefore sought to overthrow it. The Great Powers agreed upon a common purpose: to ensure their own survival by harnessing their power to the system as a whole and creating a collective security arrangement that would maintain peace and stability. This could not be achieved unless they reached a consensus on basic principles, accepting each others' existence, defining their own interests in terms of the larger good, seeing the relationship between their national security and broader international security, and agreeing upon their shared responsibility to defend what they created. They had to strike a difficult balance between the desire to pursue purely selfish objectives in rivalry, on the one hand, and the need to maintain the system as a whole in partnership, on the other. For this reason, the Great Powers did not perceive each other as implacable enemies engaged in a struggle for elimination, or a "zero-sum" contest in which any gain for one meant a loss for the others. Rather, they viewed each other as limited adversaries in their competition, while at the same time partners within the system. Armed force could be a permissible and legitimate instrument of policy as long as it was employed for limited ends. Any war that seriously threatened the existence of another member, however, and thus jeopardized the entire system, had to be prevented.

Statesmen of the period also clearly realized that they needed to develop certain **norms, methods, and rules of accommodation** in order to create restraints, establish what was regarded as legitimate and acceptable behavior, provide some regulation of their rivalries, and direct change in desired ways— all in order to maintain their system. They were not so naive as to think that the balancing and equilibrium would automatically occur, that they had created a fixed utopia, or that they had protected themselves against future crises simply by redrawing the map or by joining hands at a diplomatic conference. Instead, they recognized that conflict among themselves could not easily be prohibited or eliminated in the real world of international politics. They believed, however, that such competitive behavior need not be totally arbitrary, haphazard, or unrestrained. To deal with this, they reached consensus on a wide variety of normative values, methods, and rules to regulate their competition and keep it within mutually acceptable bounds, many of which were articulated in the widely used handbook of Carl von Martens entitled *Guide diplomatique*. This required that democracies and absolute monarchies alike accept certain self-imposed restraints, honor their commitments, and be willing to take collective action to enforce the rules if necessary. Part of this stemmed from pragmatic self-interest with the calculated knowledge that, as they said, "no Power can free itself from treaties without at the same time freeing others." Yet another part was based upon a larger sense of responsibility to the system as a whole. "The Great Powers," observed one leading statesman, "feel they have not only a common interest, but a common duty to attend to." With such attitudes and through such means, they hoped that any changes or adjustments would be *within* the system rather than *of* the system.

The results of their efforts demonstrated an imaginative array of mutual self-restraints tailored to fit specific problems and took many forms. At a very practical level, they agreed on rules of protocol for ranking diplomatic representatives and for using the French language in written communication and in the texts of treaties. On a larger scale, they collectively created procedures that enabled the Concert of Europe to promote cooperation and the coordination of their policies. They opposed unilateral action and attempted to secure the consent of all for major territorial changes. Methods of crisis management were developed and used, even as late as the time of William II. They developed sophisticated practices and ground rules for preventing crises, including employing multilateral consultation and decision making, systematizing arbitration, creating buffer states and demilitarized zones, establishing neutrality laws, localizing and restricting regional conflicts, delineating areas of special interest, and pacifically settling disputes. Moreover, they agreed that the principles of *raison d'état* and national sovereignty possessed value, that diplomacy should be a "commerce in mutual benefits," that ideology should not be a determining factor in their foreign policies, that negotiations should be conducted with discretion and in private, and that their attention should be focused not on economic affairs but rather on what they called the "high politics" of political and military affairs involving issues of war and peace.

In this regard, and with specific reference to force and statecraft, those responsible for maintaining this system agreed with the norm *that wars, if fought with limited means for limited political objectives, could be regarded as legitimate instruments of policy.* They did not try to completely eliminate wars or threats of force. Instead, they made a distinction between those that were permissible and those that were not, sometimes drawing upon just war theory. Thus, wars or threats of military action, even with the weapons increasingly made possible by the Industrial Revolution, were permitted as long as they did not threaten the vital interests of Great Powers or the system as a whole. In fact, the use of force was regarded as not only legitimate, but even necessary, if one state attempted to achieve domination, for this would destroy the balance of power itself. With the passage of time and with the bipolar alignment at the end of the century, however, the distinction between permissible and impermissible war became increasingly difficult to determine.

Among these various norms, methods, and rules of the classical system of diplomacy was also the agreement to rely heavily upon **professional**

diplomats. No system, however cleverly designed, can possibly operate itself. It is completely dependent upon people to make it work. In this regard, statesmen of the time appreciated the wisdom in the advice of de Callières that, given the enormously high stakes of international politics, only the most highly qualified individuals should be employed to conduct the demanding tasks of statecraft. Consequently, they carefully trained and selected professionals who regarded themselves as members of a like-minded elite and culturally homogeneous *corps diplomatique*, or diplomatic corps, known specifically as the European *famille diplomatique*, or diplomatic family. These cosmopolitan diplomats moved with ease within the larger system, and many in fact were employed by countries other than their own. They shared common ties of culture and historical tradition, geography, language, religion, class and social status, race, and gender. As political scientist Charles Burton Marshall writes, these professionals

> drew on a generally common fund of history. The frame of discourse among them was unified to a degree permitting any government participating significantly in world affairs to be confident of having its utterances understood by others in the sense intended. None was a revolutionary power. Ideologies were "a minor theme." ... The basis of the general order was not at issue. A common notion of legitimacy prevailed.

This made it much easier for them to achieve such a remarkable level of cohesion and consensus on the nature and purposes of what they called "the art of diplomacy," ethical values, the need to establish certain normative rules and procedures, and a sense of responsibility to make and to enforce collective decisions necessary to protect their system as a whole.

Finally, the **limited state of technology** also characterized the classical system. In terms of transportation and communication, they began the nineteenth century with the same condition as all of their predecessors in human history: no ambassador, no instructions, no replies from foreign missions, no military orders, no idea could travel faster than the speed of a horse. The pace was slow, and time, distance, weather, and geography were significant facts of life. In a revealing memorandum to his secretary of state, President Thomas Jefferson once observed, "We have heard nothing from our ambassador in Spain for two years. If we do not hear from him this year, let us write him a letter." Even in the best of circumstances, it took days for a hand-carried diplomatic dispatch to go from Paris to Vienna, weeks to go from Rome to St. Petersburg, and months to go from Berlin to Tokyo. Such delays meant that major battles still could be fought by military or naval commanders even after statesmen had declared peace. Despite the obvious limitations, such conditions did possess one great advantage: time to think and time for passions to cool. By the end of the century, railroads appeared on land and steamships on the seas, and electricity made possible the use of telegraphic communication. This eventually generated what would become a rising tide of information and the growing pressure for critical decisions to be made rapidly, the dangers of which were demonstrated all too well when leaders found themselves suddenly overwhelmed, as we shall see in Chapter 11, during the crisis of 1914 and when Austria first declared war on Serbia—by telegram.

But this would not happen until the very end, and statesmen throughout the century enjoyed small and simple foreign ministries and a relaxed atmosphere characterized by the tradition known as le thé de cinq heures, or "5:00 tea," when officials gathered to socialize. Participants fondly recalled "comparatively idle days," porters meeting horse-drawn carriages, dispatches written by hand, and time to read and reflect. "There were few bathrooms and ice was rare," wrote one diplomat looking back on his own experiences and capturing the mood of the period, "but calm abounded...; there were no telephones, no cars, no deaths on the road or in the air. There were less nerves, less noise; perhaps after all the world would give that peace which the prayer-book said it couldn't."

Weapons technology always plays a critical role in force and statecraft as well. The nineteenth century witnessed the emergence of the Industrial Revolution and with it the change from smooth-bore muskets firing solid balls to rifles projecting expanding bullets, from simple cannon to long-range artillery, from soldiers marching on their feet to being transported to battlefields by railroads, and from wooden-hulled sailing ships like the H.M.S. Victory to heavily armored and turbine-driven battleships like the H.M.S. Dreadnought. Each of these developments proved significant, but none produced anything that even came close to a weapon of mass destruction. Indeed, even if the volume, accuracy, and range of fire increased, most shots still missed. This meant that the limited state of weapons technology reinforced the limited political objectives of warfare and that the cost of diplomatic failure was not catastrophic ruin.

Yet, by the turn of the century, many of these limits and the basic simplicity and homogeneity of the system came under growing stresses and strains. The Spanish-American War of 1898 and the Russo-Japanese War of 1904–1905 revealed other actors and other races anxiously waiting to assert themselves in international affairs. At the same time, the European chancelleries experienced more frequent crises, an increase in diplomatic agreements shrouded in secrecy, and an enlargement in the number of military and naval attachés posted to embassies who were not always willing to serve as instruments of policy. Of particular importance, the Great Powers came to lose sight of their common values and the necessity of self-restraint, as became painfully evident in the summer of 1914, when leaders abandoned their sense of responsibility to the system and turned instead to a war that would unleash unimagined forces.

SUGGESTIONS FOR FURTHER EXPLORATION

The classical system of diplomacy long has fascinated students of international relations. See Keith Hamilton and Richard Langhorne, *The Practice of Diplomacy*

(New York, 2011 ed.); Markus Mösslang and Torsten Riotte (eds.), *The Diplomat's World: A Cultural History of Diplomacy* (Oxford, 2008); R. Bridge and Roger Bullen, *The Great Powers and the European States System, 1815–1914* (New York, 2005 ed.); Ralph Menning, *The Art of the Possible* (New York, 1996) with its use of primary source documentary material; Henry Kissinger, *Diplomacy* (New York, 1994); Norman Rich, *Great Power Diplomacy, 1815–1914* (New York, 1992); Paul Gordon Lauren, "Crisis Prevention in Nineteenth-Century Diplomacy," in Alexander L. George (ed.), *Managing U.S.-Soviet Rivalry* (Boulder, CO, 1983); René Albrecht-Carrié, *A Diplomatic History of Europe Since the Congress of Vienna* (New York, 1973 ed.); Charles Burton Marshall, "The Golden Age in Perspective," *Journal of International Affairs*, 17 (1963): 9–17; Hajo Holborn, *The Political Collapse of Europe* (New York, 1951); and many editions of Carl von Martens, *Guide diplomatique*.

Insightful discussions of system building and the personalities and motives that guided it include David King, *Vienna 1814* (New York, 2008); Adam Zamoyski, *The Rites of Peace* (New York, 2007); G. John Ikenberry, *After Victory* (Princeton, 2000); Paul Schroeder, *The Transformation of European Politics* (Oxford, 1994); Alan Sked, *Europe's Balance of Power* (London, 1979); Henry Kissinger, *A World Restored* (New York, 1973 ed.); C. K. Webster, *The Foreign Policy of Castlereagh* (London, 1963 ed.); and Paul Schroeder, *Metternich's Diplomacy at Its Zenith* (New York, 1962).

Those interested in the Concert system should consult Jacques-Alain de Sédoux, *Le concert européen* (Paris, 2009); Raymond Cohen, "Rules of the Game in International Politics," *International Studies Quarterly*, 24 (March 1980): 129–150; Richard Elrod, "The Concert of Europe," *World Politics*, 28 (January 1976): 159–174; Gordon A. Craig and Peter Paret, "The Control of International Violence," *Stanford Journal of International Studies*, 7 (1972): 1–21; and Carsten Holbraad, *The Concert of Europe* (London, 1970). For the balance of power, see F. H. Hinsley, *Power and the Pursuit of Peace* (Cambridge, 1963); Gordon A. Craig, "The Great Powers and the Balance of Power, 1830–1870," in *New Cambridge Modern History* 10 (Cambridge, 1960); and E. V. Gulick, *Europe's Classic Balance of Power* (Ithaca, NY, 1955). The classic treatment of war as an instrument of policy is Carl von Clausewitz, *On War*, available in several editions.

The course of international politics and nationalism are explored in Winfried Baumgart, *The Peace of Paris 1856: Studies in War, Diplomacy, and Peacemaking* (Santa Barbara, CA, 1981); Paul W. Schroeder, *Austria, Britain, and the Crimean War* (Ithaca, NY, 1972); and A. J. P. Taylor, *The Struggle for Mastery in Europe, 1848–1918* (Oxford, 1954). Italian unification is treated by D. Mack Smith, *Italy and Its Monarchy* (New Haven, CT, 1989); and Derek Beales, *The Risorgimento and the Unification of Italy* (New York, 1971); and German unification by Otto Pflanze, *Bismarck and the Development of Germany*, 3 vols. (Princeton, 1990); Lothar Gall, *Bismarck* (London, 1986); and Fritz Stern, *Gold and Iron* (New York, 1977). The Bismarckian period is discussed in Klaus Hildebrand, *German Foreign Policy from Bismarck to Adenauer* (London, 1989); George Kennan, *The Decline of Bismarck's European Order* (Princeton, 1979); William Langer, *European Alliances and Alignments, 1871–1890* (New York, 1964 ed.), and *The Diplomacy of Imperialism, 1890–1902* (New York, 1968 ed.).

Great Power relations on the eve of 1914 are discussed in James Joll and Gordon Martel, *The Origins of the First World War* (London, 2006 ed.); Zara Steiner, *Britain and the Origins of the First World War* (London, 1977); Oron Hale, *The Great Illusion, 1900–1914* (New York, 1971); and Barbara Tuchman, *The Proud Tower* (New York, 1966). More specific topics, such as naval competition, are analyzed in Paul Kennedy, *The Rise of the Anglo-German Antagonism* (London, 1980) and P. Padfield, *The Great Naval Race* (London, 1974); imperialism in Paul Gordon Lauren, *Power and Prejudice* (Boulder, CO, 1996 ed.); military interference with policy in Paul Kennedy (ed.), *The*

War Plans of the Great Powers, 1880–1914 (London, 1979) and Gordon A. Craig, *The Politics of the Prussian Army* (New York, 1955); big business and politics in Eckhart Kehr, *Battleship Building and Party Politics in Germany* (Chicago, 1975); and the impact of technology in David Paull Nickles, *Under the Wire: How the Telegraph Changed Diplomacy* (Cambridge, MA, 2003) and Stephen Kern, *The Culture of Time and Space* (Cambridge, MA, 1986 ed.).

—— 3 ——

The Diplomatic Revolution Begins, 1919–1939

I n 1814–1815, after almost twenty-five years of intermittent warfare, representatives of the European powers had been able to sit down together—in Metternich's phrase, "as friends,"—and lay the foundations for a diplomatic system that, with readjustments, worked remarkably effectively for nearly a century. The First World War, which brought this system to a calamitous end, lasted only four years, but when it was over and new leaders came together in another great peacemaking conference in Paris, their achievement fell far short of that of their predecessors at Vienna. No viable system ever emerged from their labors, and although they tried at times to pretend that it had, the fact that an even greater world war than that of 1914–1918 broke out within twenty years provided dramatic proof of their utter failure. The unprecedented destruction and dislocations of the war, as well as the personal shortcomings of the participants themselves, provide some of the explanation for this. But the larger, underlying reason for their failure to build a viable international system can be found in the beginning of a revolution, the features of which slowly emerged over a period of several years but then virtually erupted in fury before their very eyes. This was the diplomatic revolution characterized by the increase in the numbers and types of actors in international relations, expansion of the geographical scope of diplomacy, powerful domestic political forces pressing to ignore professional diplomats and instead elevate the role of public opinion and economic interests, new technology in communications and transportation as well as weapons, and the deliberate ideological rejection by many national leaders of traditional norms of diplomacy and self-imposed restraints on force and statecraft. These forces created pressures that in the end overwhelmed them all and are still with us today.

ATTEMPTS AT PEACEMAKING AND SYSTEM BUILDING

Peacemaking, even in the best of circumstances, presents formidable challenges, always serving as a reminder that it is easier to destroy than it is to create. But when the First World War ended, the problems appeared particularly difficult as Europe and the world staggered in disbelief over the carnage and disruption that confronted them. The century's new industrialized science and technology in the hands of mass, citizen-conscripted armed forces infused with intense nationalism had unleashed destruction that revolutionized modern warfare and seriously challenged many earlier assumptions of using armed force as a legitimate instrument of policy. The combination of patterns of machine-gun fire, barbed wire entanglements, artillery capable of firing exploding shells to targets several miles away, poison gas, land mines, torpedoes, submarines and battleships mobilized on a massive scale, aircraft, and armored tanks laid waste entire provinces, obliterated the traditional distinction between civilian and combatant, and killed an estimated 10,000,000 human beings.

But there was more. The war destroyed four empires and their monarchies. It precipitated seismic shocks of democratic and Communist revolutions. It loosened the bonds of imperialism overseas, and thereby began to unleash the force of self-determination and the place of colonized peoples in any future international system. In leaving little distinction between "victor" and "vanquished," the conflict profoundly signaled the collapse of many of the restraints and limited features of classical warfare and diplomacy. Moreover, the internal and external dimensions of the First World War demolished the earlier cultural and psychological homogeneity and general consensus on ethical values of European civilization itself. Death and exhaustion left, in the mournful words of German writer Erich Maria Remarque, "Fields of craters within and without." "The old Europe that we had known in 1914," wrote one French diplomat, "ceased to exist."

Structurally, for example, there was not much left of some of the best-known entities of the past. Of the five Great Powers that had dominated the classical system, more than half—the German Empire, the Russian Empire, and the Austro-Hungarian Empire—had succumbed to revolution and collapsed. The Ottoman Empire no longer existed. War and revolution radically transformed Europe and the Middle East by creating completely new nation-states, emerged from the ashes of these former empires, including Finland, Estonia, Latvia, Lithuania, a revived Poland, Czechoslovakia, Hungary, Yugoslavia, Iraq, Syria, and Saudi Arabia, among others. The war brought about direct American intervention into global affairs, thereby undermining European hegemony and setting the stage for a redistribution of world power. In addition, countries such as Canada, Australia, New Zealand, South Africa, and Japan that had played only minor or sporadic roles in international relations prior to the war now emerged with objectives and policies of their own. The peacemakers found it impossible to determine how much of a role these untried elements would play and how to fit them and the expansive process they described as "internationalization" into some kind of a diplomatic system.

Passions and pressures also greatly complicated the tasks of peacemaking. There was no question now of former friends and foes sitting down together as partners to lay the foundations of peace as they had at Vienna, and this meant that the final settlement would not constitute a consensual agreement

Europe and the Middle East Transformed by War and Revolution

among all the belligerents. The war of 1914–1918 far exceeded the conflicts of the nineteenth century in duration and ferocity. In revolutionary ways, it divorced military strategy from foreign policy, was fought not as a limited but rather as a "total" war that involved all of the resources at the command of the participants, and broke down the traditional division between the military and civilian parts of society. Indeed, the suffering of the civilian populations was greater than it had been since the horrors of the Thirty Years' War. That war, as we have seen, started as a religious conflict and ended as a political one. One could say that the First World War marked a reversal of that process, beginning as a political conflict and ending as a religious one, in which each side began to view the other not as an opponent to be defeated, but as a kind of anti-Christ who must be completely extirpated. This transition resulted not only from the extent of suffering and sacrifice, but also from the emergence of Bolshevism (and then anti-Bolshevism) and the deliberate manipulation of nationalistic passions by means of wartime propaganda. As one of the leading propagandists, George Creel, observed:

> It was in this recognition of Public Opinion as a major force that the Great War differed most essentially from all previous conflicts. The trial of strength was not only between massed bodies of armed men, but between opposed ideals ... [and] raised issues that had to be fought out in the hearts and minds of people as well as on the actual firing line.

Once aroused, these passions were exceedingly difficult to turn off. Consequently, when the war ended there was precious little patience or sympathy for the traditional practices of diplomacy, for a broad sense of proportion on behalf of the system as a whole, for letting the defeated enemies even attend the peacemaking negotiations or express their views, or for compromise and reconciliation. Instead of working in partnership to build a consensus on system-wide principles, leaders focused on rivalry and allowed themselves to succumb to the emotional impulse to seek revenge.

These domestic pressures received powerful expression in those political leaders determined to represent their countries themselves at the Paris Peace Conference in 1919, even though they often had little knowledge of history, international relations, or understanding of just how complicated it would be to make peace in the aftermath of such a devastating war. The mercurial British Prime Minister David Lloyd George had actively campaigned on a slogan not for a new legal order based on consensus, but rather for a settlement based on revenge against the Germans. "We will squeeze the orange," he ranted, "until the pips squeak!" Referring to the art of diplomacy, he stated contempt for the professionals, saying that "diplomats were invented simply to waste time" and declaring simply, "I want no diplomats." Similarly, President Woodrow Wilson of the United States (described by one career diplomat as "The Dread Amateur") asserted that the world needed a "New Diplomacy" different from the "Old Diplomacy" in its origins, objectives, and methods. They and their fellow politicians Georges Clemenceau of France and Vittorio Orlando of Italy put these sentiments into practice at the peace conference when they often rejected the advice offered by their staff experts and relied more upon popular passions or personal intuition instead of facts to solve intricate international problems. As Winston Churchill so pointedly described it:

> The peoples, transported by their sufferings and by the mass teachings with which they had been inspired, stood around in scores of millions to demand that retribution should be exacted to the full. Woe betide the leaders now perched on their dizzy pinnacles of triumph if they cast away at the conference table what the soldiers had won on the hundred blood-soaked battlefields.... The multitudes remained plunged in ignorance of the simplest facts, and their leaders, seeking their votes, did not dare to undeceive them.

All of this, of course, led to a distorted settlement, festering grievances and primal passions which could be easily exploited, and a manifest failure to secure consensus on goals and objectives, on normative values and ethics in statecraft, and on the very conceptual basis of international order itself. The negotiators in Vienna a century earlier, for example, had shared a common agreement on the principle of the balance of power to build their system. Some leaders still wanted to think in those terms and frequently pressed for treaties of guarantee to enforce the peace settlement. But this idea was directly challenged by Wilson, who believed that balance-of-power politics was a contrivance of states and that the coming of the war in 1914 had been rooted in its machinations. He set out to eliminate this system, declaring:

> There must not be a balance of power but a community of power...I am therefore proposing that all nations henceforth avoid entangling alliances that draw them into competitions of power, catch them in a net of intrigue and selfish rivalry, and disturb their own affairs with influences intruded from without....When all unite to act in the same sense and with the same purpose, all will act in the common interest and are free to live their own lives under a common protection.

Wilson and his supporters envisioned replacing the modalities of the old European order with a new "international organization to limit the burden of armaments and diminish the probability of war." Premier Clemenceau and a number of others, however, remained convinced that the balance of power would be the most effective regulator of relationships among nations, and refused to abandon this opinion because of sermons by a man whom they regarded as an idealistic schoolmaster from a country with little experience in world affairs. They wanted to avoid any self-imposed restraints and instead to punish the enemy, to be compensated for their sacrifices, and to construct a system based on treaties and legal guarantees.

Peacemaking and system building at Paris thus became the scene of intense and protracted conflict. This explains why the final Versailles Treaty reflected all of these passionately held differences, described by Romanian Foreign Minister Ioan Bratianu as "Wilsonian garlands wrapped around Napoleonic clauses." In the end, Wilson gained his major objective, the creation of the League of Nations, but only at the expense of many compromises that vitiated his own declared principles. This was particularly evident when one compared the final results with his earlier and highly publicized declarations about a "war to end all wars" and a "peace without victory." Indeed, the discrepancies between what had been promised and what was delivered were so palpable that Wilson's critics lashed out at him. His role in defeating a provision on the emotionally charged issue of international human rights and racial equality, for example, prompted the Japanese to publicly accuse Wilson of being nothing more than a hypocrite of the worst sort.

Domestic opponents within the United States were even harsher and mounted a powerful offensive against the whole settlement itself. They attacked the League as an instrument of irresponsible commitments and a dangerous international organization that would threaten national sovereignty, jeopardize the Constitution, interfere in domestic affairs, and "entangle the American nation in a European-Asiatic balance of power." Senator James Reed of Missouri, impassioned about race, even declared: "Think of submitting questions involving the very life of the United States to a tribunal on which a nigger from Liberia, a nigger from Honduras, a nigger from India…each have votes equal to that of the great United States." Thinking like this fanned the flames of bitter partisanship between Democrats and Republicans, personal feuds, and the refusal of both Wilson and his "irreconcilable" opponents to compromise, and, in the end, the Senate rejected the treaties and forbade American membership in the League entirely.

Others, despite the opposition of the U.S. Senate, hoped that their creation of the first permanent international organization in history would play a vital role in building and sustaining a new system. They believed that the significant changes taking place in international relations needed to be addressed, that the First World War had demonstrated that the "winners" appeared to lose as much as the losers, and that *raison d'état* could best be served by peace. For this reason, they attempted to design the League of Nations as an instrument to manage crises and to prevent war—a bolder, more comprehensive, and more egalitarian experiment than anything ever attempted before. Its Assembly, for example, was to meet once a year in Geneva and serve as a forum for multilateral diplomacy open to all member states represented with equal voting rights. Its Council, a smaller group composed of both permanent and temporary members, could meet at any time to deal with a crisis. Moreover, its Secretariat would establish a new actor known as the international civil servant. The Covenant called for its members to promote peace and security, to regulate their disputes by peaceful means, to honor international law and treaty obligations, and to respect and defend the territorial integrity and political independence of each other against external aggression. "Any war or threat of war," it stated, "whether immediately affecting any of the members of the League or not, is hereby declared a matter of concern to the whole League, and the League shall take any action that may be deemed wise and effectual to safeguard the peace of nations." If any nation resorted to war in violation of their promises, the Covenant provided for the possibility of joint economic sanctions and the use of armed force. In this way, those who created the League hoped that aggression would be deterred by collective security without the resort to divisive alliances and dangerous arms races as in the past.

Discussion about the League of Nations also revealed yet another aspect of the diplomatic revolution: a growing tendency, which would increase through time, to explore the relationship between peacemaking and system building and human rights. There are several reasons for this. The first is that wars disrupt and destroy, often tearing down power structures and prejudices heretofore resistant to change. In this regard, the First World War brought about new opportunities to extend rights to many, not the least of which were women. Second, one of the characteristics of total war is that in order to mobilize their full resources, governments make promises. Those who had been promised a

"New Diplomacy" of "justice," a world "safe for democracy," and "an equality of rights" as a reward for sacrifices made during the war were determined that leaders at the Paris Peace Conference and then in the League keep their promises. Third, modern wars and peacemaking, by their very nature, demonstrate the increasing international interconnectedness of shared life and death, and the fact that the fate of one country and its people and their rights are tied to those of others. Finally, peacemakers and system builders at the end of a war generally want to do what they can to avoid another deadly conflict by creating a settlement reflecting normative values designed to enhance peace. They want their wartime sufferings, in short, to be worth something. As such, many people after 1919 began to envision peace as more closely connected with security, justice, and respect for human rights. This explains why the League set about to initiate a series of path-breaking international measures to protect the rights of women, children, ethnic minorities, workers, indigenous peoples, the sick, combatants, and refugees.

Those who worked to make the League of Nations effective, however, came to realize that not everyone agreed with their efforts and that international systems cannot be built or maintained unless there is genuine consensus among the major actors to agree on basic norms, objectives, and principles, including those of self-restraints, and to actively collaborate in defending them. This proved to be a problem from the very beginning when the Americans simply refused to join, causing the League to irreparably suffer from what political scientist Inis Claude calls "the problem of the empty chair." Moreover, other important powers stood outside its membership for most of the period: Germany did not join until 1926 and then withdrew in 1933 along with Japan, while the Soviet Union did not become a member until 1934 and was then expelled five years later. Moreover, when the League attempted to take action to protect human rights, those states accused of abuse lashed out—as many do today—accusing the international community of "impertinent interference" into domestic affairs and threatening the Westphalian principle of national sovereignty. To make matters worse, the only two major nations left participating in the League, namely Britain and France, could never agree on its purposes and methods, particularly when involving force and statecraft. They continually disagreed and actually worked at cross purposes concerning the League's authority to respond to danger. The French periodically tried to put teeth into the organization by having its members sign guarantees to act automatically when confronted with threats to the peace, as with the Draft Treaty of Mutual Assistance of 1923 and the Geneva Protocol of 1925, intended to bind them into taking required action against states when necessary. But the British consistently defeated these attempts, arguing that the League should not be a body that took punitive action against wrongdoers but simply a place for debate. The League thus was forced to confront the fact that its member states were unwilling to take responsibility for collective security seriously, and this did not bode well for the future. Said one observer in frustration: "The trouble with the League is not the *League*, it is the *Nations*."

Such unwillingness to address issues of force and statecraft collectively became manifest in other ways as well. At the Washington Naval Conference of 1921–1922, leaders signed the Five Power Treaty on capital warships, but fundamentally refused to engage in creating meaningful restraints or limitations on their weapons. At exactly the same time, the Four Power Treaty on Asia and the Pacific demonstrated a similar lack of will to enforce its terms. As Senator Henry Cabot Lodge, who previously had orchestrated opposition to both the Versailles Treaty and the League of Nations, announced with pride: "There is no provision for the use of force to carry out any of the terms of the agreement, and no military or naval sanction lurks anywhere in the background or under cover of these plain and simple clauses."

In exasperation, the French attempted to build their own security system by concluding separate alliances with Belgium, Poland, and the so-called Little Entente of Yugoslavia, Romania, and Czechoslovakia. But these efforts at deterrence, as we shall explore in Chapter 9, looked far better on paper than they did in practice. The small states had disputes among themselves and could never contribute significant military force against powerful neighbors like the Germans or the Soviets. Moreover, France's resources were not sufficient to support their allies unless they received assistance from Britain, and the British were unwilling to do any such thing. In fact, when the British government signed the 1925 Locarno Pact guaranteeing the common boundary between Germany, France, and Belgium, it wanted to make it "perfectly clear" that such offers of protection would not extend to borders in Eastern Europe. When the historical advisor to the Foreign Office, Sir James Hedlam-Morley, struck a dissenting note by warning that British foreign policy always had sustained the European balance of power by supporting the weaker side against the stronger, his advice was dismissed. Weakened by this British attitude and by the high cost of military assistance to its eastern members, the French treaty arrangements appeared in shambles after the conclusion of the Nazi-Polish Pact in 1934. France cast even further doubt on its own system when it tried to complete the Maginot Line, a gigantic defensive rampart fixed along its frontier from the Switzerland to Belgium, indicating that it would stay inert on the inside of its own borders and thereby abandon others to their fate. These developments could not possibly restrain the designs of any aggressors.

Those statesmen attempting peacemaking and system building also struggled with yet other features of the diplomatic revolution: the rapid expansion in the number and types of actors in international relations and the expanding geographical scope of diplomacy. Before 1914, only about a dozen nations in the entire world took continuous interest in global affairs, and these were largely European. The Paris Peace Conference provided the first clear demonstration of how radically that condition was about to change. Up to this point, for example, no American president had ever left the United States to negotiate an international treaty, and certainly none had ever before enjoyed the influence that Wilson now possessed. One immediate result shocked the traditionalists, and this was the formal acceptance of English as a language equal to French in diplomacy. But there was much more. "THIRTY-TWO NATIONS,

PEOPLES, AND RACES...," noted one observer, "Not simply England, Italy, and the Great Powers are there, but all the little nations....Not only groups, but races have come—Jews, Indians, Arabs, and all-Asia." Another participant at the conference described it as: "Chinamen, Japanese, Koreans, Hindus, Kirghizes, Lesghiens, Circassians, Mingrelians, Buryats, Malays, and Negroes and Negroids from Africa and America were among the tribes and tongues forgathered in Paris to watch the rebuilding of the political world system and to see where they 'came in.'" This was something unknown in the annals of diplomacy, and it would continue.

One of the results of this development was the realization that it would be much more challenging to create a working system for an international community than it had been when the participating states had been few. The original membership of the League of Nations, to illustrate, numbered forty-two, including (in addition to the Europeans) Australia, Canada, China, Haiti, India, Japan, the Latin American states, Liberia, New Zealand, Persia, Siam, and South Africa. Others came to join as well. But there was something more than just numbers. This expansion brought with it a breakdown in what had once been the internal homogeneity of the small, Eurocentric system of classical diplomacy. An important reason for the relative effectiveness of the nineteenth-century system was that its members were bound together by a common historical tradition and language, by shared cultural and religious values, and by ties of race, class, and gender, all of which (despite their many other drawbacks) greatly facilitated communication and cooperation. This did not survive in the aftermath of the First World War, and the adjustments necessitated by the new heterogeneity were sometimes painful. The British found it difficult, for example, to watch the League of Nations pay as much attention to the speeches of Eduard Benes of Czechoslovakia, Nicolae Titulescu of Romania, or Haile Selassie of Ethiopia as it did to their own representatives. They showed disrespect for the small powers, and it was said of Foreign Secretary Austen Chamberlain that when he spoke in the Assembly, he seemed to be saying, "We are perfect. We are British. And yet you, you dagoes, dare to come here and criticize US!" Attitudes such as this made it difficult to build any inclusive or effective international system.

Further complications arose as a result of technology that began to transform the pace of diplomacy. The staggering power and speed of invention and practical application affected diplomats as directly as it did the lives of millions of other people. Foreign ministries found themselves replacing their horse-drawn carriages with automobiles, their candles and gas lamps with electric lights, their elegant curving staircases with elevators, and their clerks skilled in handwritten script with typists who could do the work faster. Moreover, the growing use of electronic communication and aircraft all revealed further nullifications of former practical limits heretofore imposed by distance, geographical barriers, weather, national boundaries, and—perhaps most critically—time. The speed of these new forms of communication and transportation reduced the length of time to contemplate, analyze reports, choose between alternative courses of action, assume responsibilities, and issue instructions without the relaxed luxury enjoyed just a few years before to calm emotions and reach careful judgment.

PUBLIC OPINION AND "PUBLIC DIPLOMACY"

One of the most salient features of the diplomatic revolution during this period was the heightened influence exercised by public opinion on foreign policy. There were a few, such as former U.S. Secretary of State Elihu Root, who worked to develop an informed public in an age of spreading democracy and, in a famous essay published in the newly created journal *Foreign Affairs,* stressed the necessity of serious education to help citizens learn lessons from international history and "acquire a knowledge of the fundamental and essential facts and principles upon which the relations of nations depend," including those of force and statecraft. But these were exceptions, for the new emphasis focused more on emotion than on facts for people set adrift by war and revolution. This manifested itself in excessive preoccupation with the public mood and for governments to follow rather than lead opinion in the conduct and forms of diplomacy.

Here again, it was the experience of the First World War that shattered traditional practices and the heretofore limited role of public opinion in international relations. The years and sacrifices required by "total" war and the deliberate use of nationalistic propaganda to win "the hearts and minds" of people at home and abroad brought rising and irresistible pressure from politicians, business interests, journalists, and vocal members of the public at large insistent on having a greater voice in determining their countries' foreign policies. They deplored what they called the "secret diplomacy" and class "elitism" of the past and announced their determination to end, in the words of the *Berliner Tageblatt,* "an aristocratic collegium unapproachable to the ordinary mortal, like the table of the Holy Grail." Critics, such as Arthur Ponsonby in his wartime manifesto *Democracy and Diplomacy: A Plea for Popular Control of Foreign Policy,* argued that they had remained silent and subservient long enough and thus began to insert themselves into diplomacy, creating permanent legislative committees to deal with foreign affairs and demanding that they be kept informed and consulted.

This forced the professionals in foreign ministries—who only a short time before had so assiduously refrained from providing any information at all about their activities to "the masses"—not only to respond to these public demands, but actually to attempt to shape opinion as well. They found themselves required to spend ever larger amounts of time and effort engaging in what came to be called "public diplomacy" by providing legislative or congressional briefings, guiding junketing politicians, hiring press attachés, recruiting publicists, holding press conferences, making public appearances and answering questions, producing broadcasts for the new technological invention of radio, publishing collections of heretofore classified diplomatic documents in order to win popular support, building domestic political coalitions among pressure groups in order to conduct policy, promoting their national cultural achievements abroad, and referring ever more frequently to "world public opinion." The German Foreign Ministry even created a special War Guilt Office for the sole purpose of convincing this public that Germany had not been responsible for causing the First World War. In some countries, as we shall soon see, they increasingly were required to represent and propagate the ideology of the regime they served. Professional diplomats warned ominously that such trends would replace the traditional norms of restraint and practices of discretion with cheap public displays and what they described as "the inflammation of national passions."

Such developments increasingly became a feature of diplomacy, and the retribution that public feeling could wreak upon political leaders seeking to deal with complicated problems of force and statecraft was real and intimidating. French Prime Minister Aristide Briand was forced from office by a pervasive and wholly irrational rumor that his policy at the 1922 Geneva conference had been dictated by the British. Lloyd George met the same fate when his handling of a crisis in the Middle East led to a public outcry that he had been trying to drag the country into another war. When Winston Churchill, in a 1936 House of Commons speech, accused Prime Minister Stanley Baldwin of irresponsibility for having failed to take advantage of the previous election campaign to meet the growing international dangers by calling for heightened armament efforts, Baldwin answered with a startling ingenuousness. "Suppose I had gone to the country," he replied, "and said that Germany was rearming and we must rearm, does anyone think that this pacific democracy would have rallied to that cry at that moment? I cannot think of anything that would have made the loss of the election from my point of view more certain."

Fear of alienating public opinion influenced the foreign policy of United States as well. During the Disarmament Conference of 1932, President Herbert Hoover might have persuaded the French to modify their position if he had been willing to adjust or abandon war debts owed to the United States, but he refused to do so because he believed that such an offer would be unacceptable to American opinion. Like Baldwin, he was afraid of losing an election. Similarly, when President Franklin Roosevelt warned in 1937 that the epidemic of lawlessness spreading in the world could only be checked by a quarantine imposed by the peace-loving states, the isolationist public outcry in his own country was so immediate, massive, and negative that the White House felt compelled to disavow the true intent of the speech and retreat into inactivity that lasted until the very eve of a new war.

In addition to its tendency to cripple the resolution of governments, the power of public opinion had a significant effect on the conduct of diplomacy itself. For one thing, it ended the virtual monopoly of the professionals. Popular opinion held the view that the professional diplomats and their way of doing business had been largely responsible for causing the war of 1914 and that the sooner their control was broken, the better. So strong was this feeling that political leaders sought to reduce the role of the professionals by at times actually taking over the functions of the diplomats themselves. This explains why Lloyd George so frequently dismissed the advice and sometimes even the existence of the Foreign Office and to a large extent ignored his ambassadors, traveling around with his own staff and conducting negotiations with foreign officials on complicated matters that he did not fully understand. Others did the same. Instead of letting chiefs of mission abroad do what they were trained to do, political leaders, ministers, and special missions of politicians or private citizens often took to doing their business for them. In this regard they were assisted by the new technological inventions of the telephone (that enemy of reflection, which became increasingly accepted as a means of communication) and the airplane to travel abroad and conduct negotiations themselves. A French commission later investigated the deficiencies of this practice, concluding:

> after the conclusion of the treaties of 1919, ministers had the habit of multiplying their contacts with their colleagues in other countries. The abuse of direct conversations opens the door to numerous dangers. Engagements are entered into too easily. They are often improvised. It is better to define the course of a negotiation by a note which has matured in the silence of the ministry than by chance exchanges that are likely to be imprecise.

Nor was imprecision the only danger inherent in this kind of diplomacy. When politicians engaged in the process of negotiation, they often felt that their personal reputations were at stake and that a successful result was imperative. This, in turn, could lead to ringing declarations plainly designed to convince a credulous public that great objectives had been achieved—which later, however, proved to be unsubstantiated.

Along with these transformations in personnel came changes in format. During the war, Wilson had called for "open covenants openly arrived at," and it soon became an article of public faith that "open diplomacy" represented the only acceptable procedure. The result was a rapid growth of diplomacy by conference, which took the form of either large meetings in which many states participated in discussions of subjects of general interest or what came to be called summit meetings, such as the Locarno Conference of 1925, involving heads of state or foreign ministers. While introducing some of the benefits of inclusiveness and transparency, they all too often met under the pressure of public impatience and without preliminary talks adequate to lay a basis for fruitful negotiation. Indeed, they often seemed planned more for public spectacle than for the substantive issues at stake, as evidenced by the numbers of journalists, photographers, press conferences, inspired leaks, and other inventions of modern public relations. In these circumstances, not much could be expected, except for a final communiqué that sought to convey a success where none existed. A perfect example of this could be seen in the Kellogg-Briand Pact of 1928, purporting with a simple stroke of the pen to outlaw war itself—a token gesture with no enforcement provisions of any kind, signed simply to appeal to popular sentiment.

As for summit meetings, the eminent expert on diplomatic practice, Sir Harold Nicolson, pointed out that the political leaders who participated were particularly busy and preoccupied men. "The time at the disposal of these visitors," he noted, "is not always sufficient to allow for patience and calm deliberation. The honors which are paid to a minister in a foreign capital may tire his physique, excite his vanity, or bewilder his judgment." This could be seen with striking clarity with the ill-fated Munich Conference of September 1938 in which the participants were anxious to go home with anything that might be called a success. British Prime Minister Neville Chamberlain desperately wanted to come back with something, so he persuaded Adolf Hitler to sign a hastily drafted and loosely stated "Anglo-German Declaration" of future cooperation. When Chamberlain flew home to joyous crowds, he smiled and waved the piece of paper in his hand as proof that he had secured "peace in our time." The public desperately wanted to believe him. They thus were completely shocked when, in March 1939, Hitler invaded Czechoslovakia, demonstrating that this agreement meant nothing at all.

A final result of the heightened importance of public sentiment could be seen in new efforts to shape that opinion through propaganda and a new emphasis on what might be called diplomacy by public declaration. This technique sought to use an address to send a message, not to another government, but rather to public opinion in another country, in the hope of influencing it to bring pressure upon its own leaders. The master of this was Hitler. Whenever he did something particularly outrageous, he would make a major speech in which he appealed to wishful thinking and the uneasy conscience in the West. He would explain that, far from being provocative or aggressive, what he had just done was simply a means of redressing legitimate grievances, opening up new opportunities for a better world, or removing the final obstacle to lasting peace. These speeches proved to be remarkably effective, principally because his listeners did not want war—and they *felt* more than they *thought*. This made them more vulnerable and susceptible to manipulation. As such, they could be led to believe that they could secure peace by giving dictators what they wanted, eschewing collective security, and dissuading their own governments from taking action that might have discouraged the aggressors from launching a war.

ECONOMICS AND "ECONOMIC DIPLOMACY"

The diplomatic revolution from 1919 to 1939 also was characterized by a rapidly expanding role of economics and by the insensitivity of the various powers to its potential for political damage and long-term international implications. Part of the problem, of course, flowed from the consequences of the First World War itself: millions killed in combat, millions more permanently disabled, and the unprecedented destruction of homes and farms, livestock and forests, financial resources and investments, communication and transportation networks, and industrial plants and shops. Added to this was the fact that most of Europe had relied on borrowing rather than taxation to meet the costs of the war and now found itself confronted with staggering debts and the threat of mounting inflation caused by depreciating currencies. In the face of these problems, the victors often demonstrated remarkable ignorance about the simplest of economic facts, and the tactics that they employed were so unrealistic, shortsighted, and narrowly nationalistic that they fatally weakened the possibility of maintaining any diplomatic system.

Given the losses of the war and the monumental reconstruction that lay ahead, it is not surprising that nations would intensify their economic competition. Bitter rivals increasingly spoke of each other and their postwar struggle in terms of "business enemies," "financial weapons," "commercial battles," "captured markets," and "economic warfare." Interests representing chambers of commerce, exporters, businesses, and investors consequently placed powerful pressure on their foreign ministries to engage in what they called "economic diplomacy." By this they meant making greater efforts to fuse economics with foreign policy, seeing expanding trade and finance as projections of national power. Professional diplomats thus found themselves, as never before, being forced to abandon their traditional distinction between high "political" and low "commercial" affairs, gather business intelligence and trade statistics, train more consular officers, hire commercial attachés, and include businessmen, bankers, and industrialists as active participants in diplomatic negotiations. No clearer evidence could be found than when Walter Rathenau, a part owner or director of eighty-six domestic and twenty-one international enterprises, became German foreign minister in 1922, symbolizing the role that large-scale business would play in international politics.

But passion sometimes overrode expertise and wise financial decisions, as evidenced by the determination at the peace conference to impose upon the beaten foe the burden of reparations without establishing shared goals and objectives, or thinking through the possible consequences. Some sought merely to pay for their losses of the war and to enable the victors to liquidate the debts that they had contracted during the course of the conflict. Others wanted to use reparations as an economic weapon to punish Germany and to keep it in a position of weakness for a long time. In the end, they chose to ignore the historical lessons of the generally counterproductive nature of reparations and decided to exact from Germany a punitive amount twice as large as the original estimate, even though its capacity to make such payments had been significantly diminished as a result of losing the war. These terms helped to destroy not only the democratic experiment of the German Weimar Republic but also the postwar settlement itself.

Reparations also revealed sharply divergent approaches by the British and the French as to how economics should relate to issues of force and statecraft. Lloyd George became convinced that only a scaling down of the burden imposed upon Germany would allow the diplomatic system to operate—a position that the French, under the leadership of the tough and rigid Raymond Poincaré, adamantly opposed. This irreconcilable difference between the two major powers most responsible for maintaining the peace settlement found fateful expression in January 1923 when a German default led, despite British protests, to a French and Belgian military occupation of the Ruhr mining area. The Germans responded with passive resistance, the costs of which could only be met by printing new money in such large amounts that the result was runaway inflation. This impoverished the middle class and strengthened the growing number of rapid nationalist, antirepublican, and discontented political movements, not the least of which was a group known as the Nazis. The termination of reparation payments, in turn, created a fiscal crisis and the collapse of the franc in France. In the end, the currency was saved and bankruptcy averted only when the government secured loans from the banking houses of J. P. Morgan in New York and Lazard Brothers in London.

The growing role of private bankers and business and financial experts in place of professional diplomats could also be seen in the various efforts made to devise new and reduced reparations payments and to extend loans to Germany. Indeed, they dominated the London Reparations Conference of 1924, and their decisions revealed their ability to impose serious restraints on the actions of governments. If any further doubts existed about the power of economics to alter global affairs, they were shattered by the Wall Street stock market crash of 1929 and the resulting Great Depression. In the United States, Britain, and France, this led to isolationism and trade protectionism. In Germany, it resulted in collapse and helped to bring Adolf Hitler to power. None of this could be encouraging for those who desired international peace and security.

Using economics as a tool of coercion in dealing with issues of force and statecraft received increasing attention throughout this period as well. Negotiations at the Geneva Disarmament Conference of 1932 certainly confirmed this development. Here, the British believed that everything possible should be done to help Germany restore its full sovereignty in foreign affairs, including a revision of restrictions in the Versailles Treaty on armed forces. The French adamantly opposed such a proposal unless accompanied by other security guarantees. This impasse and its impact upon the whole subject of peace brought the United States temporarily back to European councils, with President Herbert Hoover arguing that a reduction of armaments would be the best way of promoting recovery from the world depression. Some of his advisors actively encouraged him to use the war debts owed to the United States by France as economic leverage to coerce the French into changing their position. But, as we have seen, Hoover did not want to jeopardize his electoral chances with the public by any suggestion of debt reduction, even as a means of pressure to promote disarmament. This, when combined with the reluctance of the participants to accept any meaningful limitations on their armed forces, caused the collapse of the conference and the fateful consequences that would follow.

Germany, on the other hand, showed no reluctance at all in employing economic diplomacy to its fullest advantage. Bernhard von Bülow, the state secretary of the Foreign Office, designed a strategy in 1931 to create a customs union between Germany and Austria in order to exert "the pressure of economic necessity" that would "lead to a solution, scarcely conceivable by other means, of vital political interests of the Reich." He continued:

then Poland with her unstable economic structure would be surrounded and exposed to all kinds of dangers; we should have her in a vise which could perhaps in the short or long run make her willing to consider further the idea of exchanging political concessions for tangible economic advantages.

Hitler seized upon such calculations and pushed the idea of economic weapons even further. When he launched the Four Year Plan in 1936, he made it clear that those charged with making economic decisions needed to know that their sole duty was to create the basis for "the struggle for self-realization" that would enable Germany to assert itself in the world. Hitler called for a *Wehrwirtschaft*, or war economy, with an economic mobilization comparable to his military mobilization. "The German economy," he said, "must be capable of supporting war in four years." The key to his success in this effort was the economic strategy, which targeted exchanges of weapons made in Germany for foodstuffs and raw materials from Eastern Europe.

Hitler's open admission that his economic diplomacy was predicated upon war and his rapid success in penetrating Eastern Europe alarmed the professional foreign policy establishments in Britain and France. Voices were raised to argue that acquiescence in Germany's economic hegemony would violate their national interests. Proposals that economic countermeasures be employed, however, encountered strong opposition on the part of the general public, private investors, businesses, and bankers, who argued that cooperation with Germany, rather than opposition, was the best way to secure peace. Their appeasement became such a force that one diplomat bitterly complained: "In spite of all our efforts, Mr. Montagu Norman [the governor of the Bank of England] continues to carry out his own foreign policy, certainly without consulting the Foreign Office and without, I suspect, taking even the Treasury very much into consideration." Such divisions of purpose and policy made an effective answer to Hitler's economic diplomacy impossible, thereby making him the beneficiary.

A *DIALOGUE DES SOURDS* WITH CONTRASTING NORMS AND OBJECTIVES

In September 1938, when Neville Chamberlain went to Godesberg, carrying his allies' approval of the terms for a settlement of the Czechoslovakian crisis on which he and Hitler had agreed two weeks earlier, he was disagreeably surprised to find that his host had changed his mind and had rewritten the agreement, introducing severely harsher conditions. When Chamberlain was handed a paper embodying these changes, he is reported to have said angrily, "This is an ultimatum, not a negotiation!" Pointing to the title page, Hitler replied mildly, "It says memorandum."

This incident illustrates the failure of meaningful communication in the interwar period. Indeed, diplomatic discussions took place between intense rivals rather than partners, often resembling what the French call a *dialogue des sourds*, or a conversation between deaf people. Here, words meant different things to different people, sides misheard what was being said, or the participants did not really listen at all. The victories of Bolshevism in Russia in 1917, Fascism in Italy in 1922, the militarists in Japan in 1931, and National Socialism in Germany in 1933, when combined with the general marginalization of professional diplomats and their established practices, created four major states determined to actually overthrow the peace settlement and to bring about a new ideological age. With this came one of the most fateful features of the entire diplomatic revolution: the deliberate rejection of heretofore commonly accepted norms of behavior and the resulting collapse of a consensus on objectives.

The basic reason for this condition emerged from a fundamental disagreement on basic principles and a profound difference in values and aspirations. Great Britain, France, and the United States had developed in the liberal-democratic tradition, and their approach to international relations after 1919 was strongly influenced by their faith in the primacy of reason and a repugnance for war. They viewed the conduct of diplomacy as a rational pursuit among responsible powers that operated according to reasonable and generally accepted rules, self-imposed restraints, and the peaceful settlement of disputes. They believed that after the most terrible war in history, any person competent enough to rise to the leadership of a great nation would be intelligent enough to see that war was not to anyone's advantage. In sharp contrast, there were other states that deliberately rejected these values and assumptions and, like playing chess by moving bishops as if they were rooks, operated according to rules that they made up on their own.

It was clear from the very beginning, for example, that the Soviet Union had a fundamentally different approach to diplomacy from that of the West. The new Communist leaders had no hesitation in declaring an unremitting ideological war with capitalism, rejecting self-imposed restraints, and overthrowing the established international order. They repudiated the debts owed by the czarist government to its Western allies, confiscated foreign properties without compensation to the owners, published confidential treaties, and announced their intent to foment worldwide revolution. V. I. Lenin set about, as he had promised, "to prepare and conduct revolutionary war" and "to at once systematically start to incite rebellion." As a part of this strategy, he insisted on rejecting all forms of traditional diplomacy, which he regarded as no more than tools in the hands of blood-sucking capitalists. Thus, when Leon Trotsky became the first commissar for foreign affairs, he announced his determination to "issue a few revolutionary declarations to the peoples and then shut up the joint [the Foreign Office]." Based on their belief that they could never coexist with bourgeois states, the Soviets created the Comintern as a "general staff of the world revolution of the proletariat" to engage in ideological propaganda abroad and subversion to overthrow non-Communist governments. Such actions immediately provoked fear and suspicion. As U.S. Secretary of State Bainbridge Colby concluded:

> It is not possible...to recognize the present rulers of Russia as a government with which the relations common to friendly governments can be

maintained. This conviction…rests upon…facts…which none dispute [and which] have convinced the Government of the United States, against its will, that the existing regime in Russia is based upon the negation of every principle of honor and good faith and every usage and convention underlying the whole structure of international law, the negation, in short, of every principle upon which it is possible to base harmonious and trustful relations, whether of nations or individuals.…There cannot be any common ground upon which [the United States] can stand with a Power whose conceptions of international relations are so entirely alien to its own, so utterly repugnant to its moral sense.…We cannot recognize, hold official relations with, or give friendly reception to, the agents of government which is determined and bound to conspire against our institutions.

Soviet ideological beliefs and suspicions, in turn, were exacerbated by Western actions. Political leaders forced the Soviet Union into diplomatic isolation by refusing to recognize the new government and deliberately excluding it from all peacemaking and system-building efforts of the Paris Peace Conference. They then used the Versailles Treaty to take vast swaths of territory from what had been Russia and gave them to the new successor states, creating what they called a *cordon sanitaire*, or sanitary barrier, to protect against the "disease" of Communism. Its clear purpose, according to British General Sir Henry Wilson, was "to create a ring of States all around Bolshevik Russia, the object being to prevent Bolshevism from spreading; to deprive it of supplies and power of expansion, and to reduce it to absolute exhaustion." Not content with these actions, the West then actually launched a military intervention against the Communist regime in an attempt to overthrow it by armed force.

Such an intense divergence of norms and objectives and its disastrous effect on any efforts to build and maintain a viable diplomatic system could be seen in subsequent Soviet behavior. Lenin boldly announced that he had purged the diplomatic corps of every "single influential person" from the old regime and reconstituted with ideological loyalists charged with creating "a reliable Communist apparatus" for foreign affairs. This explains why Soviet negotiators like Georgii Chicherin, Maxim Litvinov, and V. M. Molotov engaged in what has been called "diplomatic guerrilla warfare." Here, they would automatically reject all initial proposals from others, persist in an uncompromising advocacy of Communist ideology, use negotiations not to reach settlements but to block or delay them, and refuse to use diplomacy as a means of reaching real understanding or agreement. Sometimes they entered into discussions largely for the purpose of propaganda or rhetorical fireworks, as they did on the eve of the Anglo-Soviet Trade Agreement of 1921, announcing: "We are convinced that the foreign capitalists, who will be obliged to work on terms we offer them, will dig their own graves." On other occasions, they engaged in negotiations primarily to ingratiate the Soviet Union with third parties, as they did during the Genoa Conference of 1922 and the Disarmament Conference of 1932.

These practices only reinforced the conviction that it was difficult under any conditions to carry on meaningful diplomatic conversations with the Soviet Union and impossible to rely on any agreements made. The belief proved to be a heavy handicap to any revision of view in the years when the Soviets, seriously alarmed by the threat of Hitler's Germany, began to seek arrangements with the West that might strengthen their position and the system of collective security. This shift in Soviet diplomacy was marked by placing the Comintern under restraint, gaining diplomatic recognition by the United States in 1933, securing admission to the League of Nations in 1934, and negotiating the Franco-Soviet Pact in 1935. But Western suspicion of Soviet motives remained unabated. Even as the war approached and attempts were made to secure an Anglo-French-Soviet alliance, British Prime Minister Neville Chamberlain remained unmoved, saying: "I must confess to the most profound distrust of Russia."

Further complications arose during these interwar years with the emergence of Benito Mussolini and his Fascist party in Italy. His previous experience in journalism left him with a preoccupation for newspaper opinion, for style rather than substance, and for a hankering after sensational strokes and dramatic coups that would look good in headlines. He was forever making emotional public statements about his contempt for conventional practices, professional diplomats, collaborative negotiations, and restraints on the use of force. Instead, he wanted to pursue what he called the *tono fascista*, or the "Fascist style" of diplomacy, which demonstrated a proud and militant bearing, constant posturing and bombast, and a determination to impose ideological purity. Its practical effect, made even worse when he appointed his inexperienced son-in-law and former propaganda chief Galeazzo Ciano as foreign minister who boasted, "In Italy, the most Fascist ministry is that of Foreign Affairs," and then forced Italian ambassadors to conduct themselves not as partners of a common diplomatic community, but rather as if they were in "an enemy camp." When one senior diplomat received the order to represent Italy in France, for example, he naturally requested instructions. "What ought I try to accomplish in Paris?" he asked. "Nothing," replied Ciano. "It will be difficult," the ambassador responded, "but I will do my best." Blatantly rejecting the norms and objectives of traditional diplomacy, Mussolini turned instead to violence, launching the Italian-Ethiopian War of 1935–1936, flagrantly attacking a fellow member of the League of Nations.

Developments in Asia produced even more challenges. The outbreak of the Great Depression not only brought untold economic hardship to Japan, but enormously enhanced the popular appeal of the Japanese nationalist extremists and expansionists in civilian patriotic societies and in the armed forces, who called for drastic changes in their country's domestic and foreign policies. They denounced their government's emphasis on international partnership and peaceful conciliation, insisting that territorial spoils existed on the mainland, ripe for the taking. Frustrated with official policy that called for "patience and restraint," Japanese army officers precipitated a crisis in Mukden in 1931 that served as an excuse for seizing all of Manchuria. As historian Norman Rich observes, the Japanese conquest of Manchuria was the first significant breach in the international treaty system established after the First World War, the first blatant example of successful "revisionism," and the beginning of the Western policy of appeasement. Emboldened with their success and their appetite whetted for more, militant Japanese military and naval officers assassinated the prime minister, abolished parliament, and became the makers rather than the instruments of policy. They marginalized the professional diplomats and directed that Japan withdraw from the League of Nations, repudiate the Washington Naval Treaties, and begin a massive arms build up. In 1937, Japan seized control of Shanghai and then engaged in the "Rape of Nanking" with brutal and shocking human rights atrocities against tens of thousands of innocent civilians. Providing evidence of a *dialogue des sourds*, the Japanese described their actions not as aggression, but as an effort to "protect" the Chinese people, to establish a New Order based on "justice," and to bring about "eternal peace."

The final element in this gathering storm was the emergence of Adolf Hitler. He had given some thought to foreign affairs well before he came to power in 1933 and actually expressed many of his ideas in his autobiography *Mein Kampf*. Here he revealed that his own personal experience in the First World War had convinced him of the necessity of manipulating public opinion through propaganda in order to create "a national passion rearing up in its strength" to stir aggressive nationalism, inflame hatred against enemies, portray international cooperation as betrayal, and justify war itself. He also articulated his dreams of creating a *Machtstaat*, or power state, by tearing up the *Diktat*, or dictated settlement of the Versailles Treaty, and by securing *Lebensraum*, or living space, at the expense of others, even going so far as to identify his foreign targets in advance. "State boundaries are made by man and changed by man," he insisted, but this is "not won through solemn appeals to the Lord or through pious hopes in a League of Nations, but only by *the force of arms*." Importantly for our consideration, he never regarded diplomacy as a means of resolving conflict or preserving peace, but rather as an instrument of preparing for expansion and war. As he wrote himself, "An alliance whose aim does not embrace a plan for war is senseless and worthless. Alliances are concluded only for struggle." It is not surprising, therefore, that Hitler had a deep distrust of professional diplomats, referred to the German Foreign Ministry as "the Idiot House," and actually removed his ambassadors from foreign posts when he thought that they might be interested in seeking peace when he desired war.

As he planned for what he regarded as his "inevitable" war, Hitler received enormous assistance from the Western policy of appeasement. It was based on ignorance of force and statecraft, a belief that everyone surely shared the same norms and objectives even when they did not, fear of war, an intense hatred of Communism, and wishful thinking that the best way to maintain peace and security was to give the aggressors what they wanted in the hope that, once satisfied, they then would play by the rules. Although practiced by others in the West, including the French and the Americans, appeasement is most frequently identified with Neville Chamberlain, a politician who had made his way to becoming British prime minister by distinguished service in domestic politics, but who knew little of international relations. Indeed, he

"Only by the Force of Arms": Hitler and Mussolini

had once been interrupted while airing his views on diplomacy by his own brother Austen, one of the authors of the Locarno treaties, who accurately said, "Neville, you must remember you don't know anything about foreign affairs." This proved in the end to be tragically true, but it never seemed to bother him. Like so many other political leaders at the time, he was headstrong in his own opinions, resented professional diplomats, sought to bypass the Foreign Office as much as possible, dismissed the criticisms of those with considerable international knowledge and experience such as Foreign Secretary Anthony Eden or Winston Churchill, and surrounded himself instead with those whose views agreed with his own. In the end, Chamberlain's critics proved to be absolutely right, and appeasement helped to bring on the very war that the prime minister sought to avoid.

This disaster, however, did not result solely from his own gullibility. Hitler possessed considerable gifts of persuasion, and Chamberlain was not the only leader deluded by his ability to mask his true intentions until he felt strong enough to strike. Hitler showed calculating skill and inventiveness in using the resources and techniques of diplomacy to advance his purposes and adroitness in playing on the prejudices and wishful thinking of what others wanted to see and hear, thereby postponing the time when the scales finally fell from their eyes.

Hitler demonstrated these abilities as he methodically designed his foreign policy through four distinct phases on the road to war. The first of these, which followed immediately upon his accession to power, may be called the diplomacy of concealment or obfuscation. Here he wanted to convince other powers that they had nothing to fear. Toward this end, he did not change the personnel in the Foreign Office or the embassies, played down whatever earlier statements appeared in *Mein Kampf*, and explained on every possible occasion that whatever unpleasant things and violations of human rights were going on inside Germany had no international implications. Hitler's public statements at this stage were pacific, disarming, and even ingratiating. All of this was designed to blunt criticism, divert attention from his real intentions, and prevent external interference while Germany was still vulnerable.

In the second phase, which began at the end of 1933 and extended through the next year, Hitler's diplomacy was intended to remove the fetters of the past and to protect the country from the possible consequences of doing so. This began with Germany's secret rearmament and withdrawal from the disarmament conference and the League of Nations, actions which Hitler carefully prepared by playing on the guilty conscience of the West with regard to the Versailles Treaty and the resentment that existed in some countries over France's uncompromising attitude. He used with effect tactics that were to be employed again: constantly raising the level of his demands so that a settlement became impossible and then walking out, claiming that the German people would no longer tolerate an imposed inequality. Hitler also devoted considerable effort to avoiding any punishment for these actions. This took the form of a flurry of public and private assurances that he was willing to make new engagements and enter into new pacts with any power, including a pact of friendship with Poland in 1934. His smooth promises had such a ring of sincerity that they lulled Western leaders into a dangerous false sense of security.

The third phase, which extended from 1935 through 1937, was characterized by a diplomacy of testing resolve, designed to discover how much resistance could be expected once Hitler decided to unmask his plans for expansion to the East. It began with the first of his "Saturday Surprises," when (after government officials and military personnel in other countries already had left for the weekend and were off-duty) he announced in March 1935 that Germany had decided to create a new air force and that it would no longer be bound by the arms restrictions of the Versailles Treaty. In a revealing example of just how skillful he could be in disarming potential antagonists, Hitler explained his decision as reasonable and a matter of honor, saying that Germany simply wanted to be free to have an air force like any other self-respecting state. Even the usually skeptical British ambassador in Berlin, Sir Eric Phipps, was won over and actually advised his government that Hitler had changed from his "old, somewhat gangster-like days at Munich" and that he could now be trusted: "His signature, once given, will bind his people as no other could."

When this deception proved to be successful, Hitler then boldly decided to invade and remilitarize the Rhineland, the last remaining protection for France against an immediate German attack. Only words (rather than actions) of protest occurred in response to this direct challenge to security, and no one marched—except for the Germans. As Hitler later admitted, "If the French had marched into the Rhineland we would have had to withdraw with our tails between our legs, for the military resources at our disposal would have been wholly inadequate for even a moderate resistance." He had tested the resolve of others to uphold the international order and found that they had none.

The fourth phase was the period of aggression, heralded by Hitler's secret meeting with his military and diplomatic advisers in November 1937, the reorganization and expansion of the army, and the appointment of the ideologically pure but completely inexperienced businessman Joachim von Ribbentrop as foreign minister. In March 1938 he sent his troops into Austria, violating yet another provision of the Versailles Treaty, completely swallowing a sovereign state and member of the League of Nations, thereby covering his southern flank and expanding the territory of his new Reich. Then, with his own successful offensive coercive diplomacy and with the help of those who appeased him at the Munich Conference of September 1938 and assisted in the dismantling of their own system by giving him everything he wanted, an emboldened Hitler took control of the strategic Sudetenland on the German-Czech border, solemnly promising that it represented his "last demand." He was true to his word—for six months. In March 1939 he tore up the agreement, ordered his military forces into Prague, seized control of the remainder of Czechoslovakia, and prepared for war against Poland. He then joined with Mussolini in signing the Pact of Steel for planned aggression. Last-minute attempts by the British and the French to practice a strategy of deterrence could not help but fail; for, as we shall see in Chapter 9, success requires credibility, and this had long since disappeared. Hitler had no reason at all to believe that they had either the will or the ability to enforce their threats.

Hitler's most stunning diplomatic stroke came in August 1939, when he suddenly signed the Nazi-Soviet Non-Aggression Pact with blinding speed, literally under the noses of the French and British. This treaty between the two powerful countries who had been deliberately excluded from peacemaking and system building in 1919 and who for their own reasons desired to overthrow the international system itself now called for a division of spoils in Eastern Europe and relieved Hitler of any immediate military threat of a two-front war. With this in his pocket, he had no further use for diplomatic tactics and thus turned to his poised and waiting troops, heavy artillery, armored tanks, Stuka dive bombers, and other new weapons made possible by the most recent technology. In marked contrast to his opposite numbers in London and Paris, he had never regarded diplomacy as a means of preserving peace but instead as an instrument for preparing for the war that he had always wanted. "After all," he said once the war had begun, "I did not raise the army in order *not* to use it." This statement underlines the fact that all of his diplomatic interactions with the Western governments, upon which they had placed such high hopes, had been nothing but a deliberately contrived *dialogue des sourds*, in which the words he used had secret meanings that the other side would not or could not hear.

SUGGESTIONS FOR FURTHER EXPLORATION

The central theme of a revolution in diplomacy is developed in Paul Gordon Lauren, "The Diplomatic Revolution of Our Time," in David Wetzel and Theodore Hamerow (eds.), *International Politics and German History* (Westport, CT, 1997); Paul Gordon Lauren, *Diplomats and Bureaucrats* (Stanford, CA, 1976); and Gordon A. Craig, "The Revolution in War and Diplomacy," in *War, Politics, and Diplomacy* (New York, 1966).

The Paris Peace Conference is treated in many books, including Margaret Macmillan, *Paris 1919: Six Months That Changed the World* (New York, 2002); Manfred Boemke et al. (eds.) *The Treaty of Versailles* (Cambridge, 1998); Alan Sharp, *The Versailles Settlement* (New York, 1991); Arno Mayer, *Politics and Diplomacy of Peacemaking* (New York, 1967); and Harold Nicolson's personal memoir, *Peacemaking 1919* (New York, 1939 ed.). For discussion on Wilson, see Lloyd Ambrosius, *Wilsonianism* (New York, 2002); the chapter entitled "The New Face of Diplomacy," in Henry Kissinger, *Diplomacy* (New York, 1994); Arno Mayer, *Political Origins of the New Diplomacy* (New York, 1970 ed.); Gordon A. Craig, "The United States and the European Balance," *Foreign Affairs*, 55 (1976): 189–198; Arthur Link, *Wilson the Diplomatist* (Chicago, 1965); and Alexander L. George and Juliette L. George, *Woodrow Wilson and Colonel House* (New York, 1964).

For diplomacy during the interwar period, see the chapter entitled "The 'New Diplomacy,'" in Keith Hamilton and Richard Langhorne, *The Practice of Diplomacy* (London, 2011 ed.); Zara Steiner, *The Lights That Failed* (Oxford, 2005); Jonathan Haslam, *The Soviet Union and the Struggle for Collective Security in Europe* (New York, 1984); G. Ross, *The Great Powers and the Decline of the European States System* (London, 1983); Sally Marks, *The Illusion of Peace* (London, 1976); R. J. Sontag, *A Broken World, 1919–1939* (New York, 1971); Arnold Wolfers, *Britain and France Between the Wars: Conflicting Strategies of Peace* (New York, 1966 ed.); and Gordon A. Craig and Felix Gilbert (eds.), *The Diplomats, 1919–1939* (Princeton, 1953).

Public opinion and foreign policy are treated in John Milton Cooper, *Breaking the Heart of the World* (New York, 2001); Richard Cockett, *Twilight of Truth: Chamberlain Appeasement and the Manipulation of the Press* (New York, 1989); Ralph Levering, *The Impact of Public Opinion on American Foreign Policy* (New York, 1978); Winston Churchill, *The Gathering Storm* (Boston, 1948); E. H. Carr, *Propaganda in International Politics* (New York, 1939); and Elihu Root, "A Requisite for the Success of Popular Diplomacy," *Foreign Affairs*, 1 (1922): 3–10. Those readers interested in economics and foreign policy should consult Paul Kennedy, *The Rise and Fall of the Great Powers* (New York, 1987); Marc Trachenberg, *Reparations in World Politics* (New York, 1980); David E. Kaiser, *Economic Diplomacy and the Origins of the Second World War* (Princeton, 1980); Charles Kindleberger, *Power and Money: The Economics of International Politics and the Politics of International Economics* (New York, 1970); Karl Polanyi, *The Great Transformation* (New York, 1944); and John Maynard Keynes, *The Economic Consequences of the Peace* (London, 1920).

For studies on Hitler, see Gerhard L. Weinberg, *Hitler's Foreign Policy, 1933–1939* (New York, 2010 ed.); Alan Bullock, *Hitler: A Study in Tyranny* (New York, 1991 ed.); Chapter 19 of Gordon A. Craig, *Germany* (New York, 1978); Klaus Hildebrand, *The Foreign Policy of the Third Reich* (Berkeley, CA, 1974); Norman Rich, *Hitler's War Aims* (New York, 1973); Hitler's own revealing autobiography *Mein Kampf;* and the multi-volume collection of captured materials published by the U.S. Department of State entitled *Documents on German Foreign Policy, 1918–1945.* For Soviet diplomacy, insights can be gained from Robert Service, *Lenin* (Cambridge, MA, 2002); Alan Bullock, *Hitler and Stalin* (New York, 1991); Anthony Read and David Fisher, *The Deadly Embrace* (New York, 1988); Andre Gromyko and B. N. Ponomarev (eds.), *Soviet Foreign Policy, 1917–1945* (Moscow, 1981); and Teddy Uldricks, *Diplomacy and Ideology* (Beverly Hills, CA, 1979). Appeasement is analyzed in David Faber, *Munich, 1938* (New York, 2009); Frank McDonough, *Hitler, Chamberlain, and Appeasement* (Cambridge, 2002); Richard Davis, *Anglo-French Relations Before the Second World War* (New York, 2001); Keith Robbins, *Appeasement* (London, 1997); and Telford Taylor, *Munich: The Price of Tragedy* (New York, 1979).

— 4 —

A New Postwar System of Security: Great Power Directorate or United Nations?

N o war in human history created more devastation than the Second World War. It lasted for years and, long before it ended, proved to be more truly global than its predecessor, more total in its demands on resources and in its impact on all classes of society, much more sophisticated in its weaponry, and infinitely more destructive in its results. Three-fourths of the world's population took part. It is estimated that more than 60,000,000 human beings met their deaths during this conflict and that, for the first time, far more civilians lost their lives than combatants. As if that were not enough, the war ended with the revelation of the existence of a new category of terrible weapons of mass destruction that promised to multiply these dreadful statistics beyond the limits of human comprehension if statecraft could not control the use of force on a major scale in the future. Allied leaders thus realized that if they failed to establish a viable postwar security system at the end of this war and at a time of an unabated diplomatic revolution, they would face the prospect of a repetition of the cataclysm—or something even worse.

LESSONS FROM THE PAST AND PLANS FOR THE FUTURE

Thoughtful men and women responsible for the conduct of force and statecraft attempt to learn lessons from history that might guide them in their formulation and implementation of policy, as we shall see in more detail in Chapter 7. This applied particularly to those who lived through the harrowing experience of systemic international collapse and the *second* world war of their lifetime. They watched their people suffer terribly from armed attacks, attempted to create and maintain the massive military coalition that British Prime Minister Winston Churchill called the "Grand Alliance," and witnessed even democratically elected leaders become virtual warlords for the duration. When it was over, they were not only eager, but desperate, to succeed where their predecessors after the First World War had failed. They wanted to avoid any repetition of those mistakes that had led to such disasters as the Great Depression, the emergence and then appeasement of the juggernaut of aggressive regimes, the rejection of existing treaties and international law, the refusal to work as partners in the collective security mechanism of the League of Nations, a catastrophic global war, the brutality of the "Rape of Nanking," and the horrific genocide of the Holocaust.

Some of the lessons they learned focused on relatively simple and pragmatic problems. They believed that one of the mistakes made by the victors in 1918, for example, had been to enter into an armistice with the German government without decisively defeating its armed forces and occupying the country. This led to subsequent claims by rabid nationalists that Germany had not really been defeated but that the army had been "stabbed in the back" by traitors. Resolved not to make this mistake again, the victors of 1945 agreed this time to convincingly defeat, disarm, and occupy Germany, Italy, and Japan.

Other lessons were more complex and profound. Their recent past forced the victors to seriously reexamine a number of previously held beliefs and to develop more sophisticated analyses of issues in statecraft that would go on to influence the responses to challenges of our own time. It became increasingly evident to them, for example, that so many of the problems in the world now were truly international in nature and scope and thus required more serious and effective partnerships instead of single nation-states acting alone or sticking their heads in the sand as isolationists. Their experiences also suggested the necessity to reconsider the meaning of "power" and of "peace and security" themselves, going beyond the narrow measurement of armed force alone and taking into account broader and multifaceted dimensions such as economic well-being, normative values of human rights, and justice. Many postwar planners insisted that another lesson to be drawn was that the traditional concept of "national sovereignty" needed to be redefined in order to appreciate not only its benefits, but also its dangers.

The results of these discussions about lessons took a variety of forms. One important lesson, for example, was drawn from the previous failure to develop economic policies and cooperation that would avoid future depressions and thereby encourage more lasting peace. The victors came to believe that the interwar years demonstrated a relationship between economic despair and political violence. Their plans for the future therefore called for a more carefully crafted form of "economic diplomacy" characterized by the removal or reduction of trade barriers, the creation of a new monetary system to stabilize currencies and facilitate the flow of capital, and the institution of policies that would expedite healthy economic development and postwar reconstruction. Toward this end, they began to hire increasing numbers of specialists in economics, finance, and business and to create such new institutions as the International Monetary Fund and the World Bank.

Many survivors of the war and genocide also came to believe, importantly, that the recent past taught them the dangers of letting governments claim special privileges by invoking the principle of "national sovereignty" as a cloak to hide gross violations of human rights against their own people that, in turn, constituted serious threats to the peace. Nations like Nazi Germany that engaged in grievous abuses, they saw, became dangerous to the countries around them. As the influential Commission to Study the Organization of Peace composed of scholars and foreign policy experts concluded:

> It has become clear that a regime of violence and opposition within any nation of the civilized world is a matter of concern to all the rest....[T]he government that rests upon violence will, by its very nature, be even more ready to do violence to foreigners than to its own fellow citizens, especially if it can thus escape the consequences of its acts at home. The foreign policy of despots is inherently one which carries with it a constant risk to the peace and security of others. In short, if aggression is the key-note of domestic policy, it will also be the clue to foreign relations.

For this reason, they declared with as much intensity as they could command: "We are determined that hereafter no nation may be insulated and wholly a law unto itself in the treatment of its people." A number of statesmen reached the same conclusion and thus began to give serious consideration to the proposition that there could be no security without peace, no peace without justice, and no justice without respect for human rights.

Other lessons emerged from the experience of the League of Nations. Many of those who watched it emerge and then collapse remained convinced of the necessity of some form of international organization, but wanted to learn from their mistakes. It was not difficult in retrospect, for example, to see the serious flaw in the Covenant of giving each and every member state the ability to veto operations by requiring complete unanimity for action. They came to believe in the error of failing to clearly delineate the responsibilities and the authority between the Assembly and the Council. In addition, they saw the mistake of restricting the League's secretary-general to the performance of only clerical and administrative duties.

With specific reference to force and statecraft, they saw a grave defect in the fact that, according to its own rules, the League could not require its members to impose serious sanctions or take military action against those who would threaten the peace. Since the Council could only "advise" or "recommend," its decisions were not binding. States did not have to contribute armed forces or participate in deterrence or coercive diplomacy unless they wished to do so. When combined with the unanimity rule, this made it easy for any single nation to kill any enforcement measures. As such, it eviscerated collective security. It is for this reason that those now planning the future spoke of the necessity for any new, postwar international organization to have "teeth" to confront aggression.

Still another lesson of history had to do with abject failure during the interwar years to obtain the support of the Great Powers for an international system to keep the peace. They learned that, for better or for worse, dreams cannot get too far ahead of political reality and that power matters. Power is not one-dimensional and can take many forms, but no international system or organization can succeed unless those with power are committed to make it succeed. The League of Nations starkly demonstrated the reality of this fact. Although the small- and medium-sized powers eagerly joined and participated, the Great Powers did not. During its existence it could claim the membership of only Britain and France, and their support was either luke-warm or sharply divided. Germany and the Soviet Union, as we have seen, were initially and deliberately excluded, and then participated as half-hearted or even antagonistic members only for a short time before they either with-drew or were expelled. After paying only lip service to the League, Japan sim-ply pulled itself out as it prepared for a war of aggression.

And then there was the United States. It had gone its own way after the First World War and remained largely unwilling to participate as a partner with other nations in the international system. It not only had deliberately refused to join the League of Nations, but even tried in the early years to thwart some of its efforts at international cooperation and collective action against aggres-sion. In addition, the United States pursued a policy of isolationism, often popular at home for reasons of domestic politics with its emotional appeal against "foreigners" and "entangling alliances," but fatal for diplomacy and collective security. This contributed significantly to the perception among the aggressors that they had little to fear, and thus led to the onset of the Second World War. Believing that this had been a most serious mistake, President Franklin Roosevelt (the first president to leave the country in wartime and the first to travel by airplane) determined that this time it was essential—for both national self-interest and for the world—to not follow the same path, but instead to cooperate with other peace-seeking countries in developing and maintaining a new postwar security system.

Such a system, in Roosevelt's view, could not possibly work unless the Great Powers that possessed preponderant force agreed to cooperate in creating and in preserving the peace. He knew that only one thing had brought the success-ful coalition partners together in war: fear of a common enemy. Once victory removed that threat, serious differences could easily and quickly emerge. The defeat of Nazi Germany, to illustrate, would create a power vacuum in Europe with serious implications for the vital interests of both the Western powers and the Soviet Union. If no international system was created in sufficient time to provide a framework within which they could cooperate, dangerous conse-quences would result.

How might one accomplish this task? One possibility would be to simply allow unbridled competition among the major powers like in the eighteenth century, seizing territories at will and creating countervailing forces to keep each other at bay by fear. But this arrangement certainly had failed in the past to bring about peace or deter Napoleon from trying to achieve hegemony, and it was likely to fail again. Britain would be too weak by itself to provide a military counterweight to Russian domination on the European continent, and any long-term American commitment appeared at the time to be highly uncer-tain. Another possibility would be to try to reduce the potential for conflict by giving each of the major powers generous spheres of influence in areas of special interest to them. Such an approach was initially favored by Churchill and Stalin, who privately reached an agreement for dividing up the Balkans between them. But Roosevelt refused to agree to this scheme. He believed that it would be unstable, would not eliminate competition for very long, and would create armed camps that might well lead to another war. In addition, he doubted that public opinion would support postwar plans for a crass spheres-of-influence agreement that directly contradicted the principles of human rights and self-determination written so prominently and publicly into the Atlantic Charter and the Declaration of the United Nations as the peace aims for which they were fighting.

The only alternative, Roosevelt concluded from his reading of lessons of the past and his own personal attendance at the Paris Peace Conference in 1919, was a continuing coalition of the victors to maintain the peace settlement modeled on the concert system established by the Congress of Vienna after the defeat of Napoleon. He called his plan the "Grand Design." He knew that one of the most serious problems after the First World War was that the final treaties had not been decided by all of the Great Powers—but by only some of them. This led not only to a settlement that lacked widespread consensus and legitimacy, but to resentment and a determination on the part of those who had been excluded to overturn the result. Consequently, Roosevelt envisioned a new, postwar security system in which all of those possessing the greatest power—the United States, Britain, the Soviet Union, and China—would serve as an executive, Great Power directorate known as the "Four Policemen." They would possess exclusive authority to decide on the use of military force, but would consult with each other as a means of collective rather than unilateral decision making. Together they would use force and statecraft to meet whatever threats might arise.

This "Grand Design" suffered from several problems. In the first instance, it did not take into account the interests and the visions for the future of the many other nations in the world who had actively participated and sacrificed in the war. Military victory had been secured by the combined forces and sacrifices of forty-six different countries, and each believed that it most assuredly had earned the right to plan for and to participate in whatever postwar security system might be created. Not one of these was willing to be excluded or to be preempted by only four nations acting arrogantly and exclusively by themselves. Proposals like this, observed one diplomat from another country that had contributed much to the war effort, amounted to no more "than an undertaking by the Great Powers to meet from time to time to discuss the situation as it appeared, and to decide what might best be done, and in taking this course they expected the assistance and collaboration of the smaller powers." Such an approach, if left unmodified, he and many others argued, would violate the democratic principles for which the war had been fought and would thereby fail to keep the peace. They knew, however, that by themselves they did not possess sufficient strength or resources to enforce collective security, and that any effective use of armed force or economic sanctions could not possibly be achieved without the Great Powers. The challenge for the small- and medium-sized countries thus was—and remains to our own day—how to get the Great Powers, who could make or break the organization, to agree to participate in it while at the same time not letting them completely control it.

Still another problem with Roosevelt's initial plan emerged with public opinion at home and overseas, which strongly supported widespread international cooperation rather than a Great Power directorate. Since so many sacrifices had been required of civilians and so many had been killed during the war under the banner of the "United Nations," and since popular support would be critical for sustaining any postwar security policy, this opinion had to be taken very seriously. As one foreign minister declared: "As we have had a people's war, so shall we now have a people's peace."

After considering all the other plans for a new postwar system of security, the best solution appeared to be the creation of and greater reliance on a new international organization, more broadly based and stronger than the League of Nations, making it more of a policeman rather than a mere mediator. Roosevelt himself eventually concluded that such an arrangement would enable the United States to work collectively with others countries to pursue its interests and secure its defense and, when necessary, accept certain self-imposed restraints and sacrifice its own freedom of action for the common good. Once this vision became clear in his mind, he worked tirelessly to build support for it. With history very much on his mind, he wanted to avoid Woodrow Wilson's mistake of failing to secure support in the Senate, and thus went before a joint session of Congress. Here he declared with as much energy as his weakened body could muster: "This time, as we fight together to get the war over quickly, we work together to keep it from happening again." Roosevelt said that the time had arrived

> to spell the end of the system of unilateral action, the exclusive alliances, the spheres of influence, the balances of power, and all the other expedients that have been tried for centuries—and have always failed. We propose to substitute for all these a universal organization in which all peace-loving nations will finally have a chance to join.

This new organization was to be the United Nations. It would come to be described as "the most ambitious order-building experiment in history."

FORCE AND STATECRAFT AS ENVISIONED BY THE UN CHARTER

Statesmen have seriously attempted to create some form of international order on four occasions: Westphalia in 1648, Vienna in 1815, Paris in 1919, and San Francisco in 1945. Each of these came about as a result of war. The horror of death and destruction from the Thirty Years' War, the Napoleonic Wars, the First World War, and then the Second World War forced them to confront the necessity of working as partners in finding new ways to manage their relations. Those delegates of the victorious coalition who now met at the most recent of these diplomatic conferences, at a time of high risk and great uncertainty, to negotiate the details of the United Nations were no exception. They had just barely survived the most catastrophic "total" war in human history, replete with genocide and some of the worst cases of man's inhumanity to man ever known. It was burnished into their minds. Hard-earned and often brutal experience, not wild-eyed idealism or naïveté, taught them that their victory against the aggressors had not come from words or moral suasion, but by the application of superior power made possible by the combined armed forces and resources of many different nations. They thus understood far better than most the dilemmas presented by both the necessity and the dangers of force in statecraft. They realized that they had a common interest in keeping the peace and were realistic in their calculation that it could be secured in the future only if they continued their cooperation through partnership and collective action by finding, in the words of Roosevelt, "the courage to fulfill their responsibilities in an admittedly imperfect world."

To do this, the statesmen gathered at San Francisco created the United Nations. It was to be composed of a small but powerful Security Council comprising fifteen members but dominated by the Great Powers through their permanent membership and their exclusive power of the veto. A large General Assembly was to serve as a barometer of global public opinion by providing a worldwide forum to discuss "any questions relating to the maintenance of international peace and security" in which each member nation participated and possessed an equal vote. An Economic and Social Council was designed to address conditions of stability and well-being, including issues of human rights. A Trusteeship Council was established to promote the interests and the rights of people in non-self-governing territories and an International Court of Justice to advance the rule of law. Finally, the position of secretary-general was instituted to serve as the chief administrative officer of the secretariat while at the same time given the authority to initiate debate and, if necessary, propose courses of action on "any matter which in his opinion may threaten the maintenance of peace and security."

Given their recent experience in war, they knew perfectly well that the threat or the use of force would be very much a part of the statecraft of the new United Nations. The question for them was not how to eliminate force, but rather how to guide and control it. They drew on lessons they had learned from recent history and described their purpose simply enough in the very first sentence of the United Nations Charter: "to save succeeding generations of the scourge of war, which twice in our lifetime has brought untold sorrow to mankind, and to reaffirm faith in fundamental human rights." Toward this end, they importantly pledged as members in partnership to "refrain in their international relations from the threat or use of force against the territorial integrity or political independence of any state" and "to unite our strength to maintain international peace and security, and to ensure by the acceptance of principles and the institution of methods, that armed force shall not be used, save in the common interest."

Agreement on this critical phrase of "the common interest," what it meant, who would define it, and how it would be defended, it was envisioned, would be determined among the members of the United Nations by diplomatic negotiation (a subject we shall explore at length in Chapter 8). According to the Charter, the general principles of cooperation in this international system, including those dealing with human rights "for all without distinction as to race, sex, language, or religion," would be discussed in the General Assembly, where every country was represented equally and where recommendations could be made. Actual authority for action on specific problems and crises, however—especially those involving force and statecraft—would reside in the much smaller Security Council, which the five most powerful nations at the time (the United States, Britain, France, the Soviet Union, and China) could control as a result of their permanent membership and power to veto any substantive action they did not like. This was the price they extracted for their participation in the organization. The preferred means of resolving conflict, of course, would be diplomacy, or what Chapter VI of the Charter called "Pacific Settlement of Disputes." Here, solutions would be sought "by negotiation, enquiry, mediation, conciliation, arbitration, judicial settlement, resort to regional agencies or arrangements, or other peaceful means of their own choice." Should these efforts fail, however, Chapter VII on "Action with Respect to Threats to the Peace, Breaches of the Peace, and Acts of Aggression" specifically addressed armed force.

Those who founded the United Nations realized that any viable international system required consensus on a number of basic principles and normative rules that restrained their competition. As the new American President Harry Truman, who had worked diligently to overcome innumerable obstacles in order to keep the vision of the organization alive, quite realistically declared at the San Francisco Conference, "We all have to recognize, no matter how great our strength, that we must deny ourselves the license to do always as we please." This principle applies to all matters of international relations, but particularly to those dealing with force and statecraft. More specifically, the framers of the Charter understood that no system could survive for very long unless its members could reach a consensus on shared norms, or if aggressors unilaterally decided on their own when they were justified in threatening or using armed force against others.

They spent considerable time, therefore, wrestling with the question of exactly how the United Nations could serve as the source of collective legitimization for the threat or use of armed force in the world and as the forum where norms on force and statecraft best could be developed, interpreted, and enforced. After intense and extensive negotiations, they agreed that only two kinds of cases would qualify for the legitimate use of armed force:

1. **Self Defense** in the event of an actual armed attack. According to the text:

   Nothing in the present Charter shall impair the inherent right of individual or collective self-defense if an armed attack occurs against a Member of the United Nations, until the Security Council has taken measures necessary to maintain international peace and security. Measures taken by Members in the exercise of this right of self-defense shall be immediately reported to the Security Council and shall not in any way affect the authority and the responsibility of the Security Council under the present Charter to take at any time such action as it deems necessary in order to maintain or restore international peace and security.

2. **International enforcement action** to maintain or restore international peace and security. The Charter reads:

> The Security Council shall determine the existence of any threat to the peace, breach of the peace, or act of aggression and shall make recommendations, or decide what measures shall be taken...[If peaceful means proved to be inadequate] it may take such action by air, sea, or land forces as may be necessary to maintain or restore international peace and security.

The Charter thus provided the Security Council with a unique status and with considerable powers and responsibilities. It provided for a number of tools of coercive diplomacy, including military demonstrations, blockades, sanctions, the severance of diplomatic relations, and threats of armed force. Should these be insufficient, the Security Council could determine to escalate by employing air, sea, and land forces. But the obligations for collective security extended to all members of the United Nations who pledged "to make available to the Security Council, on its call and in accordance with special agreement or agreements, armed forces, assistance, and facilities, including rights of passage, necessary for the purpose of maintaining international peace and security." No nation voted against this because they all wanted to guarantee that the United Nations would protect them against future wars. The Charter also created a Military Staff Committee composed of the chiefs of staff of its permanent members that would help to develop plans for "the application of armed force," for "the employment and command of forces placed at its disposal," and for "the regulation of armaments." Over time, these plans came to include various arms control agreements and arms embargoes as well as shows of force for deterrence or coercive diplomacy, peacekeeping forces, humanitarian intervention, and even war itself. In addition, the Charter allowed for the possibility of standing United Nations forces and of regional security arrangements.

These provisions on force and statecraft marked a strong and explicit endorsement of shared responsibility for collective security. They boldly proclaimed that aggression or threats to peace and security would be met by the concerted efforts of the members of the Security Council and the collective military contributions of the members of the United Nations acting in the name of the international community as a whole.

The Charter thus went considerably further than any previous treaty in history and gave every impression that the United Nations had the very real possibility of satisfying the requirements of a viable postwar security system. There seemed to be an agreement among the member states on the basic aims and objectives for creating and maintaining the system as a whole. The purposes of the organization were stated boldly: to take effective collective measures to maintain international peace and security, to develop universal principles of international law and friendly relations among states, and to promote and encourage respect for human rights and fundamental freedoms. In addition, there appeared to be a structure appropriate to the number of states interacting with each other, with a hierarchy among them and a recognition that new states likely would be added through time. The design deliberately created a global organization rather than one of merely European membership, thus accurately reflecting the ever expanding geographical scope of the diplomatic revolution. It acknowledged the principle of the equality of all nations—regardless of size, form of government, interests, or ideology—in the General Assembly. At the same time, it recognized the inequalities of the world by providing the most powerful with both privileges and responsibilities on the Security Council, thereby gaining the necessary participation of all of the Great Powers in the organization. Consequently, it seemed as though the founders of the United Nations had reached a consensus on values and procedures that would help them maintain the system as a whole, including restrictions on what could be regarded as the legitimate use of armed force. It is not at all surprising, therefore, that when the Charter was signed in June 1945, many commentators emotionally and optimistically hailed it as "an epoch-making document" marking "one of the great moments in history."

Not everyone reacted so positively. Some critics complained bitterly that the United Nations Charter did too little. In their minds, it did not fully define what was meant by expressions like "the common interest" or "self-defense." It promoted the principle of international human rights "for all" in Article 1, yet nevertheless supported the Westphalian principle of sovereign nation-states in Article 2 by sweepingly asserting that the organization could not interfere with matters "essentially within the domestic jurisdiction of any state." Such a provision seemed to provide ready-made impunity to governments who violated the rights of their people from any outside scrutiny or intervention to protect abused victims. Moreover, according to some commentators, the Charter made little effort to eliminate armed force, created an organization completely dependent on whatever power its members—jealous of their own national sovereignty—were willing to give it, and granted far too much authority and privilege to the Great Powers who controlled the Security Council. E. B. White of the *New Yorker*, for example, wrote in despair that the fundamental problem could be found in the "steady throbbing" of one, single theme: "sovereignty, sovereignty, sovereignty." *Time* magazine compared the idealistic promises made during the war with the end result and concluded in disappointment that the final agreement represented no more than "a charter for a world of power." Others complained that the Charter did too much. This applied particularly to those who valued the interests of their own nation much more than the needs of the international system. They feared that involving others in collective decision making would jeopardize their sovereignty and thereby restrict their freedom of action to pursue their own national ambitions as they saw fit.

A number of seasoned diplomats and observers viewed the United Nations Charter neither as a magnificent achievement that would suddenly create heaven on earth nor as a horrendous tragedy that would destroy the cherished nation-state. Instead, they saw it in the historical context of the time and considered diplomacy to be the art of the possible, balanced somewhere between the cynics and the perfectionists, and knew that no nation or group could obtain everything that they wanted over the course of a mere two months of negotiations. They believed that those who assembled at San Francisco had accomplished about as much as, if not more, than could realistically be expected given the traditional practices, the circumstances of the war, the magnitude of the tasks, the differences between the Great Powers and the medium and small nations, the divergent opinions of the states and nongovernmental organizations (NGOs), and the often exaggerated hopes for the future. They likely would have agreed with the later conclusion of political scientist John Stoessinger, who writes:

> In not attempting the impossible, the founders of the United Nations were realists. But in seeking to go to the very limits of the possible, they were also visionaries. And necessarily so, for the idea of the United Nations had to take into account the full import of the cruel paradox that, in the nuclear age, the national sovereignty of nations would have to be controlled by an international order, but that this international order would have to be created and even controlled by sovereign nations. The plan therefore had to combine the dictates of national power with those of international order.

It is precisely this paradox and the need to combine both the specific interests of sovereign nation states with the broader interests of the international order that present the central dilemma of any system. Collective security cannot work without the support of the most powerful, and collective security cannot work unless the most powerful can also be restrained.

Statesmen present at the creation of the United Nations proceeded with uncertainty. They had no idea about the magnitude of the challenges and diplomatic problems that lay ahead. As they attempted to learn lessons of history, however, they did know that any system required that its members be willing to make sacrifices for the common good and able to adapt to new developments in order to survive. With this in mind, Truman announced: "This Charter, like our Constitution, will be expanded and improved as time goes on. No one claims that it is now a final or a perfect instrument. It has not been poured into a fixed mold. Changing world conditions will require readjustments."

Changing World Conditions and Readjustments

The smiles and cooperation that characterized the approval of the Charter did not last long, for changing conditions and upheaval occurred much sooner than expected. Within only months, the world watched with deep concern as the United States, Britain, and the Soviet Union failed to reach agreement at the Potsdam Conference on several fundamental features of the postwar settlement, as the Soviets moved troops further into positions in Eastern Europe and entered the war in Asia, and as the Americans dropped the atomic bombs on Hiroshima and Nagasaki. With the end of the war and the elimination of the common threat that had held them together, the coalition partners of the "Grand Alliance" fell victim to their own rival national passions, histories, interests, and perspectives. Two days after the beginning of the very first session of the United Nations, the presence of Soviet troops in Iran was brought before the Security Council, quickly followed by a countermove by the Soviet Union complaining about British forces in Greece and Indonesia and the refusal of Europeans to end their domination over colonial empires. Shortly thereafter, Winston Churchill delivered his famous "Iron Curtain" speech condemning Soviets for securing their grip on Eastern Europe by forcibly imposing Communist regimes. One diplomat painfully observed that "the clouds were gathering fast," and these gave every indication that the world was rapidly moving from one war into another, soon to be called the Cold War.

Given these frightening developments, widespread global sentiment strongly believed that the United Nations remained the best hope for peace and security. Even as late as 1948, public opinion polls revealed an overwhelming majority within the United States enthusiastically supporting the organization and its mission. Some of this popular enthusiasm for the new organization was doubtless selfish, based on the hope that it would reduce American responsibilities in foreign affairs. Perhaps much more of it resulted from unreasonable expectations by those who wanted to believe that the new organization would be able to act on the international level in much the same way as a government acts on the national level. This was a profound misunderstanding, for as Brian Urquhart, a long-time civil servant posted to the United Nations, writes, "The UN is nothing like a [world] government. It has no sovereignty or power of sovereign decision-making. It is an association of independent, sovereign states which depends for its effectiveness on the capacity of its members to agree and cooperate." At times, such capacity to place the needs of the international system as a whole above those of the nation-state appeared quite limited.

This was certainly true in the case of the most powerful of its members. The dream of maintaining Great Power cooperation and consensus on principles that had formed the basis of Roosevelt's initial "Four Policemen" idea never materialized. Instead, national interests prevailed, and a pattern quickly emerged that one scholar describes as "the moral infection of Great Power disagreement." Britain and France resisted any attempts to dismantle their colonial empires, China fell into revolution and the coming to power of Mao Zedong and his Communist Party, and the Cold War rivalry between the Soviet Union and the United States seriously and dangerously escalated with no end in sight. Domestic opinion, which had so strongly supported the United Nations, began to erode. In the United States, the public was outraged when other members of the General Assembly did not agree with American positions abroad or dared to criticize racial segregation or lynching at home. Congress increasingly complained about the undue influence of "foreigners" and "the colored peoples of the world" within the United Nations or the organization's failure to prevent crises that Congress itself had not foreseen. The "Red-baiting" hysteria surrounding the McCarthy investigations provided a steady stream of highly public accusations that United Nations staff members and certain delegates were "manifesting fellow-traveler tendencies," tainted with a "scarlet hue," and no more than "un-American" "crypto-Communists."

In addition, there was a tendency on the part of many governments to belittle the achievements of the United Nations while blaming their own foreign policy failures on it, to insist that it stay out of their own particular areas of interest, or even to attempt to emasculate it. President Truman's self-styled "realist" secretary of state, Dean Acheson, contemptuously referred to those who supported the United Nations as the "True Believers" with "universal Plumb plans," criticized the Charter as "impracticable," complained that the Secretariat was no more than "a crowded center of conflicting races and nationalities," and revealed his attitudes about gender roles by asking V. L. Pandit of India, who became the first female president of the United Nations General Assembly: "Why do pretty women want to be like men?" During the critical crisis caused by Great Britain's admission that it could no longer support the governments of Greece and Turkey against external threats, Acheson bypassed the United Nations completely and eliminated all but the barest reference to it in the Truman Doctrine. A similar disregard, bordering on contempt, came in 1948 when the organization was desperately seeking a plan for partitioning Palestine that might avert a war between the Arabs and Jewish settlers, whose numbers were being rapidly augmented by refugees from Europe. This time the United States negated the negotiations and precipitated hostilities in the area by abruptly recognizing an independent state of Israel without even informing its own delegation to the United Nations of its intentions. Others tried to deliberately subvert agreement, as the British demonstrated during one series of diplomatic negotiations when they sent ciphered instructions to their representative to kill a particular proposal, but "not give the impression that we are being obstructive. We suggest our right course is to play for time, leaving it as far as possible to other delegations to bring out the difficulties." On other occasions, the permanent members of the Security Council cast vetoes if they wished to stop actions they regarded as contrary to their national interests.

When the Great Powers agreed with the secretary-general of the United Nations, they lavished him with praise; but when they disagreed, they poured out their contempt and criticism. When Secretary-General Trygve Lie of Norway condemned the North Korean attack on South Korea in 1950, for example, the United States praised him for his courage, "unusual skill," "good judgment," and "understanding mind." When he publicly supported membership in the United Nations for the new Communist-led People's Republic of China, however, the Americans condemned him as no more than "a stooge of the Reds." The British and the French sharply criticized his brilliant successor, Dag Hammarskjöld from Sweden, for trying to "interfere" during their military action against Egypt in the Suez Crisis of 1956, but then eagerly welcomed his offer to provide a face-saving way out of their mistake with some semblance of dignity. When Hammarskjöld worked to facilitate the massive process of decolonization or tackled the problem of apartheid in South Africa, the Soviet Union praised him for his courage and wisdom. But when he worked against Soviet interests in the Congo, they not only criticized him for being a "tool of the colonialists and capitalists" but actually went so far as to demand that the position of secretary-general itself be abolished. Hammarskjöld viewed this vehement attack as a challenge not just to him, but to the principles of the Charter and the larger international security system and its future. He therefore announced that he would leave whenever the majority of members wanted him to leave, but that he would not be intimidated by Great Power pressure designed to emasculate the organization. "It is not the Soviet Union or, indeed, any other big powers who need the United Nations for their protection," he said, "it is all the others." In the end, he forcefully declared, "I shall remain at my post." When he finished, the General Assembly rose to give him an emotional standing ovation.

One of the reasons for this widespread global support for the secretary-general and the organization, of course, resulted from the fact that the United Nations demonstrated remarkable success in adapting to new circumstances by facilitating one of the most momentous developments of the twentieth century: the collapse of colonial empires and the subsequent emergence of newly independent nations and peoples and the geographical expansion of the international system itself. When the delegates created the United Nations in 1945, only fifty-one states were admitted to membership. Among these, only three came from Africa, and among the mere three from Asia, only China was independent of colonial rule. The great majority of member states therefore represented the countries of Europe, the Americas, and the white Commonwealth countries. Many assumed that this political dominance by the Western world would continue in the future, as it had for centuries in the past. They were wrong, for in the simple words of one observer, "time had run out." Within a single decade and in the name of national self-determination, twenty-five new states joined the United Nations. By the end of 1965, forty-one more had been added, swelling the membership to 117. This development marked one of the greatest geopolitical changes in international history, shifting power from whites to nonwhites and liberating more than 1,000,000,000 people from Western colonial rule in Asia, Africa, the Middle East, the Pacific, and the Caribbean.

These developments profoundly changed the composition as well as the agenda of the United Nations. Expanded membership meant that the West lost its majority in the United Nations. As a consequence, America, Britain, and France became less and less able to control the direction and outcome of negotiations and thus were less inclined to view the organization as a major factor in their foreign policies. Perhaps more important, it greatly accelerated that dimension of the diplomatic revolution whereby the cultural homogeneity that had characterized diplomacy for so long increasingly gave way to heterogeneity. The shared similarly among diplomats of the European-dominated past was steadily being replaced with great differences of race, language, religious values, socioeconomic status, stages of development, and gender, among other factors. This development demonstrated the remarkable ability of the organization to realize its goal of becoming truly international in scope, as well as adjusting to the growing number of states interacting with each other within the system as a whole. The United Nations became the one place in the world where all blocs and ideologies could genuinely be represented. Nevertheless, such diversity brought about new and different assumptions about the nature of international society. These states were not as interested in the political and military questions that absorbed the attention of the superpowers and their allies of the Cold War, not as eager to maintain a static system frozen at the time of the 1945 victory, not as willing to continue letting the Great Powers alone determine the agenda of the United Nations, and increasingly convinced that genuine peace and security could not exist without the dimensions of justice and human rights. Consequently, they began to broaden the global agenda to include issues of self-determination, decolonization, racial equality, voting, religious toleration, economic and social development, "people-to people" diplomacy, relief operations, the plight of refugees, development, education, medical care, environmental protection, and the rule of law.

Indeed, this expansion of the number of actors and the new majority of small- to medium-sized states provided one of several important features of the diplomatic revolution that increasingly helped to develop and articulate new norms and place the whole subject of human rights high on the international agenda. There were other factors as well. When the technological invention of television was brought into the public deliberations of the United Nations, for example, it created what was called "media diplomacy," forcing representatives to explain abusive actions and policies of their governments under journalistic scrutiny and before the eyes of the world as never before in history. This growing openness or transparency of diplomacy in this international forum, in turn, encouraged segments of public opinion to organize pressure groups of very vocal human rights NGOs who passionately believed that respect for individual dignity was closely related not only to freedom and justice but to peace and security. It is for this reason that they often were willing to challenge traditional concepts of the prerogatives of national sovereignty and the relationship between states and their citizens or subjects by stressing the broader connection between individual, national, and international security and by developing standards and mechanisms that might bring life and substance to the vision proclaimed in the landmark Universal Declaration of Human Rights. Innovative treaties, treaty-monitoring bodies, and special procedures dealing with genocide, racial discrimination and apartheid, civil and political rights, economic and social rights, torture, and women and children, for example, all sought to provide protection to those who suffered and to transform victims of abuse from being mere objects of international pity into actual subjects of international law.

The United Nations also became the one permanent piece of diplomatic machinery that could be put to work at a moment's notice for crisis management (a topic to be discussed in Chapter 11). It served as the one body in which both traditional and democratic, bilateral and parliamentary forms of diplomacy could be brought to bear on critical problems and crises in order to avert great danger. The United Nations had great importance as a place in which contacts could be made, communication networks established, and signals and messages passed outside official diplomatic channels, thereby sometimes saving governments from the possible consequences of their own mistakes. American ambassador Philip Jessup and Soviet ambassador Jacob Malik discovered the great advantages of this during their private conversations in 1949 that prepared the way for the termination of the crisis precipitated by the Soviet blockade of Berlin. The British and the French received the same benefits during the Suez Crisis of 1956. Two years later, after an anti-government coup in Iraq, the landing of U.S. Marines on the shores of Lebanon might have invited a Soviet response had Hammarskjöld not devised a face-saving formula by which the United States withdrew its troops.

Any doubts about this potential for crisis management by the United Nations should have been put to rest after the Cuban Missile Crisis of 1962, when the world stood on the brink of possible nuclear annihilation. In this situation, Secretary-General U Thant, a Buddhist from Burma, initiated direct communication with the Americans, Soviets, and Cubans, offering his good offices, serving as a go-between, suggesting a way to avert catastrophic war, providing an impartial point of reference to which each side could respond without giving the appearance of weakness or surrender, and creating an international observation and supervision mechanism to ensure that the terms of settlement would be acceptable to the antagonists. In the end, courage and wisdom on the part of many individuals made it possible to manage and defuse the crisis, but those who knew the inside details gave U Thant and the United Nations considerable credit. A highly unusual and joint official letter sent shortly thereafter stated clearly: "On behalf of the Governments of the United States of America and the Soviet Union we desire to express to you our appreciation for your efforts in assisting our Governments to avert the serious threat to the peace which recently arose."

Such tense and dangerous crises always provide reminders to any international security system not only of the need to try to avert and, if that fails, to manage them, but also of the fact that it may be necessary at times to threaten or use force and statecraft to protect peace and security. As already discussed, this had been envisioned by the Charter itself. In working through changing world conditions and in making adjustments to new circumstances, therefore, the United Nations began to develop policies to do precisely this. Explicit provisions in the text for the possibility of collective action against aggressors or threats to the peace always provided some measure of deterrence. But if this failed, much more was needed. In an effort to practice coercive diplomacy, for example, the Security Council invoked its authority under Chapter VII in 1966 and imposed the first-ever mandatory sanctions against the white minority regime of Rhodesia, and did so until power was transferred to a black majority and the country renamed Zimbabwe. Similarly, the United Nations imposed a whole series of political, economic, and military sanctions against the white minority government of South Africa for its racial policies and occupation of Namibia, including a Security Council mandatory arms embargo in 1977. These were lifted only when Namibia gained its independence and when South Africa repealed its racist apartheid laws and successfully held its first democratic election.

Members of the United Nations also dealt directly with matters of force and statecraft by creatively developing both the concept and the practice of international peacekeeping forces, or what was described as "using soldiers as the servants of peace rather than as the instruments of war." This innovation began when the General Assembly, in the absence of leadership from the Great Powers on the Security Council, seized the initiative and called upon Hammarskjöld to set up an United Nations Emergency Force (UNEF) during the Suez Crisis of 1956 in order to keep the warring parties apart. It proved to be so successful that other military forces subsequently were sent into troubled areas to separate enemies from each other, patrol buffer zones, monitor cease-fire lines and the withdrawal of the combatants' troops from disputed territories, guard election centers, and safeguard humanitarian aid. These blue-helmeted soldiers were authorized by the Security Council and operated in the collective name of the United Nations, being deployed, among other places, in the Suez Canal and Sinai Peninsula (1956–1967 and 1973–1979), the Congo (1960–1964), West New Guinea (1962–1963), Yemen (1963–1964), Cyprus (1964 to the present), the border between India and Pakistan (1965–1966), Dominican Republic (1965–1966), the Golan Heights (1974 to the present), Lebanon (1978 to the present), and beginning in 1987 to Afghanistan, Pakistan, Iran, and Iraq. By 1988, nearly 500,000 United Nations personnel contributed by fifty-eight different nations had been involved in peacekeeping operations. Viewing all this activity, often in nearly impossible circumstances, one feels compelled to ask where the world would have been during these years without the United Nations.

The most serious challenges of force and statecraft confronting the United Nations involved those international enforcement actions taken under Chapter VII of the Charter—that is, the actual use of armed forces to enforce the decisions of the Security Council when facing acts of aggression. These cases entailed moving from limited peacekeeping to more extensive war making in the form of military "police action" in defense of states that had been attacked. The first occurred when the Soviet-equipped armies of North Korea launched a massive and well-coordinated surprise attack against South Korea in June 1950, thus beginning the Korean War and marking, in the words of one observer, "one of the great watersheds in the history of the organization." Since the Security Council found itself temporarily boycotted by the Soviets at the time, it was able to avoid any veto of opposition and thereby invoke its power to employ as-yet-untested machinery for collective security and approve support for military intervention to defend the south. The General Assembly further passed its "Uniting for Peace Resolution," indicating widespread support from the international community for this United Nations–sponsored use of armed force. Although nineteen nations contributed to the coalition, the majority of troops came from South Korea and the United States, under the command of American General Douglas MacArthur. In the end, but only after the involvement of the Chinese and a considerable loss of human lives, the North Korean invaders were repulsed and the Korean peninsula was largely restored to its prewar status quo.

It was the Security Council, in what has been called one of the most important decisions in the history of the organization, that also authorized the use of collective force when Saddam Hussein of Iraq blatantly invaded neighboring Kuwait in 1990. President George H. W. Bush, who had previously served as a U.S. ambassador to the United Nations and therefore appreciated the importance of diplomacy and collective decision making when confronting dangerous international problems, worked diligently with other leaders such as Mikhail Gorbachev of the Soviet Union to create agreement on mobilizing a coalition to force Saddam out of Kuwait. Efforts were first made to use coercive diplomacy (a strategy to be discussed in Chapter 10) to persuade the aggressor to yield to the demands of the international community. When this failed, the Security Council acted with unusual speed and decisiveness in authorizing the actual use of military force to expel Iraqi troops from the territories they occupied and "to restore international peace and security to the area." A coalition of thirty-four different nations led and orchestrated by the United States thus launched a massive land, air, and sea assault called Operation Desert Storm in January 1991 and in less than seventy-two hours successfully routed the Iraqi forces and restored independence to Kuwait. As one contributor in *Foreign Affairs* wrote, "the concept of collective security as envisioned in the UN Charter worked" and "the United Nations reclaimed a major role in international relations."

In retrospect, much of the criticism suffered by the United Nations as an international security system seems mean-spirited and ill-informed. Despite its problems, its successes in preventive diplomacy, peacemaking and peace-keeping, setting normative standards, promoting and protecting human rights, viewing peace and security as connected to justice and human rights, mediation in conflict resolution, crisis management, adaptability to an expanding and heterogeneous world, advancing international law, and the record of accomplishment made by its subsidiary bodies specializing in humanitarian aid, women and children, public health, and relief are undeniable. In addition, its support for the principle of the inviolability of borders, under which borders cannot be changed unilaterally or by military means, was seen clearly in the collective use of armed force in both the Korean and Persian Gulf wars. These achievements become even more impressive when seen in light of the sheer complexity of diplomatic challenges in the world, the claims of national sovereignty, the reality of a hierarchy in which some members are more equal than others, Great Power vetoes to protect themselves and their friends, the failure of members to honor their pledges under the Charter, and the fact that the organization can never do any more than its sovereign member states allow it to do. They—and they alone—determine its budget, its assignments, its enforcement tasks, whether they will honor its resolutions, whether they will participate in sanctions, and whether they will contribute soldiers and weapons when armed force becomes necessary. Nevertheless, throughout much of its history there ran a current of carping and criticism from those with exaggerated expectations, governments that in moments of frustration blamed the organization for problems in which they had themselves been impercipient before the event and unwilling to act after it, or adamant opponents such as those in the United States who viewed the United Nations as an alien and dangerous presence and who sought to cripple it by withholding funds. From his years as secretary-general, Dag Hammarskjöld (a man described by President Kennedy as "the greatest statesman of our century") tried to provide some perspective on all of this by employing nautical imagery:

> On the seas we sail, we have to face all the storms and stresses created by the ideological, economic, and social conditions of our world. Aboard this new *Santa Maria* we have to meet the impatience of those sailors who expect land on the horizon tomorrow, also the cynicism or sense of futility of those who would give up and leave us drifting impotently. On the shores we have all those who are against the whole expedition, who seem to take a special delight in blaming the storms on the ship instead of the weather.

Despite these kinds of problems, however, support for the United Nations as an indispensable organization in times of mounting international complexity remained strong throughout most of the world. Indeed, 1988 saw such a string of impressive United Nations successes that the often critical *New York Times* declared it "The Year of the UN." In April, after seven years of peace talks led by a United Nations mediator, the Soviet Union agreed to withdraw its forces from Afghanistan. In August, on the basis of a Security Council plan, Iran and Iraq agreed to a cease-fire in a bloody and wasting conflict that had lasted for ten years. In the same month, Secretary-General Javier Pérez de Cuéllar of Peru secured the agreement of Greece and Turkey to hold new talks on the problem of uniting Cyprus, which had poisoned relations between the two NATO allies for more than twenty years. He also began talks in August that promised to end the war between Morocco and the Algerian-backed Polisario guerrillas for control of the western Sahara. In September, the 10,000-member United Nations peacekeeping forces received the Nobel Peace Prize for their significant—and sometimes vital—contributions to international peace and security. In December, United Nations forces began to monitor the withdrawal of Cuban forces from Angola in accordance with the terms of an agreement between the Angolan, South African, and Cuban governments. During the same month, Yasser Arafat's declaration before a meeting of the General Assembly that his Palestine Liberation Organization (PLO) would recognize the binding nature of pertinent United Nations resolutions and the right of the state of Israel to exist created the necessary conditions for American Secretary of State George Shultz's decision to establish formal contact with the PLO in the hope of addressing the Palestine problem. Finally and significantly, and in sharp contrast to several decades of his country's determined efforts to limit the power of the organization and its secretary-general, Soviet leader Mikhail Gorbachev made a breathtaking announcement before the General Assembly calling for a greatly enhanced role for the United Nations in global affairs.

There also was something more. Despite its restraints and imperfections and all of the political problems and magnitude of the challenges and criticisms that confronted it, the United Nations managed to respond to pressing crises and to adapt to unforeseen challenges, thereby keeping its ambitious order-building experiment alive. It continued to hold out the vision created in the wake of a catastrophic war of a larger international community of men and women united by a common desire for a security system with peace and justice rather than a world constantly divided by human frailties and the anarchy of parochial national interests. Those who supported it knew that sometimes they would succeed and sometimes they would fail, but that, through time, their efforts would matter. In this regard, noted Hammarskjöld with insight based on considerable experience, "The United Nations reflects both aspiration and a falling short of aspiration. But the constant struggle to close the gap between aspiration and performance now, as always, makes the difference between civilization and chaos."

As a result of these considerable achievements and a realization that this struggle might be worth the effort, the United Nations began to attract considerably more attention than it had at other times. In fact, a number of states appeared to have discovered new virtues in the organization they had often neglected and abused. This, in turn, led many thoughtful observers and participants to devote considerable attention to how it might best respond to the needs of the future. "After forty-five uncertain, and sometime bleak, years, the prospects for international cooperation are brighter than at any time since the Second World War," concluded a 1990 study entitled *A World in Need of Leadership: Tomorrow's United Nations*. Others expressed similar enthusiasm for an increasingly dynamic and invigorated role for the United Nations. In a special issue called "Beyond the Year 2000: What to Expect in the New Millennium," *Time* predicted that in the future "cooperation with the UN will be the norm" and that "the world will have to utilize the powers of the UN" to solve the diplomatic challenges of our time.

Whether these predictions would be realized or not would depend—as always—on whether the Great Powers would let them happen. Historically, as we have seen, any viable order of international peace and security, including those of a balance of power, a concert of powers, or a more broadly based strategy of collective security, has been dependent on a very high level of consensus on normative values and objectives among those with the greatest power. The United Nations was no different. It depended on the support that the major powers gave it over the years and, importantly, whether they would accept any restraints upon themselves "in the common interest." Only the future would tell. The years ahead would be dramatic and would entail major upheavals in the international system and the diplomatic revolution with profound implications for force and statecraft. These would involve the collapse of the Soviet Union, the emergence of the United States as the world's only superpower, new crises in Africa and Asia, the escalation of violence in the Middle East, civil wars, genocide in the former Yugoslavia and Rwanda, "failed" states and "rogue" regimes, the proliferation of weapons of mass destruction, the attacks of September 11, 2001, and the rise of global terrorism. Further turmoil erupted when the George W. Bush administration decided to completely ignore the Charter's clear prohibition against the threat or use of force against the territorial integrity or political independence of another state by launching a war against Iraq in 2003. But these developments lay in the future and remained as yet unknown. Until then, as we shall see in the next chapter, the ability of the United Nations to function as its founders intended would be severely undermined by what happened in the grinding, debilitating, and terrifying struggle known as the Cold War.

Suggestions for Further Exploration

Paul Kennedy, *The Parliament of Man* (New York, 2006) provides a particularly insightful assessment of the United Nations as a whole. For the history of plans for a postwar security system, see Stephen C. Schlesinger, *Act of Creation* (Boulder, CO, 2004); Townsend Hoopes and Douglas Brinkley, *FDR and the Creation of the U.N.* (New Haven, 1997); Robert A. Divine, *Second Chance: The Triumph of Internationalism in America During World War II* (New York, 1967); Ruth Russell, *A History of the United Nations Charter* (Washington, DC, 1958); United Nations Information Organization, *Documents of the United Nations Conference on International Organization, San Francisco, 1945* (London and New York, 1946–1955); and Forrest Davis, "Roosevelt's World Blueprint," *Saturday Evening Post*, April 10, 1943.

Further discussions and analyses can be found in Thomas Weiss et al., *The United Nations and Changing World Politics* (Boulder, CO, 2009 ed.); Stanley Meisler, *The United Nations: The First Fifty Years* (New York, 1997); Paul Gordon Lauren, "The Diplomats and Diplomacy of the United Nations," in Gordon A. Craig and Francis Lowenheim (eds.), *The Diplomats, 1939–1979* (Princeton, 1994); Brian Urquhart, *Ralph Bunche* (Boston, 1993), and his excellent autobiographical account based on a long career within the organization, *A Life in Peace and War* (New York, 1987); John Stoessinger, *The Might of Nations: World Politics in Our Time* (New York, 1979); the pioneering Inis Claude, Jr., *Swords Into Plowshares* (New York, 1971 ed.); and Thomas Hovet, Jr., "United Nations Diplomacy," *Journal of International Affairs*, 17 (1963). On the relationship between security, peace, justice, and human rights, see Paul Gordon Lauren, *The Evolution of International Human Rights* (Philadelphia, 2011ed.).

For specific treatment of force and statecraft in the United Nations, see Vaughan Lowe et al. (eds.), *The United Nations Security Council and War* (New York, 2008); Paul Diehl, *International Peacekeeping* (Baltimore, 1995 ed.); Michael Howard, "The Historical Development of the UN's Role in International Security," in Adam Roberts and Benedict Kingsbury (eds.), *United Nations, Divided World* (Oxford, 1993 ed.); United Nations, *The Blue Helmets* (New York, 1990 ed.); the pioneering Michael Harbottle, *The Impartial Soldier* (London, 1970); and Gabriella Rosner, *The United Nations Emergency Force* (New York, 1963). On the legal aspects, see Christine Gray, *International Law and the Use of Force* (New York, 2008 ed.).

Additional information can also be found on the Internet, including the home page for the United Nations at www.un.org; the Security Council at www.un.org/Docs/sc; the UN High Commissioner for Human Rights at www.ohchr.org; and the UN Department of Peacekeeping Operations at www.un.org/en/peacekeeping. See also the reports of organizations with long-standing interests in the United Nations, including the United Nations Association of the USA at www.unausa.org; and the Stanley Foundation at www.stanleyfoundation.org.

— 5 —

The Cold War

The Cold War became one of the longest and most costly international conflicts in history. It was fought first and foremost between the United States and the Soviet Union, along with their respective allies and the Chinese, who often intertwined messianic ideologies with global geopolitical ambitions. In this epic struggle they employed as many tools and methods as possible to gain advantage, including economic aid to win friends, propaganda to manipulate public opinion and create hatreds, psychological warfare, espionage, covert action and political assassinations, persecutions, military assistance, the construction of rival alliances, guerrilla and counterinsurgency warfare, proxy wars, and a massive and terrifying arms race with weapons capable of obliterating life as we know it. The Cold War was wider in scope than any of the world wars, for it was not only fought on every continent but, considering the space race, *over* each one as well. It also proved to be one of the costliest of all of the world's conflicts. The United States alone, for example, spent more than $13,000,000,000,000 on this struggle. As the authors of *A Hard and Bitter Peace: A Global History of the Cold War* describe its impact, "For decades the Cold War dominated international relations, profoundly influenced the global economy, and to some extent affected the life of almost everyone on the planet." The magnitude and totality of what has been called this "struggle for the soul of mankind" could not help but create profound consequences for the diplomatic revolution, domestic politics and institutions, cultural and social practices, foreign and national security policy, any attempts to create a viable international system, and, most certainly, force and statecraft.

THE ORIGINS AND ESCALATION OF THE COLD WAR

In one sense, this struggle began with the Bolshevik Revolution in 1917 when Lenin announced that there always would be unremitting hostility between the capitalistic West and the communistic Soviet Union. But the immediate origins of what came to be called the Cold War emerged at the end of the Second World War, once military victory had eliminated the threat of a common enemy. The hopes that the coalition that had cooperated to win the war would continue to cooperate to win the peace were dashed. Problems surfaced immediately. As soon as he arrived at the San Francisco Conference to establish the United Nations, Soviet Foreign Minister V. M. Molotov threw down the gauntlet by speaking of the "many irreconcilable enemies in the camp of the most aggressive imperialists." President Truman reciprocated this hostility by telling his advisors that "if the Russians did not wish to join us they could go to hell." The United States, Great Britain, and France strongly opposed Stalin's brutal use of the Soviet Red Army in Eastern Europe, particularly in Poland, and vehemently protested his refusal to coordinate policies in the postwar occupation zones of Germany. The Soviets, for their part, furiously lashed out when the British and the French sought to move back into their colonial possessions and when the United States announced that it would brook no opposition to its sole occupation of defeated Japan. They also grew intensely suspicious about the American monopoly of a weapon that would become one of the defining characteristics of the Cold War with a most profound impact on subsequent force and statecraft: the atomic bomb.

Weapons in the past had always been characterized by their limited capacity to destroy. The existing state of technology imposed severe limits on their lethality, and large masses of people could never be killed at an instant. It is for

"The Fate of Nemesis": The Atomic Age Begins

this reason that Clausewitz could write with confidence about the historical experience of war genuinely being a continuation of policy by other means. Yet, this feature of all previous weapons changed in an instant with America's successful 1945 test in the desert at Alamogordo, New Mexico. As he personally witnessed the first ever atomic explosion, General Thomas Farrell was nearly overwhelmed when he realized what a critical threshold had just been crossed. He wrote in his official report:

> The effects could well be called unprecedented, magnificent, beautiful, stupendous, and terrifying. No man-made phenomenon of such tremendous power had ever occurred before.... Thirty seconds after the explosion came first, the air blast pressing hard against people and things, to be followed almost immediately by the strong, sustained, awesome roar which warned of doomsday and made us feel that we puny things were blasphemous to dare tamper with the forces heretofore reserved to The Almighty.

Serious escalation and complications followed. While visiting Fulton, Missouri, in 1946, Winston Churchill presented his blunt "Iron Curtain" speech, accusing the Soviets of brutally imposing pro-Communist regimes across Eastern Europe, warning that there might be no limits to their expansive and proselytizing tendencies, and declaring, "I am convinced that there is nothing they admire so much as strength, and there is nothing for which they have less respect than weakness." Stalin angrily shot back in response that this was nothing less than a declaration of war against the Soviet Union.

Confrontations now appeared in rapid succession. One exploded in Iran as the British and Americans struggled with the Soviets over access to vital Middle East oil concessions and Stalin supported an ill-fated revolt in Azerbaijan. Another erupted in Turkey as the former allies of the "Grand Alliance" contested who would control the strategic Bosporus and Dardanelles straits guarding naval access between the Mediterranean and the Black Sea. Yet another broke out in Greece when the British-supported government suddenly found itself teetering on the verge of collapse in a civil war against Communist insurgents. Then, in 1947, the United States dramatically enunciated the Truman Doctrine, arguing that in the emerging global ideological struggle it would provide assistance to all countries willing to resist Communism. "At the present moment in world history," Truman declared, "nearly every nation must choose between alternative ways of life"—either democracy characterized by free institutions or totalitarianism based on terror and political oppression. The Soviets responded by describing this speech as "venomous slander," "aggressive," "hostile and bellicose," and specifically designed "to interfere in the affairs of other countries on the side of reaction and counter-revolution." They, in turn, imposed tighter controls over Eastern European countries occupied by their troops, ruthlessly eliminated political opponents and replaced them with more reliable Moscow-controlled Communists, and in 1948 seriously escalated the Cold War by dismantling the democratic government of Czechoslovakia and installing a puppet government of their own and then by dramatically cutting off all Western access into West Berlin by imposing the Berlin Blockade.

This vicious cycle of action and reaction continued with other events and crises in the relations between the West and the Soviet Union. Each side believed that it alone represented the best vision for human society, and each side believed that it was behaving in a justifiably defensive manner in response to obstructionist and threatening behavior on the part of the other. The more sympathetic images that Soviet and Western leaders had held of each other at the end of the Second World War were now transformed and darkened as each side perceived the other as dangerously hostile. This is not to say that the Cold War was caused merely by mutual distrust and misperception—its origins lie deeper than that, as already indicated, in the real and important conflicts of interest that existed between the two sides—but there is no doubt that they were seriously exacerbated by the psychological dynamics of conflict escalation. False perception and psychological phenomena of this kind are, unfortunately, familiar in international relations, as they are in everyday life. Oliver Wendell Holmes once remarked that in any argument between two persons, six persons are involved: the two as they actually are, the two as they see themselves, and the two as they see each other. No wonder, Holmes exclaimed, that the two talk past each other and become angry! In international affairs, the same sort of psychological multiplication process is apt to take place, with much the same effects.

When leaders deliberately seek to manipulate negative images of their adversaries in order to generate—and then exploit—fear and suspicion, this problem becomes even worse. The Cold War greatly accelerated that feature of the diplomatic revolution whereby the domestic pressures of mass politics and public opinion came to exert enormous influence on international relations. Both sides escalated their programs of information and propaganda for "public diplomacy" and its new variant called "cultural diplomacy," employing "cultural weapons" to win hearts and minds at home and abroad. Some efforts were even more calculating. Secretary of State Dean Acheson, for example, freely admitted in his memoirs that he consciously portrayed Russia as aggressive as a means to gain approval for President Truman's policies. Others of both political parties followed suit, finding inflammatory rhetoric, hysteria, "Red-baiting," and the exaggeration of Communist threats useful political expedients. Republican Senator Joseph McCarthy became so successful, in fact, that the term "McCarthyism" was coined to describe these activities. He and his rabid followers gained sufficient political power to actually purge the professional diplomats known as the "China Hands" from the Department of State by accusing them of being "sympathizers," "fellow-travelers," or "card-carrying" members of the Communist Party. The price for doing so, of course, was a further diminution of the professionals and the elimination of America's expert eyes and ears on Asia for many years to come.

Communists, for their own part, similarly discovered that generating fear of an enemy can be a very useful tool. Soviet leaders thus began their "Hate America" campaign, depicting the United States as leading the "monopoly bourgeoisie of capitalism," "fascist sympathizers," and "reactionary elements of world imperialism" bent on subversion, military adventurism, aggression, and global domination. When Mao Zedong and his Chinese Communist Party came to power in Beijing in 1949 and created the People's Republic of China as a result of their victory over the American-supported Chiang Kai-shek, they wasted no time in portraying the United States as a

> paradise of gangsters, swindlers, rascals, special agents, fascist germs, speculators, debauchers and all the dregs of society. This is the world's manufactory and source of all such crimes as reaction, darkness, cruelty, decadence, corruption, debauchery, oppression....Everyone who does not want the people of his beloved fatherland contaminated by these criminal phenomena is charged with the responsibility of arising to condemn her, curse her, hate her, and despise her.

In this contest of words, ideology, images, and symbols, it is important to understand that the Cold War coincided exactly with the midpoint of the twentieth century's revolution in communications technology. This happened just as radio, press, and film media were maturing and television was emerging. These tools, when placed in the hands of those increasingly trained in the scientific approach to psychological manipulation, such as public relations experts, advertising specialists, and image consultants, provided governments with unprecedented capacities to target public opinion and mold it to their liking and to use psychological warfare as a means of breaking the will of the enemy. Because they could shape the way that ordinary people viewed and reacted to their perceived friends and adversaries in the world, they became powerful weapons in a global battle for hearts and minds. Indeed, according to historian Kenneth Osgood, this combination of new media technologies and communication techniques explains why the Cold War became so ideological, so pervasive, and so all-encompassing. As he writes in *Total Cold War: Eisenhower's Secret Propaganda Battle at Home and Abroad*, "In this context, propaganda and public relations emerged as integral components of statecraft, altering the ways foreign policies were formulated, implemented, and presented....The Cold War reversed Clausewitz's famous dictum that war was an extension of politics: diplomacy became an extension of warfare, and propaganda became a critical weapon in this new type of international combat."

The volatile combination of deliberately manipulated and ideologically driven perceptions, when combined with seriously conflicting national interests, escalated the Cold War to frightening proportions. In a few years, both the United States and the Soviet Union gained such strength that they came to be known not just as great powers, but as superpowers. Each moved quickly to organize and then dominate their respective alliance systems. Under the policy known as Containment, for example, the United States sought to stop the spread of Communism first by intertwining economic development with security guarantees and then by creating the North Atlantic Treaty Organization (NATO) in 1949 with Canada and Western Europeans, adding Greece and

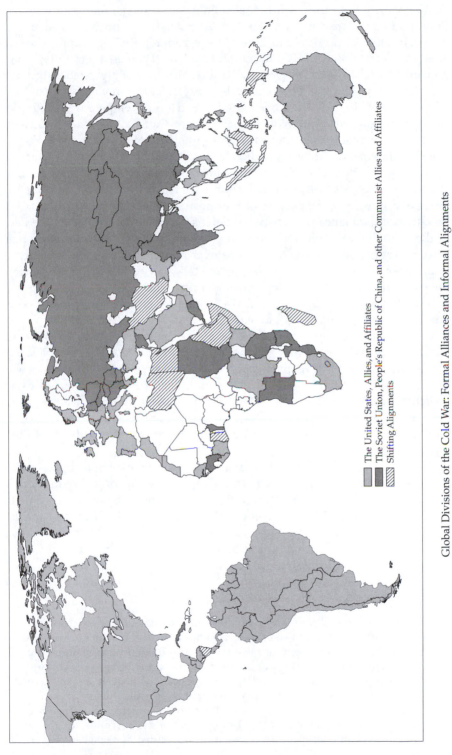

Global Divisions of the Cold War: Formal Alliances and Informal Alignments

The United States, Allies, and Affiliates

The Soviet Union, People's Republic of China, and other Communist Allies and Affiliates

Shifting Alignments

Turkey shortly thereafter. Additional military agreements followed with the Philippines and Japan in Asia, ANZUS with Australia and New Zealand in the Pacific, the Southeast Asian Treaty Organization (SEATO), and the Central Treaty Organization (CENTO) in the Middle East. Then, in a particularly significant and controversial move, the United States strongly pushed to have West Germany, which had been an archenemy defeated only ten years before, added to NATO in 1955. The Soviets condemned this development as an "imperialistic program of oppression and aggression" and a "revival of German militarism," accusing the Americans of stopping at nothing in order to secure "world supremacy." They immediately responded by creating the Warsaw Treaty Organization with their puppet states in Eastern Europe, claiming that it was "a purely defensive organization directed towards safeguarding the peace and security of the peoples of Europe and the rest of the world."

Whether an alliance is offensive or defensive, however, is often in the eyes of the beholder. Deterrence to prevent a war by one side may easily be perceived as aggression by the other. Whatever the intentions of the Americans and the Soviets at the time, and despite the talk about "peaceful coexistence," the fact remains that their policies created a powerful, bipolar structuring that divided the world during the Cold War. There were not enough major powers of relatively equal strength to make possible the reemergence of a genuine multipolar balance-of-power system. Each superpower sought to dominate its weaker allies and to keep their hegemonic alliances under tight control, while at the same time expanding their capacities to project military force. There was very little flexibility in making alliances or, for most of the weaker states, in switching them. Both the United States and the Soviet Union viewed any possible loss of an ally, even a small one, with great apprehension for fear of its effects on the rest of their alliances and thus the perceived credibility of their military threat.

These threats, like those of all military alliances in the historical past, relied heavily on trained troops armed with weapons. But during the diplomatic revolution and the Cold War there was something new, for weapons came to be distinguished as either "conventional" or "nuclear." The human capacity to destroy had never known such unlimited possibilities, and this suddenly caused serious practical and ethical problems for those charged with formulating and implementing foreign policy involving force and statecraft. In a thought-provoking book entitled *Nuclear Weapons and Foreign Policy*, scholar Henry Kissinger observed:

> In Greek mythology, Nemesis, the goddess of fate, sometimes punished man by fulfilling his wishes too completely. In has remained for the nuclear age to experience the full irony of this penalty. Throughout history, humanity has suffered from a shortage of power and has concentrated all its efforts on developing new sources and special applications of it. It would have seemed unbelievable even fifty years ago that there could ever be an excess of power.... Yet this is precisely the challenge of the nuclear age. Ever since the end of the Second World War brought us not the peace we sought so earnestly, but an uneasy armistice, we have responded by what can best be

described as a flight into technology: by devising ever more fearful weapons [of mass destruction].

In this new and terrifying environment, the Americans and the Soviets competed in the most serious, expensive, and potentially deadly arms race in human history. The Soviet Union broke the monopoly of the United States by exploding its first atomic weapon in 1949. In response, Truman's newly created National Security Council issued a strategic policy statement in 1950 known as NSC-68, later described as "one of the key historical documents of the Cold War." It predicted a future of indefinite tension and monolithic Communist aggression on a global scale and saw the contest ahead as primarily military in nature. It therefore called for more armed force: a tripling of America's defense budget, a massive increase in conventional weapons, and the building of a huge and more powerful nuclear arsenal. Even greater destruction became possible when the United States successfully exploded the first hydrogen or thermonuclear bomb in 1952. (To provide a point of comparison, the atomic bomb dropped on Hiroshima released an explosive energy equivalent to approximately 15,000 tons of TNT, whereas this bomb provided a yield of 10,500,000 tons of TNT.) The Soviets responded in kind three years later.

The arms race was on, and both sides rushed to build not only their nuclear arsenals but ever more sophisticated means of delivering these weapons to their targeted adversaries. With the first successful launch of the Sputnik satellite by the Soviet Union in 1957, the race entered space. Both nations developed intercontinental ballistic missiles (ICBMs) with a range of over 3,000 miles, thus making it possible to attack each other from one continent to another. With weapons such as these capable of destroying an enemy without ever having to launch an armed invasion as in the past, and doctrines like "Massive Retaliation" threatening the complete annihilation of an opponent, some strategists began to speak of all-or-nothing "Mutual Assured Destruction." Critics used the first letter of each word in this strategy to describe its impact on the world: MAD.

This capacity to inflict massive, annihilating destruction could not help but raise the issue of excess, or far too much, both in terms of the end result and of the process itself. The superpowers could not possibly pursue their unprecedented arms race unless they committed staggering human and material resources to the effort. To do so, they increasingly devoted the funding and bureaucratic power of their governments, the minds of their scientists, the skills and energies of their labor forces, and the capacities of their industries to their military forces. This process achieved many of its objectives, but at the same time began to present serious threats. Among those who voiced their concerns was none other than President Dwight Eisenhower. In his last day of office he delivered one of his most important and thoughtful speeches. Here he explicitly acknowledged military strength as a vital instrument in force and statement. But then he drew attention to the dangers of combining "an immense military establishment and a large arms industry [that] is new in the American experience." He ominously warned:

...we must not fail to comprehend its grave implications. Our toil, resources, and livelihood are all involved; so is the very structure of our society. In the councils of government, we must guard against the acquisition of unwarranted influence, whether sought or unsought, by the military-industrial complex. The potential for the disastrous rise of misplaced power exists and will persist.

The escalating Cold War also intensified the use of intelligence activities. Statecraft throughout time always has attempted to obtain valuable foreknowledge that might help to avoid surprise attacks or threats. Government leaders historically and typically have used a variety of means, including spies, to collect and analyze information and to protect their own intelligence sources and methods. During the Cold War, however, these traditional practices were augmented by the increased use of covert action, or clandestine operations, designed specifically to alter the course of events in another country. These included secret financial payments, weapons deliveries, subversion, paramilitary operations, destabilization of unfriendly governments, and political assassination by the superpowers to advance their interests. The Soviets developed their massive apparatus of the Committee for State Security (KGB) to coordinate these efforts, drawing on a long national experience with the czar's secret police. The United States, which up to this point had always resisted establishing a permanent intelligence organization, now created the Central Intelligence Agency (CIA). The tenor of the time is well reflected in a top-secret government memorandum recommending that American intelligence operations jettison accepted normative standards and ethical restraints and instead become

> more effective, more unique, and if necessary, more ruthless than that employed by the enemy. No one should be permitted to stand in the way of the prompt, efficient, and secure accomplishment of this mission.... It is now clear that we are facing an implacable enemy whose avowed objective is world domination by whatever means and whatever cost. There are no rules in such a game. Hitherto acceptable norms of human conduct do not apply. If the U.S. is to survive, long-standing American concepts of "fair play" must be reconsidered.... We must learn to subvert, sabotage, and destroy our enemies by more clever, more sophisticated, and more effective methods than those used against us.

Seeking Restraints Through Deterrence, Diplomacy, and *Détente*

Such unremitting hostility, unrestrained competition, and recommendations to become "more ruthless" and observe "no rules" created diplomatic challenges of the first magnitude. Without some form of restraint, as we shall see in Chapter 12, international competition becomes utterly unbridled and leads to anarchy. At this stage in the Cold War, the superpowers appeared to be careening toward destruction. Every major crisis, whether in Berlin during 1948, 1958–1959, and 1961, in Cuba during 1962, or in any other location around the world, always was coupled with the fear that *any* shooting war between American and Soviet forces, no matter at how modest a level initially, could escalate completely out of control. It therefore eventually became evident to the United States and the Soviet Union that, despite their intense rivalry, they in fact shared one essential goal in common: the prevention of a Third World War and what would very likely bring about their mutual annihilation.

The practical task thus was how to compete and use force and statecraft in the Cold War while at the same time avoiding thermonuclear war. This presented both superpowers with a serious dilemma and the necessity of choosing between preferred objectives and risks. Policy makers in the United States, for example, constantly had to confront a built-in conflict during every major international crisis: how to contain international Communism, or to roll it back if possible, and simultaneously to avoid a catastrophic war. Democratic and Republican administrations alike attempted to cope with this dilemma by considering whether in a given situation the balance of power between the Soviet bloc and the free world alliance was at stake. If a Communist success in a certain area might critically weaken them or their allies, and the balance of power was thereby threatened, American policy makers demonstrated a willingness to do what they could to prevent that particular outcome, even though to do so meant accepting some danger of war, as in Korea. If, however, a Soviet success would not seriously undermine the ability of the Western alliance to contain the future spread of Communism, then they generally were inclined not to overreact in ways that would risk armed confrontation between themselves. This explains why Eisenhower, despite all of his talk about the "liberation" of Eastern Europe, greatly feared the possibility of provoking the Soviets into a war and thus refused to intervene when the Hungarians called for help during their revolution in 1956.

In some ways, this use of balance-of-power criterion in making critical foreign policy decisions during the Cold War was similar to its employment by the Great Powers in the classical European system. But it is important to recognize that a "balance of terror" is not the same as a multipolar, system-wide balance of power, especially when the major actors lacked a consensus on basic values. The major difference, however, was the fear not of limited conventional war, as in the past, but of a thermonuclear holocaust. The sheer destructiveness of modern weapons thus provided a powerful deterrent by discouraging both the superpowers from resorting to war as a way of preventing an undesired change in the existing balance of power if to do so would result in a direct military clash between the United States and the Soviet Union.

The strategy of threatening force with deterrence, which we will explore in detail in Chapter 9, at times played an invaluable role in restraining both the Americans and the Soviets in their rivalry. But this occurred only in the most dangerous of circumstances and certainly did not cover all the other aspects of Cold War competition or of American-Soviet relations. Critics complained that the strategy of Containment, despite its steadfastness, was nevertheless static, purely reactive, and, of particular importance, provided no place for diplomatic initiative. They argued that it often failed to utilize the techniques, institutions, and practices of diplomacy developed over many centuries to help resolve conflict and to facilitate relations among states.

Fearing the consequences of such neglect, as well as the lost opportunities for negotiation that would result, some policy makers sought to learn lessons from history about diplomacy or to develop some other new method of seeking restraint, regulating rivalry, and promoting some level of cooperation. These included experimentation with crisis prevention, crisis management, and accommodation, or, as we shall see in Chapter 8, negotiation to arrive at agreements to settle or moderate certain conflicts. On some occasions, agreements were reached on arms control, as with the decision in 1958 to temporarily suspend nuclear testing. Sometimes these negotiations were conducted within the context of the United Nations when it suited the interests of the superpowers. But most of the time they were not, for neither the Americans nor the Soviets were prepared to consistently honor their obligations under the Charter. Efforts to find restraints thus were episodic and inconsistent, and often remained less than effective as long as the two superpowers persisted in placing a higher priority on winning the Cold War.

The dangers of rejecting diplomacy became painfully evident. In 1958, major confrontations occurred over the Taiwan Straits and over Berlin. Two years later, the Soviet Union announced that it had shot down an American U-2 spy plane deep inside its own territory, and armed struggle broke out in the Congo and in Laos. After his earlier bombastic threat to the West that "we will bury you," Soviet leader Nikita Khrushchev declared in 1961 that the Soviet Union would actively support "wars of national liberation" in the developing world, forced another crisis over Berlin and built a hideous wall that carved the city in two, issued menacing threats of what came to be called "nuclear blackmail," and exploded the largest thermonuclear weapon ever made with a yield of over 50,000,000 tons of TNT in order to demonstrate just how awesome Soviet capabilities had become. The fear of nuclear war became so intense that thousands of Americans began building fallout shelters in their backyards. The same year witnessed the United States launch of the ill-fated Bay of Pigs invasion of Cuba in an attempt to overthrow its Communist leader Fidel Castro and the decision of President John F. Kennedy to increase production of nuclear weapons and the missiles to deliver them, double the number of ships in the navy, enlarge the army, build up the number of tactical air squadrons, create special counterinsurgency forces to fight Communist guerrillas, and expand covert actions in order to provide what he described as a "flexible response" to as many contingencies as possible. It is thus not surprising that even the seasoned U.S. ambassador in Moscow, Llwellyn Thompson, worried aloud: "All of us are going to be dead!"

The potential for catastrophe was revealed with vivid and frightening clarity by the most acute confrontation of the entire Cold War: the Cuban Missile Crisis. In the late summer and early autumn of 1962, and despite his promises to the contrary, Khrushchev secretly deployed a number of medium- and intermediate-range ballistic missiles to Cuba, capable of obliterating most cities in the United States. When this was discovered by U-2 reconnaissance aircraft, it brought the superpowers—and the world with them—to the very brink of thermonuclear war. Rejecting the recommendation from his military advisors on the Joint Chiefs of Staff to use force immediately by launching an air strike against the missile sites, but nevertheless threatening to do so if necessary, Kennedy undertook a naval blockade of Cuba instead. American and Soviet leaders placed their armed forces on full alert, an invasion force was assembled for combat in Cuba, and Strategic Air Command planes were sent airborne with nuclear weapons and with prearranged targets. Kennedy announced ominously that he would "regard any nuclear missile launched from Cuba against any nation in the Western Hemisphere as an attack by the Soviet Union on the United States, requiring a full retaliatory response upon the Soviet Union." This brought the antagonists, in the words of one leading participant, "eyeball to eyeball." The world held its breath. In the end, as we shall analyze in more detail in Chapters 10 and 11, the combination of crisis management by both Washington and Moscow, successful diplomacy at the United Nations, and Kennedy's use of the strategy of coercive diplomacy proved effective. The crisis ceased with a quid pro quo in which Khrushchev agreed to remove the missiles in return for a pledge by Kennedy not to invade Cuba in the future, as well as a secret agreement to remove U.S. Jupiter missiles from Turkey.

Once it became more fully understood just how close the world had come to a nuclear holocaust, the impact of the Cuban Missile Crisis became even more profound. Indeed, this crisis marked one of the major turning points of recent history. It had a dramatic, catalytic effect by facilitating a transition from the era of the acute Cold War to a more serious search for a less dangerous and more viable system of peace and security, thereby demonstrating that international crisis sometimes can have positive results in improving relations between previously antagonistic states. This interesting feature is conveyed by the Chinese character for "crisis," which has two meanings. The first is the same as the standard meaning of the word in English, that is, a threat or danger. The second connotation, however, is something quite different—not "threat," but rather "opportunity." This insightful double meaning suggests that a crisis might lead policy makers to question and to revise—if not totally discard— some of the old beliefs and policies that led to the confrontation in the first place and perhaps make them more willing to reach out in new directions.

The Cuban Missile Crisis produced precisely this kind of effect. It moved the allies of the Americans and the Soviets to explore ways that they might begin to somehow disengage from the dangers of military blocs controlled by their respective superpowers whose misjudgments and arrogance might pull them into unwanted wars. It also stimulated those new states emerging from decolonization in Asia, Africa, and the Middle East with revolutionary nationalism on their minds and the bitter taste of racial discrimination still in their mouths to avoid being drawn too closely into the wakes of either the United States or the Soviet Union by seeking options that they called Third World "nonalignment." In the same way, the terrifying horror of the missile crisis provided a form of shock therapy for the leaders of the superpowers.

It brought to a sobering head long-standing fears of the Cold War on both sides and strengthened their determination to seek better alternatives. "Evil has brought some good," wrote Khrushchev to Kennedy. "The good is that now people have felt more tangibly the breathing of the burning flames of thermonuclear war and have a more clear realization of the threat looming over them....Everything in our relations capable of generating a new crisis should be erased now."

Almost immediately the two superpowers became partners in reaching what they called the Hot-Line Agreement, establishing a cable link between Washington, D.C., and Moscow in order to provide direct, secure, and rapid communication during times of crisis. Shortly thereafter they successfully negotiated the Limited Test Ban Treaty, prohibiting atmospheric nuclear tests and marking the first major arms control agreement during the Cold War. At the same time, many Americans came to transform their image of the Soviet Union from that of a total enemy to a *limited adversary* and began to see the virtues of diplomatic negotiation. Kennedy himself conveyed this change during a moving speech at American University in which he spoke of peace as "the most important topic on earth" and "as the necessary rational end of rational men," calling upon his fellow citizens to reexamine their dogmatic views on the Cold War if they wanted to save humanity from annihilation. In sharp contrast with previous presidential statements (and in some that would follow), he said about the Soviet Union that "no government or social system is so evil that its people must be considered as lacking in virtue." He called for a renewal of traditional diplomacy and warned his listeners not to take "a distorted and desperate view of the other side, not to see conflict as inevitable," and not to regard "accommodation as impossible and communication as nothing more than an exchange of threats."

Heartening as this sounded, the fact remains that people learn different lessons from history and from their own experiences, leaders change, entrenched habits and patterns of thought are hard to break, and not everyone is capable of escaping their fears or ideological shibboleths, even when it is in their interests to do so. The assassination of John Kennedy in 1963 and the removal of Khrushchev from office the next year robbed the world of the two leaders who had been most personally transformed by the dangers of confrontation. After the initial terror of the Cuban Missile Crisis had passed, some American policy makers and members of the public alike began to believe that the "success" in Cuba had been the result not of careful diplomacy, but rather of being tough and threatening to use force if necessary. Moreover, they found themselves continuing to be dominated by the hubris of thinking that their military might could solve all challenges and the tendency to view problems in simplistic terms. It was the persistent and indiscriminate assumption that all Communist regimes were identical, linked, and deadly, for example, that fostered the so-called "domino theory" (arguing that if one country fell to Communism, others automatically would do the same) and that drew the United States into the long agony of the Vietnam War. This involvement, made against military advice and without any careful assessment of costs and possible outcomes, escalated dramatically under President Lyndon Johnson, who ordered a bombing campaign known as Operation Thunder against North Vietnam in 1965. Ultimately, the United States would send more than half a million troops into the conflict. At the same time, Khrushchev's successor, Leonid Brezhnev, committed the Soviet Union to supporting America's adversaries in Vietnam, escalated the arms race by more than tripling the number of strategic Soviet ICBMs, invaded Czechoslovakia in 1968, and announced with the Brezhnev Doctrine that he would intervene militarily in other countries as well if Soviet and/or Communist interests were threatened further.

Trouble brewed in Asia as well. The People's Republic of China under Mao persecuted domestic opponents and then descended into the chaos of the Cultural Revolution, which consumed perhaps a half million Chinese lives. Its ideological fervor also permeated foreign affairs. The government charged the Soviets of losing their revolutionary zeal and becoming "soft" on capitalism, stationed troops on their border with the Soviet Union, and contributed to the conflict known as the Sino-Soviet split that greatly increased tension between the world's two largest Communist powers. China also directed its wrath against the United States, accusing America of imperialism and racism, supporting the hated rival regime in Taiwan, killing its soldiers earlier during the Korean War and its allies in Vietnam, arming its neighbors like Japan and the Philippines, excluding it from assuming its rightful membership in the United Nations, and denying it diplomatic recognition.

The renewed international dangers, as well as the severe domestic turmoil and economic costs resulting from these problems and others involving various allies and client states, forced leaders to look once again at the merits of diplomacy. To describe their efforts, they increasingly came to use the French word *détente*, taken from traditional diplomacy and meaning a relaxation of tension between adversaries by means of a conscious and more rational policy of engagement, cooperation, and accommodation. Each, for their own reasons, had strong self-interests in creating some restraints for the Cold War competition threatening to engulf them. The Americans and the Soviets thus began by negotiating an arms control agreement known as the Nuclear Non-Proliferation Treaty (NPT) in 1968. The following year, West German Chancellor Willy Brandt initiated a policy he called *Ostpolitik*, or Eastern Policy, designed to improve relations with the governments of the Soviet bloc in Eastern Europe, including Communist East Germany, and to reach an agreement on the divided city of Berlin. The Chinese had their own fears as well, not the least of which were Soviets threats and military confrontation on the Sino-Soviet border, and therefore began to consider better relations with the United States as a means of providing a counterweight to the Soviet Union. For their part, the Soviets feared the deployment of new U.S. multiple warhead missiles (MIRVs) aimed at them, continued unrest among their satellite states, and what they regarded as the unpredictable Chinese, and thus sought to find ways of relaxing a number of Cold War tensions.

These interests coincided with those of the United States trying desperately to extricate itself from the Vietnam War, which was consuming lives, creating tensions with allies, wrecking havoc with other diplomatic efforts, escalating budget deficits in order to finance the war, and (especially after the American invasion of Cambodia in 1970) intensifying public opposition to such an extent that it divided the country more than at any time since the Civil War. The United States simultaneously found itself engaged in antagonism with the Chinese Communists and confrontation with the Soviets, who were pursuing an unrestrained arms race with strategic weapons and developing an anti-ballistic missile (ABM) system to defend itself against the U.S. arsenal. These problems help to explain why Richard Nixon, despite his reputation as a militant anti-Communist and ardent Cold Warrior of the past, declared in his inaugural presidential address that America was prepared to enter a new "era of negotiation" with its major adversaries. But he and his new national security advisor, Henry Kissinger, wanted *détente* to not only mean a relaxation of tension between antagonists but to eventually create a strategic balance of power. Their own political experience and understanding of history convinced them that all nations, including their own, based their policies on what they perceived as their national interests and that this factor should be used to create some arrangement of accommodation to maintain peace and security.

To begin this process of creating restraints by using mutual interests, Nixon and Kissinger began negotiating constructive relationships with their major rivals, trying to minimize ideological differences and using a combination of threats as "sticks" and inducements as "carrots" in a triangular configuration of power for leverage. They began with China, for as Nixon had written in an article in *Foreign Affairs,* "any American policy must come urgently to grips with the reality of China. There is no place on this small planet for a billion of its potentially most able people to live in angry isolation." As a result of lengthy negotiations, the Chinese agreed to reduce their level of support for America's adversaries in the Vietnam War and to settle the issue of Taiwan by peaceful means, while the United States promised to gradually reduce its troops in Asia and to reverse their long-standing opposition to Beijing's admission into the United Nations. Both agreed to establish offices for permanent diplomatic representation in their respective capitals of Washington, D.C. and Beijing. Nixon, who personally traveled to China in 1972 to meet Mao Zedong and solidify these agreements, described his trip as "a week that changed the world."

The most critical element of *détente,* of course, involved the two most powerful nations on earth: the two superpowers of the Cold War. Here, a whole series of remarkable agreements ranging from trade and technical exchanges to strategic weapons were signed in a very short period of time. In 1971, to illustrate, the United States and the Soviet Union reached an accord on Berlin, a treaty prohibiting the emplacement of nuclear weapons on seabeds or ocean floors, and agreed to participate in a wide-ranging security conference on Europe and a separate discussion on mutual and balanced reduction of forces. The next year, Nixon and Brezhnev successfully negotiated two arms control agreements, the first Strategic Arms Limitation Treaty (SALT I) and the Anti-Ballistic Missile (ABM) Treaty placing limits on their offensive and defensive strategic missiles. "Never before," announced Kissinger, "have the world's two most powerful nations...placed their central armaments under formally agreed limitation and restraint." They also signed an accord called "Basic Principles of Relations" to define new norms and rules of cooperation and competition, pledging to prevent the development of situations that might dangerously exacerbate their relations, to do their utmost to avoid military confrontations, and to "exercise mutual restraint in their relations and be prepared to negotiate and settle differences by peaceful means." At the 1973 summit in Washington, D.C., the two leaders further signed the "Agreement on the Prevention of Nuclear War," promising to consult and "to refrain from the threat or use of force" against either "the other party" or "the allies of the other party" in situations that might raise the threat of thermonuclear holocaust.

Persistent Problems and the Final Demise of the Cold War

Given all these agreements, it was not difficult to imagine the world moving away from the intense rivalry of the Cold War. The efforts to create new restraints and to regulate conflict appeared to have a reasonable chance of success. But, as we have seen from historical experience, such efforts ultimately succeed only if the participants actually honor their commitments regarding the common aims and objectives they are seeking to advance by following the norms and procedures on which they have agreed. And this is done only if the participants regard it to be in their interest and can gain sufficient international and domestic support to do so. *Détente* suffered from both of these problems, and, by so doing, revealed much to us about the nature of efforts to create and maintain viable international systems for peace and security.

The expectation that the superpowers would act with greater self-restraint in their foreign policies, for example, was not always realized in practice. In fact, at times it seemed to be completely ignored. Both superpowers persistently refused to give up the economic, diplomatic, and military advantages that came from being the world's two largest weapons manufacturers and exporters of arms sales to other nations and rebel factions. Each continued to support their respective client states in the Middle East, with the United States announcing that it was supplying an additional forty-eight Phantom jets to Israel and the Soviet Union responding with increased military supplies to Egypt and Syria, which they promptly used to launch an attack in October 1973. The resulting Arab-Israeli War immediately escalated into superpower confrontation and demonstrated that both sides were willing to ignore their mutual pledges by trying to intimidate each other, with the Soviets threatening to intervene with troops and placing their air force and Strategic Rocket Forces on full alert and the Americans moving to DEFCON III (the maximum defense condition state of readiness short of war) to simultaneously deter and coerce. Moreover, when the citizens of Chile democratically elected a Marxist leader, Kissinger responded that "I don't see why we need to stand by and watch a country go Communist due to the irresponsibility of its own people," and Nixon approved a covert operation to overthrow the government.

This resulted in a military coup d'état that brought to power the repressive dictatorship of General Augusto Pinochet. The agreements similarly did little to restrain the Soviets and their support for what they called "progressive" and "liberation" movements in the Third World. All this raised serious doubts about whether the superpowers of the Cold War would place any restraints upon themselves or not, let alone think about the possibility of the larger international system as a whole.

In this regard, their attitudes toward and policies in the United Nations made tensions even worse. American and Soviet pledges to work together for "the common interest," as envisioned by the Charter, evaporated. Their promises to act cooperatively in partnership, to show self-restraint, to develop a sense of responsibility to protect shared values and objectives, and to harness their enormous power to advance the goals of the organization, vanished. Instead, the two superpowers continually emasculated the Security Council—designed as the focal point for managing matters of force and statecraft in international peace and security—and prevented it from taking any serious action that might threaten their perceived interests. They cast more vetoes by far, for example, than all other countries combined. As we have seen, the Soviet Union attempted to actually eliminate the position of secretary-general. Moreover, both nations chose to ignore the Charter's provisions on the legitimate use of armed force and kept the United Nations from addressing their own unilateral military action against other countries, as evidenced by the Soviets in Hungary, Czechoslovakia, and then Afghanistan, and the Americans in Central America, the Caribbean, and Vietnam.

This persistent problem plagued *détente* by contributing to its failure to gather widespread legitimacy and support. Many countries, including a number of allies, complained that whatever understandings or accommodations had been made, there could be no such thing as a truly international "system" as long as the United Nations was ignored and they, as legitimate nation-states, were deliberately excluded from negotiations conducted in secret and from a triangular structure confined exclusively to the Americans, Soviets, and Chinese.

Domestic support also proved difficult to secure. There were bureaucracies, defense industries, and constituencies that possessed vested interests in preventing any relaxation of tension or change of course. In addition, the pursuit of *détente* required a more sophisticated mental and emotional analysis than that of an ideological Cold War rivalry. Previous American leaders had developed and successfully exploited fear, hysteria, and a simplistic image: Communists were bad and anti-Communists were good, and that is all that one needed to know. The policy of *détente*, however, imposed the more complicated intellectual task of viewing the Soviets and the Chinese as limited adversaries, neither completely friend nor foe, but something in between, depending on circumstances. The nature of that "something" in the context of force and statecraft was not easy for many people to understand. Members of Congress and the public often demonstrated an inability or an unwillingness to grasp the subtleties of a strategy that combined both sticks of punishment and carrots of incentive. Whenever the administration engaged in efforts and conciliation and the bestowal of benefits, critical hawks on the Right complained that it simply rewarded Communist "adventurism" around the world and thus was nothing less than "appeasement." On the other hand, whenever the administration engaged in threats or punishments, critical doves on the Left complained that America risked the outbreak of nuclear war or the descent down a slippery slope into another Vietnam disaster. Added to this was a growing cynicism and distrust of government leaders after the Watergate scandal and revelations of shocking CIA activities conducted in the name of national security sufficient to cause Congress to pass the 1973 War Powers Act, seeking to restrain a president's ability to commit armed forces abroad. Many Americans grew weary of such abuses, of disputes and duplicity, of diplomacy that required subtlety and nuance, and of the distrust and acrobatics that accompanied balance-of-power maneuvers, and thus withheld their support.

Given all of these factors, it is not at all surprising that *détente* came to resemble a roller coaster. As Gerald Ford and then Jimmy Carter came to realize once they became president, the pursuit of consistent and effective foreign policy in the absence of public support is difficult, if not impossible. There were times when the superpowers found ways to successfully collaborate on areas of mutual interest and let pragmatism transcend ideological rivalry, as with the SALT II accords seeking to reduce a further escalation of the arms race. There were times when others would largely take the initiative in using diplomatic negotiation to reach accommodation and relax tension. This occurred, as we shall see in Chapter 8, when thirty-five nations negotiated the historic 1975 Helsinki Final Act at the Conference on Security and Cooperation in Europe (CSCE), tying individual human rights to national and international security and pledging the signatories to refrain "from the threat or the use of force against the territorial integrity or political independence of any state, or in any other manner inconsistent with the purposes of the United Nations." But there were other times when the antagonism grew worse, as when the Soviets dramatically escalated their military buildup, expanded their influence in the Horn of Africa, intervened to support their clients in the civil war in Angola and then enlisted Castro's Cuba to contribute additional weapons and eventually 11,000 combat troops to the struggle, and publicly rejoiced when radicals of the Islamic Iranian Revolution overthrew America's ally the Shah of Iran and seized hostages from the U.S. embassy shouting, "Death to America!"

But the real *coup de grâce* was delivered in December 1979, when the Soviet Union, against the advice of its military commanders, forcefully invaded neighboring and nonaligned Afghanistan. This invasion rocked American leaders to the core and led immediately to a renewal of the Cold War. A shaken and beleaguered Carter, who came into office with the intention of developing a more constructive foreign policy that stressed human rights, disarmament, and working with the Soviets to create greater global stability, condemned the invasion as "the greatest threat to world peace since the Second World War." He responded by recalling the U.S. ambassador from Moscow, cutting off sales of technology and grain, withdrawing SALT II from consideration by the

Senate, substantially increasing American military spending, accelerating the development of a Rapid Deployment Force to project military power abroad, and signing Presidential Directive 59, shifting U.S. strategic emphasis from merely deterring nuclear war to planning to actually fight and win it. *Détente* was dead.

If any doubts still existed about the renewal of confrontational attitudes in the Cold War, they ended when Ronald Reagan became president in 1981. In his first press conference, he depicted Brezhnev and other Soviet leaders as dangerous and dishonorable individuals who were bent on world domination and who would "reserve unto themselves the right to commit any crime, to lie, to cheat" in order to achieve its goals. Later, in the most widely quoted speech of his presidency, he referred to the Soviet Union as "the focus of evil in the modern world" with all "the aggressive impulses of an evil empire." With this as the premise, he challenged the Soviets to "tear down that [Berlin] wall" and called upon Americans to realize their historical destiny by becoming fully engaged in the worldwide battle with Communism—"the struggle between right and wrong and good and evil."

It was in this spirit that the Reagan administration launched its offensive of force in statecraft. The first thrust challenged the Soviet Union with a massive increase in conventional and nuclear weapons. This began with expenditures funding the largest peacetime buildup in American history, at a level doubling the national debt. Billions of dollars were spent on developing and deploying the B-1 bomber, "Stealth" aircraft capable of minimizing radar detection, Trident II submarines with their sub-launched ballistic missiles, air- and ground-launched cruise missiles, Pershing II intermediate-range missiles, the neutron bomb, and powerful and highly accurate MX missiles carrying ten independently targetable nuclear warheads. Reagan also resumed production of poison gas for chemical warfare and called for the development of a space-based defense system that mated lasers, mirrors, particle beams, and other kinetic-energy projection technology with the power of computers designed to destroy Soviet missiles before they reached their targets. He described it as the Strategic Defense Initiative (SDI). His critics dubbed it "Star Wars." From recently declassified documents and the memoirs of former Soviet leaders, we now know that they thought that the United States was preparing to launch a preemptive strike against the Soviet Union and believed SDI to be but one step toward that end.

At the same time, the United States set out to counteract any Communist attempts to spread influence in the Third World. It intervened in the civil war in El Salvador, mined harbors in Nicaragua, invaded Grenada, sent Marines to Lebanon, and conducted the largest naval exercise in history to demonstrate its power. Various forms of support went to authoritarian anti-Communist regimes, whatever their lack of democracy, rule of law, or record on human rights, such as those in Chile, El Salvador, Guatemala, Haiti, Pakistan, the Philippines, and South Africa, among others. Arms and money were covertly funneled through the Pakistani Inter-Services Intelligence (ISI) directorate to militant Islamic fighters known as *mujahideen* battling the Soviets in

Afghanistan (including one by the name of Osama bin Laden); anti-Communist forces in Angola, Cambodia, and Ethiopia; and the Contras fighting against the Communist-backed Sandinistas in Nicaragua. The obsession to promote this fight grew to such an extent that specific laws passed by Congress to restrain or even prohibit certain actions were broken. The campaign against the Sandinistas, for example, was financed in part by laundered money gained from secret arms contracts with some of the same Iranian revolutionaries who had captured American diplomats, thereby creating the Iran-Contra scandal. But critics of individual aspects of Reagan's foreign policy were outnumbered by the majority of voters, who found pleasure in seeing America strong again after a decade of setbacks and disappointments.

Popularity at home, however, does not necessarily translate into popularity abroad, and Reagan's vitriolic rhetoric and confrontational policies alarmed many other nations. Even close allies in Europe deplored the passing of *détente*, listened in horror as the Americans and Soviets openly spoke about force and "counterforce" strikes, and feared the coming of a new ice age. This was particularly true of Germany, where the Social Democratic party repudiated its own chancellor, Helmut Schmidt, because he supported deploying intermediate-range Pershing II and cruise missiles if the Soviets did not agree to remove their large number of mobile, land-based SS-20 missiles. A large and well-coordinated peace movement opposed this deployment and urged withdrawal from NATO if it took place. The Soviets took advantage of this situation to rain threats down upon the new West German government of Helmut Kohl, warning of a sharp deterioration of relations between Moscow and Bonn and the end of arms control negotiations in Geneva. In the end, the deployment took place and successfully forced the Soviets to change their strategy, but it came at a heavy price and revealed deep and widespread concerns within allied countries about the direction of superpower confrontation.

This episode served as a good reminder that diplomacy, by its very nature, involves the interaction among different states, and, within these at the time of the diplomatic revolution, each is heavily influenced by domestic politics. In this regard, a monumental change occurred in 1985 when Mikhail Gorbachev became the new leader of the Soviet Union. More energetic, better educated and traveled, more thoughtful, more skeptical of military force, and less reverential to the ideological stereotypes of the past than his predecessors, Gorbachev nevertheless faced not only an openly hostile administration in the United States, an exhausting war in Afghanistan, unrest in Eastern Europe, and tension with China, but a country in profound crisis at home. The long-term, debilitating effects of military and territorial overextension, arms race competition, bureaucratic stultification and mismanagement of a planned economy, absence of accountability, and a system that resisted independent initiative all had driven the Soviet Union into a political and economic state of near collapse.

Gorbachev attempted to salvage this situation by launching a dual policy of what he called *perestroika* (restructuring) and *glasnost* (openness) at home and "new political thinking" abroad. He announced before a meeting of his stunned diplomats that the Soviet Union needed to make a radical paradigm shift in its perception of threat. In a fundamental transformation from all previous ideologically oriented Soviet leaders who viewed the Cold War as a zero-sum contest between two diametrically opposed revolutionary and imperialist camps, Gorbachev argued that the most serious challenge facing Soviet foreign policy was no longer the class struggle against capitalism, but rather the immense danger of the arms race that threatened humankind itself with mutual destruction. He believed that the ever mounting stockpiles of nuclear weapons created dangerous insecurity rather than security, that nuclear war could never be won, and that nuclear war must never be waged. As such, he insisted on a monumental shift in the way that the Soviet Union approached not only the United States but international relations as a whole. Gorbachev thus called for a "fresh start."

Toward this end, he announced within his first year in office that he would freeze the deployment of Soviet intermediate-range missiles in Europe, begin to negotiate the elimination of all tactical nuclear weapons, impose a moratorium on Soviet nuclear testing (while expressing the hope that the United States would do the same) and replace the inflexible Andrei Gromyko, who had served as foreign minister for twenty years. He then declared that the Soviet Union no longer sought to maintain exact numeric parity in strategic armaments, but instead would shift to a new and less threatening policy of "strategic sufficiency." At the same time, Gorbachev began to cultivate a more personal relationship with Reagan, who, through time and in turn, appeared during his second term to be more willing to modify some of his earlier positions. The two leaders met at summit meetings in Geneva, Reykjavik, Washington, D.C., and Moscow, one of which yielded the remarkable 1987 Intermediate-Range Nuclear Forces (INF) Treaty that actually eliminated an entire category of weapons. He then undertook a series of surprise, unilateral actions that accelerated his course, over the objections of many of his own military and intelligence advisors. These included completely removing Soviet troops from the Afghan War, which he described as a "hopeless military adventure" and a "bleeding wound," reducing the military budget by 14 percent, cutting weapons expenditures by 20 percent, and withdrawing 200,000 troops from Asia. Then, in his electrifying 1988 speech before the United Nations, Gorbachev announced that his government would work as partners in cooperation with the international community, reduce the Soviet stock in conventional weapons, slash troop strength by 500,000, and support freedom of choice for all nations, including those in Eastern Europe—"without exception."

Such a dramatic and unexpected statement signaled that the Soviet Union would exercise military self-restraint by renouncing the use of armed force to protect its empire and prop up its puppet regimes. This initiative from above triggered a deluge from below. Within the single year of 1989, every one of the Communist governments behind the Iron Curtain—Poland, Hungary, Czechoslovakia, Bulgaria, East Germany, and Romania—either changed its political orientation or was overthrown by popular uprisings. People held free elections and crowds tore down the despised Berlin Wall, dancing joyously on its ruins. "Rarely in history," wrote one journalist, "has such a sweeping reorientation of political, economic, and military power taken place so swiftly without military conquest or bloodshed." *Time* magazine reflected on these tumultuous events and in January 1990 concluded:

> With remarkable imagination and daring, he has embarked on a course, perhaps now irreversible, that is reshaping the world.... He has been breaking up an old bloc..., altering the relationship of the Soviet empire with the rest of the world and changing the nature of the empire itself. He has made possible the end of the Cold War and diminished the danger that a hot war will ever break out between the superpowers. Because he is the force behind the most momentous events of the 1980s and because what he has already done will almost certainly shape the future, Mikhail Gorbachev is *Time*'s Man of the Decade.

Little could *Time* or even Gorbachev himself imagine what lay ahead, for these events unleashed unanticipated forces that appeared impervious to control. Although often praised abroad, Gorbachev's reforms and new policies generated great discontent, resistance, and even sabotage at home, especially among hard-line Communists, impassioned nationalists, and those in the military, KGB, and defense industries, who had vested interests in keeping the Cold War going. They watched in staggering disbelief and then anger as their power and prestige collapsed around them, as the ruble plummeted and their economy fell into chaos, as the Soviet Union's most valuable ally of East Germany ceased to exist as it was absorbed into a reunited Germany and brought into the rival alliance of NATO, and as Lithuania, Estonia, and Latvia all declared independence and broke away from centralized Soviet control.

In November 1990, the leaders of thirty-four member states of CSCE, including the Soviet Union, signed the Charter of Paris, reaffirming their belief in the intimate connection between human rights and security and pledging themselves to "a new era of democracy, peace, and unity." Several months later, the Warsaw Treaty Organization formally dissolved. This proved to be too much for some of Gorbachev's opponents. They plotted against him, and in August 1991 placed him under a humiliating house arrest and attempted a bizarre and ineffective *coup*. In the midst of all these upheavals, Boris Yeltsin, the outspoken and reformist president of Russia, asserted that the Russian Republic also would become independent and that the Communist Party would no longer hold a monopoly of power. Finally, in December 1991, he and the leaders of most of the other republics announced that the seventy-four-year experiment was finished and declared their independence. The Soviet Union ceased to exist.

Why this massive geopolitical earthquake occurred immediately became a matter of enormous controversy, and surely will remain so. Just as there are intense arguments over the origins of the Cold War, so there are over the reasons for its demise. Some, including many Americans, give the credit to Ronald Reagan, who steadfastly determined to drive the Soviet Union into an expensive arms race that they could not possibly win, challenging them from a position of strength at every turn, giving support to their enemies, denying them technical and economic assistance, and thereby driving them to collapse. Others claim that Reagan's military buildup and ideological zealotry actually prolonged the Cold War, and instead praise Mikhail Gorbachev for his assessment of how thermonuclear weapons had changed the world and the necessity to change course, his capacity to transcend ideology, his bold initiatives, and his willingness to take unilateral and unreciprocated action to reduce the level of tension between the superpowers, describing him as "the architect of a world transformation" and the "indispensable agent" most responsible for ending the Cold War. Some credit a whole series of American presidents, Democratic and Republican alike, who together contributed to the eventual shift of the balance of power toward the West and persisted in a strategy of containing the Soviet Union until it finally fell apart. Others explain these events as the logical result of the inherent weakness, impoverishment, and structural decay of the Soviet system and the failure of the ideology and the practice of Communism itself, with its centrally controlled economy and one-party state, rather than any pressure imposed on the Soviet Union by the United States, arguing that no one could indefinitely ignore market forces or such a repressive regime supposedly representing the dictatorship of the proletariat and somehow "reform the unreformable." Still others credit the ultimate power of ideas and values in the vision of liberal democracy, personal opportunity, civil society, and human rights for being able to inspire those who were oppressed with a dream of eventual freedom.

Whatever the reason, or combination of reasons, the fact remains that the struggle that had defined international relations for decades, which many people thought would last indefinitely and end in a cataclysm, now came to an end. Thus, in 1992, Mikhail Gorbachev stood at exactly the same spot where Winston Churchill years before had delivered his "Iron Curtain" speech. This time there was a new message, for he told his audience what so many had waited so long to hear: "The Cold War is over—and a new era has begun."

SUGGESTIONS FOR FURTHER EXPLORATION

For excellent treatments of the Cold War as a whole, see Melvyn Leffler, *For the Soul of Mankind* (New York, 2008); John Lewis Gaddis, *The Cold War: A New History* (New York, 2006) and *We Now Know* (New York, 1998); Ronald Powaski, *The Cold War* (New York, 1998); Walter LaFeber, *America, Russia, and the Cold War* (New York, 2006 ed.); and Edward Judge and John Langdon, *A Hard and Bitter Peace: A Global History of the Cold War* (Upper Saddle River, NJ, 1996). The statecraft of particular leaders is discussed in Gordon A. Craig and Francis L. Lowenheim (eds.), *The Diplomats, 1939–1979* (Princeton, 1994). New articles of analysis and interpretation constantly appear in the *Journal of Cold War Studies*.

A good sense of the controversy surrounding the origins of the Cold War can be gained by comparing the "orthodox" interpretation of Herbert Feis, *From Trust to Terror* (New York, 1970), with "revisionist" authors like Gar Alperowitz et al., *The Decision to Use the Atomic Bomb* (New York, 1996); Michael Parenti, *The Sword and the Dollar* (New York, 1988); and William A. Williams, *The Tragedy of American Diplomacy* (New York, 1988 ed.); and "neo-revisionist" interpretations of Thomas Paterson,

On Every Front (New York, 1996 ed.); and Melvyn Leffler, *A Preponderance of Power* (Stanford, CA, 1993 ed.).

Any student of diplomacy needs to appreciate that international relations involve the interaction among different states, rather than simply the unilateral policies of a single country. It thus is very important to examine the documents and perspectives of other nations. Good places to begin for the Cold War are Vladislav Zubok, *A Failed Empire* (Chapel Hill, NC, 2009); and official histories from the Soviet Union, including Andre Gromyko and B. Ponomarev, *Soviet Foreign Policy, 1917–1980*, 2 vols. (Moscow, 1981) and B. Ponomarev, Andre Gromyko, and V. Khvostov (eds.), *History of Soviet Foreign Policy, 1945–1970* (Moscow, 1974). For a Chinese perspective, see Chen Jian, *Mao's China and the Cold War* (Chapel Hill, NC, 2001).

The role of psychological images and perceptions is treated in Kenneth Osgood, *Total Cold War* (Lawrence, KS, 2006); John Stoessinger, *Nations at Dawn* (New York, 1994 ed.); and Alexander L. George, "The Transition in U.S.-Soviet Relations," *Political Psychology*, 12 (1991): 469–486; and McCarthyism is explored in Paul Gordon Lauren (ed.), *The China Hands Legacy* (Boulder, CO, 1987). Containment is discussed in John Lewis Gaddis, *George F. Kennan* (New York, 2011) and *Strategies of Containment* (New York, 2005 ed.); and Deborah Larson, *Origins of Containment* (Princeton, 1985). The arms race is analyzed in Ronald Powaski, *March to Armageddon* (New York, 1993); Robert Jervis, *The Meaning of the Nuclear Revolution* (Ithaca, NY, 1990); and Henry Kissinger, *Nuclear Weapons and Foreign Policy* (New York, 1957). Intelligence and covert action are treated in Loch Johnson, *America's Secret Power* (New York, 1991); Christopher Andrew and Oleg Gordievsky, *KGB: The Inside Story* (New York, 1990); and Paul Gordon Lauren, "Ethics and Intelligence," in Alfred Maurer et al. (eds.), *Intelligence* (Boulder, CO, 1985). The subject of race is discussed in Mary Dudziak, *Cold War Civil Rights* (Princeton, 2000); and Paul Gordon Lauren, *Power and Prejudice: The Politics and Diplomacy of Racial Discrimination* (Boulder, CO, 1996 ed.). Détente is explored in United States, Department of State, *Soviet-American Relations: The Détente Years* (Washington, D.C., 2007); Alexander L. George et al. (eds.), *U.S.-Soviet Security Cooperation* (New York, 1996 ed.); Alexander L. George (ed.), *Managing U.S.-Soviet Rivalry* (Boulder, CO, 1983); and Henry Kissinger's autobiographical *Years of Upheaval* (Boston, 1982) and *White House Years* (Boston, 1979).

The debate over the end of the Cold War can be seen by comparing Jack Matlock, Jr., *Reagan and Gorbachev: How the Cold War Ended* (New York, 2005); Richard Herrmann and Richard Ned Lebow (eds.), *Ending the Cold War* (New York, 2004); Peter Schweizer, *Reagan's War: The Epic Story of His Forty Year Struggle and Final Triumph Over Communism* (New York, 2002); Don Oberdorfer, *From the Cold War to a New Era* (Baltimore, 1998 ed.); Archie Brown, *The Gorbachev Factor* (New York, 1997); Richard Ned Lebow and Janice Gross Stein, *We All Lost the Cold War* (Princeton, 1995); and Francis Fukuyama, *The End of History and the Last Man* (New York, 1993).

New findings about the Cold War are increasingly being made available on the Internet, including declassified documents, material obtained under the Freedom of Information Act, and previously inaccessible archival sources once hidden behind the Iron Curtain. Some of the most valuable Web sites are those of the Cold War International History Project at www.cwihp.org; the Parallel History Project on Cooperative Security at www.php.isn.ethz.ch; U.S. Department of State, Foreign Relations Series, at www.state.gov/www/about_state/history; and the National Security Archive at www.gwu.edu/~nsarchiv.

6

The Evolving International System

The end of the Cold War and the Soviet empire created a widespread mood of euphoria. The prospect that the struggle that had dominated global politics for so long was over seemed to open up a vast new horizon of possibilities. Some reacted with strident triumphalism, believing that their own superiority had brought about victory and would now allow them to shape the world in their own image. Others, however, sighed in quiet and grateful relief that the world had managed to escape from completely destroying itself in nuclear annihilation. But despite their enormous differences of opinion, it appeared as though all sides shared one thing in common: the opportunity to think about a new future. For the first time in decades, serious consideration could be given to what the world might be like without the dangerous and costly confrontation between the superpowers. Many hoped that they would now see less reliance on the sword, as portrayed in the allegorical statue of *Diplomacy*, and greater use of the olive branch. They looked eagerly for a "peace dividend," an end to the arms race and the "balance of terror" of "Mutual Assured Destruction" (MAD), the elimination of rival alliance systems and covert action, the rule of law, enhanced human rights, and thereby greater international peace and security. U.S. Secretary of State James Baker gave expression to this mood when he proclaimed: "We live in one of the rare transforming moments in history, with the Cold War over and an era full of promise just ahead."

"A World in a Rapid State of Transition"

As we have seen from the very beginning, change occurs constantly, and any international system must be able to adapt to geopolitical shifts and to internal changes within its member states that affect its performance. With the new possibilities in a post–Cold War world, people increasingly began to speak of their hopes for a "New World Order," but realized that this could not be accomplished without addressing the issue posed directly by United Nations Secretary-General Boutros Boutros-Ghali from Egypt: "How the international community can best equip itself to respond to a world in a rapid state of transition."

Accomplishing this was not as easy as many had hoped. Indeed, it immediately led to intense debates that continue today over the best way to achieve peace and security. Boutros-Ghali, for example, strongly opposed any arrangement controlled by a single country or group of countries, no matter how great or powerful, and advocated a broad-based system centered around the United Nations. As he observed:

> History is accelerating. The pace is alarming. The direction is not entirely known. At this time of stress, the hard fact is that no power or combination of powers is prepared to take on its shoulders the responsibility for collective security worldwide.

Although he argued instead that this evolving system should be guided by strong American leadership, Henry Kissinger also acknowledged the uncertainly ahead in his book *Diplomacy*:

> Never before has a new world order had to be assembled from so many different perceptions, or on so global a scale. Nor has any previous order had to combine the attributes of the historic balance-of-power systems with global democratic opinion and the exploding technology of the contemporary period.

The challenges that they and others anticipated appeared soon enough.

One of these was the dramatic expansion of the international community itself. In 1990, Namibia and Liechtenstein became members of the United Nations. The following year witnessed the admission of North and South Korea, Estonia, Latvia, Lithuania, Micronesia, and the Marshall Islands. A remarkable twenty new states then joined over the next two years, including Slovenia, Bosnia and Herzegovina, Croatia, and former Soviet republics such as Armenia, Georgia, and Kazakhstan. Today, membership is virtually universal. A walk along First Avenue in New York City in front of the United Nations headquarters reveals a display of the national flags of 193 members. This phenomenal number represents nearly a quadrupling of independent nation-states just since the end of the Second World War, each with its own history, perceptions, interests, and values. All of these, especially when combined with the burgeoning number of nonstate actors in global politics, as we shall discuss shortly, marked a dramatic escalation of the diplomatic revolution in the sheer number of participants, expanding geographical scope, and resulting complexity within the evolving international system.

Other challenges emerged in this transformation as well, including political instability and the outbreak of violence and wars. Indeed, just when the revolutions in Hungary, Poland, Germany, and Czechoslovakia consolidated themselves and the Soviet Union began to crumble in the summer of 1990, observers in the Middle East noted an ominous massing of Iraqi forces along the border of Kuwait. For some time, it had been obvious that the Iraqi dictator Saddam Hussein's ambitions had not been diminished by his long and wasting conflict waged against Iran. Seeing nothing to hold him in check, he now blatantly breached international law by lashing out and sending his armed forces smashing into neighboring, militarily weak Kuwait. In quick response to this invasion, with its enormous geopolitical implications, President George H. W. Bush and other leaders skillfully threw themselves into mobilizing world opinion against Saddam, seeking authorization from the United Nations for action and building a multilateral military coalition. The Security Council immediately voted to employ coercive diplomacy by imposing progressively stiffer sanctions, backed by a naval blockade, and eventually accompanied by an ultimatum. Despite this pressure, Saddam stubbornly refused to disgorge his spoils. When he disregarded the deadline for withdrawal, American and allied warplanes began the Gulf War in January 1991, bombing command-and-control centers in Baghdad and Iraqi military positions in Kuwait, followed by a massive ground attack. In the end, they successfully liberated Kuwait, but Saddam remained in power, and new questions emerged about the future of the Middle East, of oil reserves, and of whether this war would have any impact on the rise of Islamic fundamentalism.

Still further challenges of warfare and the use of force and statecraft emerged, seemingly one exploding right after the other. These were complicated by the fact that they entailed very different kinds of security threats than those posed by aggressor states, involving instead civil wars, religious and ethnic violence, collapsed states, and horrific violations of human rights. Saddam Hussein, for example, continued to brutally persecute the Kurds in Iraq, prompting the dispatch of international armed forces in 1991 and the eventual establishment of "no-fly zones" to protect them. During the same year, Somalia erupted into civil war and anarchy. American and United Nations peacekeeping forces were deployed in the name of humanitarian intervention, but by 1993 the policy ended in dismal failure. At exactly the same time, the centrifugal forces in Yugoslavia began to career out of control. Slovenia and Croatia declared their independence from the Serbian-dominated government in Belgrade, and violence broke out in Bosnia in which Bosnian Serb nationalists, with the support of Serbian president Slobodan Milosevic, attempted to create an ethnically pure region by means of a ghastly process of intimidation, rape, fighting, and mass murder known as "ethnic cleansing." Member states of the United Nations responded by combining diplomacy with the sending of peacekeeping forces and imposing an arms embargo on all sides. Although such a position possessed some advantages in theory, in practice it seriously disadvantaged Bosnian government troops against the already well-equipped Serbs. This became particularly evident in 1994, with a massive mortar attack against civilians in a Sarajevo marketplace, and especially in 1995, with the shocking massacre of 8,000 men and boys of Srebrenica, an event described as "the worst human rights disaster in Europe since the Holocaust." In response, NATO deployed its Rapid Reaction Force (RRF), and President Bill Clinton authorized U.S. troops to launch Operation Deliberate Force in the Balkans. During 1994, civil war also broke out in Rwanda between Hutus and Tutsis, taking the lives of an estimated 800,000 in genocide. All this seemed to belie the dreams of those who had hoped for a post–Cold War "New World Order."

Political and military alliances also shifted in this period of transition. Once the Cold War ended and the Iron Curtain and the Warsaw Treaty Organization collapsed, states formerly bound by the straightjacket of the Soviet bloc looked for ways to draw closer to the West. They hoped that this would allow them to enjoy greater economic prosperity and to benefit from common foreign and security policies, as well as protecting them from once again being pulled into a Russian sphere of influence. This dramatic process began immediately with the absorption of East Germany into a united Germany and then into NATO in 1990. Poland, Hungary, and the Czech Republic became members in 1999. Seven other states joined in 2004, and then Albania and Croatia in 2009. At the same time, most of these states eagerly pursued membership in the ever enlarging European Union, pledging themselves to its criteria of having a democratic government, operating a free market economy, and respecting the rule of law and human rights.

These shifts provoked strong opposition from Russia, which had assumed the successor status of the former Soviet Union. It neither fit, nor was welcomed, into NATO or the EU. Resentment against Russians from Eastern Europe and the Baltic states previously under the control of the Soviet empire remained strong. Many Russian political elites reciprocated by deliberately distancing themselves from the West and turning within. As a result, Russia remained apart from the "new" Europe and the evolving international system increasingly being shaped by the United States. But things were even worse at home. Russians found themselves and their post-Communist country mired in anarchy, political instability, corruption, economic recession, violence, the disappearance of social programs, the loss of enormous state assets to privatized criminal groups and business oligarchs, and a brutal and humiliating war against separatist irregulars in Chechnya. In these circumstances, it is not surprising that people would look to a strong leader to save them and to restore their prestige. They thus elected Vladimir Putin, a former KGB officer, as president of Russia.

Dramatic transformations revealed themselves in other ways as well, particularly in technology. Over one-half of all the scientists and engineers who have ever lived are alive today, and this dramatically affects force and statecraft. The diplomatic revolution has been made all the more potent with the emergence of what is called the revolution in military affairs (RMA), especially with the application of advanced sensing and information-reporting computer technologies and precision-guided munitions (PGMs). These include cruise missiles with guidance systems capable of comparing landmarks with prerecorded maps to guide them to their targets, jet fighters with radar-evading Stealth technology based on new aerodynamic shapes and composite materials, electronic jamming equipment, night vision devices, and so-called "smart bombs" and unmanned aerial vehicles (UAVs) or drones guided by lasers, infrared signals, or cameras. Advanced research continued apace for developing and refining weapons using biotechnology, robotics, and nanotechnology manipulating matter on an atomic or molecular scale with highly sophisticated delivery systems capable of sending nuclear, chemical, or biological agents toward targets thousands of miles away. At the same time, scientists worked to develop electromagnetic pulse (EMP) weapons and new space and counter-space technologies using particle beams and kinetic energy to project military potential beyond earth's atmosphere. This enabled strategists to go beyond the previous arenas of land, sea, and air warfare into the new "fourth medium": space. Diplomats and military planners of previous generations, schooled on ideas of limitations from Clausewitz, could not have even imagined such sophisticated developments and their implications for what is today known as C⁵ISR: command, control, communications, computers, combat systems, intelligence, surveillance, and reconnaissance.

These technological transformations also greatly impact the collection, analysis, and transmission of information. A visit to the communications center of any major foreign ministry today reveals the effects of the "digital revolution" produced by the microchip and its staggering array of complex devices to encrypt and decrypt classified messages, create and store elaborate databases, compress and retrieve vast amounts of material, conduct highly complex mathematical computations, convert photons into electrons and then process these into images, and use Internet links that span the globe. Those charged with the conduct of diplomacy in the contemporary world use computers, facsimile machines, fiber optics, and various wireless devices to instantaneously send and receive satellite transmissions and maintain constant and secure mobile communications with others virtually anywhere on the planet. It is now possible for a secretary of state to sit in the Situation Room of the White House with the president and other advisors in front of a high-definition screen and literally watch the details of a clandestine raid or military operation taking place thousands of miles away in real time.

Digital technologies also have created an "information revolution" that makes it possible to gather and analyze extraordinary intelligence about others in world affairs. Capacities now exist to collect data from billions of e-mails, telephone calls, and facsimile transmissions—like specks of dust from a carpet—through technical means of electronic intercepts, embedded relay chips in telecommunications equipment, hydrophones on the ocean floors, and space-borne satellites equipped with multi- and hyper-spectral sensors and synthetic aperture radar, and then to provide analysis through sophisticated processing, such as integrating overhead photographic imagery with terrain elevation data to produce three-dimensional depictions of territory. The impressive images and data available on Google Earth to anyone with access to the Internet, for example, simply pale next to the capabilities of the National Security Agency and the National Geospatial-Intelligence Agency with its computer-assisted map tailoring and spatial-statistical and imagery analyses. The intelligence thereby provided to policy makers and military commanders when confronting challenges in force and statecraft simply staggers the imagination.

This vast amount of information and the ease of transmitting much of it to widespread audiences also contributes further to that other feature of the diplomatic revolution discussed previously: namely, the acceleration of public opinion and "public diplomacy." Indeed, one insider estimates that the staff of the U.S. Secretary of State spends 80 to 90 percent of its time thinking about the media and how policies will "play" with the public. This is further confirmed by the existence and the size of the office of the Under Secretary of State for Public Diplomacy and Public Affairs and by the fact that American Foreign Service Officers now can select a career track specifically designated as "Public Diplomacy Officers." According to their official job description, they are assigned a variety of tasks, including to "explain and defend the substance of American foreign policy to ensure that U.S. positions are well understood and that misrepresentations are corrected." In this regard, technology increasingly makes it infinitely easier to influence stories in the press, images broadcast over television, "cultural diplomacy," and information made available on the Internet. The foreign ministries of every major nation-state in the world today, in addition to the United Nations, regional organizations, and nongovernmental organizations (NGOs), maintain active Web sites full of reports, explanations, briefings, news releases, video streams, and digital images designed to provide information and influence public opinion. The U.S. State Department now produces *eJournal* and even has a Department of eDiplomacy. One recent government commission consequently concludes that "public diplomacy is a strategic component of foreign policy" and, as such, must be regarded as "indispensable" to contemporary statecraft.

These transformations in public diplomacy are matched, if not exceeded, by those in economics, thereby accelerating yet another feature of the diplomatic revolution. Business firms, bankers and financiers, manufacturers, shipping companies, chambers of commerce, private investors, and many analysts argue with increasing effectiveness that survival depends not on military success but rather on the ability of states to successfully compete in the international economic sphere and thereby provide for the well-being of their people. Diplomats, they urge, therefore must become more aggressive in promoting trade and financial investment in the global marketplace. At the same time, writes one observer,

> Governments increasingly recognized that the distribution of goods and capital abroad might be utilized as an instrument of diplomacy. Investment could buy friendships or build and solidify alliances, while monies withheld or economic reprisals could coerce opponents into making certain diplomatic concessions. Financial penetration could facilitate political hegemony in developing countries. Commercial advantages offered to foreign suppliers of strategic raw materials could strengthen security. Moreover, profits from overseas markets could contribute to national wealth and perhaps increase international prestige.

The combination of these private and public interests has resulted in foreign ministries around the world taking more determined action than ever before to protect and promote trade and investment by recruiting economic specialists, creating career tracks for "economic officers," employing commercial attachés, compiling databases of vital import and export statistics for their nationals, reporting on foreign market conditions and tariff policies, utilizing successful business men and women as trade negotiators, and upgrading the quality and professionalism in the consular services. Over time, these activities have expanded even further to include close cooperation between business and diplomacy in areas of investment, trade, technical assistance, foreign aid, and reconstruction projects. Said one high-ranking diplomat in a recent speech to his colleagues, "We are going to have to acknowledge that our economic health and our ability to trade competitively on the world market may be the single most important component of our national security....We must also become more activist in promoting American exports and in serving U.S. business interests overseas."

CHALLENGES TO NATION-STATES AND NATIONAL SOVEREIGNTY

Many of these transformations also increasingly and significantly have rendered the traditional borders and power of nation-states less consequential than in the past. Ever since the emergence of the Great Powers in the seventeenth century, as we have seen, states were regarded as the sole actors of international relations, as the only entities capable of mobilizing sufficient force to threaten the security of others, as the singular protectors and authority governing people within their own territories, and as the exclusive possessors of sovereignty whose leaders claimed immunity from any scrutiny beyond their own borders. Various features within the evolving international system, however, steadily challenged all of these features, assumptions, and claims.

One of the most direct challenges comes from the surging process of international interconnectedness and integration in telecommunications, transportation, and economics, widely known as "globalization." As a result of technologies, for example, it is possible for data in the form of words, images, and sounds to transcend national borders, geographical and cultural barriers, and to override government authority nearly at will. "Nations once connected by foreign ministries and traders," notes the Center for Strategic and International Studies report entitled *Reinventing Diplomacy in the Information Age*, "are now linked through millions of individuals by fiber optics, satellite, wireless, and cable in a complex network without central control." The capabilities of this technological globalization enable news from the most remote locations and circumstances to be uploaded, transmitted, and then downloaded from cyberspace to the Internet within seconds and then to international organizations, broadcasters such as Cable Network News (CNN), BBC World Service, Qatar's al-Jazeera, NGOs, social networking sites such as Facebook and Twitter, file exchange and video sharing sites such as You Tube, personal e-mail accounts, and blogs. Some measure of the power of this technological globalization can be seen in the efforts made by the Chinese government to erect "The Great Firewall of China" to block or censor information, of the Iranian government to stop the release of a video taken from a smartphone showing a girl named Neda bleeding to death on the streets of Tehran while protesting rigged elections, or of the American government and others to prevent WikiLeaks from releasing masses of classified diplomatic documents to the world via the Internet.

Economic globalization presents similar challenges. The evolution of a worldwide market of trade and finance similarly creates vast and interlocking networks of relationships and interests that by definition bypass nation-states. National economies are being subsumed into an increasingly integrated and complex global economy through the exchange of goods and services, the flow of capital, direct foreign investment, international production and labor markets, migration, and the spread of technologies. This results in the diminution and sometimes even the elimination of state-enforced restrictions on transactions across borders. Several trillion dollars are exchanged every day in international money markets, to illustrate, outside any government control. Try as they may, nation-states simply cannot govern this process.

Further challenges to nation-states come from problems that render borders and passports meaningless. The magnitude of these in our time simply exceeds the capacity of any single national government, even the largest and strongest, to protect their own people and territory. These include "beyond the border" problems such as the proliferation of weapons, international terrorism, cyber attacks, widespread epidemics such as the HIV/AIDS virus, ethnic conflict, environmental pollution of the atmosphere and the oceans, climate change, unsustainable pressure on what is called the "water-food-energy" nexus, demographic transformations and the existence of 7,000,000,000 people on an increasingly fragile planet, the flow of refugees, transnational crime, corruption and economic disparities, currency volatility and fiscal crises, collapsed or "failed" states, and "outlaw" or "rogue" regimes. Under these circumstances, it is not at all unusual to hear experts on statecraft increasingly speak of broad "complex interdependence" requiring "global governance," "cooperative security," and the "indivisibility of security." Indeed, as political scientists Dan Caldwell and Robert Williams argue in their book *Seeking Security in an Insecure World*, the security of individuals, nation-states, and the international system has become so interconnected in our time that narrowly defined notions of "national security" and an exclusive focus on military power are no longer relevant.

When facing these common threats, many nation-states have realized their mutual vulnerability and that they can no longer "go it alone." For this reason, they have sought greater security through partnerships and collective efforts, and have been willing to voluntarily surrender some of their national sovereignty to do so. Many have agreed to accept certain self-imposed restraints, including those directly involving force and statecraft. They thus have become parties to international legal agreements such as the Non-Proliferation Treaty (NPT) dealing with nuclear armaments and its monitoring agency of the International Atomic Energy Agency (IAEA), the 1993 International Convention on the Prohibition of Chemical Weapons, the 1996 Comprehensive

Nuclear Test Ban Treaty, and the 1997 International Convention to Ban Land Mines, as well as participating in current negotiations over the Arms Trade Treaty seeking to regulate the illicit circulation of small arms, light weapons, and their ammunition, which today cause the majority of combat deaths in the world. Other treaties address the actual use of these weapons, including the Geneva Conventions seeking to protect civilians in armed conflict, a protocol to the International Convention on the Rights of the Child prohibiting the use of child soldiers in warfare, and the 1998 Rome Statute of the International Criminal Court, designed to hold national leaders personally responsible for crimes against humanity, war crimes, or genocide. These treaties recognize that a correlation exists between respect for human rights and international peace and security and thereby emphasize the rights of individuals over the rights of nation-states.

These many developments present formidable challenges to traditional notions and claims of sovereignty. In fact, according to United Nations Secretary-General Kofi Annan of Ghana, within the evolving international system there is an evolving redefinition of sovereignty itself:

> State sovereignty, in its most basic sense, is being redefined. States are now widely understood to be instruments at the service of their people, and not vice-versa. At the same time, individual sovereignty—by which I mean the fundamental freedom of each individual, enshrined in the Charter of the UN and subsequent international treaties—has been enhanced by a renewed and spreading consciousness of individual rights. When we read the Charter today, we are more than ever conscious that its aim is to protect individual human rights not to protect those who abuse them.

The international community, for example, is increasingly willing to dismiss claims by leaders that national sovereignty allows them to do whatever they please and grants them complete immunity from any kind of accountability. One need only consider the condemnation of dictators such as Augusto Pinochet of Chile and the prosecution of war criminals such as Slobodan Milosevic of Serbia, Radovan Karadžić of Bosnia, and Thomas Lubanga Dyilo of the Democratic Republic of the Congo. In addition, there is a growing determination to use force in humanitarian intervention within the territory of other nations to protect victims who cannot protect themselves. As the International Commission on Intervention and State Sovereignty recently concluded in its report, tellingly entitled *The Responsibility to Protect*, the task at hand is to deliver "practical protection for ordinary people, at risk of their lives, because their states are unwilling or unable to protect them."

This constantly evolving meaning of national sovereignty within the larger evolving international system is unmistakable. It also is not without controversy or resistance. Whereas many states are willing to voluntarily surrender portions of their sovereignty on behalf of the larger system as a whole, others clearly are not. Indeed, some states are firmly opposed to this trend insofar as their own countries are involved and insist upon retaining the traditional prerogatives of their national sovereignty. These often include, among others, China, Iran, Israel, North Korea, and the United States.

Despite this opposition, nation-states and national sovereignty continue to be challenged by other actors with claims to actively participate in global affairs. Among these are the United Nations and its many related specialized agencies, such as the International Labor Organization and World Health Organization, as well as supranational or regional intergovernmental organizations (IGOs) such as the European Union, Organization for Security and Cooperation in Europe, North Atlantic Treaty Organization, Organization of American States, the Arab League, African Union, and the Association of Southeast Asian Nations. Other actors include the International Monetary Fund, World Bank, World Trade Organization, and commodity cartels such as the Organization of Petroleum Exporting Countries. Still another that has assumed increasing international importance is the Group of Twenty Finance Ministers and Central Bank Governors, or G-20, whose collective economies comprise over 80 percent of the world's gross domestic product, global national product, and world trade. Although composed of nation-states, each of these organizations or groups sometimes is more powerful than the sum of its parts, often challenging traditional attributes of national sovereignty itself.

Other international actors today do not represent nation-states at all and actually challenge the statist assumptions of the international order. Among the most striking of these are global, or transnational, business corporations such as General Electric, Exxon Mobil, Royal Dutch Shell, Walmart, Toyota Motor, PetroChina, Nestlé, and Siemens, among others. They carry neither the burdens nor the limitations of governing, but their size, enormous wealth, and sophisticated ability to move goods, services, and capital worldwide often gives them significant global influence far beyond the control of specific national governments or international organizations. Indeed, some possess annual revenue that far exceeds the gross national products of many nation-states. For this reason, their chief executive officers and directors can have a much greater impact on people and world events than many heads of governments. The same can be said to some extent about international crime syndicates (especially those in the drug trade), whose vast and unregulated wealth and global influence present security threats that exceed the ability of most states to protect even their own territory.

Still other actors in the evolving international system today are groups of private citizens seeking to confront nation-states and national sovereignty by advocating for particular policies and to extend citizen participation in the conduct of diplomacy by means of activist nongovernmental organizations working from below rather than from above. When the Economic and Social Council of the United Nations first granted official consultative status to NGOs in 1948, the number was forty-eight. Today it reaches nearly 4,000. The authoritative Union of International Associations estimates that the total number of recognized NGOs operating internationally now exceeds 40,000. Some of these include philanthropic organizations such as the Ford Foundation, the Rockefeller Foundation, and more recently, the Gates Foundation. Particularly in the area of human rights, NGOs work to directly challenge national sovereignty and any of its corollary claims that government leaders can do whatever

they wish to their own people without fear of being held responsible. It is estimated that there may be as many as 26,000 human rights NGOs operating in
the world today. Some of these, such as the International Committee of the Red
Cross, Amnesty International, Human Rights Watch, and Médecins sans fron-
tières, have an international influence. Others, such as the Afro-Asian Peoples'
Solidarity Organization, the Asian Coalition of Human Rights Organizations,
or the Arab Organization for Human Rights, have a focus that transcends borders within regions.

The impact of these nongovernmental organizations—greatly enhanced by
globalized communication technology that places power in the hands of those
previously excluded, and in an age of public diplomacy thereby enables change
from below rather than just from the top—sometimes has been phenomenal.
In fact, they have been credited with helping to break the monopoly of nation-
states in conducting foreign affairs as they wished by creating what has been
called the "advocacy revolution." Human rights NGOs can have great influence on public opinion and the emergence and empowerment of transnational
civil society, especially in an age of public diplomacy, as demonstrated by their
successful campaigns to enact the International Convention Against Torture,
the International Convention to Ban Land Mines, and the statute creating the
path-breaking International Criminal Court. There are times when they and
their highly motivated and Internet-connected members and cross-border networks can be mobilized long before nation-states can act or when political
constraints prevent any governmental action at all. Indeed, said one United
Nations official recently, "Without the people of the NGOs, our program for
human rights would be a mere shadow of itself."

If any doubts existed about the growth in the prominence and influence
of nonstate actors and their capacity to challenge nation-states and national
sovereignty, to threaten the ability of governments to protect their security
and the well-being of their own people, and to enormously influence contemporary global affairs in the evolving international system still remained after
all these developments, they should have been irrevocably shattered by the
premeditated terrorist attacks of September 11, 2001—a date now known simply as 9/11.

TERRORISTS AND THE "GLOBAL WAR ON TERROR"

Within less than two shocking hours on this single day, nearly 3,000 people were deliberately killed in New York City, Washington, D.C., and rural
Pennsylvania, starkly revealing the power of terrorist networks or cells to
use commercial aircraft as weapons to destroy human lives and wreak havoc.
Osama bin Laden, a radical Islamic militant, and his nonstate terrorist organi-
zation known as al-Qaeda, based in faraway Afghanistan, claimed responsi-
bility. He described the suicide strikes as "blessed attacks" against "the Great
Satan" of the United States, which he accused of supporting Israel against the
Palestinians, violating Islam's holiest sites with its military presence in Saudi
Arabia, and spreading a message of secularism and materialism that threatened

the beliefs of more than a billion Muslim followers around the globe. He had been emboldened by the successes of the *mujahideen* against the Soviets in the Afghan war and now ominously concluded: "We no longer fear the so-called Great Powers."

Terrorism possessed a long history of using violence to change policy by creating fear and violating the just war principle prohibiting the killing of innocent civilians. Attacks had been made on American and other targets previously. But never before had a single episode captured so much global attention or made the world so painfully aware of its collective vulnerability. Although the main target had been the United States, eighty different countries lost citizens in the attack on the World Trade Center, and the international community reacted with outrage. Almost all nations expressed their sympathy and support, with the leading French newspaper *Le Monde* memorably declaring in a headline: "We are all Americans now." "All of us," continued Kofi Annan, "feel deep shock and revulsion at the cold-blooded viciousness of this attack. All of us condemn it and those who planned it—whoever they may be—in the strongest possible terms....A terrorist attack on one country is an attack on humanity as a whole. All nations of the world must work together to identify the perpetrators and bring them to justice."

This devastating attack became a seminal event, thrusting the world into confronting the fact that terrorism presented a security threat that raised extremely difficult questions about the vulnerability of even the strongest of states, the effectiveness of the international system, and the impact of force and statecraft. Nearly all countries responded by taking immediate steps to combat terrorism within their own territories. But collective intelligence sources increasingly revealed the extensive and highly concealed network of terrorist cells with a worldwide reach, and this persuaded most countries that this global challenge required a global response. The United Nations Security Council and General Assembly thus quickly created the Counter-Terrorism Committee and set about to develop specific and far-reaching measures to combat international terrorist acts. NATO gave the United States its full support within twenty-four hours of the 9/11 attacks by invoking Article Five of its founding treaty for the first time, stating that an attack on one of its members was an attack on them all. Further diplomacy worked to create several international counterterrorism conventions grounded in the rule of law, to achieve much greater cooperation among intelligence services, to increase security measures and procedures, to identify and apprehend suspected terrorists, and to freeze financial assets and prohibit the transfer of funds or other material assets to those supporting terrorism.

But major issues of force and statecraft remained. Terrorist groups did not control specific territory and did not appear to be threatened or intimidated by the classical techniques of deterrence or coercive diplomacy, as used in the past against nation-state actors. The United States therefore concluded that the use, rather than the threat, of force would serve as the best response. Less than one month after 9/11, it launched cruise missile attacks and bombing raids against al-Qaeda targets and the radical Taliban regime supporting Osama bin

Laden in Afghanistan. Ground forces followed immediately with an invasion. Little did they know that they would confront some of the same individuals and Islamic fundamentalist forces that they had armed to fight the Soviets in the 1980s. Nevertheless, at the time the United States received not only widespread domestic and international support for this military action, but also the actual contributions of many states willing to commit forces and participate in one way or the other in a coalition to fight against those who engaged in terrorism.

Such remarkable and widespread support for the United States, however, did not last long. There began to be serious concerns about the escalation of the rhetoric about what American leaders increasingly, broadly, and indiscriminately called "the global war on terror." In his State of the Union speech in January 2002, for example, President George W. Bush said nothing about the Taliban or Osama bin Laden. Instead, he argued, "What we have found in Afghanistan confirms that, far from ending there, our war against terror is only beginning." Bush then went on to dangerously simplify the complexities of the world by claiming that other nations were either "for us or against us" and expansively declared the existence of "the Axis of Evil," asserting the existence of a connection between Iraq, Iran, and North Korea in their support of terrorism. His National Security Advisor, Condoleezza Rice, ominously declared that these governments now had been "put on notice." By May, this ever-expanding list included Cuba, Libya, and Syria. The Department of Defense then announced a rapid acceleration of its Integrated Global Presence and Basing Strategy to restructure and reposition combat brigades from their Cold War bases in Germany and South Korea in order to increase its military capacity to project force globally as a means of fighting a protracted struggle against terrorism.

International anxiety and alienation became even greater in September when the administration released a document entitled *The National Security Strategy of the United States of America, 2002*. This unusually combative statement enunciated the "Bush Doctrine," asserting unmatched American superiority and hegemony, declaring that armed force would no longer be considered as a last resort, and that the United States henceforth would take unilateral and preemptive action whenever it chose to do so. Other nations reacted with outrage, arguing that such strident and arrogant assertions of preeminence, preemption, and unilateralism not only violated the rule of law as embodied in the UN Charter's provisions regarding the use of force, but in the context of ever-growing and unparalleled American military capabilities, presented extraordinarily serious threats to peace and security for the entire evolving international system.

Their fears were only exacerbated when Secretary of State Colin Powell pressed the UN Security Council for a resolution explicitly authorizing the use of armed force against Iraq. He tried to argue that there existed a "nexus between Iraq and the al-Qaeda terrorist network" and that Saddam Hussein possessed stockpiles of "weapons of mass destruction" that posed an imminent threat. But most of the others believed that sufficient, credible evidence simply did not exist for these charges to be persuasive—and said so. The French and the Russians threatened to cast vetoes, as did the Chinese. Although they had participated in sanctions against Iraq and threatened significant consequences against Saddam, the majority seriously doubted that any connection existed between terrorism and Iraq and wanted United Nations inspectors to be given time to actually find the alleged weapons. This incensed President Bush, who resented being challenged. He lashed out, accusing the United Nations of making itself "irrelevant" and declaring that he did not need a "permission slip" to take military action. Knowing that he could not obtain the necessary authorization from the Security Council for a specific mandate to use force, he refused to even bring a resolution to a vote at all and launched a war in 2003 against Iraq. Bush and his advisors confidently announced that American technological superiority resulting from the revolution in military affairs would completely "shock and awe" the opponent and that victory would come quickly.

The results proved to be something very different. Indeed, the war in Iraq dragged on for years, forcing even the commander of U.S. Central Command, General Anthony Zinni, to describe the results in these words: "The wrong war at the wrong time with the wrong strategy." The National Intelligence Council itself concluded: "[T]he Iraq war made the overall terrorism problem worse." The conflict in Afghanistan became the longest war in American history. Estimates placed the cost of supporting each solider there at $1,000,000 per year. Military operations expanded into the territory of unreliable and nuclear-armed Pakistan, including the mission by Navy SEALs that killed Osama bin Laden in 2011. After ten years, more than 2,000,000 Americans had served in these wars. Nearly 8,000,000 refugees had been produced. At least 225,000 people, including men and women in uniform, contractors, and civilians had been killed, meeting their deaths from weapons ranging from sophisticated precision-guided Hellfire missiles fired from Predator drones to small handguns or simple, but very deadly, homemade improvised explosive devices (IEDs). During this same period, according to the Brown University "Cost of War" project, the United States spent up to an estimated $4,000,000,000,000 on these campaigns, almost entirely on credit, which helped to drive the country into staggering debt. Moreover, in the name of fighting the "global war on terror," the United States and several other countries at times suspended the rule of law either at home or abroad, conducting warrantless wiretaps, apprehending suspects, hiding them in "black sites," and engaging in torture.

Although further terrorist attacks on American soil were successfully thwarted, assaults actually expanded in scope and increased after 9/11. Thousands of innocent victims suffered death or maiming while simply riding on commuter trains, sleeping in their beds, shopping in stores, studying in classrooms, relaxing on beaches, drinking in bars, or trying to survive in dangerous war zones. Added to the unrelenting attacks in Bagdad, Iraq and Kabul, Afghanistan, were those of 2004 in Madrid, Spain, of 2005 in London, England, of 2008 in Mumbai, India (as will be discussed more fully in Chapter 11), of 2011 in Charsadda District, Pakistan, and of 2012 in Benghazi, Libya. These represented but a fraction of the total. At the same time, terrorist cells

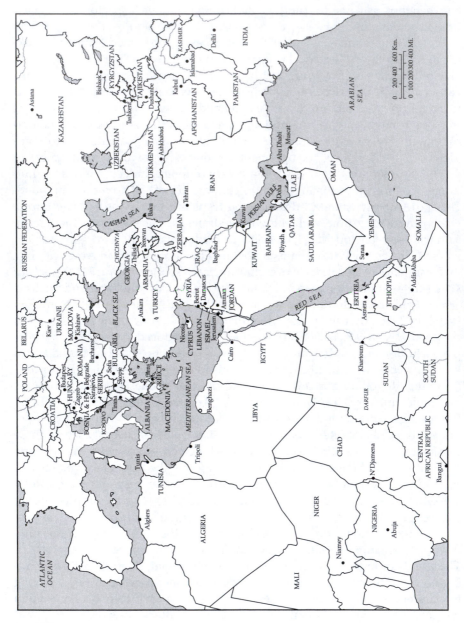

Turmoil in the Evolving System

and networks, often with increasing sophistication using the Internet and video-sharing platforms, grew in Europe, Central and South Asia, the Middle East and the Arabian peninsula, and in highly troubled areas of trans-Sahara and East Africa. The continuing turmoil of all these developments obviously raise extraordinarily difficult challenges for force and statecraft in the evolving international system.

PARTNERS AND/OR RIVALS?

The members of every international system in history always have had to wrestle with the extent to which they were partners and/or rivals with each other. They generally balanced at some point along a scale of cooperative partnership and contentious rivalry: at times readily agreeing on their shared interests, collective values, and the fact that they needed each other in facing common dangers, and, on other occasions, disagreeing and competing with each other. Their particular position at any given time depended on the circumstances of a specific case and they rarely placed themselves at one extreme or the other over a wide range of issues. But with the end of the Cold War, the collapse of a bipolar world, the emergence of America as the sole superpower, and the evolution of a new system, careful observers wondered whether this balance between partnership and rivalry would be placed in jeopardy. Questions started slowly, but took on a particular poignancy as leaders in the United States increasingly claimed special prerogatives, acted unilaterally, seemed unwilling to acknowledge the legitimate interests of others, tried to thwart a number of major international treaties, and especially when they attacked Iraq.

When the Cold War ended, attention focused on the theme of partnership in building a "New World Order." Indeed, President Bush the elder, who had considerable experience in working with the intelligence community and the United Nations, declared before the General Assembly in a widely quoted 1991 speech that although "the United States is now the world's only remaining superpower," it

> has no intention of striving for a Pax Americana. However, we will remain engaged. We will not pull back and retreat into isolationism. We will offer friendship and leadership, and in short, we seek a Pax Universalis, built upon shared responsibilities and aspirations.

In many ways, his actions were consistent with his words. When widespread starvation struck Somalia, for example, he sent American troops to help with the international effort to distribute food and save lives, announcing that he could not ignore the shared global responsibilities and aspirations "even though the United States has no military, economic, or political interests at stake in such crises."

This pattern of working as partners with others was followed by Bill Clinton when he assumed the presidency in 1993. His administration actively participated in the international community's efforts to place sanctions on Saddam Hussein, protect human rights by developing international criminal law with the tribunals for war crimes by those responsible for genocide in the former Yugoslavia and Rwanda, establish global environmental protections, and sponsor the Partnership for Peace plan for expanding the membership of NATO to eventually include the former members of the Warsaw Treaty Organization and others once subjugated by the Soviet Union. Clinton hoped that these efforts at cooperation and inclusiveness would be further enhanced in 1997 by naming former U.S. Ambassador to the United Nations Madeleine Albright as the first woman to ever hold the position of secretary of state.

Even in the most challenging area of force and statecraft, the administration attempted to work in partnership with others and to avoid unilateral military action. This was not easy. One of the reasons involved serious differences of opinion over political-military doctrine and the use of force in humanitarian intervention. Should armed force be employed in gradually restricted and limited ways, it was asked, or used overwhelmingly from the beginning on a huge scale in order to achieve a decisive outcome quickly? This was further complicated in the age of the diplomatic revolution by the emergence of an unusually hostile and partisan Congress. Still another reason had to do with the president's own personal weakness, which brought scandal to his administration and for which he had no one to blame but himself. Nevertheless, Clinton made great efforts to enlist Security Council support for the sending of American troops to Haiti to help restore democracy in 1994, and then to work in collaboration with the United Nations in Bosnia during 1995 and with NATO allies in Kosovo during 1999 to protect against genocidal "ethnic cleansing." The United States thus agreed to actively participate with others in air attacks on military and communication sites, in a peacekeeping force to separate the parties and participate in reconstruction, and in the prosecution of Slobodan Milosevic in the name of protecting human rights and advancing international criminal law.

With the election of George W. Bush in 2001, it did not initially appear that there would be any drastic change of course. He frequently declared as a candidate that he intended to work as a partner in cooperation with other nations, pursue a "humble" foreign policy, and be "judicious as to how to use the military." In his inaugural speech he announced: "We will show purpose without arrogance." Within a very short period of time, however, the new administration deliberately removed itself from several international initiatives and agreements ranging from the environmental protections of the Kyoto Accord to the banning of land mines and restrictions on the spread of small arms and light weapons, took the unprecedented step of "unsigning" the treaty establishing the International Criminal Court, refused to participate in a conference to provide verification measures for the Biological Weapons Convention, repudiated the Comprehensive Test Ban Treaty, and abrogated the Anti-Ballistic Missile (ABM) Treaty which had served as the foundation of strategic nuclear arms control.

The theme of partnership resonated loudly in the aftermath of 9/11 and the initial phases of the war against the Taliban, al-Qaeda, and Osama bin Laden in Afghanistan, but then collapsed with the unilateralism of *The*

National Security Strategy of the United States, 2002. The country's possession of "unprecedented—and unequaled—strength and influence in the world," the document declared, presented "a time of opportunity for America." To take full advantage of this unipolar moment, it announced that policy henceforth would be based not on broad norms and restraints of international order but rather "on a distinctly American internationalism that reflects the union of our values and our national interests." The United States, it declared, intended "to lead." "In exercising our leadership we will respect the values, judgments, and interests of our friends and partners. Still, we will be prepared to act apart when our interests and unique responsibilities require." Moreover, it asserted that it would tolerate no competitors and that the most critical instrument of statecraft would be armed force: "It is time to reaffirm the essential role of American military strength. We must build and maintain our defenses beyond challenge."

Such strident pronouncements about acting "apart" and armed forces "beyond challenge" provoked deep concerns among virtually all other nations in the world, but they marked only a prelude to the veritable chasm that opened when the United States invaded Iraq in March 2003. The launching of this war could hardly be described as an act of "self-defense" by any stretch of the UN Charter. It was a *preventive* war against an uncertain and potential threat in the distance, rather than a *preemptive* war against a direct and imminent threat at hand that could only be averted by force. As such, for many it crossed a threshold of legitimacy and thereby created a crisis over the fundamental principles that should guide the evolving international system and its search for peace and security. No one posed the central question more directly than German Foreign Minister Joschka Fischer, who asked pointedly: "What kind of world order do we want?"

For some Americans, the answer to this question could be found in the *National Security Strategy of the United States, 2002,* and its call for them to become the undisputed leader of a unipolar world, wielding unsurpassed military superiority. They embraced the view expressed by President George W. Bush, Vice President Richard Cheney, Secretary of Defense Donald Rumsfeld, and Deputy Secretary of Defense Paul Wolfowitz that America was entitled to act alone, using its unparalleled power to full advantage without the restraints of international norms or collective decision making. They welcomed the much-quoted opinion piece by David Frum and Richard Perle, American authors of *An End to Evil,* who argued that the United Nations had become "an obstacle to our national security," sliding "from irrelevance to oblivion," and boasted: "The U.N. member states know that the United States will in the end do whatever it has to do, regardless of what the United Nations says."

For those who looked to partnership and collective security to maintain order in the evolving international system, these positions presented nothing short of an existential threat. President Jacques Chirac of France described America's unilateral and preventive use of force as "one of the gravest trials" in the history of the United Nations, saying that it "undermined the multilateral system." "In an open world," he continued, "no one can live in isolation, no one can act alone in the name of all, and no one can accept the anarchy of a society without rules." Kofi Annan delivered an unusually impassioned and sharp condemnation of American policy, declaring that "unilateralism" amounted to an assault on the "collective action" envisioned by Franklin Roosevelt and others who created the United Nations. He warned:

> This logic represents a fundamental challenge to the principles on which, however imperfectly, world peace and stability have rested for the last fifty-eight years. My concern is that, if it were to be adopted, it could set precedents that resulted in a proliferation of the unilateral and lawless use of force, with or without justification.

Annan concluded that "we have come to a fork in the road. This may be a moment no less decisive than 1945 itself when the United Nations was founded."

The outrage intensified. To most other governments and to the hundreds of thousands around the globe who protested at the beginning of the Iraq War, as well as to critics within the United States itself, America's unilateralism and claims to be the unrivaled leader of the world demonstrated a sharp turn from partnership into rivalry, as well as a simultaneous rejection of a balance of power, broad-based international security, and the just war tradition. Criticism from adversaries and extremists who bitterly detested America's powerful global influence could be expected, but now it came from close friends and allies. Long-time members of NATO began speaking openly of American "arrogance," "aggressive nationalism," "unilateralism," "hegemony," "self-indulgence," "bullying," and "imperialism." They referred to the United States as a "hyperpower" and "the new Rome," accusing it of being bent on domination and insistent upon refusing to restrain its own power as a part of the broader international order. Even British Prime Minister Tony Blair, who closely allied himself with the United States, felt compelled to openly warn before a joint session of the U.S. Congress: "What America must do is show that this is a partnership built on persuasion, not command." Even the normally friendly BBC began a series of critical broadcasts in 2004 on the subject of the American "Age of Empire," which concluded that the United States could end up being "not only the most powerful country in the world but also the most distrusted country in the world."

As this distrust grew, it became a disaster for public diplomacy. Indeed, the highly respected Pew Research Center, which conducted thousands of interviews in many different countries as part of its Global Attitudes Project, discovered a dramatic shift from a spontaneous outpouring of sympathy toward the United States after 9/11 to a surge in anti-American attitudes following its invasion of Iraq and revelations (made even worse by shocking photographs of prisoners subjected to torture) of illegal actions in its "global war on terror." Those surveyed expressed growing suspicion of its motives, anger over what they characterized as its "my-way-or-the-highway" approach and failure to take others into account as partners in a broader system, and outright fear of its unleashed—and unchecked—power projected across the globe. Many actually perceived the United States as the greatest threat to peace and security, more menacing than Iran, North Korea, or even terrorism itself. They saw massive force, but little statecraft.

Extremely negative opinions about the United States and its role in the world continued, according to the Pew researchers, until two factors emerged in 2008. One of these was the onset of the global financial crisis. This caused international opinion to reassess America's overall power somewhat differently in light of its struggling economy. The other was the election of Barack Obama as president of the United States.

From the beginning, Obama received far more than just the benefit of doubt. Global opinion polls reached nearly astronomical ratings of support, revealing widespread anticipation that he and his new administration would turn away from rivalry and move toward more serious partnership. In a number of areas their hopes appeared justified, starting with a highly acclaimed speech in Cairo, Egypt, in which he called across the chasm opened by the 9/11 attacks for a "new beginning" and a "partnership between America and Islam," "based on mutual interest and "mutual respect." Obama followed this with an address before the 2010 graduating class of the U.S. Military Academy at West Point. The United States, he said, was "clear-eyed about the shortfalls of the international system," but needed to fully appreciate that history taught important lessons about the dangers of "acting alone" and "stepping out of the currents of cooperation." "The international order we seek," he declared, "is one that can resolve the challenges of our times." To achieve this goal, he concluded, America must understand where its interests and values coincide with others in the world, support universal human rights, have its military forces work more closely with statecraft and the renewed engagement of its diplomats, actively shape stronger international norms and institutions, and "build new partnerships."

Several new policies clearly marked a change of direction, and Secretary of State Hillary Clinton began to speak of the necessity of formulating what she called "21st Century Statecraft." To begin, Clinton, a Democrat, developed a close working relationship with Secretary of Defense Robert Gates, a Republican, to better coordinate force and statecraft. One indication of this could be seen in the significant increase in the number of advisors from the Bureau of Political-Military Affairs within the State Department attached to the Pentagon and posted to component commands, major headquarters, and embedded in military units assigned to combat areas. Clinton then decided to follow the Pentagon's practice of formulating strategic evaluations of performance and needs in order to prepare for challenges ahead. This resulted in the 2010 *Quadrennial Diplomacy and Development Review*, which, among other things, drew renewed attention to the new security agenda encompassing the relationship between security, peace, justice, and human rights, as well as the principle of the "indivisibility of security." International and national security, it noted, increasingly depend on individual security or whether civilians enjoy some measure of their human rights; for where they do not, the proven results are escalating violence, mass atrocities, violent extremism, and humanitarian disasters.

In addition, the Obama administration went on to successfully negotiate the New Strategic Arms Reduction Treaty (START) with Russia, initiate the Nuclear Security Summit (NSS) of world leaders to create ways of keeping weapon-grade nuclear material out of the hands of terrorists, work with the Security Council to coordinate policy toward Iran and North Korea, partner with the Arab League and the United Nations and then NATO in a multilateral mission in defending civilians from attacks by the dictatorship of Muammar Gaddafi in Libya, and finally ending the exceptionally unpopular American-led war in Iraq. The United States stood for election and then actively participated in the new UN Human Rights Council, strongly supported the shift from a narrow G-8 to the wider membership of the G-20 (thereby including Brazil, China, and India) in serving as the major forum for leading international cooperation in economic growth and financial stability, engaged in negotiations to join the Trans-Pacific Partnership (TPP), and backed reforms to give emerging powers more influence over decision making in the International Monetary Fund and governance of the global economy. At the same time, both Hillary Clinton and her successor John Kerry spoke frequently with other nations about "shared security."

These efforts at partnership certainly did not eliminate all differences and rivalries, however. International opinion remained critical of Obama's surge in the number of troops sent into the continuing war in Afghanistan, the escalation of military operations into Pakistan and Yemen with drone strikes, inability to end the widely discredited military trials of terrorist suspects held indefinitely at the prison camp at Guantanamo Bay in Cuba, lack of cooperation in reaching agreement on mitigation strategies for global climate change, and failure to use American influence on Israel to protect the rights of Palestinians and to advance peace in the Middle East. Some critics blamed Obama personally, while others directed their wrath on domestic politics that produced an intensely partisan and often dysfunctional Congress. Yet, regardless of who served as president or which party held the majority in Congress, those who looked seriously at the international system as a whole came back again and again to two critical and sobering facts: that the United States alone maintains an estimated 900 military bases or facilities of various sizes in at least 130 foreign countries, and that it alone spends nearly as much on its military budget as all of the other countries of the world combined.

Given this one-sided preponderance of the most extensive and technologically advanced military power in the world, it is not surprising that other nations and peoples increasingly speak of the need to develop what they call "a counterweight to the United States." Ironically, such a natural reaction to any hegemon has been enhanced by the fact that while American resources were being bled by wars in Afghanistan and Iraq, potential rivals were husbanding their energies and growing. One of these is the European Union. With its twenty-seven member nation-states, the EU serves as the home to the largest number of Fortune 500 companies and constitutes the largest single market in the world. The idea that it should serve as a counterweight, according to opinion polls, is popular among a new generation of Europeans who no longer share the gratitude of their parents or grandparents to the United States for saving them from tyranny during the Second World War. Some look not to "the rise of the West" but rather "the rise of the rest," such as the recently established group known as BRICS (comprised of Brazil, Russia, India, China, and South Africa), urging them to leverage their growing economic power into greater geopolitical clout. Among these, Russia not only presents the country with the largest mineral-rich landmass in the world but possesses a powerful nuclear arsenal. Some look to a more focused network of three emerging powers known as IBSA (comprised of India, Brazil, and South Africa), beginning to flex their collective influence and self-confidence on behalf of Asia, Latin America, and Africa. Others seek balance from countries in the Middle East that derive power from their huge oil reserves. Still others turn to Africa, as indicated when a summit of the heads of state of all African governments considered the possibilities for the evolving international system if they combined their vast territories, resources of oil and diamonds, and populations. As one spokesman declared: "We have the capabilities that would allow us to be as strong as the United States and the European Union, and this is a good thing, so there could be balance in the world. When there is no balance, there are wars and conflicts."

Among single nation-states in the world, only China appears to have the potential of presenting any serious counterweight to the United States. During the years of Mao Zedong, the country pursued revolutionary and ideologically motivated foreign policies that resulted in rivalries with both superpowers, a rejection of many international norms, an undertrained diplomatic corps, economic autarky, and isolation from the broader system. With the emergence of Deng Xiaoping and the end of the Cold War, however, China moved to normalize diplomatic relations and seek partnerships with other countries, seriously prepare its diplomats, and present a non-confrontational posture that would attract foreign investment and enable it to grow economically. Under the leadership of Jiang Zemin and Hu Jintao, it served as one of the founding members of the Asia-Europe Meeting to discuss mutual interests, signed the Comprehensive Nuclear Test Ban Treaty, ratified several major arms control and non-proliferation accords, joined the World Trade Organization, aggressively extended its economic muscle, and became very active as a permanent member on the UN Security Council. China's influence thus continued to grow, often exceeding the expectations even of its own leaders. Indeed, today China possesses the world's biggest population (1,000,000,000 more than the United States), the world's most extensive market, and the world's largest army. With force and statecraft in mind, since the 1990s its military budget increased threefold, and in 2011 it tested a new stealth fighter and launched its first aircraft carrier. The self-confidence that accompanies these developments is reflected in the writings of Chinese strategists, marking a critical shift in their view of the evolving international system and China's role in it, emphasizing the need to develop a more muscular posture as a means of redressing perceived humiliations at the hands of the West in the past, to use both land and sea power to protect its network of economic resources, to "share global responsibilities," and to adopt what they call "Great Power mentality" (*daguo xintai*). All this helps to explain the appearance of so many new books with titles such as *China's Rise*; *A Contest for Supremacy: China, America, and the Struggle for Mastery in Asia*; *China, Inc.: How the Rise of the Next Superpower Challenges America and the World*; and *When China Rules the World: The End of the Western World and the Birth of a New Global Order.*

These calculations and speculations about counterweights are nevertheless complicated by heated disputes about the best means of attaining peace and security, the uncertain trajectory of relative power and shifting coalitions among the actors, and by the nature of the challenges themselves. Although there are many who see benefits in geopolitical rivalries balanced against each other, for example, others are fearful. As Tony Blair warns: "There is no more dangerous theory in international politics than that we need to balance the power of America with other competitive powers, different poles around which nations gather." Although the financial resources of the EU are impressive, the sovereign debt crises within some of its members creates serious fissures and weaknesses. Although the economic strength of a number of emerging countries is rising, that does not necessarily translate into the experience or the tools for security problems, including military strength that might be required for force and statecraft. Although China's power is a fact, the question arises about how long its leaders will be able to sustain equilibrium between economic growth, social stability, and political control by the Communist Party. Moreover, although America remains the most powerful nation on earth, it can no longer simply get its way because of its own unique position. This raises serious questions about the nature and extent of American leadership and participation in the evolving international system. As political scientist Bruce Jones describes the challenge:

> The greatest risk lies not in a single peer competitor but in the erosion of systems and institutions vital to U.S. interests and a stable order. U.S. power is indispensable for international order, but not sufficient. No longer the CEO of Free World Inc., the United States now holds a position akin to that of the largest minority shareholder in Global Order LLC. Can the United States use its changed position to shape the emerging order?

In shaping this evolving order, many observers believe that America, like all other shareholders, must learn to go "beyond blocs" by creating broad partnerships to take collective action.

Such attention to partnership often finds itself directed toward the United Nations. After the acute crisis created by the American war against Iraq, many governments responded by increasing their efforts to make this organization succeed. Instead of viewing it as being "irrelevant," they saw how much more active and robust the organization had become once freed from the emasculating straightjacket of the Cold War and insisted that it was now "indispensable." At the World Summit of 2005 held at UN headquarters in New York, national leaders committed themselves to forging "a new consensus on which to base collective action." Many increased their financial contributions dramatically and went on to commit tens of thousands of military forces and civilian police to United Nations–mandated peacekeeping missions, which today are found around the world. Renewed vigor also can be seen in their support for and participation in counterterrorism strategies, sanctions, international criminal tribunals, humanitarian intervention, international administration in post-conflict areas, and willingness to authorize the use of force when necessary to address threats to peace and security.

Yet, even while working in partnerships within the United Nations, it is important to remember that rivalries are never absent. The organization is, after all, a collection of, by, and for governments of nation-states. Blocs and alignments that divide the world thus are readily reflected in negotiating and voting behavior. Nowhere is this contention more acute or the questions more difficult—as always—than in matters of force and statecraft. What should be done in the Security Council, for example, when the five permanent members refuse to adapt to change by continuing to resist expansion or restructuring that might allow the growing influence of Brazil, Germany, India, or Japan to jeopardize their privileged status, frozen in time as a result of their military victory in the Second World War nearly seventy years ago? If these most powerful members are necessary to enforce collective security, what happens if they decide that the rules of the system do not apply to them or to their allies and friends? Given the fact that since the Cold War ended the main threats have come more from conflicts within states than from external aggression by one state against another, what should the Security Council do about using force in the name of "Responsibility to Protect" to intervene within the domestic affairs of a country whose own national sovereignty is accorded special status under the Charter? Can any threat be judged to be "imminent" enough to justify preemption, and who makes that judgment? Who determines what is a "last resort" and when diplomacy has been fully exhausted? Similarly, who makes the decision of whether "self-defense" is legitimately at stake when armed force is employed? Attempts to find answers to these questions and to devise both substantive rules and institutional arrangements to govern force and statecraft present formidable challenges.

Those seeking to develop greater international cooperation by means of strengthening the United Nations, as historian Paul Kennedy observes in *The Parliament of Man: The Past, Present, and Future of the United Nations*, have cause for both optimism and despair. They know that the organization can never do more than its member nation-states allow it to do, that debate sometimes occupies more attention than action, and that the powerful and the wealthy cannot always be counted on to be partners. But they also know that the United Nations, despite all of the structural limitations and the rival political forces aligned against it, has not only survived but in certain areas has even prospered. Its development of international norms and contributions to peacekeeping and humanitarian intervention, peace building, preventive diplomacy, mediation and conflict resolution, relief operations in the face of tragic

"Aspiration and Performance": Efforts to Find Peace and Security Through the United Nations

disasters, advancement of human rights, promotion of democracy, extension of social and economic development, assistance to refugees, campaign for international criminal law, and efforts to address globalization and complex interdependence all mark undeniable achievements. For these reasons, they view the United Nations as an imperfect but indispensable instrument in guiding the evolving international system toward peace and security in a dangerous world, taking hope from the observation made by Dag Hammarskjöld concerning slow but steady steps toward an ultimate goal, when he said: "The United Nations reflects both aspiration and a falling short of aspiration. But the constant struggle to close the gap between aspiration and performance now, as always, makes the difference between civilization and chaos."

At the same time, there are others who seek to advance international partnerships by adapting existing institutions or by creating new ones as a means of structuring the relationships among actors in order to meet changing circumstances, shared interests and values, and common threats. This can be seen in the efforts of those governments who work to reform and strengthen not only the United Nations but also other multilateral organizations such as the International Atomic Energy Agency, the International Monetary Fund, the Organization for Economic Cooperation and Development, or the G-20. Others have considerably less confidence in the capacity of nation-states to avoid dangerous rivalries among themselves or to solve complex problems and threats, and thus look to nonstate actors such as transnational corporations or NGOs to create networks that mobilize those with shared interests and values across national borders. One of these is the World Economic Forum, an independent, nonpartisan organization established to help set the agenda for shaping the evolution of the international system and finding solutions to global challenges by creating collaborative partnerships. This is done throughout the year by bringing together multiple and interdependent stakeholders from business, government, and civil society, including heads of state or government, cabinet ministers, ambassadors, senior officials from international organizations, business leaders and entrepreneurs, academic experts, scientists and technology pioneers, journalists, religious leaders of different faiths, labor organizers, and NGO activists to interact and address specific challenges. Some indication of its impact can be seen in the fact that its annual gatherings in Davos, Switzerland, often are called the "Summit of Summits."

The future direction of the evolving international system will depend—as it always has in the past—on the extent to which the participants view themselves as partners or rivals. There can be no such thing as a system unless there is some measure of cooperative partnership among the major actors, but at the same time no system can expect to completely eliminate the competition between those same actors. It is for this reason that diplomacy has always taken place in a complex dynamic, moving somewhere along a scale between collaboration on the one hand and contention on the other. Statecraft requires an understanding of this commixture and the capacity to find a way to live with elements of both partnership and rivalry. This is why policies that are based on simplistic notions of either "friend" or "foe," or "you are either for us or against us," are so fraught with peril.

No international system thus can possibly function or survive unless competition can be sufficiently balanced or restrained by an essential agreement among its actors on their shared interests and values. One of the great insights of those who created and maintained the classical system of diplomacy, as we have seen, was the realization that a balance of power can inhibit the capacity to overthrow a system, but that consensus on basic values inhibits the desire to do so. They reached the conclusion that realistic and pragmatic calculations, rather than idealistic impulses, made it essential for them to be responsible stakeholders in and of the system by defining their own interests and *raison d'état* in terms of the larger collective that could regulate their rivalries, address shared threats, and preserve peace and security. But the lessons learned are not always understood or accepted by those who follow, the quality of leadership changes, and agreement on fundamental values often is extraordinarily difficult to achieve.

Just as those in the past had to confront the specific challenges of their time, so will those responsible for statecraft in our own time. In this endeavor, the powerful movements of globalization and complex interdependence will encourage, if not compel, the participants to see that some threats are so widespread and so difficult that no single nation or even blocs of nations, however strong, can possibly solve them alone. They will call attention to the fact that global problems require global solutions and thus the forging of cooperative partnerships. These include international terrorism, the proliferation of weapons of mass destruction, human rights abuses, indebtedness and development, infectious diseases, transnational crime, poverty, population growth, and environment degradation. Other issues instead will provoke division and exacerbate rivalries. Among these, one can point to the arguments over the necessity and legitimate use of armed force, conflicting claims of traditional national sovereignty and those of collective security, the relationship between human rights and security, the future of United States leadership and what its presence—or its absence—would mean, the role to be played by the United Nations, the continuing conflict between the Israelis and the Palestinians, the consequences of the upheaval known as the "Arab Spring" of 2011 in which several leaders in North Africa and the Middle East who had clung to power for decades were removed, fanaticism and xenophobia that perceive international cooperation as betrayal, economic competition and the growing worldwide divide between the rich and the poor, divisions of race and religion, and the intensifying clash of cultural and political differences at home and abroad.

Whether the evolving international system follows the path of malice and danger or that of peace and security—and whether it can find shared values in the midst of the continuing diplomatic revolution or not—will be determined by where we choose to be along that scale of partnership or rivalry. In doing so, our future may well depend on whether we can learn the lessons of how and why others have succeeded or failed when dealing with the challenges of force and statecraft in the past. It is, consequently, to this matter that we now turn in Part Two.

SUGGESTIONS FOR FURTHER EXPLORATION

Many accounts of, and broad prescriptions and strategies for, the evolving international system appeared at the end of the Cold War. Some of these include Alexander L. George, "The Role of Force in Diplomacy," in H. W. Brands et al. (eds.), *The Use of Force After the Cold War* (College Station, TX, 2003 ed.); John Mearsheimer, *The Tragedy of Great Power Politics* (New York, 2003); Bruce Jentleson (ed.), *Opportunities Missed, Opportunities Seized* (Lanham, MD, 2000); Karen Mingst and Margaret Karns, *The United Nations in the Post-Cold War Era* (Boulder, CO, 2000 ed.); George Bush and Brent Scowcroft, *A World Transformed* (New York, 1998); Center for Strategic and International Studies, *Reinventing Diplomacy in the Information Age* (Washington, DC, 1998); Samuel Huntington, *The Clash of Civilizations and the Remaking of the World Order* (New York, 1998 ed.); Boutros Boutros-Ghali, *Agenda for Peace* (New York, 1996 ed.); Henry Kissinger, *Diplomacy* (New York, 1994); and Gareth Evans, *Cooperating for Peace* (St. Leonards, Australia, 1993).

Challenges to the traditional state system and claims of national sovereignty are analyzed in Paul Gordon Lauren, *The Evolution of International Human Rights* (Philadelphia, 2011); Stephen Krasner, *Power, the State, and Sovereignty* (New York, 2009); T. V. Paul et al. (eds.), *The Nation-State in Question* (Princeton, 2003); International Commission on Intervention and State Sovereignty, *The Responsibility to Protect* (Ottawa, 2001); Royce Ammon, *Global Television and the Shaping of World Policy* (New York, 2001); Charles Kegley and Gregory Raymond, *Exorcizing the Ghost of Westphalia* (Upper Saddle River, NJ, 2001); Joseph Nye, Jr., and John Donahue (eds.), *Governance in a Globalizing World* (Washington, DC, 2000); Martin van Creveld, *The Rise and Decline of the State* (Cambridge,

2000); and Kofi Annan, "Two Concepts of Sovereignty," *The Economist*, September 18, 1999, pp. 49–50.

On terrorism and the "global war on terror," see the official assessments in "Country Reports on Terrorism" of the U.S. Department of State at www.state.gov; Dan Caldwell, *Vortex of Conflict* (Stanford, CA, 2011); Peter Galbraith, *Unintended Consequences: How War in Iraq Strengthened America's Enemies* (New York, 2009); Ahmed Rashid, *Descent Into Chaos* (New York, 2009); Michael Scheuer, *Imperial Hubris* (Dulles, VA, 2005); Richard Clarke, *Against All Enemies* (New York, 2004); National Commission on Terrorist Attacks Upon the United States, *The 9/11 Commission Report* (New York, 2004); David Frum and Richard Perle, *An End to Evil* (New York, 2003); Peter Bergen, *Holy War, Inc.* (New York, 2002); Richard Falk, *The Great Terror War* (New York, 2002); and Bob Woodward, *Bush at War* (New York, 2002).

The always present theme of partnership and rivalry has assumed much greater importance in recent years, generating considerable and often heated debate. Interesting and sometimes provocative treatments can be found in Bruce Jones, "Largest Minority Shareholder in Global Order LLC," *Brookings Institution Policy Paper No. 25* (Washington, DC, 2011); Pew Research Center, "From Hyperpower to Declining Power," press release of September 7, 2011; Jack Matlock, Jr., *Superpower Illusions* (New Haven, 2010); Fareed Zakaria, *The Post-American World* (New York, 2009); Stefan Halper and Jonathan Clarke, *America Alone* (Cambridge, 2004); Andrew Bacevich, *American Empire* (Cambridge, MA, 2004); UN High-Level Panel on Threats, Challenges, and Change, *A More Secure World: Our Shared Responsibility* (New York, 2004); Zbigniew Brezezinski, *The Choice: Global Domination or Global Leadership* (New York, 2004); Robert Kagan, *Of Paradise and Power* (New York, 2004 ed.); William Odom and Robert Dujarric, *America's Inadvertent Empire* (New Haven, 2004); Ivo Daalder and James Lindsay, *America Unbound* (Washington, DC, 2003); Michael Hirsh, *At War With Ourselves* (New York, 2003); Charles Kupchan, *The End of the American Era* (New York, 2003); Joseph Nye, Jr., *Paradox of American Power* (New York, 2003); Clyde Prestowitz, *Rogue Nation* (New York, 2003); and United States, White House, *National Security Strategy of the United States, 2002* (Washington, DC, 2002).

PART TWO

HISTORY, THEORY, AND PRACTICE

7

Lessons of History and Knowledge
for Statecraft

"Those who cannot remember the past," philosopher George Santayana once famously observed, "are condemned to repeat it." His thought-provoking statement is quoted so frequently because it seems to resonate intuitively with how we learn from experience, trying to understand ourselves and make sense of the world in which we live with others. We believe that we do and should learn from our past, trying to avoid previous mistakes and to replicate behavior that brought success. It seems natural, therefore, to seek to apply this principle to the broader canvas of the human condition as a whole, exploring whether and how people gain *insight from hindsight*. With specific reference to diplomatic challenges in force and statecraft, for example, we want to know if leaders have learned any lessons from past failures and successes—or not. Almost every statesman and general has professed to having learned from history, but there are times when the evidence certainly suggests otherwise. There is often confusion and dispute about precisely how leaders learn, what they learn, how they deal with seemingly conflicting lessons, and whether the analogies that they take from the past are appropriate to specific problems at hand. With these factors in mind, it is important to explore in Part Two of this book how knowledge for statecraft might be gained and to consider the opinion of the distinguished historian of the Renaissance, Jacob Burckhardt, who once remarked that the true use of history should be not to make leaders more clever for the next time but to make them wiser forever.

CLASSICAL WRITERS ON THE IMPORTANCE
OF HISTORICAL LESSONS

Virtually every writer who has ever seriously analyzed force and statecraft has stressed the critical importance of learning historical lessons. They have strongly believed that whatever guides exist for survival in the present or future can be found only in the past, arguing that if we do not know where we have been, we cannot possibly know where we are or where we are going. Knowing background and context can provide enormous assistance in avoiding unnecessary and costly mistakes. The study of history, they have maintained, can reveal patterns and invaluable insights about human behavior, the nature of diplomatic challenges, the range of choice between partnerships and rivalries, likely reactions to certain policies, continuities and changes, the evolution of international systems, the relationship between capabilities and intentions, and the role of ethical values and restraints, among many, many other factors. For this reason, they have stressed time and time again the critical necessity of learning from history.

It is consequently not surprising that Thucydides would write his insightful and path-breaking book, *The History of the Peloponnesian War,* with precisely this purpose in mind. He was not interested in telling a story for entertainment or simply chronicling the long life-and-death struggle between ancient Athens and Sparta, but rather in sustained inquiry into history as a means of discerning meaning about the world and human behavior that might be useful to policy makers. Thucydides took seriously the fact that the Greek word *historeo* meant to learn or gain knowledge by objectively gathering evidence, providing accurate descriptions, applying reasoned analyses, and offering critical judgments about the past in such a way as to move from the particular part to the larger whole, or from the specific event to underlying patterns. He analyzed the negotiations with Argos, for example, to appreciate the more encompassing nature of negotiations as a whole, the defensive alliance between Athens and Corcyra to understand the strategy of deterrence, the disastrous Athenian expedition against Sicily as instructive of the results of arrogant ambition and incompetent leadership, the threats conveyed in the Melian dialogue to gain knowledge of the nature of coercive diplomacy, and the wars themselves to learn why normally law-abiding people sometimes resort to passion and violence. Indeed, as he wrote in his introduction, he sought to learn lessons and wanted his words to be "judged useful by those who want to understand clearly the events which happened in the past and which (human nature being what it is) will, at some time or other and in much the same ways, be repeated in the future." In this regard, he wanted his work to provide wisdom, guidance, and good and useful estimates (not absolute certainty) for leaders who would face similar problems in the future. Some testament to his success in doing so can be seen in the fact that his book has been taken seriously over millennia and that no course on diplomacy or war is likely to fail to discuss it.

This theme of the practical use of history as a guide for statecraft received substantial reinforcement from Niccolò Machiavelli in the early sixteenth century. Indeed, as he expressed in *The Prince*: "My hope is to write a book that will be *useful* ... and so I thought it sensible to go straight to a discussion of how things are in real life and not waste time with a discussion of an imaginary world." In order to create this handbook for policy makers, Machiavelli engaged in what he described as "a constant study of the past," drawing evidence from history about those who exercised power, with failures and successes ranging from Moses of the Old Testament, Alexander the Great, and Severus of the Roman Empire to Cesare Borgia and other leaders of Renaissance Italy. From these he drew a number of conclusions—or lessons—designed to help leaders govern and advance the interests of their states. This matter became so important to Machiavelli that he returned to it again in his subsequent book, *The Discourses*, and concluded directly:

> Whoever considers the past and the present will readily observe that all cities and all peoples are and ever have been animated by the same desires and the same passions; so that it is easy, by diligent study of the past, to foresee what is likely to happen in the future.

Hugo Grotius reached similar conclusions by drawing extensively from history. As he argued in his famous seventeenth-century *On the Law of War and Peace*, past experience provides rich examples of human behavior and a solid basis of judgment because people will "act in a similar way under similar circumstances." The events of his own time, he believed, revealed lessons not only about the dangers and the costs of continuing long wars but also of treaties that seek to destroy or punish enemies as compared to creating guarantees of mutual beneficial stability against the renewal of war.

François de Callières echoed exactly this theme in his masterful eighteenth-century *On the Manner of Negotiating with Princes*. The entire purpose for writing his book, he explained, was to develop the skills and the habits of thought necessary to deal with the critical issues of statecraft on which the whole fortunes, peace, and security of states depended. He worried that there had been "no discipline or fixed rules" by which "good citizens destined to become negotiators might instruct themselves in the knowledge necessary for this kind of employment." From his own considerable experience, astute observation, and careful reading of the past, de Callières believed that the conduct of diplomacy required very special kinds of skills: "It demands all the penetration, all the dexterity, all the suppleness which a man can possess. It requires a wide-spread understanding and knowledge, and above all, a correct and piercing discernment." The development of such understanding, knowledge, and discernment, he argued, could be found in studying alliances, military establishments, the interests and personalities of foreign leaders, the languages and customs of other countries, and "above all" and "of first importance," the study of history. Frederick the Great reached the same conclusion a few years later, observing: "What is the good of experience if you do not reflect?"

During the nineteenth century, Carl von Clausewitz's monumental and insightful *On War*, focusing directly on force and statecraft, reiterated and then further elaborated precisely the same theme. In fact, he opened his chapter on the use of history with these words: "Historical examples clarify everything and also provide the best kind of proof in the empirical sciences." He explained this by describing how history can assist policy makers by providing explanations of ideas, showing applications in the form of specific examples, offering support for various possibilities, and presenting evidence to deduce a particular doctrine or theory. Clausewitz's text on the relationship between means and ends, on war as a continuation of policy, consequently drew heavily on historical evidence. He nevertheless cautioned that the use of history in this way required considerable effort and sophistication. In one of his most perceptive observations, Clausewitz warned against those who fleetingly look to find historical examples for quick answers for policy or the development of theory, who "never rise above anecdote," and who draw vast lessons from only an individual case, "starting always with the most striking feature, the high point of the event, and digging only as deep as suit them, never getting down to the general factors that govern the matter."

These classical writers, who stressed the vital importance of historical lessons for statecraft, heavily influenced generations of successors. One thinks, for example, of Henry Kissinger who wrote a thesis on the subject of "The Meaning of History" and whose first book, *A World Restored*, focused on the experience of forming a successful coalition against Napoleon and holding the Congress of Vienna in 1814–1815 as a means of exploring larger and enduring issues of personalities, alliances, balances of power, legitimacy, national interests, peacemaking, and the nature of stability and security within an international system. "No significant conclusions are possible in the study of foreign affairs...," he concluded, "without an awareness of the historical context. For societies exist in time more than in space." Whether Kissinger appropriately applied the historical lessons he wrote about as a scholar when he served as a policy maker, of course, will be debated for years to come, but there can be little doubt about his conviction in the value of history for the conduct of statecraft.

Other recent scholars and practitioners reach similar conclusions. Political scientist Klaus Knorr introduced his influential book, entitled *Historical Dimensions of National Security Problems*, by writing that

> the understanding of past events and problems can be part of a learning process that assists us in understanding present events and problems. Without knowing how past societies coped with problems similar to our own, the options they considered, the choices they made, and the consequences entailed by these choices, we can only arrive at a flat, poorly constructed understanding of our present problems.

Seeking to learn as much as he could from the past that would assist in addressing contemporary challenges of force and statecraft, General David Petraeus focused his entire doctoral dissertation on the subject of *The American Military and the Lessons of Vietnam*. Here, he drew on the thoughts of a number of classical writers as well as contemporaries, including Army General and Chairman of the Joint Chiefs of Staff John Vessy, who insightfully observed, "We don't learn new lessons. We relearn old lessons that we haven't paid attention to."

The Historical Habit of Mind

Acknowledging the necessity of learning—and relearning—lessons from history, however, is not the same as understanding what it is that history actually teaches about force and statecraft. In seeking to address precisely this question, the Scottish historian D. P. Heatley decided in the aftermath of the upheaval of the First World War to write a book entitled *Diplomacy and the Study of International Relations*. He began his work by discussing the importance of learning historical lessons and then presented a direct proposition: "Political Science without History, it has been said, has no root; and History without Political Science has no fruit." With this in mind, Heatley argued that anyone who wanted to understand international relations must begin first with the study of how people of earlier times attempted to solve their diplomatic challenges, and this he regarded as the foundation and "training ground" of statesmanship. The best way to approach this task was not with some kind of simplistic memorization of names and dates, but rather with an exploration of important phenomena and patterns from the richness of historical experience. He demonstrated what he meant by this with thoughtful treatments about the traditions and practices of diplomacy, the classical writers from Thucydides and Machiavelli to de Callières and Clausewitz, treaties and maps, the qualities required of diplomats, the conduct of negotiation, the challenges confronting those persons charged with the formulation and execution of foreign policy, the restraints imposed upon them, the impact of ethical values, and the relationship between statecraft and its most drastic instrument of policy, armed force. With such an approach, Heatley believed, students of the past could avoid becoming mere chroniclers of what happened in international relations and could instead become much more thoughtful interpreters and sophisticated analysts of how and why it happened. Fundamentally, he maintained that the study of history, more than anything else, could lead to reflection and wisdom by developing "the habit of mind that is required for appreciating questions of foreign policy."

It is exactly this habit of mind that helps to develop essential skills in understanding the world of diplomacy and the instruments of foreign policy by establishing perspective and a basis for reasoned judgment. Thinking in focused ways about history trains the mind to make comparisons and to recognize certain patterns or reoccurrences in issues, problems, and human behavior; to identify important variables and causal mechanisms; to analyze both the similarities and the differences, or continuities and changes, between cases; and, especially, to appreciate the critical significance of context. It can never pretend to provide the gift of certain prophecy, a precise recipe book for action in every contingency that arises, or detailed and highly accurate predictions about a specific outcome if a particular choice is made. Instead, the great value of such a habit of mind, or way of thinking, can be found in its power to use broad and wide-ranging knowledge of the past in such a way as to sharpen thought, to formulate questions that need to be asked and suggest what kind of evidence might be necessary to answer them, to warn about what is or is not likely to happen and what might go wrong, and to stimulate reflection on previous human behavior for the diagnosis and prognosis of current and future events.

1. People. Students of history seeking to gain knowledge for statecraft, for example, develop a habit of mind that realizes the critical importance of individual people. Nation-states, governments, organizations, departments, or groups do not make choices or take actions themselves—real people do. These are the leaders and their advisors, the ambassadors and strategic planners, the diplomats and intelligence officers, the generals and the foot soldiers, the admirals and sailors, the negotiators and crisis managers, the politicians and bureaucrats, the business investors and human rights activists, and the local warlords and terrorists, among many others. History demonstrates time and again that policies are determined and implemented—as they only can be—not by abstract entities, but by the human element of living men and women within their own contexts, each with his or her own personality, strengths and weaknesses, ability to handle stress, beliefs and normative values, casts of mind, and historical memories. All of these shape how they perceive the reality around them, their interests, their politics and culture, what happens in the world, threats and opportunities, and their visions of what might be achieved. People determine the extent to which armed force is necessary and is dangerous. Force possesses bargaining influence in deterrence and coercive diplomacy only insofar as people are willing and able to use it, or others think they are willing and able. Ethics and international norms have no power to restrain behavior unless people feel bound to honor their obligations and make choices that protect the well-being of others. The whole concept of diplomacy itself is significant only insofar as it is put into practice by people. They may be wise or foolish, rational or irrational, able or incompetent, compassionate or vengeful, deliberative or impulsive, confident or frightened, flexible or rigid, and capable of seeing events from the perspective of others or not, but because of design or chance, office or character, people matter.

When these factors about ourselves and about others are forgotten or ignored, the results can be disastrous. Having been so instrumental in directing the American war in Vietnam, for example, former Secretary of Defense Robert McNamara spent much of the rest of his life trying to understand what went so wrong and to learn lessons that he hoped future leaders would heed. "Our misjudgments of friend and foe alike," he sadly concluded in his memoir, "reflected our profound ignorance of the history, culture, and politics of the people in the area and the personalities and the habits of their leaders."

2. Process. History also trains the mind to be attentive to process. Those who study the past tend to think processionally: of time passing. They view time as a stream, sometimes calmly meandering and sometimes smashing in cascades, but always aware not only of the present and future emerging from the past, but also in turn becoming the past. Historians analyze how events and developments evolve, as demonstrated in Part One, which addressed international systems and the diplomatic revolution, paying particular attention to sequence, to cause and effect, and to change and continuity. They examine those elements that are transformed through time and those that stay the same, for example, exploring how the diplomatic challenges of our time are both similar and different from those of the past. This applies whether the discussion centers on the advice of François de Callières or Kofi Annan, the international system-building efforts of Clemens von Metternich or Woodrow Wilson, or the use of force by Frederick the Great or George W. Bush. As David Trask, the former historian of the U.S. Department of State, argues, such a habit of mind is indispensable for statecraft. "The policy maker," he observes, "has no alternative but to make use of historical information and historical thought simply because he [or she] is specifically concerned with process, the bread and butter of historians."

3. **Possibilities.** Reading and thinking about history similarly opens the mind to an extraordinarily wide range of possibilities. The systematic study of people and events over extended periods of time and space provides a wealth of vicarious experiences with a rich and varied array of imaginable or possible actions and strategies and likely reactions, which expands and far exceeds what any one person could ever possibly learn from personal experience in his or her own short lifetime alone. Knowing that certain things already have occurred—of paths taken and not taken—affords an enormous inventory or database of information about human behavior, replete with specific evidence, examples, variables, ideas, analogies, thresholds, interpretations, patterns, trends, benchmarks, and precedents that otherwise may have remained completely beyond our imagination. History thus offers not only a spectrum of multiple choices, policy options, or range of alternative solutions that have been practiced and previously tried by others, but also some basis for judgment and diagnostic value about whether the strategies were appropriate or not and why they may have resulted in success or failure. This is precisely the point made by a recent RAND Corporation study prepared for the Department of Defense with reference to the insurgency in the war against Iraq. The report sharply criticized the tendency of American leadership "not to absorb historical lessons" and strongly recommended setting up some means "for exposing senior officials to possibilities other than those being assumed in their planning."

4. **Perspective and Proportion.** Historical study also creates a habit of mind that can develop a sense of perspective and proportion. In a marvelous essay entitled "The Historian's Opportunity," Barbara Tuchman argued that the task is to tell what history is about, what the forces are that drive us, and how we interact as humans. History, she wrote, "being concerned as it is with reality and subject as it is to certain disciplines," must see these various elements "in proportion to the whole":

> Distillation is selection, and selection...is the essence of writing history. It is the cardinal process of composition, the most difficult, the most delicate, the most fraught with error as well as art. Ability to distinguish what is significant from what is insignificant is *sine qua non*.

Study of the past involves not only making precisely these distinctions, but creating scales or measuring rods against which actions are judged and establishing a contextual background against which people and events are viewed. One aspect of this entails developing a capacity to see not only ourselves, but the perspectives of other actors and how they view their interests and themselves. Another element entails the perspective of time, or acquiring the ability to avoid the dangers of "presentism" by looking both backward over a long period and forward in such a way that a seemingly isolated event can be seen as a part of a larger pattern or process and is given meaning beyond a mere immediate or single occurrence. These are precisely the tasks of those responsible for statecraft as well, who must be able to make intelligent, objective judgments about the relationship of specific parts to the whole, compare one case to others, and prudently determine what is important and possible—and what is not. It has been observed, for example, that one of the qualities that made Otto von Bismarck such a successful statesman was his extraordinary sense of perspective and proportion, which enabled him to discern how specific problems were related to larger issues and to appreciate the range and the limitations of choice among human actors. The study of historical experience is excellent training for developing just such skills. Indeed, it was Bismarck himself who once said that fools learn from their experience, while the wise learn from the experience of others.

The Challenges of Learning and Applying Lessons of History

To emphasize the importance of learning and then applying lessons from history, however, is not the same as actually being able to do it in practice. The fact remains that many challenges confront those who seek to do so. Some of these involve the very process and nature of learning lessons themselves. In the first place, the study of history, although fascinating and often enjoyable, is nevertheless difficult. It is complex and requires the time, effort, and ability to study and to analyze the evidence of intricate human interactions, the particular skills and personalities of people, forces of continuity and change, ideas and beliefs, domestic and foreign influences, the nature of restraints, and the state of technological development, among many, many other factors and variables, and then to reach conclusions about their meaning. Second, as a result of the inherent complexity, there is no such thing as a single, easily understandable *lesson* from history. Instead, history presents many faces and produces a variety of innumerable *lessons*. Third, these various lessons do not necessarily point in a single direction or reach a single conclusion. Indeed, at times they appear to be ambiguous, inconsistent, or even contradictory. Certain cases from historical experience, for example, might indicate that diplomatic compromise serves the best course for preserving peace and security, whereas other cases might suggest that concessions only encourage further demands and aggression by opponents.

A fourth challenge stems from the fact that lessons are often selectively learned and disproportionally recalled, depending on many factors that include different perspectives, different purposes, and the context of learning itself. Preconceived biases, ideology, the psychological propensity to take mental shortcuts or to persist in holding beliefs about the past even in the face of evidence to the contrary, or the level of firsthand participation and associated trauma resulting from particular events can produce very different results. Differences between people (including those between one generation and the next, or between one culture and another) affect how and what they learn. Studies in cognitive psychology, for example, reveal that people have a strong tendency to draw much more frequently and intensely on recent cases and on those they have experienced personally, rather than those from another place or of a more distant past. It is understandable, therefore, why there can be different interpretations, conflicting conclusions, and passionate disagreements (even among historians) about the most appropriate lessons to be learned from particular historical cases.

These problems of learning are further compounded by the further challenge of application, or the realities and processes of policy making and implementation. It often has been said that diplomacy is the art of the possible. All leaders face various kinds of restraints that necessitate trade-offs, as we shall explore in Chapter 12, and even those who have learned lessons from history are not always free to apply all that they may know. The desirable, in other words, is not always feasible. As a consequence, observes Kissinger, "Any statesman is in part the prisoner of necessity." He therefore concludes that all those responsible for statecraft must face "a continual struggle to rescue an element of choice from the pressure of circumstance."

There is another difficulty of applying lessons of history to policy. Studies show that leaders frequently make serious mistakes due either to their ignorance of the range of possible choices based on historical experience or to the related tendency to draw on a lesson from a single historical case. Decision makers often possess a very limited and simplified knowledge of the past, or prepare to fight the last war, or deal with the previous crisis rather than the current one. In doing so, they incorrectly choose a case and misapply a lesson to a new situation that differs from the past in important ways. As historian Ernest May wrote in *"Lessons" of the Past: The Use and Misuse of History in American Foreign Policy*, leaders ordinarily do not take the time or make the effort to seriously study the past or to analyze the full nature of their immediate international crisis or diplomatic challenge. Instead, they resort to analogy and

> tend to seize upon the first one that comes to mind. They do not search more widely. Nor do they pause to analyze the case, test its fitness, or even ask in what ways it might be misleading. Seeing a trend running toward the present, they tend to assume that it will continue into the future, not stopping to consider what produced it or why a linear projection might prove to be mistaken.

May's subsequent study, written with his political science colleague Richard Neustadt under the title *Thinking in Time: The Uses of History for Decision Makers*, explores this problem even further. They observe that, all too often, leaders are seduced by simple and inappropriate analogies that make little or no effort to separate the *known* from the *unclear* and the *presumed,* or to seriously compare the *likenesses* with the *differences* or the continuities with the changes between cases in history and those of the present.

The enormous dangers created for peace and security by this overly simplistic and careless approach have attracted the attention of other scholars as well. Among these are political scientist Yuen Khong's study employing insights from social psychology, entitled *Analogies at War,* and, most recently, security studies specialist Jeffrey Record's *Making War, Thinking History: Munich, Vietnam, and Presidential Uses of Force from Korea to Kosovo.* They reveal how American leaders often have made choices about whether or how to use force in statecraft based on seriously oversimplified and inappropriate analogies and, therefore, misapplied lessons of history. Time and time again, Truman, Kennedy, Johnson, Reagan, the senior Bush, and Clinton chose one of only two analogies that they thought they knew best. One of these was "Munich," referring to the Munich Conference of 1938 and its role in bringing about the Second World War, which they believed taught that appeasement only encouraged aggression, that armed force was necessary, and that there should be "no more Munichs." Or, they used "Vietnam," which they believed taught the dangers of armed force without clearly defined missions and sufficient domestic support and that there should be "no more Vietnams."

One of the most frequently misapplied historical analogies has been that of Munich. Reasoned compromise always had been part of classical diplomacy as a means of finding common ground and lowering or even eliminating the possibility of war. But the failed attempt to accommodate Adolf Hitler and his aggressive designs was subsequently etched into the consciousness of several generations of policy makers and foreign policy specialists, who often interpreted the experience as demonstrating the need to always avoid even talking to adversaries, being lulled by negotiation, and to immediately and directly meet force with force. Although President Harry Truman wrote in his memoirs about his love of history, his historical knowledge was sketchy and his range narrow, and he perceived that North Korean aggression in 1950 was "just like" Nazi expansion during the 1930s, wherein aggression unchecked led to aggression unleashed. Rather than trying to determine under what conditions appeasement might constitute a viable strategy for avoiding war and under what conditions it might dangerously increase the likelihood of a worse war in the future, his impulsive fixation on what he regarded as a completely analogous situation to Hitler's aggressive expansion led him to send troops into Korea and to vastly extend the American Cold War strategy of Containment from Europe to Asia. British Prime Minister Anthony Eden used the same analogy during the Suez Crisis of 1956, arguing that Egyptian President Gamal Nassar was "the same as" Hitler and that if action were not taken in response to his seizure of the Suez Canal, it would be "just like" the occupation of the Rhineland and would be followed by acts of aggression against all of his other neighbors. George

Bush the elder invoked the analogy of Hitler and Munich when dealing with Saddam Hussein during the Persian Gulf Crisis of 1990–1991, as did Bill Clinton when confronting Slobodan Milosevic at the time of the Kosovo Crisis of 1999. More recently, and even though the cases were vastly different, when U.S. Secretary of Defense Donald Rumsfeld addressed Asian leaders in Singapore during 2004, he warned them that any efforts to make deals with terrorists would only be "repeating the mistakes of the nations that tried to appease Adolf Hitler in the 1930s."

Although these misuses of historical analogy often appear to be the norm rather than the exception, there are occasional successes. Among these, the thoughtful deliberations and high quality of analysis demonstrated by the Kennedy administration during the intense Cuban Missile Crisis come to mind. When intelligence sources suddenly revealed that the Soviet Union was secretly placing missiles in Cuba, the president and his advisors seriously debated and agonized about how they should respond. The records of their meetings indicate that, as a group, they were remarkably familiar with history and drew not on one, but a range of historical cases during their deliberations. They spoke about the outbreak of First World War in 1914, Franklin Roosevelt's "Quarantine Address" of 1937, the unfulfilled British and French deterrence guarantees to Poland in 1939, the Japanese attack of 1941, the Berlin Crisis of 1948, the Suez and Hungarian crises of 1956, and the decision to place American missiles in Turkey during 1957, among others. As Robert Kennedy records in his memoir of the crisis, *Thirteen Days*, the president's knowledge of history played a decisive role in his actual decisions. When the suggestion was made for a surprise military attack against Cuba, for example, it was met with rejection on the grounds that America could not possibly maintain a strong moral position at home or abroad if it became responsible for "another Pearl Harbor." As John Kennedy watched the crisis escalate and the knot of conflict being pulled tighter and tighter, he similarly considered lessons from the disastrous mismanagement by leaders in 1914 who seized upon preexisting war plans, refused to create pauses or employ diplomatic alternatives, and issued demands to opponents without thinking of the consequences. He had recently finished reading Barbara Tuchman's *Guns of August* and said to his brother Robert, "I am not going to follow a course which will allow anyone to write a comparable book about this time, *The Missiles of October*. If anyone is around to write after this, they are going to understand that we made every effort to find peace and every effort to give our adversary room to move."

This kind of reasoning by historical analogy is common, and the analogies selected matter. Sometimes they matter a great deal, particularly in the selection and rejection of policy options. Hard-pressed leaders under stress in the complex and uncertain environment of international politics quite naturally seek a mechanism or framework that will help them cope by interpreting where they and the problem confronting them fit into some comprehensible and meaningful context or pattern. As they try to process incoming information and engage in decision-making tasks, they look for guidance as to what should or should not be done and assume that the future in some way will resemble the past. Indeed, according to political scientist Yaacov Vertzberger in his stimulating book *The World in Their Minds: Information Processing, Cognition, and Perception in Foreign Policy Decisionmaking*, it is not only natural but essential that policy makers responsible for major decisions—especially those dealing with force and statecraft—attempt to use analogies from previous experiences in history. When used critically, they help in the management and resolution of complexity and uncertainty by providing information as well as a diagnostic framework that offers a sense about the nature of the problem at hand and the issues at stake, concrete examples and illustrations, possible direction, and a sense of the dangers and prospects of alternatives that might otherwise be completely overlooked.

But, as he and other writers, like political scientist Robert Jervis in *Perception and Misperception,* observe, if the reasoning is unsound, this process can be notoriously inadequate and even hazardous. Some leaders possess detailed knowledge and a considerable database of history, while others have only a rudimentary sense of the past and a superficial awareness of a very small number of cases. Some are capable of perceiving and comprehending historical perspective and making sophisticated judgments on the basis of evidence, while others clearly are not. Moreover, no event or situation is ever exactly the same in detail as another. Conditions change, and sometimes they change dramatically. It is risky, therefore, to assume that a particular outcome can be predicted with exactitude or that a past event can be quickly grasped as an accurate model for a present one. These dangers become particularly acute if policy makers draw hasty and unwarranted conclusions with little scrutiny from a sample of only one: a single and narrowly drawn case that most quickly comes to mind, that belittles significant contextual differences, that tends to confirm their own preconceived biases and preferred policies, and that gives them an illusory sense of "knowing" history. In order to address this problem, it is critical to seek a much broader range of historical experiences and cases on which one might draw and then to analyze and synthesize them in such a way as to develop a greater understanding of international systems and their actors as they confront the challenges of force and statecraft.

STRUCTURED, FOCUSED COMPARISONS

If it is hazardous for policy makers to rely, as they sometimes do, upon a single historical analogy in deciding what to do in practice, how then can experience from the past be utilized to deal effectively with a new situation that appears to bear a certain resemblance to previous cases but at the same time possesses some different features? The answer lies in developing a broad historical habit of mind, expanding the range of cases from history to be examined, and then carefully and systematically focusing on a phenomenon or problem that is repeatedly encountered in the conduct of statecraft over time. By comparing a particular strategy under different circumstances, with different actors and in different settings, one can identify more closely the conditions under which it is likely to succeed or fail. This, in turn, can lead to an identification and articulation of certain conditional generalizations, or lessons, regarding the efficacy of certain strategies or instruments of diplomacy. Without such an approach, whatever lessons from the past that one might learn are acquired completely at random and are often misapplied if not appropriate to fit particular circumstances.

In Part Two of this book, we seek to demonstrate more specifically how lessons of history can be combined with theory and used to gain knowledge for statecraft. To do this, we indicate how individual historical cases of a particular problem can be systematically studied and analyzed within a well-defined framework that enables a comparison and cumulation of results in order to develop a more sophisticated appreciation of its uses and limitations. More specifically, we explore the extremely important, instructive, and recurring phenomena of negotiation, deterrence, coercive diplomacy, and crisis management. In each chapter, we analyze the nature of one of these strategies, the issues and problems that are likely to arise in attempting to implement it, as well as the conditions or causal mechanisms derived from historical cases that either favor success or contribute to failure.

The method that we have developed for this purpose is that of structured, focused comparison. Our many students over the years and readers of previous editions have told us that they have found this approach to be especially helpful in providing an analytical framework to study history, articulate principles and concepts of theory, identify critical variables, and develop diagnostic skills in making judgments about the uses and limitations of particular strategies and the conditions on which their effective use depends. This methodology requires careful specification of the strategy to be studied, selection of historical cases in which it was employed, the variables of interest, and analysis of why it succeeded or failed in those cases. It also requires that a systematic research protocol and structural format of analysis be developed, specifying the same set of issues to be addressed and the same questions to be asked of each case, thus providing a close and careful comparison of case explanations in such a way that they can be cumulated for broader knowledge.

1. Theory. Toward this end, each chapter in this section begins with an explicit delineation of a general theory or conceptual model that addresses a particular diplomatic challenge. These theories or models are constructed of basic principles that tell us much about the logic and intended purposes of policy. Although the theories are not strategies themselves, they do serve as valuable starting points for understanding and constructing them. Strategies derived from conceptual models tell us what must be done in general to achieve the desired objectives. But to actually do this in specific cases, the principles must be analyzed within a framework of *strategy variants* tailored to fit the situation at hand and likely to influence a particular actor. Thus, for example, while there is only one basic theory or model of deterrence or coercive diplomacy, there are a number of different strategies for each. The effectiveness of each, however, is highly *context dependent*; that is, the outcomes are influenced by many variables, the interactions between them, and especially the abilities of those people who try to apply them. The choices of strategy variants consequently encounter considerable uncertainty when dealing with the dilemmas of using force or threats of force as instruments of statecraft. This challenge is well understood by experienced policy makers and analysts. As George Bush the elder once observed, careful judgments have to be made about

> when the stakes warrant, where and when force can be effective, where no other policies are likely to be effective, when its application can be limited in scope and time, and where the potential benefits justify the potential costs and sacrifice. There can be no single or simple set of fixed rules for using force....

2. Case Studies. To demonstrate the critical importance of context, and thereby avoid the limitations and hazards of mere abstractions, each chapter then presents three specific historical case studies of each theory or conceptual model. Each empirically based case is selected for its intrinsic interest, its capacity to link theory with practice, and its insights that might assist in the elaboration, testing, and development of lessons and more differentiated theory. The first historical case is drawn from the classical system of diplomacy during the nineteenth century. The second comes from the twentieth century. The third is a more recent case, taken from contemporary international affairs. We spread and compare the three cases in this way in order to provide evidence of how a given strategy was and is affected by both the continuities and the changes in the diplomatic revolution that constitutes a major theme of this book as a whole.

3. Analysis. These three cases are then subjected to an analysis. Here, a *standard set of questions* is asked of each of these historical cases. Such a controlled procedure or protocol makes it possible to actually compare evidence in a systematic way in order to refine an understanding of when, judging from past experience, this strategy is or is not likely to be viable and how best to implement it. This results in the formulation of guides for thinking and conditional generalizations, which are not designed to be "decision rules" but rather tools for diagnosing the nature of the problem and then determining what choices might be available and whether favoring conditions are present. In diplomacy, as in medical practice, accurate diagnosis must precede a determination for the best course of treatment in trying to solve a problem. Each analysis also includes concluding observations that summarize the major findings, draw on additional research, and reiterate how the case studies can help us learn lessons of history and thereby contribute to knowledge required for statecraft.

SUGGESTIONS FOR FURTHER EXPLORATION

Among the many classic writers who stress the importance of learning lessons from history, one should consult Thucydides, *The Peloponnesian War*; and its most recent analysis in Donald Kagan, *Thucydides: The Reinvention of History* (New York, 2010); Niccolò Machiavelli, *The Prince* and *Discourses*; Hugo Grotius, *On the Law of War and Peace*; François de Callières, *On the Manner of Negotiating with Princes*; and Carl von Clausewitz, *On War*; which are available in many modern translations and editions. On Henry Kissinger's efforts to find and use historical lessons, see his own *Diplomacy* (New York, 1995), *The White House Years* (New York, 1979), and *A World Restored* (New York, 1973 ed.); the observations of John Lewis Gaddis, "Rescuing Choice from Circumstance: The Statecraft of Henry Kissinger," in Gordon A. Craig and Francis Loewenheim (eds.), *The Diplomats, 1939–1979* (Princeton, 1994); and Peter Dickson, *Kissinger and the Meaning of History* (New York, 1978). See also Klaus Knorr (ed.), *Historical Dimensions of National Security Problems* (Lawrence, KS, 1976); and the perspectives provided in the journals *Diplomacy and Statecraft* and *Diplomatic History*.

Discussions about the historical habit of mind can be found in Gordon A. Craig, "The Historian and the Study of International Relations," *American Historical Review*, 88 (February 1983): 1–11; Paul Gordon Lauren, "Diplomacy: History, Theory, and Policy," Gordon A. Craig, "On the Nature of Diplomatic History: The Relevance of Some Old Books," and Samuel F. Wells, Jr., "History and Policy," all in Paul Gordon Lauren (ed.), *Diplomacy: New Approaches in History, Theory, and Policy* (New York, 1979); David Trask, "A Reflection on Historians and Policy Makers," a speech released by the U.S. Department of State in 1976; Barbara Tuchman, "The Historian's Opportunity," *Saturday Review* (February 1967): 27–31; Gordon A. Craig, *From Bismarck to Adenauer: Aspects of German Statecraft* (New York, 1965 ed.); and D. P. Heatley, *Diplomacy and the Study of International Relations* (Oxford, 1919).

Insightful and thought-provoking treatments about the challenges of learning and then applying lessons of history can be found in a number of studies, including Dan Caldwell, *Vortex of Conflict* (Stanford, 2011), especially Chapter 14, "Lessons and Legacies"; Margaret MacMillan, *Dangerous Games: The Uses and Abuses of History* (New York, 2009); Jonathan Stevenson, *Learning from the Cold War* (New York, 2009 ed.); Minxin Pei and Sara Kasper, Carnegie Endowment Policy Brief 24 (May 2003), "Lessons from the Past: The American Record on Nation Building"; Jeffrey Record, *Making War, Thinking History: Munich, Vietnam, and Presidential Uses of Force from Korea to Kosovo* (Annapolis, 2002); John Lewis Gaddis, *The Landscape of History* (New York, 2002); Stephen Rock, *Appeasement in International Politics* (Lexington, KY, 2000); Russell Leng, *Bargaining and Learning in Recurring Crises* (Ann Arbor, 2000); Jack Levy, "Learning from Experience in U.S. and Soviet Foreign Policy," in Manus Midlarsky et al. (eds.), *From Rivalry to Cooperation* (New York, 1994); William Jarosz with Joseph Nye, Jr., "The Shadow of the Past: Learning from History in National Security Decision Making," in Philip Tetlock et al. (eds.), *Behavior, Society, and International Conflict* (New York, 1993), pp. 126–189; Yuen Khong, *Analogies at War* (Princeton, 1992); Michael Howard, *The Lessons of History* (New Haven, 1991); Marc Trachtenberg, *History and Strategy* (Princeton, 1991); Yaacov Vertzberger, *The World in Their Minds* (Stanford, 1990); Richard Neustadt and Ernest R. May, *Thinking in Time: The Uses of History for Decision-Makers* (New York, 1986); Robert Jervis, *Perception and Misperception in International Politics* (Princeton, 1976); Ernest R. May, *Lessons of the Past: The Use and Misuse of History in American Foreign Policy* (New York, 1973); Will and Ariel Durant, *The Lessons of History* (New York, 1968); and Francis Loewenheim (ed.), *The Historian and the Diplomat* (New York, 1967).

The methodology of structured, focused comparisons is most clearly articulated in Alexander L. George, "Case Studies and Theory Development," in Paul Gordon Lauren (ed.), *Diplomacy: New Approaches in History, Theory, and Policy* (New York, 1979). Greater elaboration of the broader issue of converting lessons of history into a more comprehensive, differentiated theory and the diagnostic use of theory and knowledge for policy making is discussed in Alexander L. George and Andrew Bennett, *Case Studies and Theory Development in the Social Sciences* (Cambridge, MA, 2004); Joseph Lepgold and Miroslav Nincic, *Beyond the Ivory Tower* (New York, 2001); and Alexander L. George, *Bridging the Gap: Theory and Practice in Foreign Policy* (Washington, DC, 1993).

8

Negotiation

"The art of negotiation," wrote François de Callières in the very first words of his classic *On the Manner of Negotiating with Princes*, "is so important that the fate of the greatest states often depends upon the good or bad conduct of negotiations and upon the degree of capacity in the negotiators themselves." A "single word or act" in high-stakes negotiation, he emphasized, "may do more than the invasion of whole armies."

His insight has provided guidance to statesmen from the early eighteenth century, when it was first written, to the present. It certainly influenced those who guided the complex diplomatic negotiations that took place over the course of five years from 1958 to 1963 dealing with nuclear testing. By this time, the unimpeded arms race and the development of intercontinental ballistic missiles had made the possibility of mutual annihilation through nuclear war a reality. The Americans, the Soviets, and the British began to understand all too well that the fallout from their atmospheric tests dangerously elevated the level of the radioactive isotope, Strontium 90, contaminating the earth and entering the food chain, becoming especially concentrated in milk. This set off considerable alarm about the health and safety of the planet and its inhabitants. Although these three states recognized that they had a common interest in addressing this problem, they all feared falling behind if they halted their own testing program while the others continued. In an attempt to resolve their mutual dilemma over the advantages and disadvantages of testing or not testing, the parties engaged in what political scientist P. Terrence Hopmann describes as "one of the most important negotiations of the second half of the twentieth century." Despite considerable political and bureaucratic resistance at home to any restrictions at all and enormous external disruptions caused by the shooting down of the American U-2 spy plane by the Soviet Union in 1960, the Berlin Crisis of 1961, and the Cuban Missile Crisis of 1962, the negotiators persisted. Finally, their long and difficult labors resulted in the watershed 1963 Limited Test Ban Treaty, allowing nuclear tests underground, but prohibiting all those in the atmosphere, underwater, and in outer space. This agreement not only demonstrated the capacity of states to negotiate as partners in the midst of intense domestic opposition and international crises over profound issues of life and death, but marked the first breakthrough to slow the arms race with self-imposed restraints, the first arms control agreement between the Cold War rivals, and a major turning point in American-Soviet diplomatic relations as a whole.

Negotiation, as this case clearly illustrates, lies at the very core of diplomacy and provides one of the indispensable tools of statecraft. Indeed, from the earliest evolution of diplomatic practice to our own time, as we saw in Part One, negotiations have profoundly shaped history, confirming that armed conflict is not an inevitable outcome when interests clash. They characterize the way in which actors collectively seek to solve their common problems, promote mutual interests, and regulate their patterns of rivalry and partnership with one another. By offering an alternative to the use of force and violence, negotiations provide the means by which parties can coordinate their activities and develop mutually acceptable agreements. They are both promoters and products of stability within an international system and cooperative relations among its members. As Cardinal Richelieu once wrote in a celebrated passage:

> States receive so much benefit from continuous foreign negotiations…that it is unbelievable….I am now so convinced of its validity that I dare say emphatically that it is absolutely necessary to the well-being of the state to *negotiate ceaselessly, either openly or secretly, and in all places….*

Diplomatic negotiations thus have been—and remain, especially today when the destructive power of modern weapons of mass destruction makes the resort to military force a highly dangerous option—the primary means for resolving conflicts by peaceful means. It is precisely for this reason that the *Oxford English Dictionary* actually defines diplomacy itself as "the conduct of international relations by negotiation."

PRINCIPLES OF NEGOTIATION

Negotiation and bargaining are closely related concepts. There are elements of each in the other, and on occasion they semantically are used interchangeably. Both negotiation and bargaining involve an *interaction* and *interdependence* among actors, each seeking an outcome that will benefit its own interests, but nevertheless confronting a situation in which the positions and behavior of one influence the expectations, interpretations, counter-positions, and reactions of the other. In this dynamic, the actors consequently—and paradoxically—become both *rivals* and *partners* at the same time and are joined into what has been called an "adverse partnership." Despite this similarity, however, it is useful to distinguish the differences between the two.

Bargaining in statecraft is normally regarded as a *contest* in which each side attempts to maximize its own gains at the expense of the other. It involves manipulating or influencing an adversary's behavior by a freewheeling exchange of verbal and nonverbal communication, threats and counterthreats, and demonstrations of power and military might, designed to make the other back down or capitulate. Here the emphasis is on rivalry, competition, the conflicting issues that divide the antagonists, taking and holding firmly to fixed positions, and developing strategies to defeat an opponent. The greater the distance between the interests and positions of the parties, the more serious will be the extent of bargaining, or what strategic theorist Thomas Schelling describes as the threat or use of armed force to manipulate the behavior of others through "arms and influence" and "the diplomacy of violence," as we shall see in Chapter 9 on deterrence and Chapter 10 on coercive diplomacy.

Negotiation, by way of contrast, is the term usually employed to describe *more formal discussions and structured procedures for collaborative problem solving*. It is normally characterized by explicit agendas, exchanged proposals, face-to-face meetings between representatives in agreed-upon settings of time and place, established rules of accommodation, and sometimes lengthy deliberations. Here there is a recognition of conflict, but a much greater emphasis is placed on partnership and an appreciation of the fact the parties have a *shared* risk, a *mutual* desire to avoid the consequences of an enforced threat, and a *common* interest in solving problems. A premium is thus placed on joint, rather than unilateral, action and finding a win-win solution. For these reasons, political scientist Fred Iklé succinctly observes in his book *How Nations Negotiate*, "two elements must normally be present for negotiation to take place: there must be both common interests and issues of conflict. Without common interests there is nothing to negotiate for; without conflict there is nothing to negotiate about."

With this perceptive observation in mind, it is helpful to try to discern why some negotiations succeed and why others fail. Historical evidence and experience, as well as considerable research on the nature of negotiation, suggest that several important factors or conditions play vital roles.

1. Shared Interest in an Agreement. One of these conditions is a shared interest in reaching an agreement. Both sides (in cases of bilateral negotiations) or all sides (in cases of multilateral negotiations) must recognize that they share a common problem, admit the other's claim to participate in finding a diplomatic resolution, and agree that the issue of conflict between them is not so intractable as to prevent a genuine possibility of together forging a satisfactory solution. That is, they perceive that whatever it is that divides them, cooperation and joint problem solving is in their best interest and is possible. Traditionally, and at its best, this has entailed the desire and the will among parties to accept certain rules of accommodation and enter into negotiations in good faith to try to reach a mutually acceptable, formal agreement that serves their interests.

2. Resistance Points. Another important condition for negotiating success is the ability to ascertain and address each other's resistance points. In negotiating over an issue of conflict, parties typically possess both maximum and minimum demands. At one end of the spectrum are their preferred outcomes, or all the things they ideally would like to obtain. These can be seen in the familiar practice of parties in negotiations initially asking for more than they ever expect to get. At the other end is the minimum for which, at least at the beginning of negotiations, they are willing to settle, the bottom line beyond which they expect to make no further concessions. This is frequently described as the *resistance point*. Reliable information about each side's resistance point and the set of interests, concerns, and attitudes that lies behind it, as one might imagine, is not always easily or quickly obtained. There may be a significant difference between a negotiator's "declared" and "real" resistance points, for example, and negotiators generally are very reluctant to reveal their minimal demands unless and until they are convinced that others are prepared to do the same. These factors emphasize the importance of patience in negotiations until some level of trust and a spirit of reciprocity and partnership can be established.

Once the respective resistance points can be more clearly ascertained, the negotiators are in a position to better assess the significance of the gap between their minimum demands and those of the other side, and thereby determine how far apart they are from an agreement and whether there is space for negotiation. At this point, the negotiators must make a judgment about the value of agreement versus the value of no agreement, or what scholars Roger Fisher and William Ury describe in their book *Getting to Yes* as the *best alternative to a negotiated agreement* (now known in the vocabulary of negotiation by its acronym, BATNA). An agreement will be acceptable only if it produces a better result than each party could obtain in the absence of an agreement. With this in mind, the negotiators may conclude that the distance between their resistance points is simply too great, that it is better to have no agreement than a poor one, that they have reached a stalemate, and, consequently, that it is useless to continue the negotiations at all. On the other hand, they may conclude that the other's minimal requirements may be weakened or changed, or that there are ways of satisfying the other's irreducible demands without seriously jeopardizing one's own interests. Most important, they believe that somewhere between their respective resistance points, as the figure below suggests, there exists a "settlement range" that would provide mutual benefits.

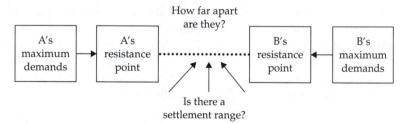

3. Settlement Range. The shared interests and objectives among the parties to any negotiation are best discovered in that area between the resistance points known as the *settlement range*. It is in this space where the possibilities of partnership become most clearly evident and where negotiators seek some degree of convergence of their interests in reaching an agreement. The possibilities of finding settlement, of course, generally are easier in bilateral negotiations when there are only two parties involved, as compared to highly complex multilateral negotiations in which there may be many actors, each with their own interests, preferred outcomes, initial maximum demands, and resistance points, and, therefore, a wide variety of possible coalitions and combinations. Moreover, in multilateral negotiations it may take all to say yes, but only one to say no. On occasion, an impasse may be bridged and the scope for a settlement increased if one party can strengthen the other's perception of their broader common interests, thus causing it to modify its minimum demands. This sometimes is attempted by means of the strategy of *linkage*, whereby one side encourages the other to be more conciliatory by persuading it that, depending on how the current dispute is resolved, it stands to benefit or suffer in other areas. The final agreement may be a comprehensive settlement dealing with many issues, or it may be a settlement dealing with more narrowly focused matters. In all cases, however, the parties secure benefits that they would not have been able to obtain on their own by peaceful means without negotiation.

4. Shared Benefits. For this reason, negotiations will not succeed unless there is a perception of shared benefits. Shared interests and objectives are in large part a function of whether the participants believe that an agreement will serve their fundamental interests and bring them some advantage that they otherwise would not be able to secure on their own or at a risk or prohibitive price. They each may secure gains in different ways and at different levels, depending on their respective interests and asymmetries of power, influence, and alternatives—but they must benefit in one way or another. This is why de Callières wisely advised that "the great secret of negotiation is to bring out prominently the common advantage to both parties." Any agreement that did not satisfy this condition, he warned, "is apt to contain the seeds of its own dissolution."

Such mutual benefits may take a variety of forms. Some of these include *extension agreements* designed to provide a formal ratification and continuation of existing arrangements, such as extending tariff agreements, renewing an alliance, or reaffirming access to overseas bases. Some may be *normalization agreements* devised to terminate an abnormal or dangerous situation, such as reestablishing diplomatic relations, ending a trade war, or putting a ceasefire into effect. Others may be *redistribution agreements* that change territorial boundaries or divide market shares. Still others may be *innovation agreements* that set up new arrangements or undertakings that benefit the parties, such as the creation of NATO or the International Criminal Court. The types of agreements, as well as the contexts of the negotiating process, may differ, depending on which kind of shared benefits are being sought.

5. Skilled Negotiators. The final factor necessary for successful negotiations, of course, is the human dimension of skilled negotiators. None of the factors or conditions described thus far automatically exists or operates on its own, but must be interpreted, shaped, and mobilized by people who possess the requisite skills for the art and the science of negotiation. As Victor Kremenyuk writes in *International Negotiation*, "The center of gravity in this process of negotiation is the negotiator." This explains why writers from de Callières to contemporaries like Michael Watkins and Susan Rosegrant in their recent book, *Breakthrough International Negotiation: How Great Negotiators Transformed the World's Toughest Post-Cold War Conflicts*, despite their individual approaches, all stress that negotiation requires certain kinds of skills.

Among these are the abilities to correctly diagnose the structure of the negotiating situation, evaluate the parties and their interests, establish clear procedures and assess the agenda, analyze the complexities, identify and try to minimize the barriers to agreement, ascertain and address the respective resistance points, determine the value of the best alternatives to a negotiated agreement, and, above all, to understand that the process of negotiation is both dynamic and interactive. Others include the capability to actually shape the negotiation process itself, offer incentives when possible, maintain flexibility on means and firmness on goals, build and sustain momentum, focus on larger principles rather than personalities, foster productive working relationships with other negotiators, and find or create a viable settlement range. Still others entail the ability, as we shall explore in Chapter 11, to practice crisis management, avoid escalation, and defuse tensions. In the process of developing these skills, virtually all writers on negotiation agree on the importance of understanding previous case studies, analyzing why negotiators in the past either succeeded or failed, and learning lessons from history.

These principles apply, in one degree or another, to all cases of international negotiation. The negotiations themselves may range widely over many different subjects, depending on the interests of the actors and the problems they face within their particular historical context. Among some of the most challenging, serious, and far-reaching negotiations are those that seek to establish restraints on force and statecraft. As the eighteenth-century French writer Fortuné Barthélemy de Felice observed: "Without negotiation, armed force is an instrument that is both too fragile and too hard that will break in the hands of the one who employs it." It is thus to this matter that we now turn.

The Congress of Vienna, 1814–1815

One of the most famous of all cases of international negotiation occurred with the Congress of Vienna. The leaders of the Great Powers clearly realized that just as their military victory over Napoleon and his vast empire, which threatened them all, had been made possible only by close collaboration, so too peace and security would be completely dependent on their ability to cooperate with one another. They understood, as we saw in Chapter 2, that all of them (including the defeated country of France) shared a vital interest in reaching mutually acceptable agreements on how best to create and maintain a viable international system that could regulate their patterns of conflict and cooperation with each other. For this reason, they all agreed to organize a diplomatic conference that would enable them to participate together in formal, collective negotiations over their respective interests and positions. As Prussian Ambassador Wilhelm von Humboldt, who largely devised the agenda and procedures, wrote:

> The Plenipotentiaries of all the Princes and States that in some way or the other took part in the War were summoned to the same place. In this way, the risk of State-to-State negotiations producing dangerous misunderstandings can be avoided. It is also ensured that the arrangements that come out of the negotiations are not contrary to the general interest and also that they be provided with more force through general sanction or at least common recognition. Finally, it will be possible to agree on some general arrangements contributing to the peace and well-being of Europe.

To accomplish these challenging tasks, the Great Powers sent an unusually gifted and far-sighted group of negotiators to Vienna from September 1814 to June 1815. Chief among them was the host of the congress, Prince Clements von Metternich, a man who had become the Austrian foreign minister in 1806 at the age of thirty-six and continued to serve in that position until 1848, a term unequaled by any other European diplomat and one indicative of the uncommon talents that he possessed. Far from being narrow in his perspectives, he looked at the international system as a whole, believing that the conflicting interests of states should be reconciled for the common sake of general peace and stability, and showed a genius in conducting negotiations that made such reconciliation possible. He was joined in this broad outlook by the leading British delegate, Foreign Secretary Viscount Robert Castlereagh, who desired to create an equilibrium, or balance of power, in which all states played their appropriate role. Prince Charles Maurice Talleyrand-Périgord served as the chief representative of France, believing that his own country's best interests would be served by recognizing the legitimate interests of others and by maintaining relations with them on the basis of reciprocal respect. Prince Karl von Hardenberg, who as chancellor and foreign minister headed the Prussian delegation, was joined by the Russian Foreign Minister Count Karl Robert Nesselrode. Both possessed impressive negotiating skills, but constantly had to contend with the volatility of their sovereigns, Frederick William III and Alexander I, who insisted on coming to Vienna.

Even though these delegates all shared a mutual interest in reaching an agreement, each started off with extensive demands that established serious distances between their positions. Indeed, even before they formally assembled, they began to assert all the things they wanted to obtain. Each of the Great Powers insisted on securing territorial acquisitions that would benefit them the most. In some cases, the demands of one conflicted directly with the demands of others who wanted the same real estate for themselves. Major differences emerged over the practical meanings of "just equilibrium" and "order," over the nature and political orientation of new or reconstituted governments, and over the agenda and organization of the negotiations themselves. Indeed, an indication of the degree of tension and distance between the initial resistance points appeared so great at one stage that three of them created an alliance against the other two, the powers readied their armies, and a renewal of war itself seemed highly likely. The Russians made the mistake (repeated by other historical as well as contemporary negotiators) of assuming that military might alone would be sufficient for them to get their way. As one of their generals arrogantly boasted: "One does not need to worry much about negotiations when one has 600,000 men under arms."

Despite such attitudes and differences, after several months of negotiations the parties began to reach a clearer understanding of their own genuine interests and to ascertain more accurately each others' actual resistance points. Although many of the difficulties already had been resolved during their deliberations, the process certainly was enhanced when Napoleon shockingly escaped from his imprisonment on Elba at the end of February and was not defeated at Waterloo until June. This experience forced them to be reminded of their shared interest in reaching an agreement and to realize that they could create a settlement range in which their respective interests might be successfully accommodated. In this regard, the negotiators came to learn that such a range could be increased if they paid less attention to specific details or annoying personalities and focused instead on larger principles of settlement. These included "compensation" (for costs incurred in the effort to defeat Napoleon), "legitimacy" (respect for the prerogatives of pre-Napoleonic rulers and the restoration of their thrones), and "balance of power" (an equilibrium of armed force between the Great Powers so as to deter unilateral aggression on the part of any of them). Yet another principle emerged as well, and this was one of ethics and human rights, for they all agreed to recognize religious toleration and to condemn the international slave trade as "repugnant to the principles of humanity and universal morality."

Once they created the range of settlement, the negotiators then could proceed to create the actual terms of formal agreements that would provide all the Great Powers with specific benefits. Britain gained Heligoland in the North Sea, Malta in the Mediterranean, Cape Colony in South Africa, Ceylon in the Indian Ocean, and several islands in the Caribbean. Austria obtained possessions on the Italian peninsula, along the eastern coast of the Adriatic Sea, and in Poland. Prussia secured almost half of Saxony, parts of Poland, and extensive holdings in the Rhineland. Russia received Finland, vast Polish provinces, and land along the Black Sea formerly belonging to the Ottoman Turks. And, although they imposed a war indemnity, they remarkably allowed France to restore the Bourbon monarchy and to keep most of its original territory.

These individual gains were enhanced by the larger benefit to them all of securing a balance of power and what the negotiators hoped would be an international system based on compromise and consent, bringing them peace and security after years of nearly continuous and convulsive war. In this regard, they were extremely mindful of issues of force and statecraft. They agreed to a combination of significant reductions in the size of their standing armies, mutual restraints, and the inclusion of specific military provisions within their final settlement. This included creating buffer zones and neutralizing those areas most likely to provoke competition among themselves. Fearing that French, Prussian, and Austrian rivalries might all intersect at the common point between them and explode, for example, they promised to guarantee the neutrality of Switzerland. Similarly, to prevent rival claims of the Russians, Prussians, and Austrians that converged precisely at Cracow from the danger of escalating into war, they agreed to demilitarize the city and its surrounding territory by pledging that "no armed force shall be introduced upon any pretense whatever." Around France, however, the negotiators wanted to station troops or to have them close by. They thus positioned the armies of the Dutch and the Prussians along its northern borders and stationed the armed forces of Austria and the Royal Navy of Britain not far away, should they become necessary. In the Second Peace of Paris of November 1815 they agreed to deprive France of several strategic fortresses in the north and east and to maintain an army of occupation for three to five years, depending on the country's progress in the reestablishment of order and tranquility. At the same time, in the Quadruple Alliance they agreed to constitute themselves as the Concert of Europe and hold diplomatic conferences "for the purpose of consulting upon their common interests" and, as we shall explore more fully in the next chapter, to use their armed forces as a deterrent for collective security to enforce their negotiated settlement. Now, for the first time in a quarter century, statesmen could turn their attention to problems of peace rather than preparations for war.

The Conference on Security and Cooperation in Europe, 1972–1975

For students of negotiation, the landmark Conference on Security and Cooperation in Europe (CSCE) stands out as one of the most intricate, innovative, and interesting cases in modern diplomacy. It emerged at the time of *détente* as a result of the dissatisfaction generated by the failure to hold a general peace conference following the Second World War and the dangerous tensions created by the division of Europe during the Cold War, as we saw in Chapter 5. In seeking to address a number of the resulting security issues through negotiation, however, the conference actually set into motion forces that would grow to be of revolutionary importance.

The negotiating marathon began in November 1972 after the government of Finland invited several states to participate in preparatory talks about principles and procedures for a wide-ranging security conference. It took them months to reach any agreement; but once they did, it paved the way for the foreign ministers of the participating nations to meet in Helsinki during July 1973 to launch CSCE. They understood that this would mark the first postwar gathering of all of the states of Europe (except for Albania, which chose not to attend), the United States, and Canada; the first meeting of the two military alliances of NATO and the Warsaw Pact, along with the neutral and nonaligned states; the first time for both Germanies to openly and jointly take part in an international conference; and the first time among these participants, both large and small, that each would have an equal vote in the negotiations. As the Finnish President Urho Kekkonen observed: "This is no meeting of the victors of war; nor is it a meeting of the Great Powers. Our Conference is the common endeavor of all concerned governments on the basis of mutual respect and equality to reach solutions on vital questions concerning all of us."

With these thoughts very much on their minds, thirty-five separate delegations gathered together in Geneva to formally and officially conduct serious and substantive negotiations from September 1973 to July 1975. Given this long period of time, the need to have widespread collaboration among so many participants, the rotation of committee chairs, and the impact of numerous government agencies, along with changing domestic politics, there was little opportunity for a single individual negotiator to stand out in name or reputation above the rest. The tasks at hand, however, required extraordinary levels of negotiating skills. For this reason, all delegations (with the single exception of the United States, which eventually was pressured to change) arrived headed by diplomats of ambassadorial rank.

The delegations at CSCE hoped to reach an agreement that would improve security and cooperation in Europe, but they all initially wanted something very different. One observer described them as "a pack of dogs warily circling and sniffing at one another." The Soviets, who had pushed for such a conference for years and attached great significance to it, demanded that the negotiations be confined only to borders, insisting that official recognition be accorded to the territorial and political order that they had imposed by the force of arms on Eastern Europe at the end of the Second World War. For their part, the Communist governments of Eastern Europe wanted to gain legitimization as normal members of the international community, guarantees of nonintervention (their historical memories of the Soviet invasions of Hungary in 1956 and Czechoslovakia in 1968 remained strong), and access to Western technological advances and economic opportunities. The Western Europeans who were members of NATO and the European Communities—and under pressure from human rights nongovernmental organizations (NGOs)—declared that their most important objective was to bring about peaceful change by means of greater freedom, and thus insisted that security could not be considered without respecting justice and human rights. Neutral and nonaligned countries such as Austria, Finland, and Switzerland, among others, also took a firm stand on advancing human rights, particularly behind the Iron Curtain, and on promoting *détente* by defusing the acute tension between the superpowers and their allies. In sharp contrast, the United States, guided by Secretary of State Henry Kissinger, remained skeptical and largely uninterested in the negotiations at all.

It took almost two years of protracted and complex negotiations in Geneva to determine the respective resistance points of the participants and to find some range of settlement. Achieving consensus among *all* thirty-five delegations representing their own interests and sometimes those of a bloc or alliance on an agreement seeking to address vital and multifaceted problems presented an enormous challenge. Their common interests and issues of conflict were seen in both broad principles and subjects. The principles involved sovereign equality, which entitled the participants to act and be treated as states in their own right, the inviolability of borders, the territorial integrity of states, the peaceful settlement of disputes, and respect for human rights, among others. The negotiators decided to organize specific subjects into different categories or "baskets": security affairs; cooperation in economics, science and technology, and environmental protection; human rights; and follow-up meetings to monitor compliance. Various texts were submitted over and over again to small working committees in order to try to narrow the differences and find a settlement range. It became very clear to all the negotiators in this process that there would be linkage between the principles and the subjects, and that in order to obtain what they wanted in one or more areas they would have to make concessions in others. This generated great frustration, particularly among the Soviets and their premier, Leonid Brezhnev, who had staked his personal prestige on the outcome, as they watched what they hoped would be a simple and quick conference about borders turn into a lengthy negotiation about the whole meaning of comprehensive security and cooperation.

In the end, the terms of the Final Act of CSCE, signed by all the heads of state in a concluding ceremony in Helsinki in August 1975, depended on the relative balance between these principles and subjects and the concrete benefits that they bestowed upon the parties. As one of the participants cogently observed: "The principles are valueless without the practice." All agreed on their common responsibility to settle their disputes by peaceful means and fulfill their obligations under international law. Of particular importance to force and statecraft, they believed that they all would benefit by mutually pledging themselves to lessen confrontations that risked armed force, to develop confidence-building measures by providing advanced notification of major military maneuvers and exchanging military observers, and, most significantly, to

> refrain in their mutual relations, as well as in their international relations
> in general, from the threat or use of force against the territorial integrity
> or political independence of any State, or in any other manner inconsistent
> with the purposes of the United Nations and the present declaration.

"No consideration," they emphatically established, "may be invoked to serve to warrant resort to the threat or use of force in contravention of this principle."

The final agreement provided other benefits as well. All parties anticipated that they would gain from their promise to increase economic cooperation by expanding trade and business opportunities, to share scientific and technological knowledge and to conduct joint research projects, and to take measures that would help protect their shared environment. The Soviet Union obtained the one major objective that it regarded as essential to its security and so desperately had sought: formal recognition of the existing borders of Eastern Europe. A number of critics in the West responded by accusing the negotiators of "selling out" and "capitulation" by conceding this provision. What they failed to appreciate, however, is that in order to secure this benefit, the Soviet Union had to grant major concessions, both of which would play unanticipated and profound roles in the near future. One of these was to refrain from any form of armed intervention or threat of such intervention against another participating state, as it had done in the past. The other was a pledge to respect human rights.

Despite strong and determined resistance from the Soviet Union, which described the whole subject as "interference in internal affairs" and an "unjustified waste of time," other participants insisted on making human rights an integral part of their negotiations. They argued that peace and security in their broadest and most meaningful sense are composed of many different and interrelated dimensions. In this regard, they insisted on a recognition of what they called the "indivisibility of security" in which genuine international security, national security, and the security of individuals are all strongly linked together. In fact, they described this connection as an "essential factor" for security and cooperation in Europe and refused to budge on other matters unless this was acknowledged and given practical effect. The final agreement consequently contained what has been called "the most spectacular innovation of the Helsinki process" and one "nothing short of revolutionary": explicit provisions linking respect for human rights with security and establishing that how sovereign nation-states treat their citizens is a legitimate matter of international scrutiny. The text boldly declared that the participating states "will act in conformity with the purposes and the principles of the Charter of the United Nations and with the Universal Declaration of Human Rights," recognizing civil and political rights, freedom of thought and conscience, and the right of individual citizens "to know" about these rights and to "act" accordingly.

Armed with this highly publicized agreement on human rights, individuals trapped under oppressive Communist regimes began to organize NGOs for the purpose of monitoring compliance with the promises. The Final Act proved to be a beginning rather than an end, for it gave them both hope and legitimacy, and they seized it. Noted Soviet dissidents like Yuri Orlov, for example, immediately formed the Moscow Helsinki Group and began to speak out at great personal risk—but with the knowledge that others could help. "We do not have the means by which to reach our [own] government," he explained. "My appeal to Brezhnev probably got as far as the regional KGB office." "The crucial question," however, was that now, with the CSCE agreement, Soviet officials could be reached "through the governments of other countries." Others realized this fact as well, including activists who instituted Helsinki Watch (eventually Human Rights Watch) in Poland, dissident (and future president) Václav Havel, who created Charter 77 in Czechoslovakia, and those who established the larger International Helsinki Federation for Human Rights to draw public attention to any violations that might occur. Although persecuted, arrested, broken at labor camps and psychiatric hospitals, and exiled by their own governments fearful of losing power, they courageously persisted and watched these seeds sown at CSCE assume political importance and thereby change the world they had known, playing powerful roles in eventually leading to the Velvet Revolution, the fall of the Iron Curtain, the collapse of the Soviet Union and its empire, and then the end of the Cold War itself.

CONTEMPORARY NEGOTIATIONS OVER NUCLEAR WEAPONS
IN NORTH KOREA

Ever since the highly secretive, Communist, and feudal family-based government of North Korea first began developing its nuclear capabilities in the mid-1950s, others feared the implications of proliferation. Various international and regional efforts attempted to halt this development, but nothing seemed to work and suspicions ran deep, for the founder of the country, Kim Il Sung, remained acutely aware of large numbers of American troops stationed in South Korea and that U.S. General Douglas MacArthur had requested that nuclear weapons be used against him during the Korean War. Tensions began to spiral dramatically in 1993 when U.S. intelligence photos revealed hidden storage tanks, the International Atomic Energy Agency (IAEA) demanded special inspections on suspected nuclear sites, and North Korea, in a fit of anger, announced its intention to withdraw from the regulations of the Non-Proliferation Treaty. When the United Nations Security Council began to discuss the possibility of imposing sanctions, North Korea announced that it would regard any such actions as "acts of war" and would respond accordingly. The next year, it expelled international weapons inspectors, threatened to turn Seoul into a "sea of fire" if necessary, and removed enough plutonium-rich fuel rods from the core of its reactor to provide the raw material for several nuclear bombs. This provocative action not only revealed that North Korea had no intention of participating in efforts to control worldwide proliferation, but possessed the capacity to quickly produce weapons of mass destruction, which, in turn, could escalate an arms race in Asia, could seriously threaten South Korea and American troops stationed there, and perhaps could be sold to bidders like Iran, Libya, Pakistan, and Syria. As the rhetoric became more bellicose and preparations for possible war intensified, U.S. Secretary of Defense William Perry declared that the situation "poses the greatest security threat to the United States and the world today."

The newly installed Clinton administration first tried to respond to this crisis by considering the use of coercive diplomacy, a strategy that we will explore in Chapter 10. But it quickly became apparent that provocative threats would be completely counterproductive and might well push North Korea over the edge into war. The Americans consequently reached the conclusion, in the words of one official, that it was "best to engage in dialogue." The question, however, was how could serious negotiations be started? The answer came in a rather unconventional way that demonstrated once again the impact of individual people. Kim Il Sung invited former President Jimmy Carter to visit North Korea to intervene in the dispute, open a channel of communication, and help to find a way to bring the parties together. The reaction of American officials ranged from vague hope to skepticism to horrified alarm, but in the end Clinton decided to let him go, not as a government representative but as a private citizen. Carter quickly established a relationship of trust and created a breakthrough that allowed both sides a face-saving way out of their impasse, thus sending their skilled negotiators back to the negotiating table with a new seriousness of purpose. The Americans selected Assistant Secretary of State for Political-Military Affairs Robert Gallucci, a man with two decades of non-proliferation experience, to lead their delegation. The North Koreans sent Vice Foreign Minister Kang Sok Ju to head their team. Then, suddenly, just as the delegations were beginning their deliberations in Geneva, Kim Il Sung, who had controlled his country with an iron fist since 1948, died. The negotiators hoped that this, too, would facilitate their work.

Not surprisingly, the two sides began with opening positions that were very far apart. At times, they appeared diametrically opposed. As one of the American negotiators describes it:

> We played hard initially, hoping that the North Koreans would come around, and we sat there and we butted heads. We'd make our points, they'd make their points, we'd go back [and] the interagency would say, "No, we don't want to change our position." So we'd go back...say the same thing, they'd say the same thing, and we'd go back to our country and say, "We're still butting heads," but the principals would say, "No, we're still not going to give in."

In this process, both sides gradually came to a serious assessment of their own interests, realizing that military solutions presented no credible options, that there were few viable alternatives, that they shared an interest in reaching an agreement, and that they needed to adjust their initial resistance points in order to find a range of settlement. One State Department official recalled:

> I can remember one of their guys, as we were breaking for lunch, saying to me, "Please look very carefully at what we said." And we went back and looked at it, and the message that came out of it was, "If we're willing to take some steps, you have to take some steps as well." That took us a while to figure out—what we could do and how far we could go.

With the cautious approval of Washington and Pyongyang, Gallucci and Kang were able to craft an agreement known as the Agreed Framework of 1994 that they hoped would bring them shared benefits. To do this, they attempted a strategy of what we will call "conditional reciprocity." That is, they sought to overcome a lack of mutual trust by creating coupled reciprocal conditions over a period of time. Mutual adherence to the conditional actions called for in the early and middle phases of the agreement, they believed, would improve confidence in order to encourage continued adherence to the remaining set of actions. The United States, for example, would secure the substantial gain of limiting nuclear proliferation because North Korea agreed to immediately shut down and eventually dismantle its particularly dangerous gas-graphite nuclear program, including its existing reactor and plutonium reprocessing facility. In exchange—and to compensate North Korea for energy lost from its closed reactor—the United States agreed to provide shipments of heavy fuel oil for heating and electrical production and to oversee construction of two proliferation-resistant, light-water reactors. Before the delivery of any of the sensitive components for these new power plants, however, North Korea had to submit to any inspections deemed necessary by the IAEA and, as the parts began to arrive, to begin shipping the dangerous spent fuel rods out of the country. These measures, it was hoped, would provide a step-by-step normalization of political and economic relations between the two countries. Benefits, in other words, would be conditioned by reciprocity, and both sides thereby would be able to avoid war.

Despite the celebration that followed the negotiations and Gallucci's observation for force and statecraft that "it was a wonderful mating of the military instrument being ready and the diplomatic instrument being used," the Agreed Framework nevertheless suffered from a number of problems. The text, for example, failed to provide specific schedules for coordinated and reciprocal moves and gave the United States an usually long period of time ("by the target date of 2003") to fulfill its obligation to provide the new and much safer reactors. In addition, it did not provide for any entity to monitor compliance, to supervise implementation with the provisions of conditional reciprocity, or to make midcourse adjustments that might become necessary. Given the historical context of distrust, these flaws magnified the probability that each side would be keenly sensitive to any signs, real or imagined, that the other might not be meeting its commitments. Sharp criticism also emerged from the IAEA and those states in the region with vital interests in the danger of nuclear weapons in North Korea who nevertheless had been excluded from the negotiations.

Further and very serious problems emerged from domestic politics. Shortly after the Agreed Framework was signed, members of the Republican Party gained control of Congress and publicly announced their intention to undermine the agreement. Such pronouncements and the subsequent U.S. failure to honor its obligation to construct the light-water reactors infuriated North Korean leaders. They therefore decided to initiate a clandestine nuclear weapons program and fire an unarmed test missile over Japan. These actions, in turn, contributed to George W. Bush's determination to isolate rather than engage the regime, to accelerate national missile defense to protect against threats from "rogue states" like North Korea, and then, in his 2002 State of the Union Address, to accuse it of being in league with Iraq and Iran as part of what he called "the Axis of Evil." This highly provocative statement, especially when coupled with his administration's proclamation of the doctrine of preemption, could not help but contribute to North Korea's perception that it might be the victim of an attack by the United States and that it therefore should create a nuclear deterrent for its own security. Consequently, North Korea withdrew from the Nuclear Non-Proliferation Treaty, restarted its nuclear reactor, forced the IAEA inspectors out of their country, and accused Bush of being a "shameless charlatan." The United States subsequently decided to invade Iraq in 2003 and announced that it would abandon the Agreed Framework. Each side blamed the other for the collapse. When U.S. Secretary of State–designate Condoleezza Rice described North Korea as "an outpost of tyranny," the government of Kim Jong Il responded by claiming that it possessed nuclear weapons to defend itself against any attack and insisting that it would never negotiate in the face of such "hostile" American policy.

Despite this intense level of rhetoric and hostility, the parties realized through time, as many other diplomats have in the past, that it was in their mutual interest to continue to negotiate and thereby try to avoid the risks of miscalculation, escalation, and possible war. As a consequence, the United States, North Korea, South Korea, China, Japan, and Russia initiated multilateral Six-Party Negotiations in Beijing later in 2005. Their efforts resulted in an agreement by which Kim Jong Il would restrain his nuclear weapons program in exchange for economic aid and desperately needed food assistance. Nevertheless, serious problems persisted, causing the negotiations to start, to stop, and then to start again. The next year, for example, North Korea conducted its first underground nuclear weapons test, and the United Nations responded with sanctions of coercive diplomacy. Negotiations resumed three months later. In 2007, North Korea began to dismantle its plutonium reactor and, in a move most unusual for this regime shrouded in secrecy, handed over many details of its nuclear program. The United States responded by taking it off the list of state sponsors of terrorism, thereby making more assistance possible. But disputes arose over whether the information provided by North Korea was correct and complete and whether the United States was fulfilling its promise of foodstuffs. At this point, North Korea launched two provocative missile tests and announced in 2009 its intention of pulling out of negotiations completely. Relations deteriorated even worse the next year, when it sunk a South Korean naval warship, shelled a border island with a loss of civilian lives, and revealed that it possessed a modern uranium enrichment facility. By 2011, U.S. Secretary of Defense under the Obama administration, Robert Gates, ominously concluded that North Korea "is becoming a direct threat to the United States."

In the midst of this highly unstable setting, all parties became acutely aware of the dangers. Indeed, even the erratic Kim Jong Il personally traveled to China and Russia, where he discussed restarting negotiations. The United States, in response, named a new full-time envoy with specialized experience in nuclear issues to engage in discussions. At precisely this stage, Kim Jong Il died, leaving power and the fate of his isolated yet nuclear-armed regime in the hands of military commanders and his young, untested son Kim Jong Un. In January 2012, North Korea announced its willingness to resume the long-suspended Six-Party Negotiations over its nuclear weapons program. The next month, it agreed to accept IAEA inspectors, to stop its uranium enrichment, and to cease testing its long-range ballistic missiles in exchange for 240,000 tons of critical food aid from the United States to help feed its starving population. Yet, just as relations seemed to be improving, Pyongyang launched several new missile tests, in direct violation of the agreement. The United States immediately suspended all planned food shipments and the UN Security Council condemned the launches as raising "grave security concerns" and imposed a series of new sanctions. When it conducted a highly provocative underground nuclear weapons test in February 2013, even its only protector China insisted that North Korea "swiftly return to the correct channel of dialogue and negotiation."

ANALYSIS

These historical cases certainly reveal the central role that negotiation plays in high-stakes diplomacy and confirm the observation of de Callières that the very fate of nations can hinge on the success or the failure of negotiations involving force and statecraft. In addition, a focused comparison of these cases can help us to more fully understand the broader principles of negotiation, to consider some lessons that might be drawn, and to appreciate how recent transformations in history have affected the tasks of negotiation in our world today.

It is clear, for example, that negotiations cannot succeed unless there is a shared interest in reaching an agreement. All parties must recognize that they have an interest in jointly finding a diplomatic solution to a problem or issue of conflict that they share in common. Those who gathered at the Congress of Vienna in 1814–1815 understood this. They realized that, despite their intense competition over the distribution of territory and their different visions of the roles that they should play to maintain peace and security, they shared a vital interest in creating a viable international system and in preventing another Napoleon from arising in their midst. Although they entered into the negotiations with many diverse interests that drove them apart, the thirty-five delegations at the Conference on Security and Cooperation in Europe also fully appreciated the fact that it was in their mutual interests to reach a formal agreement to safeguard their future. Despite the efforts of the United Nations, the United States, and four neighboring countries to check nuclear proliferation, however, the lengthy and tortuous route of negotiations certainly reveals that North Korea has not yet shared the same interest in reaching an agreement.

These cases from history also demonstrate that negotiations will fail if the participants are unable to see beyond the initial and often posturing demands and to correctly ascertain and address their respective resistance points. All negotiators must determine what they are—and are not—willing to concede and must assess their best alternative to a negotiated agreement. Despite a number of outrageous opening positions and the opinion of the Russians that since they possessed such formidable military power they did not even need to negotiate at all, for example, the delegates assembled at Vienna eventually came to understand what they and their fellow participants regarded as their barest minimums, or bottom lines beyond which they were unwilling to grant further concessions in order to reach an agreement. The same process occurred during the Helsinki and Geneva negotiations for CSCE, as it became evident that the Soviet Union would not be granted the recognition of borders it so desperately sought unless it addressed the resistance point of the West that human rights provisions be included in the Final Act. In the negotiations that led to the Agreed Framework, the United States made it clear that they would not make concessions unless the North Koreans agreed to freeze their nuclear program, while the North Koreans stated that the negotiations would collapse unless they received a commitment from the United States to provide oil shipments and two new reactors to compensate for energy lost from their closed nuclear reactor. This initially worked, but as conditions and leadership changed, so too did the respective resistance points.

Successful negotiations also require the ability to discover shared interests and objectives that exist in a settlement range somewhere between the respective resistance points. The negotiators must be able to find or create an area where their interests converge and where they might become partners rather than simply rivals. Diplomats at the Congress of Vienna discovered that their settlement range expanded considerably when they agreed that they genuinely needed each other and that they should focus less on specific details and more on the larger principles of compensation, legitimacy, and balance of power. Those involved in the negotiations over CSCE came to learn the same lesson, although it took almost two years to do so. Agreement was facilitated when the delegates realized their common interests in the broader "indivisibility of security" and the linkage among its various elements, such as the inviolability of frontiers, the peaceful settlement of disputes, refraining from the threat or use of force, and respect for human rights. Similarly, although the settlement range between the United States and North Korea was extremely narrow due to the wide gap between their positions and their lack of trust, the negotiators managed to find enough common ground to result in the Agreed Framework that successfully froze plutonium production on the Korean peninsula for several years.

Both individually and collectively, these cases also show that negotiated agreements will not be reached unless all sides perceive that they have secured some advantage that they otherwise would not have been able to obtain peacefully without negotiation. That is, there must be shared benefits. In the final settlement of 1814–1815, for example, all of the Great Powers benefited from their new collective security arrangement, and each of the victors obtained significant gains of territory that they had not possessed previously. CSCE was even more remarkable in this regard, for thirty-five separate delegations needed to be convinced that they would gain from the agreement. By 1975, all participants came to believe that they would benefit from the provisions reaffirming the principles of the United Nations and international law, military confidence-building measures, and increased economic opportunities, among others addressing comprehensive security and cooperation. More specifically, the Soviets secured recognition of existing borders, the Eastern Europeans attained guarantees against armed intervention, and the West, along with neutral and nonaligned countries, gained provisions about human rights. Although the Agreed Framework gave both parties benefits, these were short-lived due to the fact that neither side fully lived up to its promises. This sowed distrust and embittered relations, making it much more difficult to pursue further negotiations.

The critical importance of skilled negotiators is also demonstrated in each of these cases. None of the issues of conflict between the parties resolved themselves. Final agreements were reached only because of extremely able human negotiators with the skills to find common interests, ascertain resistance points, formulate settlement ranges, and create mutual benefits. These include the abilities to identify and minimize the barriers to agreement, to evaluate the parties and their interests, to shape the process of negotiation, and to build and sustain momentum. Those responsible for guiding the Congress of Vienna to reaching an agreement, for example, included Metternich and Castlereagh, two of the most impressive negotiators in the annals of diplomacy. The complex and intricately interconnected provisions of the Final Act of CSCE, which provided benefits of security and cooperation for all parties, could only have been produced by very skilled negotiators. Similarly, even the detractors of the Agreed Framework agreed that Gallucci and Kang possessed remarkable negotiating skills to reach any agreement at all in an atmosphere characterized by enormous hostility and an almost total lack of trust. Nevertheless, the case of North Korea serves as a reminder that, despite the skills of particular negotiators, they are instruments of policy themselves, and if that policy is completely inflexible or wildly erratic, there is little they can be expected to achieve.

Finally, one of the great advantages of analyzing cases of negotiation ranging from the beginning of the nineteenth century to our own time is that it helps to reveal the impact of what we have called the historic diplomatic revolution. Part of this phenomenon has been the expanding number of actors who have demanded active participation in important international negotiations. At the Congress of Vienna, the opinions of only the five Great Powers of Europe made any serious difference. Although other parties sometimes had intense interests at stake in the negotiations, they either played little role in the deliberations or were not invited to participate at all. In sharp contrast—and indicative of the expansion of the diplomatic community—not only did a total of thirty-five delegations (including two from North America) participate in CSCE, but each, regardless of size or level of power, demanded an equal vote. Since the rules of accommodation required consensus, this gave even the smallest of states extraordinary influence. This proved to be of great frustration to the superpowers, who discovered that they could no longer dictate to others and that their vast arsenals of sophisticated weapons and armed force were of little use in advancing their national interests in this kind of setting. The impact of the number of actors was also seen in the negotiations over nuclear proliferation in North Korea. Part of the weakness in both the substance and the legitimacy of the Agreed Framework resulted from the fact that others with vital interests in the outcome had been excluded from the formal deliberations, including the great and small nations of East Asia, as well as all of those parties to the Nuclear Non-ProliferationTreaty, represented by the IAEA, who were deeply worried about proliferating weapons around the entire world.

Numbers, of course, do not tell the whole story of the growing complexities in negotiations, for yet another change in the diplomatic revolution has been the transformation in the types of actors. In traditional diplomacy, such as that of 1814–1815 at the Congress of Vienna, the only meaningful actors were nation-states. Those called upon to negotiate on behalf of the national interests of their countries did not have to worry about influences outside their immediate and closed circle, known as the "inner ring." By the time of

CSCE, much had changed dramatically, for as one observer noted, "it involved not only governments and their representatives talking behind closed doors but also citizens and their organizations hammering on those same doors." Transnational corporations seeking trade opportunities, labor associations advocating jobs, NGOs and religious bodies promoting human rights, and scientists urging increased research cooperation, among many other interest groups, all mobilized their energies in such a way as to make a profound impact on the Final Act. NGOs and international bodies such as the IAEA not only played, but continue to play, significant roles in negotiations over nuclear proliferation in North Korea. Further examples of the enormous impact of nonstate actors on negotiations involving issues of force and statecraft can be seen in the creation of the Mine Ban Treaty prohibiting antipersonnel land mines and the establishment of the International Criminal Court. As scholars Fen Osler Hampson and Michael Hart observe in their book *Multilateral Negotiations*, these many different types of actors "see themselves as direct stakeholders and thus seek to affect outcomes by bringing pressure to bear on their national government. Many of these groupings also have an international constituency...enabling them to mount effective campaigns at the national and international levels." They conclude, therefore, that negotiation today "is, in essence, a coalition-building exercise involving states, nonstate actors, and international organizations."

International negotiations also have been complicated by the growing impact of domestic politics. The negotiators at the Congress of Vienna gave little thought to political opposition that might arise to challenge their deliberations and decisions. In fact, Castlereagh condemned even the prospect of public opinion influencing them, describing it as a dangerous element "to force...upon the nations, at the expense of their honor and of the tranquility of the world." By the time of the Paris Peace Conference of 1919, this situation had changed dramatically. Here, the negotiators constantly confronted the pressures of what they called the "New Diplomacy," with its "open diplomacy" and "public diplomacy" generated by opinion and domestic politics in their own countries. Delegates at CSCE similarly found their deliberations widely covered by the press and heavily influenced by political and bureaucratic factors at home. To the frustration of Henry Kissinger, several members of Congress paid very careful attention to the deliberations, and some even insisted on going to Geneva to attend the negotiations in person. In the case of North Korea, the majority of Republican members of Congress determined that they deliberately would sabotage the Agreed Framework negotiated by the Democratic Clinton administration, and continued initiatives often brought protestors into the streets of South Korea.

Modern technological developments and the growing complexity of security issues also have characterized the diplomatic revolution and challenged negotiations. Delegates at the Congress of Vienna conducted their deliberations slowly, with the knowledge that it took nineteen days for instructions to travel from London to Vienna, and with narrow conceptions of security based on a balance of power defined largely in terms of territory and military forces

Public Opinion Attempting to Influence Negotiations: Protestors in the Street

armed with relatively simple weapons with limited ranges and destructive capacities. Those who negotiated at the CSCE, in comparison, maintained constant contact with their foreign ministries and political leadership by electronic (and sometimes encrypted) means. They also worked mightily to understand the various dimensions of "complex interdependence" and the "indivisibility of security," exploring the many interconnections between military force, economic strength, technological advances, environmental health, and human rights. In contemporary negotiations over proliferation in North Korea, highly advanced technology is used for the gathering of intelligence, particularly spy satellites. The sheer complexity of the issues at stake is revealed by the fact that American delegations include highly trained specialists and scientists from the Department of State, Department of Defense, National Security Council, Central Intelligence Agency, National Reconnaissance Office, and Department of Commerce, among other agencies. Overshadowing all of their efforts, of course, is the stark realization that they are dealing with deadly nuclear materials and weapons of mass destruction.

Finally, the whole process of international negotiation has been enormously affected by the transformation of cultural values and norms. Those negotiators who assembled at the Congress of Vienna shared many of the same traditions, characteristics, and basic goals and objectives for their international system. Diplomats of this classical era agreed on and generally adhered to reasonably well-defined rules of procedure and accommodation, appreciated the need for mutual respect and self-restraint, and felt obligated to reciprocate concessions. They literally spoke the same language. This cultural homogeneity greatly facilitated diplomatic negotiations by making it possible to secure consensus on the time, place, agenda, the level of representation, and other modalities of conference arrangements, all designed to address the first principle of negotiation in reaching a mutually acceptable, formal agreement.

In sharp contrast, today's world is characterized by a vast cultural heterogeneity. The many differences in politics, religion, ideology, perceptions, assumptions, patterns of communication and decision making, language, normative values, and the passions that they arouse create a profound impact on human negotiators and their negotiations. It is not unusual, for example, to find highly divergent negotiating styles and different conceptions of negotiation itself. There are times when certain actors demonstrate little self-restraint, do not show respect for others, regard negotiation as another form of combat rather than an instrument for moderating or resolving conflict, and do not fear being unreasonable or abusive. Sometimes parties cannot even agree on rules of accommodation, or one side or the other argues tenaciously over seemingly minor procedural matters. The agenda setting and procedural arrangements surrounding the Korean War truce, the Vietnam peace talks, and the conference following the Arab-Israeli War of 1973, to illustrate, were all plagued by prolonged and bitter wrangling over such trivial subjects as the shape of the table and seating of the participants. Other manifestations of difference, particularly in an age of public opinion and mass media, occur when nations enter into negotiation not because they either expect or desire an agreement, but rather for show or "side effects." They may conclude that a refusal to begin deliberations might be politically damaging at home or present an image of inflexibility abroad that may harm relations with allies or neutrals, as indicated by the reluctant agreement of the United States to even participate in CSCE. Or, nations may enter into negotiations to size up an opponent, to acquire information, to deceive by stalling for time or to delay the possible use of force, to "maintain contact," to extract propaganda advantages, to demonstrate toughness, or to extract concessions, as indicated by the on-and-off-again talks, high level of rhetoric, and often "non-negotiable" policy positions surrounding nuclear weapons in North Korea.

Such an analysis of historical cases thus reveals much about the critical importance of negotiation to diplomacy, the principles of negotiation in partnership and rivalry, and a number of valuable lessons that might be learned. It also demonstrates not only the impact of the expansion and heterogeneity of the international community, the increased influence of public opinion and domestic politics, and the dramatic transformations in communication and weapons technology, but also the serious challenges that these factors present to negotiating matters of force and statecraft during the diplomatic revolution of our time.

SUGGESTIONS FOR FURTHER EXPLORATION

Many new studies on the importance, theory, and practice of negotiation have appeared. These include the prescriptive Roger Fisher, William Ury, and Bruce Patton, *Getting to Yes* (New York, 2011 ed.); Brigid Starkey et al., *International Negotiation in a Complex World* (New York, 2010 ed.); Richard Solomon and Nigel Quinney, *American Negotiating Behavior* (Washington, DC, 2010); Dennis Ross, *Statecraft* (New York, 2007); Howard Raiffa et al., *Negotiation Analysis* (Cambridge, MA, 2007 ed.); Harvey Langholtz and Chris Stout (eds.), *The Psychology of Diplomacy* (New York, 2004); Christer Jönsson, "Diplomacy, Bargaining, and Negotiation," in Walter Carlsnaes et al. (eds.), *Handbook of International Relations* (London, 2002); Victor Kremenyuk (ed.), *International Negotiation* (New York, 2002 ed.); Michael Watkins and Susan Rosegrant, *Breakthrough International Negotiations* (San Francisco, 2001); and P. Terrence Hopmann, *The Negotiating Process and the Resolution of International Conflicts* (Columbia, SC, 1998 ed.). Very recent scholarship can be found in the *Journal of Conflict Resolution, International Negotiation*, and *Negotiation Journal*; books in the "Negotiation, Diplomacy, and Foreign Policy" series published by the U.S. Institute of Peace; and the work of the Process of International Negotiation (PIN) project at www.iiasa.ac.at.

Earlier, but still valuable, analyses can be found in Martin Patchen, *Resolving Disputes Between Nations* (Durham, NC, 1988); I. William Zartman and Maureen Berman, *The Practical Negotiator* (New Haven, CT, 1982); Fred C. Iklé, *How Nations Negotiate* (New York, 1964); and Thomas Schelling's seminal "Essay on Bargaining" in *The Strategy of Conflict* (Cambridge, MA, 1960). The classics remain Cardinal de Richelieu, *Testament politique*, Louis André (ed.), (Paris, 1947 ed.,); Fortuné Barthélemy de Felice, "Négociation," in *Code de l'Humanité*, vol. 9 (Yverdon, 1778); Antoine Pecquet, *Discours sur l'art de négocier* (Paris, 1737); and, of course, François de Callières, *De la manière de négocier avec les souverains*, can be found in translation as *On the Manner of Negotiating with Princes* in many editions.

For the negotiations at Vienna, see Christophe Dupont, "History and Coalitions: The Congress of Vienna," *International Negotiation*, 8 (2003): 169–178; Henry Kissinger, *A World Restored* (New York, 1973 ed.); Harold Nicolson, *The Congress of Vienna* (London, 1945); and other appropriate studies as cited at the end of Chapter 2 and Chapter 9.

Studies on CSCE include Paul Gordon Lauren, *The Evolution of International Human Rights: Visions Seen* (Philadelphia, 2011 ed.); Daniel Thomas, *The Helsinki Effect: International Norms, Human Rights, and the Demise of Communism* (Princeton, 2001); Vojtech Mastny, *The Helsinki Process and the Reintegration of Europe* (New York, 1992); the eyewitness account by American negotiator John J. Maresca, *To Helsinki: The Conference on Security and Cooperation in Europe, 1973–75* (Durham, NC, 1985); the documentary materials in Igor Kavass et al. (eds.), *Human Rights, European Politics, and the Helsinki Accord* (Buffalo, NY, 1981); Luigi Ferraris (ed.), *Report on a Negotiation*, Marie-Claire Barbere (trans.) (Alphen a/d Rijn, 1979); and *Yearbook of Finnish Foreign Policy, 1975* (Helsinki, 1975).

Excellent discussion about the Agreed Framework and subsequent developments can be found in Mike Chinoy, *Meltdown* (New York, 2009); Charles Pritchard, *Failed Diplomacy* (Washington, DC, 2007); Joel Wit, Daniel Poneman, and Robert Gallucci, *Going Critical* (Washington, DC, 2004); Victor Cha and David Kang, *Nuclear North Korea*

(New York, 2003); Michael O'Hanlon and Mike Mochizuki, *Crisis on the Korean Peninsula* (New York, 2003); Selig Harrison, *Korean Endgame* (Princeton, 2002); the discussion in *Breakthrough International Negotiation* (2001), as cited above; Robert Litwak, *Rogue States and U.S. Foreign Policy* (Baltimore, 2000); and Leon Sigal, *Disarming Strangers* (Princeton, 1998). Evolving developments can be followed by exploring—and comparing—the Web sites of the states participating in the Six-Party Negotiations.

The study of diplomacy is filled with cases of negotiation. For some of those that deal specifically with matters of force and statecraft, see the London Conference on Belgian Neutrality (1831), Convention on the Dardanelles and Bosphorus (1841), Paris Peace Congress (1856), Hague Peace Conferences (1899 and 1907), Paris Peace Conference (1919), Washington Naval Conference (1921–1922), Test Ban Treaty (1958–1963), United Nations Disarmament Conference on the Non-Proliferation Treaty (1967–1968), Strategic Arms Limitation Treaties I and II (1968–1972 and 1977–1979), Mutual Balanced Force Reduction (MBFR) in Europe (1973–1990), Camp David Accords (1978), Strategic Arms Reduction Treaties I and II (1991–1993), Oslo Accords (1992–1993), Ottawa Conference on the Mine Ban Treaty (1996–1997), New Strategic Arms Reduction Treaty (2008–2010), and the Nuclear Security Summit (2010– present).

9

Deterrence

In the dangerous standoff of the Cold War, each of the superpowers greatly feared that its adversary might somehow be tempted to launch an attack against them, their allies, or their interests. To prevent such a frightening event from ever occurring became their highest priority, and they engaged in creating rival alliance systems and in acquiring weapons that dramatically increased their capacity to inflict staggering damage upon the other. Each calculated that the very threat of using armed force would be sufficient to deter the other from ever attacking in the first place. Nothing, of course, could generate more fear than weapons of mass destruction. It is for this reason that, as early as 1952, the leading Republican spokesman for foreign affairs, John Foster Dulles, wrote an impassioned article entitled "A Policy of Boldness," in which he called for going beyond the limitations of conventional weapons and drawing on the deterring power of new nuclear weapons. The nation, he said, "must develop the will and organize the means to retaliate instantly against open aggression by Red armies, so that, if it occurred anywhere, we could and would strike back where it hurts, by means of our own choosing." Dulles argued that this hopefully would create such tremendous fear in the minds of adversaries that it would "stop open aggression before it starts." To fail to do so, he warned, could create a "catastrophe" and "it will be because we have allowed these new and awesome forces to become the ordinary killing tools of the soldier when, in the hands of the statesmen, they could serve as effective political weapons in defense of peace." When Dulles became secretary of state, he put his strategic plan into practice, ominously warning the Soviet Union and all other Communist regimes in a highly publicized speech that any aggression would be met by the "massive retaliatory power" of nuclear weapons from the arsenal of the United States. He and others proudly described this threat as "the ultimate deterrent."

This strategy, known as "Massive Retaliation," was not the first nor the last case of using threats of force as instruments of statecraft to deter opponents. Indeed, deterrence is as old as the arts of diplomacy and warfare themselves. Throughout history, city-states, kingdoms, empires, and nation-states all have sought to prevent the actions of rivals dangerous to their interests. In his *History of the Peloponnesian War,* for example, Thucydides recounted how leaders mobilized troops and positioned fleets to make others "think twice before attacking." Machiavelli also wrote about "shows of force" as being economical means of persuading an adversary that the costs and risks of launching an attack would be too high. Thomas Hobbes made the same point in *Leviathan* when he observed that armed force could deter aggression by creating "a fear of the consequences" and by providing the power to frighten men into "the performance of their covenants by the terror of some punishment greater than the benefit they expect by breach of their covenant." The nineteenth century's balance of power operated on the same idea.

These long-standing practices of deterrence in statecraft, however, were not accompanied by any explicit conceptual framework or analyses of principles. Statesmen and generals in the past simply based their actions on historical lessons that they had learned and on the belief that if they presented a credible threat of using armed force, an adversary might fear the consequences, "think twice," and therefore be persuaded not to launch an attack. This rather basic approach was reinforced by at least two factors. In the first place, if threats proved to be an insufficient deterrent, war was considered to be a legitimate instrument of foreign policy that resulted in limited rather than catastrophic costs. Second, it was difficult to elaborate a sophisticated theory of bargaining with threats of force when limited technological capabilities prevented any sharp distinction from being made between the power to hurt and the power to destroy. From the time of the ancients to the first half of the twentieth century, it was virtually impossible to seriously hurt enemies—to burn cities, ruin crops, seize property, and inflict pain—without first having defeated their military forces.

This situation changed dramatically with the advent of strategic bombing. For the first time, military technology made it possible to hurt an opponent terribly before, or even without, destroying their armed forces. With the development of this possibility, the *threat* to hurt could be separated—in fact as well as in theory—from the threat to engage and destroy their military capabilities. This particular distinction, when coupled with the differentiation between the threat and the use of armed force, appeared all the more critical with the emergence of nuclear weapons and sophisticated delivery systems. The new extent of potential devastation convinced many strategists that war no longer could be considered a rational policy option, as it had been in the past. A prescient book entitled *The Absolute Weapon* confirmed this attitude at a very early stage. In the words of its editor, Bernard Brodie: "Thus far the chief purpose of our military establishment has been to win wars. From now on its chief purpose must be to avert them. It can have almost no other useful purpose."

Many scholars and policy makers alike thus increasingly began to believe that, given the destructiveness and the unacceptable costs of modern weapons of mass destruction, the first task of diplomacy and strategy must be *to prevent rather than wage war.* How to do this through deterrence and yet maintain security in the context of first the Cold War, then the post–Cold War world, and then global terrorism thus became a matter of absolutely vital concern. This acute problem has elevated the role of deterrence strategy to a preeminent position in the study of force and statecraft and, therefore, has resulted in a great deal of serious thinking about the fundamental principles of deterrence.

PRINCIPLES OF DETERRENCE

Deterrence consists essentially of an effort to persuade opponents to refrain from taking certain action, such as an armed attack, that is viewed as being highly dangerous to one's interests by making them fear the consequences of such behavior. It tries to convince an adversary that the costs and risks of aggression that they might undertake will far outweigh any possible benefits that they hope to gain. "To deter," write political scientists Robert Art and Kenneth Waltz in *The Use of Force: International Politics and Foreign Policy*,

> literally means to stop someone from doing something by frightening him...dissuasion by deterrence operates by frightening a state out of attacking, not because of the difficulty of launching an attack and carrying it home, but because the expected reaction of the opponent will result in one's own severe punishment.

In this kind of persuasion, or bargaining with threats of force, the relationship between the adversaries is clearly *psychological rather than physical*. Deterrence attempts not to destroy opponents or to physically restrain them, but to affect their motivation or *will*. The key, therefore, lies in the minds of people. The strategy seeks to persuade them that their interests would be served best by not embarking on a particular course of action at all. In this sense, it is largely designed to defend the status quo and attempts to end wars before they ever begin. As Hobbes described it: "That miserable condition of war is necessarily consequent to the natural passions of men when there is no visible power to keep them in awe and tie them by fear of punishment."

By directing threats against an opponent's will, therefore, deterrence attempts to influence their future behavior. Adversaries are warned in advance that if they initiate action contrary to the interests of the state practicing deterrence, they will suffer unacceptable consequences. In this situation of shared risk, opponents thus are told that any pain or suffering is contingent upon *their* behavior, and that *they* are the ones who must make the agonizing decision to proceed toward a clash. If they act, then the threats will be carried out. If they do nothing, then they can avoid the threatened punishment indefinitely. As strategic theorist Thomas Schelling colloquially described it in *Arms and Influence*, one state basically says to another:

> If you cross the line we shoot in self-defense, or the mines explode....If *you* cross it, *then* is when the threat is fulfilled, either automatically, if we've rigged it so, or by obligation that immediately becomes due. But we can wait—preferably forever; that is our purpose.

To accomplish this objective, a number of factors must be taken into account.

1. Weighting Interests. The formulation of a strategy of deterrence must begin by weighing the genuine interests of one's country that may be threatened by hostile action and assessing their importance. Vital and central interests, such as protecting one's people and territory from attack, call for unambiguous defense. Less important or peripheral ones, however, would suggest different levels and forms of protection.

2. Commitment to Defend Those Interests. The next step is to create and convey a commitment to defend those interests. This is done by making *threats of punishment* if the opponent acts. In this process of bargaining with threats of force, communication is essential to convince an opponent of one's resolve and strength to enforce the threats. Some states attempting deterrence may prefer to do this by explicit personal messages between heads of government, diplomatic notes, or public speeches. Others may rely more on nonverbal means of conveying threats, such as troops stationed along a border, ships deployed in nearby waters, strategic superiority in weaponry, alliances, or historic patterns of defense. Regardless of the form of communication, however, the strategy of deterrence says to any potential aggressor: whatever you *hope* to achieve *will* be outweighed by the punishment.

3. Credible and Potent Threats. To be effective, such threats must be both credible and sufficiently potent in the eyes of the opponent. That is, they must pose a level of costs and risks that the adversary regards as of sufficient magnitude to overcome its motivation to challenge the defending power's position. Deterrence, in other words, is not simply a matter of announcing a commitment and then issuing threats. In order to successfully operationalize this strategy, the threats must be credible. When the potential power to hurt is used as bargaining power, the threat will deter an aggressor only if it is persuasive by being believable and does not sound like inflated bluster or rhetorical bluff.

There are two interdependent dimensions that provide credibility to threats. First, the deterring power must possess the *ability or capabilities* to inflict considerable harm and/or to prevent the adversary from accomplishing its objective by mounting an effective and punishing defense. A state must actually hold—and be able to persuade an opponent that it holds—the strength and usable capabilities to do what it threatens to do; otherwise it will not be believed. When Bismarck set out to deter France from launching any attack for revenge after 1871, decision makers in Paris had every reason to believe that the powerful German army possessed the ability to back up his threats. Similarly, when Nikita Khrushchev wanted to establish credibility for his country's own deterrent, he declared in a famous 1960 speech:

> The Soviet Army today possesses such combat means and such firepower as no army has ever had before. I stress once again that we already have enough nuclear weapons—atomic and hydrogen—and enough rockets to deliver them to the territory of a possible aggressor, and that if some madman should cause an attack on our state or on other socialists states, we could literally wipe out the country or countries that attack us off the face of the earth.

Coming in the wake of the successful launch of the Sputnik satellite, few doubted that the Soviet Union possessed such capabilities. But even having weapons of mass destruction does not necessarily ensure credibility. Indeed, one of the basic flaws of "Mutual Assured Destruction" was the nagging belief that nuclear weapons simply were not at all usable in any practical sense.

Second, statesmen implementing a strategy of deterrence must convey to the opponent that they have the *will or resolution* to defend the interests in question and to carry through on their threats if necessary. Leaders may possess considerable and perhaps even overwhelming military power that they are willing to threaten as a deterrent, but they may be unwilling to actually use it. That is, if a crisis begins to intensify well beyond its verbal stages and it becomes clear that the deliberate use of provocative threats and manipulation of risks is resulting in dangerous and unwanted escalation and perhaps even inadvertent war, as we shall see in Chapter 11 on crisis management, the increased probability of considerable costs might well erode the original motivation to enforce deterrent threats, thereby reducing credibility. Or, it may appear after reflection that the interests at stake are not as important as originally thought and thus not worth the price that might have to be paid for their defense.

4. Credibility and Vital Interests. In this regard, it is essential to recognize that the validity and credibility of a given commitment is directly related to its possessing a reasonable relationship to the deterring state's vital national interests. The credibility of will is in large part a function of just how serious a challenge to the status quo might be. Few would doubt the determination of a state to employ *strategic deterrence* to defend its vital and central interests against an invasion of its own territory or those of its closest allies if attacked. But what about *extended deterrence*, or the willingness to honor a commitment to weaker allies, neutral states, or questionable interests? In these cases, is someone else's well-being part of one's own vital national interest, and thus worth the costs of war—or not? If such doubts arise in the mind of an opponent, they seriously compromise the credibility of the commitment. The policy of "Massive Retaliation" suffered from exactly this problem, for although no doubts existed over the awesome power possessed by the United States, few believed that it would be willing to risk nuclear holocaust and its own destruction to defend territory thousands of miles from its own shores, say, in Korea or Vietnam.

5. Motivation of Opponent. Finally, any analysis of the principles of deterrence must also take into account what is *demanded of*—or, more appropriately, *denied*—an opponent and how this influences their motivation to refrain from initiating action. A strategy designed to deter may seek to deny adversaries something that they consider to be extremely valuable. This might include strategic strongholds, territory for expansion, access to mineral wealth or oil, or vague but nevertheless important notions of prestige or reputation. A leader highly motivated to obtain such things may conclude that inaction means being denied these objectives and is, for whatever reason, too high a price to pay. The threat may well be communicated clearly and credibly but, at the same time, ultimately be insufficient to deter. An aggressor may calculate, as did the Japanese in 1941 when they determined that to be denied the opportunity for expansion would be tantamount to "national suicide," that although the costs of launching a campaign might be relatively high compared to the prospective benefits, they are worth the risk. This concept is very important for deterrence in revealing that it is the initiator's "utility calculation"—not that of the defender—that determines whether or not a challenge will be made against the existing order.

The historical cases chosen for analysis in this chapter help to explain these principles more clearly and offer perspective on deterrence in action. All confirm the fact that deterrence does not take place in isolation, but in a broader context.

COLLECTIVE SECURITY FOR THE POST-1815 SETTLEMENT

Those leaders who led the struggle to defeat Napoleon understood that they could win neither the war nor the peace that would follow unless they worked together as partners. They calculated that the strong and seasoned French forces could not possibly be defeated unless confronted with a successfully mobilized military coalition. At the same time, they wisely looked beyond the immediate task toward the future, believing that whatever peace settlement and postwar order they might establish could be sustained only if they simultaneously created a system of collective security to serve as a deterrent against any possible resurgence of French aggression. For this reason, Britain, Austria, Russia, and Prussia agreed in 1814 to sign the Treaty of Chaumont. Here they agreed to establish a system of collective security. Their clearly communicated text provides a classic example of deterrence:

> The High Contracting Powers, reserving to themselves to concert together, on the conclusion of a peace with France, as to the means best adapted to guarantee to Europe, and to themselves reciprocally the continuance of the Peace, have also determined to enter, without delay, into defensive engagements for the protection of their respective States in Europe against every attempt which France might make to infringe the order of things resulting from such Pacification. To affect this, they agree that in the event of one of the High Contracting Parties being threatened with an attack by France, the others shall employ their most strenuous efforts to prevent it....

If any doubts existed about the wisdom of their thinking about the need to deter aggression, they quickly vanished when in March 1815 Napoleon escaped his exile on Elba, announced before adoring and tumultuous French crowds that he would again raise an army to gain fresh victories, and then launched a new campaign against Europe.

The fact that they had to renew military operations and finally defeat Napoleon in June once and for all at Waterloo immediately exposed the fragility of a system of peace and security without force to protect it. This vastly increased the motivation of the victorious powers to make sure that this did not happen again. They therefore renewed their commitment to implement a strategy of deterrence by means of collective security with even greater determination. To convey the credibility of their will, they openly pledged for all to see in the formal Quadruple Alliance of 1815 that they would collectively protect their new international system against any aggression from France. According to the text, they sought "to fix beforehand by a solemn treaty the principles which they propose to follow, in order to guarantee Europe from the dangers by which she may still be menaced." They thus formally threatened that should they be attacked, they would be "obligated to place themselves on a war establishment against that Power."

Interestingly enough, statesmen like Metternich and Castlereagh saw the wisdom of combining force and statecraft. They believed that deterrent threats of armed force often were necessary in international relations, but they also wisely understood that exclusive reliance on such threats in the absence of consensus on basic principles and a sense of responsibility to the system as a whole would only bring dangers. For this reason, they simultaneously stated in the text of the Quadruple Alliance itself their determination to actively employ diplomacy as well. They pledged to hold conferences and congresses to discuss any threats that might emerge and thereby act together in concert "for the purpose of consulting upon their common interests, and for the consideration of the measures which...shall be considered the most salutary for the repose and prosperity of Nations, and for the maintenance of the Peace of Europe."

This important combination was evident in other ways as well. The leaders of the Great Powers understood that solemn and explicitly conveyed words and treaty commitments can greatly increase the credibility of deterrent threats. But they also appreciated that whereas verbal and written communications can convey a certain level of resolve and intention, they are rarely sufficient to give credibility to the actual ability to enforce or carry out threats. Consequently, those who were determined to establish and maintain their post-Napoleonic international system made every effort to carefully create and orchestrate the collective military strength of the members of the Concert of Europe. They thus deployed occupation forces within France and stationed troops around its borders. The purpose of these forces, wrote Metternich with considerable insight, was to possess a "strong union of States" to deter "the storm" of possible aggression and revolution against the system as a whole. Few could doubt the strength of the Austrian army or the British navy at this time, or that of any of the Great Powers. Indeed, it was the criteria of armed force that allowed them to use the designation of "Great" in the first place.

These capabilities of the *individual* Great Powers, however, represented only part of the equation for deterrence. Perhaps the most critical feature came from the fact that credibility was enormously enhanced whenever threats could be made and enforced by *collective* security. After their terrifying experience in defeating Napoleon, the statesmen assembled at the Congress of Vienna, as we saw in Chapters 2 and 8, strongly believed that their safety could only be attained by creating a balance of power. They consequently designed a structure and a strategy that would inform any potential aggressor in advance that any attempt to impose hegemony would be met forcefully by the collective military might of the others aligned or balanced against them. They further understood and appreciated that this could be enhanced even more by avoiding rigid alliances against seemingly permanent enemies and by creating maximum flexibility that could enable weight to be shifted in one direction or the other, depending on circumstances. The fact that France was restored to its Great Power status as early as 1818 and invited to play its appropriate role as the fifth member in the equilibrium, for example, indicated that this long-term strategy of deterrence was not designed for vengeance or directed against one particular state, but against any state that might endanger the international system as a whole. A strong France, they reasoned, could help guard against an expanding Prussia to the north or assist others in checking Russia to the east. This warning of countervailing power was given in advance to deter: to create a fear of the consequences by means of a credible threat that would convince any leader tempted to launch a war that the costs of doing so would far outweigh any possible benefits.

Deterrence by collective security is always difficult, for both the common and conflicting interests of all parties must constantly be taken into account, and these vary according to time and circumstance. The Great Powers after 1815 certainly experienced their own share of disagreements about how best to threaten and to use their armed forces. Significant arguments emerged, for example, over the meaning of Tsar Alexander I's so-called "Holy Alliance," what they should do about revolutions in Naples and Spain, the legitimacy of intervening in the internal affairs of other states, or the dangers posed to foreign affairs at the time by the dynamic forces of liberalism and nationalism. These were to be expected. Nevertheless, the statesmen of the time remarkably managed to overcome their differences and act together as the Concert of Europe when serious threats to the system emerged. Indeed, their strategy of deterrence through collective security, when combined with other features such as the balance-of-power structure and the shared goals among the major actors within the system, proved to be so impressively successful that not one war occurred between the Great Powers for forty years.

BRITISH AND FRENCH ATTEMPTS TO DETER HITLER, 1939

Well before he even became the *Führer* of the Third Reich, Adolf Hitler had written in his venomous autobiography *Mein Kampf* that if he were ever placed in a position of power, he would seek to build a powerful German state by using armed force to crush domestic enemies at home and foreign enemies abroad. Among the latter, he focused his attention on those nations that stood in the way of his expansionist dream of *Lebensraum*, or living space, including Czechoslovakia and Poland. Rather than causing alarm, however, his dangerous ideas were largely dismissed or discounted by those who practiced a policy of appeasement, as explained in Chapter 3. Political leaders in Britain and France hoped that if they gave Hitler what he wanted he would be satisfied and therefore would refrain from any aggressive moves that might threaten the international system as a whole. Prime Minister Neville Chamberlain thus returned from the Munich Conference in September 1938 and told cheering crowds that he had secured "peace in our time." He acknowledged that the partition of the Sudetenland from Czechoslovakia had been given to Hitler as a sacrifice, but said that it was a small price to pay for peace. What he had secured in return, he announced as he waved the agreement triumphantly in the air, was Hitler's solemn word and actual signature on paper that this would be his "last territorial claim in Europe."

Hitler remained true to his word—for six months. Then, suddenly and in flagrant violation of the Munich Agreement, he ordered German troops in March 1939 to invade and completely subjugate the rest of Czechoslovakia. This not only eliminated Czechoslovakia as an independent state and member of the League of Nations, but ominously placed the armed forces of Germany all along the southern as well as the western borders of Poland, which Hitler had identified years before as one of his major targets for future expansion. Winston Churchill, who had been warning against the acute dangers of appeasement since its inception, consequently declared simply but accurately, "We are in the presence of a disaster of the first magnitude."

With the invasion of Czechoslovakia, the scales fell from the eyes of Chamberlain. "Is this the last attack upon a small state," he asked publicly, "or is it to be followed by another? Is this in fact a step in the direction of an attempt to dominate the world by force?" Chamberlain now came to realize that Hitler could not be trusted at all and that without credible force to back them up, any agreements with him had no permanent value whatsoever. This called for a complete and abrupt reversal of policy if war was to be averted. He found himself joined by the French government in this conviction. Both Britain and France consequently determined to adopt a new strategy of deterrence. Toward this end, they belatedly began to build what they hoped would be a bulwark against further German aggression by increasing the size and the state of readiness of their armed forces, introducing conscription, concluding a mutual assistance pact with Turkey, and promising support for Greece and Romania. The most important change by far, however, was the deterrent threat they issued to Germany by pledging to guarantee the integrity of Poland. On March 31, 1939, Chamberlain declared in Parliament:

> In order to make perfectly clear the position of His Majesty's Government...I now have to inform the House that...in the event of any action which clearly threatened Polish independence and which the Polish Government accordingly considered it vital to resist with their national forces, His Majesty's Government would feel themselves bound at once to lend the Polish Government all support in their power. They have given the Polish Government an assurance to this effect

In an effort to try to enhance the credibility of the threat, Chamberlain said, "I may add that the French Government have authorized me to make it plain that they stand in the same position in this matter as do His Majesty's Government."

Hitler was both surprised and angered by this declaration of deterrence and its threat to thwart his plans. When the news came from London, he flew into a rage, hammered his fist on a table top, stormed up and down his office, and shouted at those who witnessed the whole spectacle. As the French *chargé d'affaires* in Berlin reported to his superiors in Paris:

> For the first time the Third Reich has come up against a categorical no; for the first time a country has clearly expressed its determination to oppose force by force, and to reply to any unilateral movement with rifles and guns. This is the kind of language that is understood in Germany. But they have not been used to hearing it for a long time.

Yet, he added with some noteworthy unease in a sentence at the end of his dispatch, "It has also been difficult for them to believe their ears...."

Difficult to say the least. Given the previous years of appeasement, could this threat be believed or not? The British and French attempt to deter Hitler from attacking Poland, of course, would have been greatly enhanced if it had been a part of a larger system of credible collective security, like that of the Great Powers during the post-1815 settlement. But where were the others? Italy under Mussolini saw only advantages in aggression and actually signed the Pact of Steel with Hitler for future military adventures. Japan was busy planning its own attacks in Asia and the Pacific and similarly drew closer to Nazi Germany. The United States remained immobilized in isolation and stubbornly refused to join the League of Nations or to become involved in partnership with others in global affairs at all. China continued its descent into domestic chaos and weakness, rendering itself unable to play any significant role. This left only the Soviet Union as a potential source of military strength for deterrence, and certainly no effective opposition to Germany could be mounted in Eastern Europe without it. The threat of the countervailing power of Britain, France, and the Soviet Union, whose military forces not only outnumbered those of Germany but together presented a prospect of a two-front war, could have produced highly realistic fear in Hitler.

Yet, all of the efforts by the Soviets to do precisely this by seeking collective security arrangements against possible German aggression throughout the 1930s had been rebuffed by a West intensely distrustful of any Communist regime. Moreover, Poland had every reason to be suspicious of Soviet motives and to question whether Joseph Stalin's "protection" or Adolf Hitler's threats presented the greatest danger. At this stage, Stalin now found Hitler particularly eager to strike a deal. If the Soviet Union promised not to go to war against Germany if he attacked Poland, Hitler would pledge not to wage war against the Soviet Union and, in a secret protocol, would agree to let it take vast swaths of territorial spoils in the eastern half of Poland, Finland, the Baltic States, and Romania. Stalin, seeking to delay any military clash with Germany as long as possible while at the same time grabbing as much land as he could, took the bait. The two dictators therefore struck a ruthless bargain in the Nazi-Soviet Pact of August 1939.

With this agreement in hand, Hitler calculated that he had little to fear, at least in the short run. There likely would be no war in the east against the Soviet Union until he decided to launch one himself. There might be a war in the west against the British and the French, but who could tell? The British continually and explicitly conveyed their intent to carry through on their promise to defend Poland. Even as late as the end of August, Chamberlain drew on the historical lesson of what could happen with unclear signals and tried to make this deterrent threat as credible as possible. "It has been alleged that if His Majesty's Government had made their position more clear in 1914 the great catastrophe would have been avoided," he wrote with urgency to Hitler. "Whether or not there is any force in this allegation, His Majesty's Government are resolved that on this occasion there shall be no such tragic misunderstanding." In order to make sure that Hitler knew precisely where the British stood, he warned as explicitly as he possibly could that "they are resolved, and prepared, to employ without delay all of the forces at their command."

This was a clear warning communicated directly, but neither the British nor the French had taken any meaningful action to stop Hitler's aggression since he came to power. Indeed, he revealed his contempt for their weakness by describing them with one word: "worms." At the last minute, when the disastrous prospect of war confronted them directly, their will might falter again and they might renege on their pledge and abandon the Poles as they had the Czechs. After all, plenty of people in both London and Paris still asked openly in letters to the editor why they should have to die to save people they did not even know in far away Danzig. But if for some reason they actually did honor their commitment, Hitler reasoned, they would have great difficulty in rendering any significant military support in time to save Poland. In his mind, no one had the will or the ability to enforce their threats. Hitler therefore resolved to employ the force of arms to crush Poland without delay. "We have nothing to lose," he told his generals, "we have everything to gain." At dawn on September 1, 1939, German guns opened fire against Poland. This marked not only the complete failure of deterrence for the British and the French but, once they decided to fight, the beginning of the Second World War.

CONTEMPORARY AMERICAN DETERRENCE OVER TAIWAN

A newscast on BBC in July 2004 ran under the ominous headline: "Beijing Warns of War with Taiwan." This followed an earlier RAND study that concluded:

> Critical differences between Mainland China and Taiwan about the future of their relations make the Taiwan issue the most intractable and dangerous East-Asian flashpoint—and the one with the greatest potential for bringing the United States and China into confrontation in the near future.

To prevent such an outcome is the purpose of contemporary American deterrence over Taiwan.

This policy began with the onset of the Korean War in June 1950. Fearing that the new Communist government of Mao Zedong and the People's Republic of

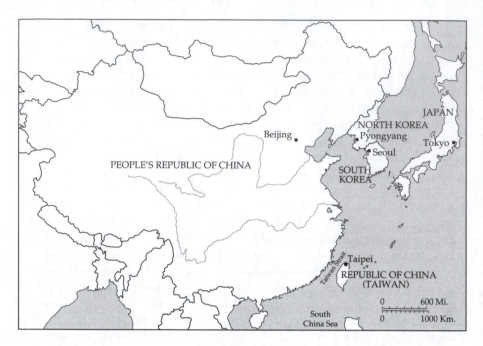

Contemporary Asia

China (PRC) would see the war as an opportunity to crush the U.S.-supported and rival Republic of China (ROC) of Chiang Kai-shek on the island of Taiwan, forcing it to unify with the mainland and thereby depriving the United States of what General Douglas MacArthur described as its "unsinkable aircraft carrier" midway up China's seaboard, President Harry Truman ordered the Seventh Fleet into the Taiwan Strait. The aim, he declared, was to deter Beijing by threatening that any aggression against Taiwan would be met by armed force and thereby "prevent the conflict from spreading." This threat received greater and more serious credibility when the United States formally signaled its intention to defend Taiwan by signing the bilateral Mutual Defense Treaty in 1954. Together, the fleet and the treaty constituted the beginning of the challenging and often changing American commitment to defend Taiwan by attempting to develop and maintain an acceptable and credible strategy of extended deterrence.

Some of the difficulties and complications of this strategy became readily apparent during the Taiwan Strait crises of 1954–1955 and 1958. Both of these began when the PRC decided to probe the extent of the American commitment far from its own shores by initiating heavy artillery barrages against ROC forces on the offshore islands of Quemoy and Matsu. When this occurred, considerable domestic political pressure was exerted on Congress and the White House by supporters of Chiang Kai-shek, collectively known as the "China Lobby," to strengthen the deterrent threat even further. For this reason, President Dwight Eisenhower in a press conference felt obliged to threaten that the United States would use tactical nuclear weapons against the Chinese Communists if war should break out. Chiang simultaneously expanded the size of his own armed forces and increasingly tried to push American leaders far beyond the mere defense of Taiwan into supporting any effort that he might make to invade the mainland and "liberate" China from Communist rule. That he attempted to bind the United States more firmly to his own aspirations in this way is understandable, but it served to demonstrate that extended deterrence can create serious dangers when it provides tempting opportunities for a weak ally to manipulate and embroil the much stronger deterring power in struggles that may not be in its best interests.

In June 1962, for example, Chiang once again threatened an invasion of the Chinese mainland, prompting the PRC to undertake military precautions and deployments. In this escalating situation, President John Kennedy feared that the United States could well be pulled into a wider conflict that it did not want, and therefore employed diplomatic channels to assure the Chinese Communist leaders that his country would not support any such ROC action. At the same time, however, he felt it necessary to remind them of America's commitment to defend the offshore islands and Taiwan. These positions, especially when combined with subsequent U.S. and Communist Chinese support for opposing sides during the Vietnam War, continued to exacerbate American relations with both the PRC and Taiwan for years.

A major transformation of America's deterrence strategy occurred when President Richard Nixon and his National Security Advisor Henry Kissinger concluded that the dramatic shifts in the geopolitical world of the Cold War necessitated that the United States and the People's Republic of China engage in *détente* and strive to reduce tensions. The first major indication of this change occurred with the signing of their 1972 Shanghai Communiqué, in which Nixon and Kissinger agreed with Beijing's highly motivated insistence that there could no longer be "two Chinas," that it alone represented the sole legal government of China, and that Taiwan must be considered an integral part of the People's Republic of China. This commitment was repeated and reinforced six years later, under the Carter administration, in a joint U.S.-PRC communiqué that reestablished formal diplomatic relations between the two states. At the same time, however, the United States announced that it would "maintain cultural, commercial, and other unofficial relations with the people of Taiwan."

Yet, the deliberate vagueness of these agreements and what appeared to supporters of Taiwan within the United States to be a diminution of deterrence provoked domestic political forces that prompted members of the U.S. Congress to reject the recommendation from the State Department and to pass the Taiwan Relations Act in 1979. According to the text, the key rested "upon the expectation that the future of Taiwan will be determined by peaceful means" and that anything else would be "a threat to the peace and security of the Western Pacific area and of grave concern to the United States." The act sought to strengthen the credibility of the deterrent threat by announcing that America would engage in arms sales and provide "defense articles and defense services in such quantities as may be necessary to enable Taiwan to maintain a sufficient self-defense capability." The president and Congress, it stated, would determine "appropriate action" in response to danger. Thus, although the Taiwan Relations Act asserted a deterrence commitment of some kind to oppose the use of force against the ROC, it left unclear exactly how the United States might respond if this actually occurred. The resulting uncertainty of this particular formulation thus came to be called "strategic ambiguity."

Further complications arose as a result of changing leaders and conditions. Domestic forces transformed the Republic of China into a democratic government. This enabled its Democratic Progressive Party to appeal to public opinion by asserting that Taiwan should never be absorbed into the PRC and become a sovereign independent state in its own right. Chinese Communist leaders became enraged at such statements and in 1996 initiated a war-threatening crisis with military exercises that rehearsed a missile attack and invasion of Taiwan. President Bill Clinton responded by signaling both resolve and capability by sending two U.S. aircraft carrier battle groups into the area (the largest display of U.S. military power in Asia since the Vietnam War). But at exactly the same time, he also dispatched National Security Advisor Sandy Berger and Undersecretary of State Peter Tarnoff to Taiwan to bluntly warn its leaders that U.S. deterrence did not mean a blank check and that America would not defend them if they unilaterally declared their independence. Secretary of State Madeleine Albright reiterated the same point at a news conference shortly thereafter in Beijing.

Ambiguities and difficulties continued. Taiwan's President Chen Shui-bian gained popularity at home by increasing his advocacy of sovereignty. The People's Republic of China launched an ambitious military modernization program and issued strident warnings that it might attack Taiwan before the 2008 Olympics if his pro-independence agenda persisted. President George W. Bush responded by describing the PRC as a "strategic competitor," sent National Security Advisor Condoleezza Rice to Beijing to issue tough deterrent warnings, and approved arms acquisitions by Taiwan that would enable them to strike high-value targets deep within the mainland. At the same time, the Bush administration warned Chen Shui-bian against taking any action that might alter the status quo, stressed that the growing economic ties between the United States and China would not be placed at risk, and worked with the PRC on common strategic interests in trying to restrict the nuclear weapons program of North Korea.

This challenge of trying to find a delicate balance in "strategic ambiguity" haunted the Obama administration as well. Although Taiwan's new President Ma Ying-jeou changed course to seek much greater accommodation with the mainland—and did so with the support of the United States—his government at the same time sought to significantly increase its military capabilities. Despite severe warnings from Beijing to not do so, President Obama notified Congress in 2010 of his intent to sell Taiwan several billion dollars worth of weapons, including Blackhawk helicopters, Patriot and Harpoon missiles, two mine-hunting ships, and upgrades for its F-16 A/B jet fighters. This sale was substantial, but it deliberately refrained from giving everything that Taiwan wanted. Nevertheless, Beijing reacted vehemently, declaring that the arms sale would create "severe harm" and "repercussions that neither side wishes to see."

The dangers and geopolitical complications grow more evident. China's motivation regarding Taiwan under the new leadership of Xi Jinping remains intense, not only because of domestic issues but because control would grant it enormous strategic advantage in projecting its naval power in Asia and in the South China Sea with its gateway to the Indian Ocean and to the world's oil transport routes. Taiwan's vulnerability is exacerbated by the fact that it lies only 100 miles away from China, whereas its major defender is half a world away. All parties are aware that as China continues to develop more sophisticated military capabilities, it diminishes the ability of the United States to deter. Indeed, a recent RAND study concluded that by the year 2020 the United States will no longer be able to defend Taiwan from a Chinese attack. Yet, if the United States abandons Taiwan to Beijing, it risks jeopardizing relations with Japan, South Korea, the Philippines, and other allies in the Pacific who will question the credibility of Washington's deterrent commitments to them. Political scientist Charles Glaser thus writes in a recent article in *Foreign Affairs* entitled "Will China's Rise Lead to War?" that contemporary American deterrence over Taiwan is "the most obvious and contentious flash point between the United States and China," full of dangers. "A crisis over Taiwan," he concludes, "could fairly easily escalate to nuclear war."

All of these developments and their implications for security in the East Asia–Pacific region have created a most difficult challenge for the United States to explicitly differentiate and then make credible what has come to be a strategy of dual deterrence over Taiwan. The first objective still remains to deter an armed invasion by the PRC against Taiwan (at the same time that Beijing seeks to practice counter-deterrence to prevent America from intervening in what it regards as its own internal affair). The second objective is to deter Taiwan from asserting a claim to be a separate sovereign state and making a unilateral declaration of independence that would trigger military attack from the mainland, thereby forcing the United States to decide whether it is willing to go to war with a nuclear power of more than 1,000,000,000 people. The American commitment to aid in the defense of Taiwan thus must tread a very fine and precarious line and make an extremely careful distinction between deterring *an unprovoked PRC attack on Taiwan* and the possibility of PRC military action *in response to a declaration of independence by Taiwan*. This, in turn, presents a very difficult security dilemma: how to dissuade one side without encouraging the other. Too much pressure against Beijing might encourage the Taiwanese to take greater risks in incrementally seeking what is described as "creeping independence," whereas too much pressure against Taiwan might encourage the PRC to harden its own position. In seeking to deter both sides, the United States runs the risk of deterring neither.

Such a policy of dual deterrence would be challenging even in the best of times, but it is rendered even more complicated by changing circumstances.

Commitments in deterrence are complex political-diplomatic-military phe-nomena, given to protect an ally or client against some dangers, under some circumstances, for some time, and each of these can change. As such, the evolving case of deterrence over Taiwan, like the others, serves as a valuable reminder that events do not take place in a vacuum but in a particular histori-cal context.

ANALYSIS

Having examined these three cases within the framework of both general principles and history, it is now possible to build upon that foundation and further explore what other lessons and insights might be discerned from past experience and how more recent changes in the context of our own time have influenced the strategy of deterrence.

One of the most important observations we can make is that, despite its attractions, the strategy of deterrence possesses a number of serious limita-tions and dangers. When compared with military strategies, bargaining with threats is understandably alluring. Threats are infinitely more palatable than the actual use of force. If successful, they can achieve policy objectives with much less money and loss of lives, fewer psychological and political costs, and less risk than strategies that rely directly or exclusively on unleashing force to influence international behavior. But these enticing features cannot be allowed to distract from the fact that bargaining with threats of force is inherently dangerous and comes with high risks. No policy maker in the world likes to be threatened with harm or punishment. Historical experience demonstrates again and again that intimidation can easily provoke anger, pride, suspicion, frustration, or a highly emotional reflex rather than a carefully calculated response that might actually encourage a desire for retaliation or revenge in the form of a response in kind, counterthreats, an arms race, or even preemp-tive war, among other undesired consequences. Although deterrent threats are designed to discourage and are *intended as defensive*, they often are *perceived as offensive* and therefore provoke. As the Russian representative to NATO said most recently in response to that portion of the American ballistic missile defense system (BMDS) stationed in Eastern Europe, "You say Defense, we see Threat." By their very nature, threats are escalatory and, as we saw in Chapter 8 and shall see in Chapter 11, can quickly violate the requirements of both negotiation and crisis management. Given these dangers of deterrence, politi-cal scientist Patrick Morgan warns that we may want to seriously "reconsider our willingness to continue trusting our fate to our capacities for violence."

Inherent in the calculus of deterrence, as seen in all of these cases, lies the assumption of a unitary, "rational" opponent—that is, one who can be deterred from taking a particular course of action by carefully calculating that the costs and risks of pursuing it clearly outweigh any benefits to be gained. But there are grave dangers lurking in oversimplification here. The adversary may be, in fact, a failed state, an ideological radical, a terrorist cell, or small group of several individuals who differ from each other, who must share power, and who must strike compromises within their group. Similarly, although some leaders, past and present, appear to have a much better ability than others to make rational calculations about unacceptable costs and potential benefits, not all actors see the world or calculate the value of gains and losses in the same way. Differences in beliefs, culture, ethical values, attitudes toward risk taking, knowledge of history and international politics, ability to handle stress, perceptions of logic, and views of themselves and others, among other factors, can vary greatly. A specific actor's mind-set, preferred way of behaving, degree of self-control, and how these might correspond or conflict with one's own are difficult to obtain, interpret, and apply correctly in assessing intentions or predicting responses. Moreover, as de Callières noted many years ago, when it comes to force and statecraft, many leaders demonstrate "passion and temperament more than reason."

The efforts at collective security after 1815, for example, were constantly challenged by the seemingly irrational desires of Tsar Alexander I to suppress "liberal" regimes, of the British to support them, and of the French to extend revolutionary fervor and renew the glory that was once theirs under Napoleon. Chamberlain's policy of appeasement rested upon a seriously incorrect image of Hitler and wishful thinking, and it foundered for the most part on the rocks of Hitler's completely insatiable appetite for conquest and his willingness to launch a war to get what he wanted. U.S. deterrence policy over Taiwan similarly had to confront an extremely hostile and highly ideological Communist regime in Beijing, which constantly condemned America for its capitalism, imperialism, racism, and support for archrival Chiang. Although some of the more bombastic rhetoric has changed today, some Chinese leaders still exhibit characteristics of paranoia and entitlement and have repeatedly said that they would be willing to risk defeat in war rather than allowing China to be permanently divided and denied the strategic assets of Taiwan.

Any power seeking to deter another also must consider the critical issue of weighing both its own and its opponent's interests in order to calculate the utility of various policy options. It is often difficult to rationally determine one's own national interests, let alone those of an opponent, but failure to do so can result in the disintegration of even the best deterrence strategy. This can be readily seen in the way in which the balance of power and the congress system sufficed to deter French or any other aggression after 1815, but started to show signs of strain as the divergent interests of the Great Powers began to manifest themselves. Likewise, the British and French attempt to deter Hitler's attack on Poland was hampered by the highly divergent interests between the Soviet Union seeking to expand its influence, on the one hand, and those trying to obtain its participation in the security agreement while at the same time limiting its penetration of Eastern Europe, on the other. Lastly, as the expressions of "strategic ambiguity" and "dual deterrence" imply, the United States has had great difficulty establishing and articulating its own tangible interests in its relations with Taiwan and the People's Republic of China, particularly in light of their own respective, easily understood, and intensely held vital national interests.

After assessing its own and the other party's interests, the deterring power then must make and convey an explicit or implicit commitment to defend the ally, territory, or interest it perceives as being threatened. This, too, is not as simple a task as it might first appear. The members of the Quadruple Alliance clearly communicated their commitment to deter further French military action beyond its borders by articulating the terms of their treaty and pledging a specific quantity of troops in the event of any violation. Their determination to defend the post-1815 system by using the countervailing weight of the balance of power, however, was certainly serious, although it remained much more general in its expression and was not directed against any particular country. Chamberlain's attempt to practice deterrence suffered from many problems, but an explicit communication was not among them, for he repeatedly made his pledge to Poland as clear and unambiguous to Hitler as he possibly could. The articulation of a clear commitment thus is neither a simple nor a sufficient means of implementing successful deterrence. In contrast, the American policy of "strategic ambiguity" toward Taiwan may afford the United States maximum flexibility, but at the same time it creates considerable uncertainty and presents more questions than answers about the actual extent of its deterrent commitment.

As discussed earlier in this chapter, the deterring power must back up its commitment with threats that are both credible and sufficiently potent in the eyes of aggressors to prevent them from attempting the undesired course of action. The credibility of a threat is comprised of two components, the first of which is the ability or capabilities to inflict considerable damage upon an opponent. In this regard, the members of the Quadruple Alliance were demonstrably capable of actually doing what they threatened to do. The combined strength of the Great Powers, acting in concert with their countervailing military and naval might, could defeat France or another state that might endanger the maintenance of the international system. The United States similarly possesses sufficient capabilities to inflict staggering damage on China in the event of an armed attack against Taiwan. During the 1939 case attempting to deter Hitler, in contrast, the British and the French had significant military and naval forces, but without the support of the Soviet Union, these were insufficient to create a fear of unacceptable losses within Germany in the short run or to render timely assistance to their ally of Poland. Thus, the issue of a deterring power's capability can be seen as a critical element in the development of a successful strategy.

The possession of vast capabilities, however, sometimes presents its own dangers. That is, it can easily create the illusion among the most powerful that simply threatening to use their armed forces will get them what they want. Capability fails in those instances when the force possessed by the deterring power is either inappropriate or unusable in a given situation. All of Britain's vaunted sea power of the Royal Navy could not deter France's 1822 intervention in Spain to restore the Bourbon monarchy if the other great land powers approved of the action. In examining other historical cases, it can be seen that the superpowers were continually frustrated throughout the Cold War by the fact that their powerful nuclear weapons appeared to have so little impact on preventing military conflicts in the Third World. Despite providing large qualities of arms to their respective Arab and Israeli allies, for example, neither the Soviets nor the Americans were able to deter invasions in the 1973 Arab-Israeli War. Similarly, there are many today who find it difficult to understand why America's huge and unparalleled arsenal of military might cannot fully deter terrorist attacks.

The second component of credibility comes from the will and resolution of the deterring power to defend the interests in question. In the successful examples of deterrence among the case studies, it is evident that there exists a strong correlation between the demonstration of firm resolve and the success of the policy. The validity of a given commitment, of course, is directly related to the degree to which it is related to the nation's vital interests. Metternich, Castlereagh, and other statesmen who met in 1814 and 1815 strongly believed that their interests would be best served by peace and security, and thus they were firmly resolved to not allow France or any other country to launch another set of wars. They manifested their determination by using occupation troops in conjunction with firm commitments in international treaties. In sharp contrast, in 1939 the will and resolve of the Allied powers was seriously in doubt in Hitler's mind as a result of years of appeasement. As Churchill described it in *The Gathering Storm*, whatever credibility the British and the French once possessed to enforce their threats had been "squandered and thrown away." Whether the United States will view its interests as requiring the defense of Taiwan in the event of a Chinese invasion with its consequent likelihood of monumental costs, of course, remains an open question that will be answered only through time.

But using force and statecraft together in deterrence is difficult, and even capabilities and resolve are not fully sufficient to guarantee success. An analysis of efforts to deter also must take into account what is being denied to opponents and how this influences their motivation to seriously challenge the status quo. Here the level of an opponent's motivation is the key. After 1815, the newly restored monarchy in France had no motive for adventurism or starting another series of disastrous wars and thus submitted willingly to the restrictions placed on it by the Quadruple Alliance and then the Concert of Europe. Although the People's Republic of China is highly motivated to seek unification, it nevertheless appears to be content to bide its time and not risk a military confrontation with the United States as long as Taiwan does not unilaterally declare its independence, perhaps hoping that American deterrence will weaken by stages rather than collapsing all at once. When the British and the French announced that they would defend Poland, on the other hand, Hitler declared that his motive for territory was too strong to be denied and that he had no intention of being deterred from his course. "I am determined," he shouted after receiving the threat, "to continue to march on this path!" It can be seen, then, that a sufficiently potent deterring force must exist not only in reality but, perhaps more importantly, in the mind of the potential aggressor as well.

For all these reasons, it is critical to appreciate that deterrence is most effective when it is employed in conjunction with other instruments of statecraft, that is, when it is used as one among several means of foreign policy and not as a substitute for skillful diplomacy. The Allied powers of 1815 clearly recognized this fact when they allowed for the rapid rehabilitation of France in the international system and established their deterrence commitments accordingly. By reintegrating France, providing incentives, and establishing the Concert of Europe, the members of the Congress of Vienna laid the groundwork for a system that prevented a major war in Europe for four decades. This was truly a successful application of the strategy of deterrence in conjunction with other diplomatic means. Similarly, while maintaining its deterrent threat over Taiwan, the United States has worked to establish many diplomatic, economic, and cultural ties of cooperation to avoid war with the People's Republic of China. The same cannot be said for the period after the First World War, for in their efforts to deter Germany from aggression and to isolate the Soviet Union to prevent the spread of Communism, the victorious powers employed only threats. They thereby created two "pariah" nations that would later combine to thwart the deterrent provisions of the Versailles Treaty by concluding the 1939 Nazi-Soviet Pact, paving the way to the Second World War.

Research on the successes and the sobering failures of deterrence also demonstrates that an exclusive reliance on negative threats precludes any possibility of using positive reassurance, incentives, or inducements to help resolve serious differences. Similarly, if the power to hurt is seen only in terms of armed force, military might, or physical punishment, then valuable nonmilitary and nonlethal instruments are completely dismissed. International disputes arise over many different and complex issues, but not all problems are military problems that can be solved by military means. It is therefore instructive to consider the possibilities of nonmilitary threats short of force. Lessons drawn from the richness of statecraft in the past would suggest that these might include withdrawing from negotiations, recalling ambassadors, terminating commercial relations, or imposing economic sanctions, among many other possibilities. A recognition of these gradual and differentiated measures may encourage leaders to consider a more flexible, careful, and specific tailoring of threats to fit the unique circumstances of each bargaining situation, rather than an automatic and exclusive reliance on military might alone. Such refined distinctions may become increasingly important, for as some forms of armed force become less and less usable in certain cases, other kinds of threats, in combination with diplomatic efforts, become all the more critical.

This theme of the need for greater differentiation and sophistication brings us to our final conclusion that, like all other strategies, deterrence is heavily dependent on context. Each and every historical and contemporary case occurs within a time, a place, and with particular people that condition the possibilities and the constraints under which the principles of deterrence operate. As such, deterrence cannot possibly compensate for a deficient foreign policy ill adapted to the specific challenges at hand.

The particular circumstances of each case thus must be seen within the broader historical context of the diplomatic revolution, or those dramatic changes that have transformed certain features of diplomacy and the evolving international system through time. Moving from the more distant to the most recent of the three cases studied in this chapter, for example, one can see the increasing impact of public opinion. Although it had minimal influence on the statesmen at the Congress of Vienna, public opinion greatly influenced governments in 1939 and certainly continues to do so in the contemporary American deterrence policy over Taiwan. Similarly, although neither Metternich nor Castlereagh paid much attention to economics, extensive investment and trade play an especially powerful role in deterrent threats and incentives in Chinese-American relations today. The shared culture and norms of diplomacy among the Great Powers that made collective security possible after 1815 were shattered at the time of Hitler, Stalin, and Mussolini. One of the most dramatic transformations, of course, can be seen with the profound impact of technology. Advances in transportation and communication certainly played their role in moving people and messages from one capital to another, but this has been overshadowed by those changes in weapons technology that transformed deterrent threats of war with smooth-bore muskets after the Napoleonic wars into contemporary threats of war with weapons of mass destruction.

Indeed, it is precisely this revolution in weapons technology—and the dangers that it possesses—that leads some foreign policy specialists and even some officials to sharply challenge the efficacy of much of the dominant American strategy of deterrence. They point particularly to today's inherent dangers of threat-based strategies, the possibility of incalculable damage and loss of lives, and the hair-trigger problems and high risks caused by launch-on-warning alert systems, vulnerabilities in command and control, and the acute dangers that new developments in weapons of mass destruction pose to their owners as well as to their targets. In addition, some critics also argue that deterrence during the Cold War may have provoked as much as it restrained the Soviets and actually prolonged superpower tensions by a "balance of terror" dependent on "nuclear blackmail." Moreover, they observe, at the time of the Cold War there was an assumption by Americans that Soviet and Chinese leaders would behave rationally and prudently in the face of threats of severe punishment if they challenged the vital interests of the United States. But times and adversaries have changed, argue these critics, and this fact requires a reassessment and a much more careful and sophisticated analysis of a particular opponent's thinking, beliefs, and approaches to risk calculation and risk acceptance. In our time, there may well be those who are completely insensitive to deterrent threats.

One of the most significant features of the diplomatic revolution, for example, is the emergence of nonstate actors and, even more specifically, of terrorists and suicide bombers. As the attacks of September 11, 2001, against the World Trade Center and the Pentagon revealed with shocking clarity, some adversaries calculate costs and benefits in very different ways and are not at all deterred by threats of military action. These actors are intensely moti-vated—indeed, they are eager and willing to sacrifice their lives—to achieve their objectives. Some do not fear force as punishment, but believe that it actu-ally enhances their legitimacy and increases their support. Other difficulties stem from the fact that terrorists generally lack developed decision-making structures, well-defined and reliable lines of authority, effective command and control over operational units, and many identifiable assets, such as massed armies in the field or territory with specific borders, that can be located and targeted. Each of these factors greatly complicates or even defeats efforts to employ strategies of deterrence against them. The implications of these prob-lems will be discussed in the Conclusion, which presents ongoing and future challenges for force and statecraft.

SUGGESTIONS FOR FURTHER EXPLORATION

The general theory of deterrence can be found in Alexander L. George and Richard Smoke, *Deterrence in American Foreign Policy: Theory and Practice* (New York, 1974). Many other stimulating treatments also exist, including NATO, "Deterrence and Defense Posture Review, 2012," at www.nato.int; T. V. Paul et al. (eds.), *Deterrence in the Twenty-First Century* (Chicago, 2009); Nick Ritchie, "Deterrence Dogma?," *International Affairs*, 85 (January 2009): 81–98; Robert Art and Kenneth Waltz, *The Use of Force* (New York, 2009 ed.); Thomas Schelling, *Arms and Influence* (New Haven, CT, 2008 ed.); Keith Payne, *The Great American Gamble: Deterrence Theory and Practice from the Cold War to the Twenty-First Century* (Fairfax, VA, 2008); Curtis Signorino and Ahmer Tarar, "A Unified Theory and Test of Extended Immediate Deterrence," *American Journal of Political Science*, 50 (July 2006): 586–605;Lawrence Freedman, *Deterrence* (Boston, 2004); Patrick Morgan, *Deterrence Now* (New York, 2003); Richard K. Betts, *Nuclear Blackmail and Nuclear Balance* (Washington, DC, 1987); Robert Jervis, Richard Ned Lebow, and Janice Gross Stein, *Psychology and Deterrence* (Baltimore, 1985); Paul K. Huth and Bruce M. Russett, "What Makes Deterrence Work?: Cases from 1900 to 1980," *World Politics*, 36 (July 1984): 496–526; Paul Gordon Lauren, "Theories of Bargaining with Threats of Force," in Paul Gordon Lauren (ed.), *Diplomacy: New Approaches in History, Theory, and Policy* (New York, 1979); John Foster Dulles, "A Policy of Boldness," *Life*, XXXII (May 19, 1952); and Bernard Brodie (ed.), *The Absolute Weapon* (New York, 1946).

Deterrence and collective security during the post-Napoleonic period is discussed in G. John Ikenberry, *After Victory* (Princeton, 2000); Paul Schroeder, *The Transformation of European Politics* (Oxford, 1994); Alan Sked, *Europe's Balance of Power* (London, 1979); Henry Kissinger, *A World Restored* (New York, 1973 ed.); Paul Schroeder, *Metternich's Diplomacy at Its Zenith* (New York, 1962); Clemens von Metternich, *Mémoirs: documents et écrits divers*, Alfons von Klinkowström (ed.) (Paris, 1881–1886).

Treatments of the failure to deter Hitler can be found in Frank McDonough, *Hitler, Chamberlain, and Appeasement* (Cambridge, 2002); Richard Davis, *Anglo-French Relations Before the Second World War* (New York, 2001); Keith Robbins, *Appeasement* (London, 1997); D. C. Watt, *How War Came* (London, 1989); Allan Bullock, *Hitler: A Study in Tyranny* (New York, 1962 ed.); Winston Churchill, *The Gathering Storm* (Boston, 1948); and materials from the British Foreign Office in *Documents on British Foreign Policy, 1919–1939* (London, 1946–1985) and from the French Foreign Office as *Documents diplo-matiques, 1938–1939* (Paris, 1939).

The case of Taiwan is analyzed in Charles Glaser, "Will China's Rise Lead to War?," *Foreign Affairs*, 90 (March/April, 2011): 80–91; Nancy Bernkopf Tucker, *Strait Talk* (Cambridge, MA, 2011); C. Fred Bergsten et al., *China's Rise* (Washington, DC, 2009); the 2009 RAND report "New Opportunities and Challenges for Taiwan's Security"; Nancy Bernkopf (ed.), *Dangerous Strait* (New York, 2005); "Beijing Warns of War with Taiwan," BBC News, July 30, 2004; David M. Lampton, "Is Pentagon Fueling Tensions in Taiwan Strait?," *Straits Times*, July 22, 2004; Douglas McCready's 2003 Strategic Studies Institute report, "Crisis Deterrence in the Taiwan Strait"; Robert S. Ross, "Navigating the Taiwan Strait: Deterrence, Escalation Dominance, and US-China Relations," *International Security*, 27 (Fall 2002): 48–85; Pan Zhongqi's 2001 Stimson Center report, "The Dilemma of Deterrence"; and the 2000 RAND report entitled "Taking Charge." Evolving developments can be followed by exploring—and comparing—the Web sites of the U.S. Department of State at www.state.gov, the Foreign Ministry of the People's Republic of China at www.fmprc.gov.cn, and the Foreign Ministry of the Republic of China at www.mofa.gov.tw.

History abounds with many cases of deterrence for those interested in further exploration. Among some of the more suggestive are America's Monroe Doctrine against Europe (1823), Britain and France against Russia (1853), the North's efforts to deter British intervention in the American Civil War (1862–1865), Bismarck against Austria (1870), Germany against France after 1871, the Anglo-German naval arms race prior to 1914, the Berlin Blockade (1948), the United States and NATO against the Soviet Union after 1949, Chinese Communist intervention in the Korean War (1950), the Eisenhower Doctrine in the Middle East (1957–1958), American "Pactomania," the Berlin Crisis (1961), outbreak of the Arab-Israeli War (1973), Operation Desert Shield to deter Saddam Hussein from attacking Saudi Arabia and Israel (1990–1991), the creation of no-fly zones over Iraq to protect Shi'a Muslims and Kurds from attacks (1991–2002); arms sales to Saudi Arabia to deter Iran (2010); and ongoing Pakistani-Indian relations.

—10—

Coercive Diplomacy

In the intense heat of August 1990, Saddam Hussein's well-armed Iraqi troops invaded neighboring Kuwait and quickly overran its ill-prepared defenses. This blatant act of aggression imperiled security throughout the Middle East, threatened oil supplies, and shocked world leaders and peoples alike as they contemplated what would happen if they acquiesced to this action and thereby passively allowed the strong to conquer the weak at will. A remarkable international consensus rapidly emerged, therefore, to demand that Saddam pull his forces completely out of Kuwait. To make this happen, and in accordance with the provisions of the UN Charter, members of the Security Council authorized the application of coercive diplomacy against him. They began by imposing sanctions, instituting an embargo, and freezing financial assets to hurt him economically, keeping the threat of resorting to military force in the background. When this gradual turning of the screw failed to erode his motivation, they dramatically escalated their level of coercion. Working closely with other countries as partners, President George Bush the elder obtained consensus and support for an explicit ultimatum backed by the threat of force. They demanded a complete withdrawal from Kuwait and threatened "to use all necessary means" unless full compliance occurred by the deadline of January 15, 1991. To enhance the credibility of this threat, more than 500,000 troops, armed with highly sophisticated weapons, were positioned for an attack. As U.S. Secretary of State James Baker described it: "Iraq must either comply with the will of the international community and withdraw peacefully from Kuwait or be expelled by force." Despite this threat and the overwhelming military power poised against him, Saddam Hussein refused to comply. His motivation to retain his conquest was greater than his motivation to avoid war. Diplomatic coercion consequently failed and the Persian Gulf War began.

This certainly represented neither the first nor the last effort at coercive diplomacy. Due to profound concerns about brutal violations of human rights and their impact on security, NATO attempted to coerce Slobodan Milosevic to pull all of his forces out of Kosovo in 1999. For much the same reason, many members of the United Nations, the European Union, and the Arab League tried to compel Muammar Gaddafi during 2011 to stop unleashing bloodshed against his own people and to relinquish his control of Libya, as they did in 2011–2013 against Bashar al-Assad of Syria. Each of these recent cases, among many others, came in a long line of efforts to employ diplomatic coercion. For centuries, thoughtful practitioners and observers have recognized that although dangers and limitations certainly exist, attempts to gain objectives by threatening—as compared to actually using—punishment might be accomplished with fewer costs and less bloodshed than resorting to war. Over 2,300 years ago in China, Sun Tzu wrote in *The Art of War* about the value of threatening to use force to intimidate and thereby influence an adversary's will. Thucydides similarly observed in his *History of the Peloponnesian War* at approximately the same time how the Greek city-states often engaged in making threats in order to get what they wanted. He recounted how in one of the most famous cases of coercive diplomacy, the powerful Athenians issued demands to the much weaker Melians, threatening that failure to comply would result in great punishment. "You, by giving in," they declared, "would save yourself from disaster . . . [for] your actual resources are too scanty to give you a chance of survival against the forces that are opposed to you at this moment." Machiavelli in his *Art of War* and *The Prince* provided other suggestions about employing threats, as did Hobbes in his *Leviathan* when emphasizing the "coercive power to compel." Even the refined and restrained François de Callières maintained that every diplomat must understand the significance of pressure in order to be effective in persuasion and bargaining.

Statesmen of the classical period of diplomacy possessed a general knowledge of these writings and, through time, increasingly made coercive diplomacy an integral part of their conventional wisdom and practice of statecraft. They never systematically articulated the principles of the strategy, however, or explicitly identified its various characteristics. Instead, they simply observed through their own successes and failures that as a political-diplomatic strategy of bargaining by using threats, it provided a valuable alternative to an exclusive reliance on military action. They learned through time, for example, that strong threats could sometimes persuade an opponent to stop an invasion or give up territory. They also came to learn that coercive diplomacy could be a seductive strategy that held hidden limitations and dangers, for sometimes threats could backfire and escalate, even to war.

These broad and rather simple generalizations about coercive diplomacy, like those about deterrence, prevailed until military technology made it possible to distinguish the power to hurt from the power to destroy. Once this occurred with strategic bombing, the threat to inflict harm could be separated, in fact as well as in theory, from the threat to destroy military capabilities. With the increased dangers made possible by nuclear weapons and sophisticated delivery systems during the Cold War, it thus became critical to make a distinction between *threats* and the actual *use* of armed force in statecraft. As a consequence, theorists and strategists began to devote serious and attention to identifying and understanding the principles of coercive diplomacy.

Principles of Coercive Diplomacy

In his pioneering study entitled *The Strategy of Conflict*, theorist Thomas Schelling observed that "most conflict situations are essentially *bargaining* situations." For this reason, he argued with considerable insight that statecraft should be concerned not "with the efficient *application* of force but with the *exploitation of potential force*." In *Arms and Influence*, he further discussed how nations use threats of their capacity for violence as bargaining power:

> To inflict suffering gains nothing and saves nothing directly; it can only make people behave to avoid it. The only purpose, unless sport or revenge, must be to influence somebody's behavior, to coerce his decision or choice. To be coercive, violence has to be anticipated. And it has to be avoidable by accommodation. The power to hurt is bargaining power.

With this in mind, he therefore concluded, "There is a difference between taking what you want and making someone give it to you....It is the difference...between action and threats."

These particular observations, in addition to the work of many other theorists, help us to understand that the strategy of coercive diplomacy, or forceful persuasion (or *compellance*, as some prefer to call it), employs threats to persuade an opponent to do something. It seeks to convince an adversary to call off or undo some encroachment, such as removing troops or weapons from a particular area, halting an invasion in progress, or giving up territory that has been occupied. To do this, coercive diplomacy—like deterrence, with which it is frequently compared—generally bargains with threats of force. But unlike deterrence, which attempts to dissuade an opponent from undertaking action that *has not yet been initiated*, coercive diplomacy attempts to reverse actions that *are already occurring or have been undertaken* by an adversary. Deterrence tries to *inhibit* behavior by fear of the consequences. To deter, a state incurs an obligation to defend or digs in and waits—in the interest of inaction. Coercive diplomacy, in contrast, tries to *initiate* behavior by fear of the consequences. To coerce, a state puts into motion a policy to make the other move—in the interest of action. It is the opponent who must act in order to avoid a collision.

Another distinction lies in the difference of purpose. Although each attempts to influence behavior, deterrence is basically a defensive strategy, while coercive diplomacy can be either defensive or offensive in nature. Defensive coercion may be attempted by a single nation, a collective group or alliance of states, or the United Nations to persuade an opponent to stop or undo an encroachment that is viewed as highly dangerous to the maintenance of the status quo or the international system, and it is often employed when deterrence has failed. Offensive coercion, on the other hand, may be attempted in order to blackmail adversaries to give up something that they already possess, rather than having to forcefully take it.

Coercive diplomacy thus is different from the crude use of military force, for it seeks to *persuade* opponents to stop their aggression or change course, rather than physically bludgeoning them into doing it. Like deterrence, coercive diplomacy tries to employ threats not to harm an adversary physically or negate their capabilities, but to affect their motivation or *will*. It attempts to convince an opponent that their interests would be best served by changing the direction of their behavior and thereby avoiding the threatened punishment, giving them the opportunity to stop or back off before employing force or escalating its use. They are told that it is *they* who must turn aside if catastrophe is to be avoided. As such, the behavior of one is contingent upon the behavior of the other—and neither one is capable of having full control of the other. Coercive diplomacy, therefore, is essentially a *diplomatic* strategy backed by the threat of force. The volatile nature of the bargaining, however, when coupled with the employment of threats and perhaps the demonstration of just enough exemplary military force to emphasize one's determination to use more if necessary, often requires careful and appropriate diplomatic communication and signaling, bargaining, negotiating, and crisis management with the opponent.

This strategy offers the possibility of achieving one's objective economically, with little bloodshed, fewer political and psychological costs, and often with much less risk of escalation than does traditional military strategy. For this reason, it is often dangerously beguiling. Leaders of militarily powerful countries are sometimes arrogantly tempted to believe that they, with little risk to themselves, can issue demands and make threats that easily intimidate weaker opponents. But most people do not like to be threatened or have demands made against them, and even a superpower can fail to coerce a weak adversary and may find itself drawn into a costly and prolonged conflict. If a recalcitrant opponent refuses to comply and, in effect, calls the bluff of the coercing power, the latter will be caught somewhere between backing down and thereby risking the loss of credibility and future bargaining power, or waging war and thereby risking loss of life and military defeat. Because both outcomes are possible, leaders should never undertake coercive diplomacy without the greatest of care.

Given the obvious dangers and high risks of this strategy, it is therefore important to identify the conditions that favor its success, or by their absence, mitigate against it. Comparisons of historical cases suggest that five are of critical importance.

1. Motivation. Since coercive diplomacy is directed toward an opponent's will, a coercing power must convey that it is more highly motivated to achieve its stated demands than the adversary is to oppose them. It must, in other words, communicate the message that there is an asymmetry of motivation: that, for whatever reason, its own propensity for creating and tolerating risks is by far the higher of the two. In this regard, as we saw with deterrence, the motivation of a state attempting coercive diplomacy becomes more convincing if it can demonstrate that its vital national interests are genuinely at stake and that these are acknowledged by strong domestic and international support. But motivation is affected by many psychological, political, and cultural factors, and these can be influenced by what is demanded, what is threatened, what is offered, and what amount of time is offered for a resolution.

2. Nature of Demands. Careful attention, for example, must be given as to what is demanded of an opponent, for this can greatly affect the balance of motivation. The demand that an adversary *stop* a particular course of action requires appreciably less than a demand to *undo* whatever has already been gained at the cost of time, money, prestige, and perhaps even lives. This distinction is extremely important for an obvious reason: if one demands a great deal, the opponent's motivation to not comply will likely be strengthened. But if the coercing power can carefully limit its demands to what is essential to itself without thereby humiliating or engaging the vital interests of the opponent and is clear about the precise terms of settlement, then it is more likely to create an asymmetry of motivation that favors the success of the strategy as a whole.

3. Credible and Potent Threats. Motivation also is affected by fear. Coercive diplomacy—like deterrence—requires threats that are both credible and sufficiently potent in the mind of the opponent to create a fear of *unacceptable punishment* if there is noncompliance with the demands. To do this, the coercing state must demonstrate that it has both the *ability or capabilities* and the *will and resolution* to inflict unacceptable damage on something that opponents value more than the object of dispute, and thereby to persuade them to overcome their natural reluctance to comply with demands and to take the kind of action that will avert punishment. These threats might involve economic sanctions, the severance of diplomatic relations, demonstrations of force, blockades, limited invasion, declaration of war, or escalating the targets or the types of weapons used in a war already in progress, among many other possibilities. Regardless of the precise nature of the threat, however, the potential power to hurt is used as bargaining power to induce adversaries to avoid it.

4. Incentives. Coercive diplomacy is far more than just "the art of making threats," for the offer of positive incentives can have a profound impact on motivation as well. Practitioners of coercive diplomacy often mistakenly rely solely on threats of punishment and thereby completely overlook the often critical importance of offering incentives. Yet, there are times when diplomatic objectives can be achieved only if one offers genuine and even substantial concessions. Coercive diplomacy thus is best conceived as a flexible strategy in which the "carrots" of incentives are combined with the "sticks" of threats in such a way that both bargaining sides believe they are getting "something for something."

5. Urgency. Finally, those practicing the strategy of coercive diplomacy need to decide how much of a sense of urgency to create in the adversary's mind to achieve compliance with the demands. In crisis situations, time is short and resolution is normally sought sooner rather than later. On some occasions, leaders adopt a "try-and-see" approach. In this variant of the strategy, a coercing power makes modest threats and waits to see whether they will suffice to persuade the opponent before escalating and taking the next step to further action. This approach is consistent with the principles of crisis management, for it attempts to slow the momentum, provide time for communication and thoughtful decision making, and gradually turn the screw of coercion by an incremental progression of pressure if necessary. When, on the other hand, strategists wish to deliberately create an acute sense of urgency, they go to the other extreme and employ a full-blown ultimatum, complete with a demand, a threat, and the characteristically short time limit for compliance. Historically, such limits have ranged from a few weeks or days down to only a few hours. The 1939 British ultimatum to Hitler after he invaded Poland demanded a positive rely within two hours, for example, and the American ultimatum to Germany in 1916 demanded compliance "immediately." Since they are designed to speed up the pace of bargaining, it is not at all uncommon for ultimata to announce that "the clock is ticking toward a showdown" or that "time is running out."

These five components, of course, are not always fully present or tailored to fit the context and unique circumstances of each situation. This fact makes coercive diplomacy fraught with risks and much more difficult and problematic than is often thought. The motives and interests at stake in the conflict may be vague or incorrectly perceived, the demands made on the opponent may lack clarity or specificity, the threat of punishment for noncompliance may be ambiguous or of insufficient potency or credibility, a coercing power may not fully convey a sense of just how urgently it wants to find a solution to the conflict at hand, or the target of coercive diplomacy may engage in unjustified wishful thinking. Moreover, people normally do not respond well to coercive demands and threats made against them. They may lash out in an emotional response, launch a preemptive strike, or dig in their heels, creating a response that is the complete opposite of what was desired. Unlike deterrence, in which a target easily can comply while claiming that it never intended to change its behavior in the first place, coercion requires that the target visibly alter its behavior in overt submission with a great loss of face. All this helps to explain why success in the application of coercive diplomacy is not easy to achieve, why the strategy so often fails, and why disaster can be just a single decision or mistake away.

American "Gunboat Diplomacy," 1852–1854

The expression "gunboat diplomacy" came into general usage during the nineteenth century as maritime powers increasingly saw that in conspicuous demonstrations of armed force, navies often served better than land-based armies as instruments of coercive diplomacy. Warships mounted with heavy guns could be easily dispatched and withdrawn, displayed and moved about in various combinations with other vessels, flexibly tailored to incrementally adjust the amount of armed force required by particular circumstances, and generally were able to be controlled for purposes of crisis management. They could project armed force and make highly credible threats over great distances, particularly if there were significant asymmetries of power and technological capabilities, as the Americans and Europeans discovered in Asia, Africa, Latin America, and the islands of the

Pacific. For all these reasons, as one naval officer observed, navies could "best unite force with persuasion."

With this in mind, the U.S. government determined in 1852 that its navy would make an excellent tool to coerce the Japanese into changing their long-standing closed-door policy that thwarted American interests and influence in the Pacific. Japan had deliberately and successfully secluded itself from other powers for two centuries, refused to engage in international trade, and forcefully resisted any efforts by foreigners to penetrate their country. In 1852, President Millard Fillmore wanted to break this policy, which stood in the way of his dreams of expansion. He therefore ordered the stern-looking Commodore Matthew C. Perry, who had considerable personal experience with "gunboat diplomacy" in Africa and Mexico, to cross the ocean with a squadron of ships and to demand that the Japanese "open" their country. American leaders sought to entice them with trade and to intimidate them with a credible threat to inflict harm. Naval superiority and technological sophistication, they believed, could demonstrate capabilities better than anything else and would be able to simultaneously show the leaders of Japan "both the emblem of peace and the cannon's mouth."

The instructions issued to Perry provide a most interesting and classic case of coercive diplomacy. The Department of State warned him that in bargaining situations like this, "it is manifest, from past experience, that arguments or persuasion addressed to this people, unless they be seconded by some imposing manifestation of power, will be utterly unavailing." He was therefore instructed to begin with a friendly and conciliatory approach to the Japanese, but in words that deserve to be quoted directly:

> If, after having exhausted every argument and every means of persuasion, the commodore should fail to obtain from the government any relaxation of their system of exclusion...he will then change his tone, and inform them in the most unequivocal terms that it is the determination of this government to insist....
>
> Do everything to impress them with a just sense of the power and greatness of [the United States] and to satisfy them that its past forbearance has been a result, not of timidity, but of a desire to be on friendly terms with them.

Thus, when Perry sailed his squadron, including four men-of-war, two of which were impressive steam frigates that carried eight-inch guns and were among the fastest ships in the world at the time, into what is now Tokyo Bay in July 1853, he sought to inspire fear and thereby gain psychological advantage. It worked. According to firsthand accounts, as the Japanese, who had never before seen steamships, watched them come belching smoke, actually moving against a strong wind, and displaying power in their own harbor, they became terrified. As historian Arthur Walworth writes in *Black Ships Off Japan*, to the rice farmers watching from the shore "the ships seemed sullen, masterful, full of pent-up force," believing that the wrath of these "floating volcanoes" would be unleashed against them. To drive the point home further, Perry landed on shore with a thirteen-gun salute, nearly 400 officers and men, two heavily armed black bodyguards, and a band playing "Hail, Columbia!" Here he delivered a letter from Fillmore boasting about the power of the American navy and demanding that Japan open itself to trade and provide access to shipwrecked seamen and coaling stations. If the Japanese refused to comply, Perry threatened menacingly, he could not "hold himself accountable for the consequences."

The Japanese immediately replied that the impertinent letter and its demands were an insult, contrary to their laws and their interests, and ordered Perry to leave. Although somewhat taken aback, the commodore had studied as much about the history of Japan as he could in advance, and this led him to conclude that a positive answer would require time and thoughtful deliberation in which its leaders carefully weighed the consequences of noncompliance. He could play on the fact that they were internally torn at the time between the traditionalists, on the one hand, and those who favored progressive change, on the other, and that these groups would debate both the advantages of incentives and the disadvantages of punishment coupled within his coercive diplomacy. The incentives, or inducements, could be found in the benefits that might flow from the offer for commercial trade and access to advanced Western technology. The punishment for noncompliance also had to be considered, for they already had seen the success of Western "gunboat diplomacy" in Asia and had the object lesson of China's earlier humiliation at the hands of the British navy before them. Perry consequently sailed away in ten days, but did so only after using forceful language in combination with his gunboats, pointedly threatening that he would give them several months for an answer and would return if necessary with even more force. As he wrote to the emperor:

> Many of the large ships-of-war destined to visit Japan have not yet arrived in these areas, though they are hourly expected; and the undersigned, as an evidence of his friendly intentions, has brought but four of the smaller ones, designing, should it become necessary, to return to Yedo in the ensuing spring with a much larger force. But is it expected that the government of your imperial majesty will render such a return unnecessary....

Perry's second arrival in Japan during March 1854 sought to ratchet up the level of coercion, for he wanted to intimidate by demonstrating beyond any reasonable doubt both the will and the capability of the United States to use armed force if the Japanese did not comply with his demands. This time he came with even more naval power, including three modern steamers out of a total of nine warships. As one of his crew members described the scene, there was a "long line of boats crowded with men glittering with bayonets, the brass...guns blazing in the sun ready to vomit forth death and destruction." He also brought gifts, particularly a miniature railroad train and telegraph designed to impress the Japanese with American technological prowess and superiority. For added effect, Perry presented a copy of a published history of the American war against Mexico, which included dramatic sketches of the results of the devastating bombardment by the U.S. fleet against Veracruz in Mexico.

Not surprisingly, the leaders of Japan engaged in serious and often agonizing debate about how best to respond to these threats. Some argued that they should never give in or meekly comply with the outrageous and arrogant American demands, whatever the cost, for it would be a "disgrace" to national prestige and "honor." Others, like advisor to the Shōgun, Naosuke Ii, rationally and pragmatically calculated that the Americans possessed sufficiently potent will and ability to harm them and, consequently, that the Japanese had reason to fear the consequences if they failed to comply. As he wrote in his revealing memorandum:

> Since 1609...we have had no warships capable of opposing foreign attack on our coasts with heavy guns....There is a saying that when one is besieged in a castle, to raise the drawbridge is to imprison oneself and make it impossible to hold out indefinitely; and again, that when opposing forces face each other across a river, victory is obtained by that which crosses the river and attacks. It seems clear throughout history that he who takes action is in a position to advance, while he who remains inactive must retreat.

To avoid disaster, he therefore proposed a tactical retreat:

> Even though the Shōgun's ancestors set up seclusion laws, they left the Dutch and the Chinese to act as a bridge [to the outside world]. Might this bridge not now be of advantage to us in handling foreign affairs [with the Americans], providing us with the means whereby we may for a time avert the outbreak of hostilities and then, after some time has elapsed, gain a complete victory?

With these rather carefully calculated thoughts in mind, the leaders of Japan determined that they would reluctantly comply with the American demands.

The result took the form of the 1854 Treaty of Kanagawa. Here, the Japanese accepted the incentives that were offered and agreed to open two ports for obtaining coal and other supplies, establish consular privileges in these locations, and assist shipwrecked American crews. Beyond these concessions, however, they refused to do more or open up their entire country. Perry wisely understood that he could not achieve anything else without risking extended war far from American shores, and thus he accepted the terms. He returned home triumphantly declaring that his success was but a foretaste "that the people of America will, in some form or other, extend their dominion and their power, until they shall have brought within their mighty embrace the islands of the great Pacific, and place the Saxon race upon the eastern shores of Asia." The Japanese, in sharp contrast, viewed their concessions as merely a temporary expedient designed to avoid immediate disaster and buy time for modernization until, in the words of Naosuke, the circumstances changed in their favor such that they might secure "complete victory." The memory of this "gunboat diplomacy" lasted for decades, with the Americans believing that they could successfully intimidate Japan whenever they wished and the Japanese vowing that they would never allow themselves to be coerced in such a way again.

THE CUBAN MISSILE CRISIS, 1962

When the American intelligence community discovered the Soviet Union secretly deploying medium- and intermediate-range ballistic missiles in Cuba during October 1962, the world found itself suddenly plunged into the most dangerous crisis of the entire Cold War. This discovery produced stunned surprise and anger among American leaders. Once it was realized that as soon as the missiles became operational they could strike almost any city within the United States, anger turned to an acute sense of peril. Members of the Joint Chiefs of Staff immediately and unanimously advised that the use of armed force was "essential," declaring that "military steps were the only ones the Soviet Union would understand." President Kennedy rejected their advice, for he believed that even surgical air strikes against the missile sites alone would lead to war and absolute disaster. He perceived Khrushchev as sufficiently intelligent to retreat if opposed resolutely and given sufficient time to calculate his interests. Rather than employing military force in the first instance, therefore, Kennedy decided to try the strategy of coercive diplomacy to compel Khrushchev to undo his action by removing the missiles himself.

To begin, Kennedy determined that he would impose a naval blockade around the island of Cuba. This would be short of armed combat but nevertheless would provide dramatic, forceful, and highly credible coercive pressure that the Soviets could easily understand. Moreover, such a blockade could be more easily controlled than troops on the ground in an invasion force and could be quickly increased if the circumstances warranted. Although the naval blockade could prevent additional Soviet missiles, warheads, and military equipment from reaching Cuba, it obviously could not remove the missiles already there and in the process of being made operational. Kennedy nevertheless hoped that the blockade and preparations for a possible air strike or invasion of Cuba would demonstrate his resolution, give Khrushchev time to consider that he had greatly miscalculated the likely American reaction, and exert enough bargaining leverage and pressure to coerce Khrushchev into withdrawing the missiles.

There was no assurance, however, that coercive diplomacy was a viable strategy or that it could be applied without setting into motion developments that would result in a war that neither side wanted. In an age of weapons of mass destruction, the risks of catastrophe were enormous. What would happen if Khrushchev, who denounced the blockade as an "act of war," ordered Soviet vessels and submarines to smash through it and test Kennedy's resolve? Might this lead to combat on the high seas or Soviet retaliation elsewhere that could lead to uncontrollable escalation—perhaps even a thermonuclear war? Would Khrushchev, who had invested so much in the missile deployment, be capable of such a public retreat before the eyes of the world? What if neither Kennedy nor Khrushchev could practice some measure of crisis management or maintain top-level civilian control of their own military forces as instruments of statecraft?

It is precisely these kinds of questions that reveal a striking tension between coercive diplomacy and the principles of managing a crisis in order to avoid triggering unwanted escalation and possibly war. This is why Kennedy exercised deliberate restraint and initially chose to ignore the advice from his military hawks to use force immediately, employing instead the "try-and-see" variant of coercive diplomacy at the outset. During the first five days of the confrontation, for example, the president deliberately avoided issuing Khrushchev a time limit for compliance with his demand for removing the missiles or explicitly threatening him with an air strike or invasion for noncompliance. As for Khrushchev, even though he blustered and issued coercive threats of his own in an effort to undermine Kennedy's resolve, he nonetheless went to great lengths to avoid a clash at sea. Within hours after Kennedy announced the blockade, to illustrate, Khrushchev chose to resist his own hard-line military advisors, whom he described as "maniacs," and directed Soviet vessels carrying missiles and other military equipment to Cuba to turn around. Both Khrushchev and Kennedy appreciated the risks associated with the use of force, and thus they behaved with sober prudence and reasonable skill to avoid escalation and to extricate themselves from the war-threatening crisis.

Events nevertheless seemed to take on a life of their own, and both leaders experienced disturbing new challenges to their ability to synchronize their interaction and to manage the crisis. The context and meaning of possibly critical moves and communications became confusing, and deciphering the intentions and calculations behind specific moves of the opponent became difficult. Leaders in Washington puzzled over the discrepancy between Khrushchev's personal and more accommodating private letter, in which he hinted at a deal for withdrawal of the missiles in return for an American pledge not to invade Cuba, and his more formal hard-line letter of the next day, which advanced new demands. Other disturbing events occurred. Soviet military officers shot down a U-2 spy plane over Cuba without an explicit order from Moscow to do so, Cuban air defense forces fired on two other U.S. aircraft as they swooped low over the missile sites, an American reconnaissance plane wandered by mistake over Siberia, aggressive antisubmarine activities by the U.S. Navy forced all Soviet submarines in the area to the surface, and ominous reports arrived that the Soviet consulate was burning classified papers. Any of these developments could have triggered escalation into war. Policy makers in the White House anxiously speculated that the Kremlin was now taking a harder line and determined to test U.S. resolution, that perhaps Khrushchev was no longer in charge, or that Moscow was trying to extract a higher price for removal of the missiles. To make matters worse, each passing day of work by Soviet technicians in Cuba brought the missiles closer to operational.

A new sense of urgency now gripped Kennedy and his advisors, and they determined to make two drastic changes in their strategy of coercive diplomacy. The first of these was to convert the weaker try-and-see approach into the more serious variant of the ultimatum. To do this, the president sent his brother Robert to personally deliver a much more potent threat and a time limit of twenty-four hours to Soviet Ambassador Anatoly Dobrynin, telling him:

> We had to have a commitment by tomorrow....He should understand that if they did not remove those [missile] bases, we would remove them....Time was running out. We had only a few more hours—we needed an answer immediately from the Soviet Union. I said we must have it the next day.

Kennedy thereby focused his demand on the limited objective of the removal of the missiles rather than the broader and more extensive issue of changing the Communist regime of Fidel Castro. He wanted to convince Khrushchev that the United States' motivation to get the missiles out of Cuba, only a few miles from its shores, was higher than that of the Soviet Union to keep them there—and that he had the resolution to achieve precisely that objective. The credibility of this urgent threat received further potency from the fact that preparations for an armed invasion of Cuba by the United States just had been completed and that Soviet and Cuban intelligence sources warned Moscow that American military action was imminent.

The second important change was the decision to couple this additional coercive pressure with inducements to make it easier for the Soviet leader to agree to remove the missiles. That is, Kennedy determined that he would create a carrot-and-stick approach, coupling the ultimatum with certain concessions that he had earlier refused to discuss. He offered to call off the naval quarantine and then, most significantly, to pledge that the United States would not invade Cuba if the Soviets removed their missiles under appropriate United Nations observation and supervision. He also secretly agreed to remove U.S. Jupiter missiles stationed in Turkey on the border of the Soviet Union. The combination of this quid pro quo and mutual reassurance—along with the growing urgency and intense fear generated by the possibility of thermonuclear war—created powerful incentives on both sides to prevent unacceptable escalation. Within just a few hours of receiving these offers, Khrushchev accepted Kennedy's formula.

CONTEMPORARY COERCION AGAINST IRAN

One of the most serious challenges of our time is the proliferation of nuclear weapons. Any increase in the number of states or terrorists who gain possession of the capability to inflict mass destruction is widely seen as a danger to the world. It is for this reason that the international community has viewed the nuclear enrichment program of highly volatile Iran with such alarm.

The seeds of nuclear development here were first sown under Mohammed Reza Shah Pahlavi, with the assistance of Europeans and the Americans with their "Atoms for Peace" program, designed to generate fuel for civil energy. But this collaboration changed abruptly with the revolution of 1979, the overthrow of the shah, and the advent of the Islamic Republic of Iran. The new government held deep suspicions of the West and "the influence of foreign powers," especially the United States. This was the country they described as "the Great Satan" that had engineered the overthrow of the democratically elected Iranian Prime Minister Mohammad Mosaddeq in 1953 and installed the unpopular shah, imposed trade sanctions on them after the seizing of American diplomats as hostages during the revolution, protected their arch-enemy Israel, supported their adversary Saddam Hussein during the wasting Iran-Iraq War of 1980–1988 (the longest conventional war of the twentieth century), placed them on its list of state sponsors of terrorism, and described Iran as a part of an "Axis of Evil" after 9/11, warning of the possibility of an armed attack. To rebuild their severely war-damaged existing nuclear infra-structure and/or to develop their military capabilities—either for defense to protect themselves from attack or for added prestige and clout at home and in the region—Iranian leaders began a program of nuclear enrichment, this time turning to Russia, China, and Pakistan for assistance. Sometimes they proceeded openly, sometimes clandestinely.

International concern and suspicion increased when in 2002 a London-based Iranian opposition group disclosed details about two secret enrichment facili-ties. The president of Iran, Mohammad Khatami, responded by repeating the long-held—and accurate—position that the Nuclear Non-Proliferation Treaty legally acknowledges the "inalienable right" of parties "to develop...nuclear energy for peaceful purposes." Nevertheless, the International Atomic Energy Agency (IAEA) insisted on an inspection. Their findings led them to conclude that Iran "has failed to meet it obligations...with respect to the reporting of nuclear material, the subsequent processing and use of that material, and the declaration of facilities where the material was stored and processed." Tehran denounced the report, accusing the IAEA and others of applying double stand-ards by not addressing Israeli nuclear weapons and by being hopelessly under the influence of "pro-West" and "anti-Iranian" "corrupt powers." Thus began an intense, highly public, and politically charged controversy about whether Iran's nuclear program was designed solely for peaceful purposes, as claimed by Iran, or for weapons development, as feared by others.

The situation did not improve. The administration of George W. Bush refused to engage in any direct negotiations, issued threats without any induce-ments, and continually called for "regime change" in Tehran. On the part of Iran, denial, deception, and concealment continued. Several uranium enrich-ment processing sites were placed under military rather than civilian control. Iranian officials refused to provide assurances and escalated their rhetoric with strident public statements insisting that they could pursue their enrichment program if they wished. The problem was made even more complicated by the fact that the technology used to enrich uranium needed for peaceful nuclear power also can be used to enrich it to the higher level required for a nuclear weapon. All of this increased alarm and fed suspicions. The IAEA Board of Directors thus expressed an "absence of confidence that Iran's nuclear pro-gram is exclusively for peaceful purposes" and voted in 2006 to refer this case to the United Nations Security Council for action.

After considering the mounting evidence, the Security Council, including all of its permanent and veto-wielding members, decided to employ coercive diplomacy. Its 2006 resolution explicitly *"Demands* . . . that Iran shall suspend all enrichment-related and reprocessing activities . . . to be verified by the IAEA." The Council combined this with the threat that if Tehran did not respond positively within one month, they would "adopt appropriate measures under Article 41 of Chapter VII of the Charter of the United Nations to persuade Iran to comply," warning that "further decisions will be required should additional measures be necessary." The following day, Iranian President Mahmoud Ahmadinejad reacted by declaring: "Those who think they can use the language of threats and force against Iran are mistaken. If they don't realize that now, one day they will learn it the hard way."

Iran's motivation for continuing its enrichment program remained intense. At the same time, the precise credibility and the potency of the threat remained unknown. The Iranians thus refused to be intimidated or to comply with the demand. The Security Council therefore responded by stating that it was *"Determined* to give effect to its decisions by adopting appropriate measures to persuade Iran to comply." To do this, its members gave Iran a sixty-day time frame to take action in order to avoid the punishment of sanctions. When Iran refused, they escalated their coercive diplomacy by increasing the potency of costs for noncompliance. They created the Iran Sanctions Committee and imposed sanctions targeted against the transfer of nuclear and ballistic missile technologies and froze the assets of key individuals and companies involved with the enrichment program. Over the next few years, they ratcheted up the level of punishment by extending financial sanctions to additional persons and entities, imposing travel restrictions, and prohibiting certain kinds of exports. By 2010, sanctions included an arms embargo on Iran, cargo inspections and seizures of illicit materials, and the freezing of funds and assets belonging to the Iranian Revolutionary Guard Corps and the Islamic Republic of Iran Shipping Lines. At the same time, some nations decided to work closely with United Nations–authorized coercive diplomacy by imposing sanctions of their own on Iran. These included the United States, Australia, Canada, Japan, Norway, South Korea, and the European Union. Together, they often used their collective capabilities to pursue a "dual-track" approach, offering a combination of incentives along with threats.

Despite these efforts, Iran remained defiant. Its leaders refused to change their behavior and halt their nuclear enrichment program. President Ahmadinejad continued to describe the sanctions as "intimidation" imposed by "arrogant powers," vowing that he would "not yield to pressure." "You can issue as many resolutions as you like and dream on," he declared, asserting that Iran "will not retreat one iota." Indeed, although still claiming that the program was intended only for peaceful purposes, in 2010, on the occasion of the celebration of the 1979 Iranian Islamic Revolution, he proudly proclaimed that Iran was now a "nuclear state." Even experts wondered precisely what that meant. The IAEA raised the stakes even higher when it issued a damning report in November 2011 presenting new evidence

Nuclear Material for Peaceful Energy—or Weapons? President Ahmadinejad Inspecting
Uranium Enrichment Facilities

concerning increased numbers and the use of sophisticated centrifuges to
speed progress in enriching uranium, computer modeling of high yield
detonations, and experiments with weaponization and payload integration
into a missile delivery vehicle, concluding that Iran had carried out activities "relevant to the development of a nuclear explosive device." Intelligence
reports believed that Iran did not yet have nuclear weapons, but was well
along on the road to developing the capabilities of making them if they
chose to do so.

It became evident at this stage of escalating tensions and high-stakes
brinkmanship that coercive diplomacy, employing sanctions, had successfully leveled economic and diplomatic punishment in disrupting and delay-
ing Iran's nuclear enrichment program—but not in stopping or reversing
it. Iranian leaders continued to resist, to obfuscate, to play for time by dan-
gling the possibilities of compromise and negotiation, and to find weaknesses in the coercion against them. In early 2012, both the United States
and the European Union determined "to ratchet up the pressure" to force
Iran to recalculate and "think again" about the costs of continuing its course
of action. They significantly increased the punishment by imposing more
severe sanctions, freezing the assets of Iran's Central Bank, and this time
striking at a particularly important and vulnerable target by banning all
crude imports from Iran's oil industry in order to strangle the lifeblood of
its economy. They also shut Iran out of the Society for Worldwide Interbank
Financial Telecommunication (SWIFT), the major clearinghouse used by

virtually every nation and corporation in the world to electronically convert currencies and process payments.

Threats of force were added to this mixture as well. President Obama announced that "military options" were "on the table," pointedly asserting: "I don't bluff." The Americans and the British sent additional naval vessels into the Persian Gulf off the coast of Iran in 2012 to demonstrate their power and their resolve. Some public figures began to call for an even greater use of force. Speaking before the Armed Services Committee, Senator John McCain declared, "The list goes on and on of the threats that we have made to the Iranians and so far no action.... We keep pointing the gun. We haven't pulled the trigger yet, and it's about time we did." A number of Israeli senior officials made even more threatening statements, insisting that time was "running out" and warning that they might soon launch an armed, unilateral, preventive attack on Iranian nuclear facilities. This threat produced great alarm since it could easily trigger a much wider conflagration and because Israel had demonstrated its willingness and ability to use force to destroy a nuclear reactor in Iraq in 1981 and another in Syria in 2007, and already stood accused of assassinating several Iranian nuclear scientists in covert operations and (along with the United States) of using a highly sophisticated computer worm to launch a cyber attack against Iranian uranium enrichment facilities. Iranian Supreme Leader Ayatollah Ali Khamenei angrily responded by accusing those powers seeking to coerce in the name of nonproliferation as hypocrites with double standards when it came to the possession of nuclear weapons by Israel, a country that he described as a "cancerous tumor that should be cut and will be cut." He refused to allow IAEA inspectors to visit suspected weapons development sites, announced a series of air defense war games dubbed "Sarallah," or "God's Revenge," to practice protecting these sensitive facilities from any attack, and counter-threatened to close the strategic Strait of Hormuz, through which much of the world's seaborne oil passes. "Pressures, sanctions, and assassinations," he boasted, "will bear no fruit. No obstacles can stop Iran's nuclear work."

This case serves as a reminder of the high level of risk inherent in coercive diplomacy, especially when the positions are so diametrically opposed and the parties seem to be on a collision course. It is at times like this when the challenges of force and statecraft are particularly acute—and dangerous.

ANALYSIS

Coercive diplomacy is an attractive, indeed sometimes a beguiling, strategy because it offers strong powers the possibility of achieving their objectives without war. Yet, like deterrence, it typically assumes a type of simple, uncomplicated rationality on the part of the opponent. If the opponents are "rational," they will surely see in any cost-benefit analysis that it is in their interest to comply with the demands made against them and back down. This assumption, however, oversimplifies the roots of motivation, passions, and the considerations that may influence those who are the targets of coercive diplomacy. Governments are not unitary actors, and there is frequent competition among various bureaucracies, military branches, interests, and personalities that may have very different perceptions, values, ideas about what constitutes the "national interest" or "honor" and calculations of possible benefits or "unacceptable" costs. Moreover, there is no way to confidently or successfully predict what leaders will do when subjected to the harsh demands, threats, and time limit of an ultimatum. An opponent's reluctance to undertake a humiliating retreat, as cognitive psychology repeatedly emphasizes, can activate psychological tendencies to engage in wishful thinking, to discount evidence that challenges existing preconceptions, and distort the ability to correctly anticipate the behavior of others, thereby leading to critical misperceptions and miscalculations. This is particularly important to appreciate since coercive diplomacy is not a physical attack, but a psychological tool designed to influence and persuade. Historical cases thus reveal that successes and failures entail a complex and sometimes quite subjective matrix of psychological, cultural, and political variables.

Those Japanese leaders who complied with the demands of Admiral Perry's "gunboat diplomacy," for example, did so in part because they held a much longer perspective of history than did the Americans and believed that their action was a mere tactical move to buy time until circumstances changed in their favor, which ultimately would bring them victory. At the onset of the Cuban Missile Crisis, Khrushchev initially and mistakenly perceived Kennedy as a young, inexperienced leader who could be pushed around. Moreover, as the crisis escalated, it revealed that Soviet policy makers subjected to days of stress, sleep deprivation, and decisions made under pressure became emotional and erratic. Even among "the best and the brightest" Americans, wrote Robert Kennedy from firsthand experience, there were those "of the highest intelligence" who "because of the pressure of events...appeared to lose their judgment and stability." When members of the international community employed coercive diplomacy against Iran, it did not instill a fear of unacceptable punishment as hoped, but instead produced just the opposite reaction: it provoked Iranian leaders to dig in their heels and become even more determined to pursue their nuclear enrichment program, often becoming more reckless in their policies.

Coercive diplomacy, by its very nature, is a strategy that induces stress. Unlike negotiation, it shifts attention away from common interests and focuses instead on conflict. It can trigger shock, anger, and a sense of desperation that easily can exacerbate rather than resolve a crisis and thereby actually provoke the very kind of behavior it sought to avoid. Acute stress can seriously degrade performance by creating decisional pathologies among fatigued leaders forced to make critical decisions under the pressure of time when the costs of failure are high. Crisis-induced stress can easily provoke emotional outbursts and increase cognitive rigidity, impairing the ability to accurately process new information that challenges existing beliefs, reducing creativity and the ability to improvise, narrowing the range of perceived alternatives or options and limiting the degree of toleration for ambiguity. One would like to believe that the fateful decisions of war and peace are not influenced by such factors, but they often are.

An analysis of these historical cases also reveals the absolutely critical importance of motivation or will—for both sides. Success is more likely if the state employing coercive diplomacy can create an asymmetry of motivation by conveying that it is much more motivated to achieve its objectives than the adversary is to oppose them. Admiral Perry took great efforts to convince the Japanese, for example, of the overwhelming determination of his country to realize its goal. During the Cuban Missile Crisis, Kennedy made it clear that absolutely vital American interests were at stake just off its shores and that he would actually risk the possibility of thermonuclear war in order to remove the missiles. When coercing Iran, however, most nations possessed a serious interest in preventing the proliferation of nuclear weapons in an already volatile region, but that interest was somewhat removed from their immediate borders and did not appear to necessarily be threatened as long as uranium enrichment remained at a low or medium grade. In sharp contrast, Iranian leaders were intensely motivated to resist coercion, viewing their acquisition of nuclear technology as vital to their interests, their national security, their prestige, and even their legitimacy. Certainly at home, where they faced severe divisions and discontent, they found that refusing to be intimidated by threats enabled them to demonstrate that they could stand up to the world, divert attention away from their internal repression, and evoke patriotic zeal. Indeed, as even the former director of the IAEA, Mohamed El Baradei, observed: "The line was 'Iran will buckle under pressure.' But this issue has become ingrained in the Iranian soul as a matter of national pride."

Historical cases also reveal that motivation sometimes can be deliberately enhanced or diminished by the nature and extent of what is actually demanded of an opponent. The quite natural motivation of the Japanese to resist American coercion in the nineteenth century, for example, was significantly reduced by the fact that the United States did not demand any more than a relatively modest opening of a few ports for trade and assistance to shipwrecked American sailors. Similarly, during the crisis over Cuba, Kennedy's limited demand, confined to the objective of removing the missiles alone, significantly helped to persuade Khrushchev that he could comply without threatening the wide-ranging and vital national interests of the Soviet Union. Nevertheless, the seemingly limited demand on Iran that it stop its nuclear enrichment program and open its facilities to international inspection did not lead to compliance because its motivation to continue proved to be greater.

These revelations about motivation should serve as warnings to those who believe that the credibility and strength of threats is *the* critical factor on which successful coercion depends. Leaders of militarily powerful states may be tempted at times to believe that they can, with little risk, simply throw their weight around and intimidate weaker opponents into giving in to their demands. But the militarily weaker state may be intensely motivated by what it has at stake and, for this reason, may actually harden its position and refuse to back down.

Credibility and potency nevertheless are often of critical importance to coercive diplomacy. In each of our historical cases, those employing this strategy sought to create a fear of unacceptable costs by attempting to convey that they possessed both the will and the ability to carry through with the threatened punishment in the event of noncompliance. They wanted to use their potential power to hurt as bargaining power to make their opponents act in order to avoid it. Admiral Perry's use of "gunboat diplomacy" effectively threatened to use American superiority in military technology to inflict punishment on Japan. When Kennedy threatened Khrushchev in 1962, he focused very specifically on the potential use of armed force to attack the missile sites in Cuba in order to destroy the weapons before they became operational. This, in turn, raised an even greater fear: if the threat were carried out, neither side would be able to control the devastating consequences. Coercion against Iran, however, suffered from problems of both credibility and potency. Leaders in Tehran knew they had friends, like Russia and China, in the Security Council who would protect them from severe punishment and would make certain that resolutions provided for nonmilitary actions and voluntary rather than mandatory sanctions. They knew that many governments and multinational corporations favored modest sanctions because of their fear of disrupting an already fragile world economy. In addition, they knew they often could circumvent sanctions by turning to the black market. Only after several years did the United States and the European Union make the punishment for noncompliance much more costly by targeting the assets of the Iranian Revolutionary Guard Corps and the Central Bank, shutting Iran out of SWIFT, and imposing a ban on its vital oil industry.

The existence of incentives also can play a particularly significant role in the success or failure of coercive diplomacy. Few international problems are ever resolved by simply making threats. But, as these historical cases reveal, incentives—like threats—also must be credible and have sufficient potency in order to affect the motivation of opponents to comply with demands made against them. When attempting to coerce Japan in the nineteenth century, the United States effectively coupled inducements with its threats. Perry offered to extend the benefits of commercial trade and access to Western technology, and this possessed considerable appeal, at least to the progressives in the Japanese court. Kennedy offered substantial inducements: a promise to call off the naval quarantine, to not invade Cuba, and to remove the U.S. Jupiter missiles from Turkey. These concessions played a profound role in altering Khrushchev's balance of motivation to comply. The incentives offered to the leaders of Iran to provide civilian nuclear technology for peaceful purposes were credible, but never potent enough or sufficiently attractive to persuade them to change course.

Coercive diplomacy also can be affected by the level of urgency. In one way or another, states determine how much time they will give an opponent to reflect on the costs that are likely to follow if the threats of punishment are carried out. They can vary their choices between a mild try-and-see approach or a much more extreme ultimatum that dramatically escalates the pressure by setting a definite time limit for compliance. American "gunboat diplomacy" in 1853 and 1854 utilized the former, actually giving the Japanese eight months for what they hoped would be ample time for thoughtful deliberation. Coercion against Iran began by setting time limits of one month and then sixty days before the actual imposition of sanctions, but this pattern then continued for several years. During the Cuban Missile Crisis, Kennedy's ultimatum gave the Soviet Union twenty-four hours to remove the missiles. Soviet compliance in this particular case, however, appears to have much more to do with the asymmetry of motivation, enormous fear of war, and the existence of potent incentives rather than the press of time. Indeed, extensive research on other historical cases suggests that ultimata with short time limits easily can add unnecessary stress and provocation to already dangerous confrontations and may not be successful in facilitating resolution by peaceful means.

Finally, these cases, ranging from Japan to the Soviet Union and Iran, from the Pacific to the Caribbean and the Strait of Hormuz, from the nineteenth century to the twenty-first, and from gunboats to missiles, all provide invaluable demonstrations of the fact that coercive diplomacy, like all strategies of force and statecraft, is highly dependent on the historical context. Each occurred with particular leaders making decisions within the range of possibilities and restraints afforded by their own time and place. Moreover, each was affected by the broader diplomatic revolution that changed many features of diplomacy and the international system itself.

Public opinion and the media, for example, played a relatively small role in shaping the agenda or influencing international relations in the nineteenth-century case of American coercion against Japan. There was little knowledge or even interest among either the American or the Japanese public in the other, and Perry actually received specific instructions to refrain from any communication with the press. In an age of extensive television coverage, Kennedy and his advisors were forced to devote considerable effort during the Cuban Missile Crisis to calculating the impact of their decisions on domestic opinion at home, fearing the severe political consequences of appearing to be "weak" on the eve of an election. In addition, they regarded global opinion to be particularly important and thus worked hard to present a favorable impression among allies in Latin America and Europe, whose support they sought, and at the United Nations before what they called "the courtroom of world opinion." When members of the Security Council determined to use coercive diplomacy against Iran, they too were greatly influenced by global opinion fearful of proliferation. President Obama found himself under enormous pressure from nongovernmental organizations, lobbyists, and political rivals to take extreme positions, ranging from softening sanctions and initiating negotiations to "don't speak to evil" and launching an armed attack. Leaders in Tehran, for their part and in the context of deep and passionate distrust of foreign powers, knew that polls throughout Iran consistently indicated enormous popular support (at times bordering on nationalistic frenzy) for defying external coercion and pursuing their nuclear enrichment program, even among those who detested the regime itself and despite its serious international implications.

The number of actors in the international system further demonstrated the growing challenges and complexities of diplomacy. When America employed "gunboat diplomacy" against Japan in 1853 and 1854, it knew for all intents and purposes that it needed to calculate only the relatively isolated interests and reactions of itself and Japan. During their confrontation of 1962, both Kennedy and Khrushchev were painfully aware of the fact that their decisions (made all the more complicated by the ideological contest of the Cold War) would affect the entire planet. As Robert Kennedy ominously explained, the crisis "was my life—and for Americans and Russians, for the whole world, it was their life as well." In the case of Iran, the large number of actors had the effect of both strengthening the widespread legitimacy of the United Nations through multilateral (as compared to unilateral) sanctions while at the same time weakening the actual coercion by increasing differences of opinion over the precise nature of the demands, the threats, and the urgency of time. The difficulty of obtaining consensus within the Security Council, the European Union, and among other powers led to a lack of cohesion and thereby diminished credibility and potency, despite global fears of nuclear proliferation.

Technological changes obviously have greatly impacted the context of coercive diplomacy as well. Strategic information during the 1850s for Admiral Perry and everyone else, in the words of one observer, was gathered and shared by "mouth-to-mouth" communication and "rumor." By 1962, the advanced technology of U-2 spy planes flying miles above the earth made it possible to show dramatic photographs of the Soviet Union placing missiles in Cuba and thereby convincingly counter Khrushchev's claims to the contrary. Such intelligence also had the enormous advantage of providing warning of pending danger and allowed the Americans to discover the missiles before they became operational—and thus design their coercive diplomacy accordingly. When employing coercive diplomacy against Iran, spy satellite imagery from vast distances in space could precisely locate enrichment facilities, determine which ones had been fortified to withstand armed attacks, and through isotopic detection of air samples ascertain the level of uranium enrichment.

But the greatest change has occurred in weapons technology. When the United States engaged in "gunboat diplomacy," the weapons at the disposal of the navy were much more sophisticated than those possessed by the Japanese, but nevertheless very limited. If coercion had failed in 1854, it would have taken months to mobilize additional force across the ocean, and, even then, the amount of damage that could have been inflicted remained very small. These limitations changed dramatically in the next century. Indeed, by 1962, both Kennedy and Khrushchev understood that their sophisticated delivery systems, nuclear weapons, and the radioactive fallout resulting immediately from their use would lead to unprecedented catastrophe. As Mohamed El Baradei notes in his recent book, *The Age of Deception: Nuclear Diplomacy in Treacherous Times*, such calculations and the fears that accompany them are renewed whenever issues of proliferation arise. Indeed, as one of the leading decision makers at the time of the Cuban Missile Crisis put it, with modern weapons the failure of coercive diplomacy could lead to "the abyss of nuclear destruction and the end of mankind."

The potential extraordinary costs resulting from the deliberate manipulation of risks through the use of demands and threats, especially in our own time, have led any number of scholars and policy makers alike to become acutely aware not only of the uses of this strategy but also of its difficulties, limitations, and dangers. A broad-ranging and insightful study entitled *The United States and Coercive Diplomacy*, edited by Robert Art and Patrick Cronin, to provide but one example, explores several post–Cold War cases. It focuses on coercive diplomacy's more recent targets, ranging from Serbia and Afghanistan to Haiti and North Korea, and from nonstate actors like warlord Mohammed Farrah Aideed in Somalia to terrorists like Osama bin Laden. The authors point out that policy makers are not always well schooled in matters of force and statecraft, are often insufficiently sensitive to the risks of coercive diplomacy, and do not fully appreciate the complexities of how difficult it is to apply theoretical principles to actual policy in particular circumstances or to predict outcomes. They observe that possession of military superiority over an opponent is not at all sufficient for success and that targets may refuse to back down for reasons such as honor or prestige and may develop "counter-coercion" techniques of their own. They also find that this strategy is more difficult in the case of nonstate actors like terrorists or suicide bombers, who are intensely motivated to resist and who possess few tangible assets that can be threatened with punishment. After carefully exploring these cases and analyzing the evidence, they conclude that coercive diplomacy has sometimes worked—but more often has failed.

All systematic analyses of case studies of coercive diplomacy reveal that this strategy, perhaps even more so than deterrence, is highly context-dependent. It does not take place in a vacuum, and thus must be tailored in an exacting way to fit the unique configuration of each situation and to take into account the background of relationships and particular behavioral characteristics of a specific adversary. But the many details of a crisis in which coercive diplomacy may be employed are seldom clearly visible to any policy maker, miscalculations and unintended consequences are likely, and, as a result, the strategy can easily fail. Efforts to engage in coercive diplomacy therefore rest heavily on skill at correctly assessing adversaries and their perspectives, appreciating limits, maintaining proportionality between the objectives being pursued and the leverage being applied in their pursuit, providing reassurances, adjusting to ever-changing circumstances, and relying more on explicit diplomatic communication rather than military signals alone. Leaders employing coercive diplomacy must continually evaluate the risks of what they are doing and must slow the momentum of events as necessary in order to give the opponent time for sober reflection. They must choose and time their actions carefully to make them compatible with the opponent's ability to appraise the evolving situation and to respond appropriately. Moreover, they must always leave the adversary with a way out of the crisis that avoids the extremes of either war or abject humiliation. As all of these observations suggest, coercive diplomacy includes some of the important requirements of crisis management, a topic to which we now turn in the next chapter.

SUGGESTIONS FOR FURTHER EXPLORATION

The theory of coercive diplomacy can be found in Alexander L. George and William E. Simons (eds.), *The Limits of Coercive Diplomacy* (Boulder, CO, 1994 ed.); and Alexander L. George, *Forceful Persuasion* (Washington, DC, 1991). Other very helpful discussions are available in Thomas Christensen, *Worse Than a Monolith* (Princeton, 2011); Thomas Schelling, *Arms and Influence* (New Haven, CT, 2008 ed.); Bruce Jentleson, "Coercive Diplomacy: Scope and Limits in the Contemporary World," Stanley Foundation Policy Analysis Brief (2006); Robert J. Art and Patrick M. Cronin (eds.), *The United States and Coercive Diplomacy* (Washington, DC, 2003); James A. Nathan, *Soldiers, Statecraft, and History* (Westport, CT, 2002); Daniel Byman and Matthew Waxman, *The Dynamics of Coercion* (Cambridge, 2002); Kenneth Schultz, *Democracy and Coercive Diplomacy* (Cambridge, 2001); Donald Daniel et al., *Coercive Inducement and the Containment of International Crisis* (Washington, 1999); Lawrence Freedman (ed.), *Strategic Coercion* (Oxford, 1998); Peter Jakobsen, *Western Use of Coercive Diplomacy After the Cold War* (New York, 1998); Alexander L. George, "The Impact of Crisis-Induced Stress on Decision Making," in Frederic Solomon and Robert Marston (eds.), *The Medical Implications of Nuclear War* (Washington, DC, 1986); Russell J. Leng, "When Will They Ever Learn," *Journal of Conflict Resolution*, 27 (September 1983): 379–419; Thomas Schelling, *The Strategy of Conflict* (Cambridge, MA, 1981 ed.); Paul Gordon Lauren, "Theories of Bargaining with Threats of Force: Deterrence and Coercive Diplomacy," in Paul Gordon Lauren (ed.), *Diplomacy: New Approaches in History, Theory, and Policy* (New York, 1979); Charles Lockhart, *Bargaining in International Conflicts* (New York, 1979); Barry Blechman and Stephen Kaplan, *Force Without War* (Washington, DC, 1978); and Paul Gordon Lauren, "Ultimata and Coercive Diplomacy," *International Studies Quarterly*, 16 (1972): 131–165.

The case of "gunboat diplomacy" in Asia is treated in Thomas Patterson et al., *American Foreign Relations* (Boston, 2009 ed.); Akira Iriye (ed.), *Mutual Images: Essays in American-Japanese Relations* (Cambridge, MA, 1975); Roger Pineau (ed.), *The Japan Expedition of 1852–1854: The Personal Journal of Commodore Matthew C. Perry* (Washington, DC, 1968); Samuel Eliot Morrison, *"Old Bruin"* (Boston, 1967); William G. Beasley (trans. and ed.), *Select Documents on Japanese Foreign Policy, 1853–1868* (London, 1955); Arthur Walworth, *Black Ships Off Japan* (New York, 1946); and Francis L. Hawks (ed.), *Narrative of the Expedition of an American Squadron* (Washington, DC, 1856). For broader discussion of navies as instruments of coercive diplomacy, see Robert Mandel, "The Effectiveness of Gunboat Diplomacy," *International Studies Quarterly*, 30 (1986): 59–76; James Cable, *Gunboat Diplomacy, 1919–1979* (New York, 1986 ed.); and Edward Luttwak, *The Political Uses of Sea Power* (Baltimore, 1974).

Much has been written about the Cuban Missile Crisis, including David Gibson, *Talk at the Brink* (Princeton, 2012); Michael Dobbs, *One Minute to Midnight* (New York, 2009 ed.); Sheldon Stern, *The Week the World Stood Still* (Stanford, CA, 2005); Ernest May and Philip Zelikow, *The Kennedy Tapes* (Cambridge, MA, 2002 ed.); Robert Kennedy, *Thirteen Days* (New York, 1999 ed.); Alexandr Fursenko and Timothy Naftali, *One Hell of a Gamble* (New York, 1998); and James Nathan (ed.), *The Cuban Missile Crisis Reconsidered* (New York, 1992).

The case of Iran can be explored by reading the UN Security Council resolutions on sanctions, particularly 1737 (2006), 1747 (2007), 1803 (2008), and 1929 (2010), at www

.un.org/Docs/sc. Analysis and discussion can be found in Trita Parsi, *A Single Role of the Dice: Obama's Diplomacy with Iran* (New Haven, CT, 2012); Mohamed El Baradei, *The Age of Deception* (New York, 2011); Barry Blechman and Daniel Brumberg, *Engagement, Coercion, and Iran's Nuclear Challenge* (Washington, DC, 2010); Alireza Jafarzadeh, *The Iran Threat* (New York, 2007); and Ray Takeyh, *Hidden Iran* (New York, 20006). See also the reports of the International Atomic Energy Agency at www.iaea.org, and the positions of the Iranian Ministry of Foreign Affairs at www.mfa.gov.ir, the U.S. Department of State at www.state.gov, and the European Union at eeas.europa.eu/iran/nuclear_en.htm.

Many other cases of coercive diplomacy exist in the annals of force and statecraft. Some of the more suggestive of these include the Great Powers against Mehemet Ali of Egypt (1840); Britain against Greece in the Don Pacifico Affair (1850); Britain against the United States in the *Trent* Affair (1861); the French ultimatum against Siam (1893); Italy against Turkey (1911); the ultimata leading to the outbreak of the First World War (1914); Hitler against Czechoslovakia (1938); Britain and France against Hitler after the invasion of Poland (1939); the United States against Japan (1938–1941), Laos (1961–1962), North Vietnam (1965), Nicaragua and Libya (1981–1989), Somalia (1992–1994), Haiti and North Korea (1994), Saddam Hussein and Iraq (1990–2002), Bosnia (1995), Serbia (1998), and terrorism (1993, 1998, and 2001); and the international coercion against Libya (1992–2003 and 2011) and Syria (2011–2013).

——11——

Crisis Management

"$\mathbf{T}$ he most dangerous moment in human history."—This is the way that historian Arthur Schlesinger Jr. describes the Cuban Missile Crisis. When the two superpowers teetered on the very brink of possible annihilation, the deeply worried Soviet leader Nikita Khrushchev sent a personal letter to President John Kennedy warning that if they both continued to escalate their actions against each other, the result would be global disaster. "The more the two of us pull," he warned, "the tighter the knot will be tied." In this process, Khrushchev poignantly observed,

> a moment may come when that knot will be tied so tight that even he who tied it will not the have the strength to untie it, and then it will be necessary to cut that knot, and what that would mean is not for me to explain to you, because you yourself understand perfectly of what terrible forces our countries dispose. Consequently, if there is no intention to tighten that knot, and thereby doom the world to the catastrophe of thermonuclear war, then let us not only relax the forces pulling on the ends of the rope, let us take measures to untie that knot. We are ready for this.

Because both leaders came to understand that they were not only *rivals* but *necessary partners* in avoiding the frightening consequences of an inadvertent war that neither wanted, they sought to actively manage the crisis, taking urgent and deliberate steps to prevent it from spiraling out of control. In the end, they succeeded. But the experience had been terrifying, and shortly thereafter Secretary of Defense Robert McNamara remarked soberly, "Today there is no longer any such thing as military strategy; there is only crisis management."

His words are an overstatement and a simplification of the lessons to be learned, but they serve to emphasize the critical importance in statecraft of keeping war-threatening situations under control. The history of relations among states is studded with innumerable international crises that resulted when negotiation, deterrence, and/or coercive diplomacy all failed. Some of these were managed peacefully, but others ended in war that neither side wanted. In each crisis, policy makers found themselves called upon to make high-stake and delicate diplomatic and military decisions under great stress.

They knew that their decisions might result not merely in success or failure for their own nations, but in the preservation or the destruction of the international order itself. Today, with the existence of weapons of mass destruction, a nearly overwhelming volume of information in an age of instantaneous communications, and the intense pressure of time and events, crisis management becomes even more essential. Indeed, this explains not only the creation of the independent and nonpartisan Crisis Management Initiative, based in Helsinki, and the International Crisis Group, headquartered in Brussels, but also the fact that the highly secure Operations Center in the U.S. Department of State maintains a twenty-four-hour Crisis Management Support team to alert, brief, and advise the secretary of state on how to manage dangerous international crises in our world today.

PRINCIPLES OF CRISIS MANAGEMENT

Leaders who are responsible for major decisions about force and statecraft from the historical past to the present have understood that crises provide one of the most fascinating and most frightening features of international affairs. They generally break out suddenly, present serious threats to vital interests, demand quick decisions under intense stress, and stand on the threshold of war or peace. There are times when they are resolved or defused and other times when they explode into armed conflict. If one state deliberately intends to launch a premeditated, preemptive, or preventive war to achieve its objectives, of course, there is little that another can do to prevent it. But what about

Crisis Managers and Crisis Management: The Cuban Missile Crisis

those cases that escalate into an inadvertent war that neither side wants or expects at the outset of a diplomatic crisis? How does one account for the fact that some international confrontations end peacefully and some result in war? To what extent does the ability or failure of the adversaries to apply principles of crisis management explain the outcome? And, more basically, what exactly are these principles of crisis management?

As a tool for resolving conflicts and avoiding inadvertent war, crisis management was a familiar phenomenon during the classical system of diplomacy. Its techniques and modalities were developed over time by trial and error with a certain level of prudence, self-restraint, and good judgment, coupled with the advantages of limited armed force and the shared norms of cultural homogeneity, but never with any explicit theory of principles to guide policy makers. There were accounts of the kinds of mistakes that statesmen had made at moments of high crises, but certainly never a systematic effort to articulate lessons from the past or to write handbooks of how to actually manage a crisis once it broke out. This began to change with the terrifying Cuban Missile Crisis, the experience of which created an infinitely greater sense of urgency about managing crises in the age of weapons of mass destruction. It prompted scholars and policy researchers to seriously study crisis management in considerable detail. As a result, we now know much more about problems of information processing and decision making under crisis conditions, of command and control, of coordinating diplomatic and military actions, of communication with opponents, and of the special tasks required for practicing crisis management.

1. From Conflict to Crisis. Analyses of historical cases, for example, quickly reveal that *it is only because neither side is willing to back down that a perceived conflict of interest results in a crisis* in the first place. Confrontations between adversaries can easily be managed and terminated—in fact, avoided altogether—if one side is willing to back away. In fact, in many situations it requires a deliberate policy decision to transform a conflict of interest or a misunderstanding between states into an actual crisis. President Truman, for example, was urged by important advisers not to oppose the Soviet-imposed blockade of land access to West Berlin in 1948, based on the grounds that it would be highly disadvantageous for the United States to become involved in military operations to defend a military outpost lying well inside East Germany. He ignored that advice and decided to accept this challenge from the Soviet Union to change the status quo in its favor. This marked the beginning of the Berlin Crisis.

2. Tension Between Resolve and Restraint. Once a crisis is set into motion, there is a *built-in policy tension for each side*. That is, each side *feels compelled to do what is needed to protect or advance what it perceives as its most important interests.* At exactly the same time, however, *these very interests force it to recognize the necessity for self-restraint and to avoid actions that could trigger unwanted escalation.* It is the tension between these two objectives—protecting one's interests and showing resolve while simultaneously avoiding measures that could trigger undesired escalation and possibly war—that creates the essential dilemma that all policy makers must solve if they hope to successfully practice crisis management.

3. Appropriate Strategy. The resolution of this dilemma at the time of a war-threatening crisis requires leaders *to develop a careful political-military strategy that combines force and statecraft in a way appropriate to the situation at hand*. They need to be particularly sensitive to both diplomatic and military considerations, balancing the two in such a way as to avoid the extremes of relying either exclusively on weapons or exclusively on words. In this regard, they need to be aware that military preparations and threats of force are often indispensable for supporting diplomatic efforts in crisis situations, but that the logic of military operations—even logic based on sound military doctrine— can conflict with the logic and requirements of diplomacy. Quickly deploying troops or naval assets may make perfect sense as a means of conveying resolve or of getting ready to fight if war should erupt, for example, but at the same time may present grave dangers by working against the political and diplomatic necessities of proceeding slowly and building in pauses for thoughtful deliberation and communication. Successful crisis managers need to combine both of these factors but must understand that threats and movements of military forces, as Clausewitz observed many years ago, must be commensurate with limited objectives and carefully employed as instruments of policy, not as substitutes for policy.

4. Limited Objectives. In developing such a strategy, it is of considerable importance to recognize that management is greatly facilitated if both sides resist the temptation to inflict a damaging and humiliating defeat on the other and instead *carefully limit the objectives that they pursue in the confrontation*. Why is this self-restraint important? The more ambitious or "offensive" the aims intended to alter the existing situation at the expense of adversaries, the more strongly motivated they will be to resist. Less demanding or "defensive" aims, by way of contrast, tend to provide lesser threats to vital interests and thereby increase the probability of accommodation. In the end, all parties must recognize each other's legitimate interests and must strive to find a mutually acceptable formula for terminating the crisis.

5. Limited Means. Successful crisis management also requires creating *proportionality between the objectives being pursued and the leverage applied in their pursuit*—that is, *the limitation of the means is matched to limited ends*. A power such as the United States, for example, has unparalleled military forces for attacking and destroying any number and variety of targets. What is described as "gross military capabilities" of this character, however, do not necessarily provide a president with viable "usable options" in conflicts in which armed forces need to be carefully tailored to the peculiarities of a particular situation. The use or threatened use of excessive force during the critical opening stages of a diplomatic crisis laden with the potential for dangerous escalation might well signal a desire to militarily impose one's will on an adversary rather than to actually manage the crisis by means of diplomacy.

During the Cuban Missile Crisis, to illustrate, Kennedy managed to limit both ends and means. He rejected the advice that he aim at a regime change or the removal of Fidel Castro and confined the objective to the removal of the immediate danger of the missiles themselves. Similarly, he rejected the recommendation from the Joint Chiefs of Staff that he launch air strikes against the missile sites or an armed invasion against Cuba itself, deciding instead to combine the means of a naval blockade with those of diplomacy for crisis management.

6. Operational Principles and Conditions. Studies of historical cases also indicate that *all* sides in an international confrontation must understand, create, and adhere to other *operational principles and conditions that favor crisis management*. Limited objectives and means alone, in other words, will not ensure control over the danger of escalation and inadvertent war. Leaders also must seek to maintain control by consciously avoiding stress-induced decisional pathologies such as cognitive rigidity, feelings of desperation, or passive resignation, with its notions of "inevitability," and instead create conditions that favor managing a crisis well enough to avoid war. Such favoring conditions are highly context dependent, and the importance of each varies from one crisis to another; although none guarantees success, they all have been found likely to make a difference and affect outcomes. Each arises, in one way or another, from the necessity of policy makers to deal with the inherent dilemma of force and statecraft that we have examined throughout: the need on occasion to use both, even though there is a tension that often exists between the military and the diplomatic measures that they employ in a crisis.

These favoring principles and conditions include:

1. *Maintaining top-level civilian control of military institutions and actions.* This certainly involves command and control over the selection and timing of military options, including specific tactical maneuvers and operations such as alerts, deployments, and movements that might lead to an undesired clash with the opponent's forces.
2. *Creating pauses in the tempo.* The momentum must be deliberately slowed down in order to provide adequate time for the two sides to exchange communications, assess the situation, reflect, make decisions, respond to proposals, and engage in consultation.
3. *Coordinating diplomatic and military moves.* Whatever military actions are undertaken must be made consistent with political-diplomatic efforts as part of a carefully integrated strategy for managing the crisis without war.
4. *Confining military measures to those that constitute clear demonstrations of one's resolve and yet are limited to the crisis at hand.* Proportionality between ends and means, in other words, must be maintained.
5. *Avoiding military moves that give opponents the impression that one is about to resort to large-scale warfare and, thereby, force them to consider preemption.* The task is to manage the crisis, not escalate it.

6. *Choosing diplomatic-military options that clearly signal a desire to negotiate rather than seek a military solution.* In this regard, confusing signals, inflammatory rhetoric, or extraneous "noise" that might lead to misperception must be avoided.

7. *Employing a strategy that leaves opponents a way out of the crisis that is compatible with their fundamental interests.* Management and accommodation are much more likely if the costs can be minimized.

7. Skilled Managers. Effective adherence to these principles and conditions requires skill, judgment, and flexibility in adapting to unexpected developments as a crisis unfolds. Such qualities, however, are not easy to obtain during war-threatening crises of intense pressure and acute stress, when rationality and objectivity can easily give way to confusion, shock, fear, anger, cognitive rigidity, and impulsiveness. Individual leaders, for example, may or may not possess the necessary skills. Some may rise to the occasion and become successful managers, while others may become completely overwhelmed by events and fail disastrously. Similarly, appropriate crisis management often imposes stringent constraints on the use of military force, and this can easily lead to serious tensions that strain the experience, imagination, and patience of diplomatic and military professionals alike. Civilians may have imperfect control over their military forces, or those forces may have been designed and structured in ways that rob them of the flexibility needed in a crisis. Moreover, efforts by leaders to use armed forces in the service of offensive and assertive foreign policy may well find that they lose their capability to be used when needed as highly refined, discriminating instruments for crisis management.

Utilizing these broad principles, it is possible to compare the relative performance of policy makers in different historical cases in such a way as to come to a deeper understanding of the nature of crisis management, the importance of context and the impact of what we have called the diplomatic revolution, and the more far-reaching issue of how success or failure in crisis management can result in the preservation or destruction of the international system itself.

BISMARCK AS AN "HONEST BROKER" IN THE CRISIS OF 1878

The origins of the Crisis of 1878 can be found in the slow disintegration of the Ottoman Empire, violations of human rights, and Great Power ambitions in the Balkans. Sensing a unique opportunity to expand its influence and territory, Russia declared war on the Ottoman Turks the previous year and sent its army marching south. When the Turkish resistance collapsed, General Nicholas Ignatiev sought to exploit the temporary military advantage to the fullest. He deliberately disregarded his instructions from civilian authorities to do everything possible to avoid any foreign suspicion that might lead to intervention. Instead, he recklessly imposed the Treaty of San Stefano with seemingly unlimited objectives that would virtually destroy Turkey in Europe and unilaterally expand Russian territory and influence in the Balkans, the

Black Sea, and the Straits. These provisions not only directly violated previous agreements but granted advantages only to Russia that, if implemented, would completely upset the balance of power. The other powers therefore concluded that the treaty was completely unacceptable. France and Italy announced that the provisions threatened their national interests. Austria mobilized troops in its southeastern provinces, declaring that it would oppose any Russian expansion by war if necessary. The Turks began assembling forces in and around their capital and erecting earthworks. Britain also threatened war, calling up its reserves, issuing orders for its navy to be sent through the Straits into the Sea of Marmara, and bringing several thousand Indian troops to strategic stations in the Mediterranean as a demonstration, all while crowds in London began to sing the belligerent chant that gave the word "jingosim" to the world:

> We don't want to fight, but by jingo if we do,
> We've got the men, we've got the ships, we've got the money too!

At exactly the same time, Russian troops were only one day's march from the very gates of Constantinople, poised to attack if necessary. A very localized conflict thus was poised on the brink of escalating into a large inadvertent war involving Europe as a whole. The situation became so tense, in fact, that one British commentator in retrospect ominously observed, "If even a midshipman had lost his temper, he might have run the country into war." Indeed, as historian William Langer concludes, "peace hung by a hair."

In this crisis situation, German Chancellor Otto von Bismarck saw the possibility that any war involving several powers would bring catastrophic consequences upon the entire international system that he had been trying to construct since the unification of Germany. He was never particularly bothered by competition and rivalry, but wanted to avoid general war at all costs. Bismarck understood that the maintenance of peace and stability would not just happen on its own but required serious and deliberate efforts at crisis management. Of particular importance, he viewed the crisis itself as the real enemy. That is, he saw the task of management in this case as one not of advancing one's own power at the expense of an opponent, in which a gain by one side amounted to a loss for the other, but rather of convincing all the antagonists that they were partners in shared risk and had a common interest to avoid escalation that could lead to inadvertent war. In response to the suggestion of the Austrian foreign minister and in keeping with the earlier norms and practices of the Concert of Europe, Bismarck consequently offered the hospitality of Berlin for an international conference and announced that he would attempt to serve as an "honest broker" to help manage the crisis.

The Congress of Berlin thus assembled in the German capital in June 1878. In addition to Bismarck, the representatives included most of the leading statesmen and foreign ministers of Europe, including the Earl of Beaconsfield (Benjamin Disraeli) and Lord Salisbury of Britain, Prince Gorchakov and Count Shuvalov of Russia, Count Andrassy of Hungary, William Waddington of France, and Count Corti of Italy, in addition to representatives of Turkey and observers from the Balkans. It lasted one month and was easily the most distinguished diplomatic gathering between the Congress of Vienna of 1814–1815 and the Paris Peace Conference of 1919. In fact, the knowledge that the congress would even be held and that they would have to actually face each other greatly encouraged the antagonists to work toward negotiating at least some agreements in advance.

In accordance with diplomatic custom, the delegates elected Bismarck, as the head of the hosting government, to be its president. But he emerged as the leader in more than name. Bismarck became the vital crisis manager, dominating the meetings, setting the pace and tone, rigorously insisting that the most serious issues of dispute be addressed first, skillfully combining both incentives and threats, working sometimes in formal sessions and sometimes in private, and constantly reminding all parties of the requirements for crisis management, particularly when great tension and strain threatened the collapse of the congress itself. His success as an impartial "honest broker" cannot be better illustrated than by the fact that all sides accused him of having favored their opponents. Indeed, in the end, all of the participants of the congress agreed that without Bismarck and his personal skills, the effort would have ended in failure.

The key, of course, resided in adhering as closely as possible to the operational principles of crisis management. Delegates at the Congress of Berlin, for example, worked to maintain civilian control over their respective military forces. Bismarck—who had far more experience than he ever wanted in constantly struggling to insist that the German General Staff be an instrument rather than a maker of foreign policy—hardly needed to be convinced of the critical importance of this requirement. No troops or naval forces were allowed to threaten others during the course of the diplomatic deliberations, military commanders (like General Ignatiev, who had done so much to precipitate the crisis in the first place) found themselves kept under strict control, and military experts were invited to participate only as consultants during certain stages of the congress. This enabled the managers to coordinate diplomatic and military moves and to use armed forces to signal resolve and limited crisis objectives rather than to create impressions of large-scale warfare. Neither the Russians nor the British were willing to withdraw their forces from existing positions, for example, but both deliberately refrained from sending them any closer to Constantinople or using them in any way that might encourage the other to escalate. All parties desired to avoid what they called an "untoward event" like a midshipman losing his temper or some other incident that could trigger unwanted war.

As we have seen, it is not uncommon in situations of crisis for the antagonists to employ a combined political-military strategy for coercive diplomacy, used simultaneously with crisis management, even though the requirements of each might actually conflict with each other. In this case, the evacuation of Russian troops from the boundaries of Bulgaria and the matter of who would replace them became a major point of contention between Russia and Britain. When it appeared that negotiations had failed, the British issued an ultimatum and threatened that they would abandon the congress entirely if a solution could not be found. Rather than concluding that the situation was beyond control or that there was nothing he could do, Bismarck remained determined not to have the conference collapse, and labored indefatigably to secure a last-minute Russian concession.

Bismarck also used other techniques of crisis management throughout the congress. He constantly built in pauses in order to give all sides adequate time to communicate with each other, assess the situation, make decisions, and respond to proposals. When progress began to stall over the highly contentious issues of Bulgaria or the lines of military occupation, to illustrate, he engineered the postponement of the discussion for several days. In addition, he and his fellow delegates selected diplomatic-military options that signaled a desire both to negotiate, rather than seek a military solution, and to leave opponents a way out of the crisis that was compatible with their fundamental interests. They came to understand the necessity of mutual restraint, of recognizing each other's interests, and of having limited objectives. The final settlement of the Treaty of Berlin consequently was based on reciprocal compensation in which none of the powers received everything it desired, but all obtained something that they wanted. Britain gained Cyprus, France received permission to take Tunis, and Austria obtained authorization to occupy Bosnia and Herzegovina. The Turks were relieved of the excessive terms imposed by San Stefano and perhaps of another war that might result in the total dismemberment of their country, religious minorities within the Ottoman Empire received a level of international recognition and sanction for the protection of certain human rights, and although Russia was forced to give up its original grandiose aims, it nevertheless secured control over a new Bulgaria, the mouth of the Danube River, and several strategic strongholds at the eastern end of the Black Sea. The Italians and Germans obtained no additional territory but were spared the agony and the costs of having to choose sides between the other powers and thereby further fracture the international system if armed conflict had broken out. In this way, the crisis was successfully managed, and an inadvertent war that easily could have engulfed all of Europe was avoided.

THE "GUNS OF AUGUST," 1914

If the Congress of Berlin provides evidence of skillful leaders practicing successful management, the crisis of 1914 that led to the outbreak of the First World War reveals a tragic instance of inept mismanagement. Several years of imperial rivalries, economic competition, arms races, war plans, and a bipolar alliance system of "two armed camps"—pitting the Triple Entente of Britain, France, and Russia against the Triple Alliance of Germany, Austria, and Italy—had contributed to a series of one-after-another crises. But each of these had been controlled, or at least localized, and many observers assumed that this practice would continue with nations going to the brink of war and then resolving the crisis by diplomacy at the last moment. What they did not realize, however, was that the cumulative effect of these heightened tensions created a context that vastly compounded their peril by making succeeding crises more difficult to control. Each time, their countries assumed more severe levels of risk, unwarranted by national interests or rational strategic objectives. Each time, the commanders of their armed forces became more autonomous of civilian control, creating inflexible war plans prioritizing military over political requirements and speed rather than reflection. Of particular importance was the fact that the leaders were more interested in not appearing weak than in keeping the peace and frankly possessed neither the understanding nor the skills necessary to conduct effective crisis management.

All of this began to be painfully evident in the decisions made and the events that transpired after the assassination of the Austrian Crown Prince Franz Ferdinand at the hands of Serbian-sponsored terrorists on June 28, 1914. This assassination was not, as the popular metaphor would have it, a match thrown onto a powder keg that automatically, and in a deterministic way, resulted in war. In fact, one of the more curious features of the crisis is that it started out very slowly and evolved over the course of six weeks. The Austrians, for example, took nearly one month to decide how to respond, and many of the troops remained on harvest leave, gathering crops rather than preparing for war. Prior to taking any serious action, they carefully sought to ascertain whether their ally Germany would support them or not. Rather than carefully assessing his nation's vital interests at stake in the Balkans, or urging a diplomatic rather than a military solution, or insisting on some measure of management, however, the German Kaiser William II acted impetuously. He granted a foolhardy "blank check" to Austria on July 5, telling them that he would support whatever they decided to do. In doing so, wrote historian Sydney Fay, the kaiser and his advisors were "putting a noose around their necks and handing the other end of the rope to a stupid and clumsy adventurer who now felt free to go as he liked." Insensitive as ever to the international implications of his decisions, William II then simply abandoned his responsibilities and left for a holiday cruise.

With this unqualified support in their hands, the Austrians drastically escalated events by issuing a forty-eight-hour ultimatum to the shocked Serbs with demands so deliberately harsh that they guaranteed rejection. British Foreign Secretary Edward Grey said that he had never seen one government send another government "a document of so formidable a character." When the Russian Foreign Minister Sergei Sazonov saw the text of the ultimatum, he was aghast and shouted to the Austrian ambassador: "This means European war. You are setting Europe alight!" The Serbians composed a masterful reply that actually acceded to most of the Austrian demands. In fact, when William II read it, he wrote happily, "Every reason for war now disappears!" But by this time the Austrians were not interested in compromise or limited objectives. They rejected the Serbian response, dismissed a British proposal for a conference that might have helped to manage the crisis, and declared war on Serbia on July 28, 1914.

Rather than building in pauses in the tempo, or avoiding military moves that give an opponent the impression that one is about to escalate, or choosing diplomatic-military options that signal a desire to negotiate rather than seeking a military solution—as required by crisis management—in order to keep the war confined to the Austrians and the Serbs alone, Russia decided to support Serbia by ordering partial mobilization against Austria. At this point, Tsar Nicholas II was shocked to discover that the only plan his military staff had prepared called for full and simultaneous mobilization against both Germany and Austria and to hear his commanders insist that any restraint would only lead to disaster. To make matters worse, instead of carefully coordinating diplomatic and military moves, at the same time that their armed forces were moving west toward the German border, Russian diplomats were telling the Germans that they had nothing to fear. The Germans perceived that threatening actions spoke louder than soothing words. They responded with the extreme variant of an ultimatum demanding that if Russia did not stop its mobilization within twelve hours, they would follow suit. The Russians refused, and Germany declared war against Russia on August 1, thereby expanding the conflict exponentially. All of these developments occurred, remarkably, without a single serious discussion between St. Petersburg and Berlin about the substance of the crisis or the need for diplomacy and in the absence of any major, tangible dispute between the two countries.

This pattern of mobilization, with its resulting escalation, was repeated by others, and each successive step made the crisis more difficult to manage. Within only days of the Austrian declaration of war against Serbia, every one of the major European powers called up its armed forces. Each claimed that its military mobilization constituted a defensive measure only, taken merely as a response to the dangers posed by others. They all feared that disastrous consequences would occur if a potential adversary gained even a momentary advantage in mobilizing its army and navy. This encouraged them to see the military incentives of moving as quickly as possible rather than the diplomatic advantages of building in pauses for thoughtful deliberation and negotiation. They also hoped that their own mobilization might serve as a deterrent, warning others against taking similar action. But in a context of fear, misperception, and seemingly total lack of empathy for the perspectives of others, this produced exactly the opposite reaction. Every mobilization, in turn—especially since they were never accompanied by serious efforts of diplomatic negotiation—gave all the others the overwhelming impression that large-scale warfare might be imminent and that they should consider countermeasures and preemption in order not to be placed at a serious disadvantage.

Crisis management, of course, requires the firm determination to actually manage or maintain control over events. Thus, the most serious mistake that any leader can make is to believe that there is nothing he or she can do to prevent war or that management is not possible. In a crisis situation, therefore, anyone seeking to manage must avoid falling prey to that dreaded word "inevitable." Yet, this is precisely what the leaders of 1914 failed to do. Time and time again, and even at early stages of the crisis, they concluded that they were helpless, passively resigning themselves to whatever fate awaited them. Paul Cambon, the French ambassador in London, for example, stated that he saw "no way of halting the march of events." Arthur Nicolson, the British

Permanent Under Secretary for Foreign Affairs, wrote, "I am of the opinion that the resources of diplomacy are, for the present, exhausted." In a telling comment written in his own hand, Wilhelm II declared in despair, "My work is at an end!" Similarly, one of the leading generals in Russia advised the foreign ministry that "war had become inevitable."

As the inflexible Russian war plan severely limited the options for civilian crisis managers, so too did the German counterpart, known as the von Schlieffen Plan, which called for a quick military attack, first against France and then against Russia. The French, seeing an opportunity for revenge for their loss of territory during the Franco-Prussian War, had no interest in urging restraint upon their ally and instead actually encouraged Russia to resist German demands and promised unconditional support in doing so. At this stage, the kaiser suddenly began to fear a two-front war and tried to persuade his Chief of the General Staff, General Helmuth von Moltke, to change the plan in such a way as to divert German attention away from France and toward the more immediate threat of Russia. Barbara Tuchman captures the memorable scene in *The Guns of August* with these words:

> Moltke was in no mood for any more of the kaiser's meddling with serious military matters....He saw a vision of the deployment crumbling apart in confusion, supplies here, soldiers there, ammunition lost in the middle, companies without officers, divisions without staffs, and those 11,000 trains, each exquisitely scheduled to click over specified tracks at specified intervals of ten minutes, tangled into grotesque ruin of the most perfectly planned military movement in history.
>
> "Your Majesty," Moltke said to him now, "it cannot be done. The deployment of millions cannot be improvised. If Your Majesty insists on leading the whole army to the East it will not be an army ready for battle but a disorganized mob of armed men with no arrangements for supply. Those arrangements took a whole year of intricate labor to complete"—and Moltke closed upon that rigid phrase, the basis for every major German mistake, the phrase that launched the invasion of Belgium and the submarine war against the United States, the inevitable phrase when military plans dictate policy—"and once settled, it cannot be altered."

In fact, it could have been altered and, in accordance with the operational principles of crisis management, should have been altered. These plans were made by men and could have been changed by men. But Kaiser William II, like Tsar Nicholas II, was not wise enough or strong enough to exert and maintain civilian control over military options or the military machinery that he had done so much to create, and both simply acquiesced to their generals who insisted that an all-or-nothing war plan must determine policy and that priority should be given to military necessity over political consequences.

To make matters even worse, almost no effort was made to coordinate diplomatic and military actions or communications as part of a carefully integrated strategy. On the very day that the German Chancellor Bethmann-Hollweg sent a telegram to the Austrian cabinet stressing the need to exercise restraint and accept mediation in the conflict with Serbia, for example, Moltke sent his own telegram to the Austrian chief of staff Conrad von Hötzendorf urging him to mobilize his army at once. These completely contradictory messages not only signaled confusion to leaders in Vienna but made them quite naturally ask whether civilians or military commanders were really in control in Berlin. Similarly, instead of confining military moves to those that were appropriate to limited crisis objectives or selecting diplomatic-military options that would leave opponents a way out of the crisis compatible with their fundamental interests, these leaders foolishly plunged their countries and the world ever closer toward full-scale war—and catastrophe. Germany, to illustrate, issued an ultimatum to France demanding neutrality in the event of war and sent another ultimatum to Belgium that demanded free passage for German troops. When both were rejected, Germany declared war on France and launched an invasion of neutral Belgium on August 3, revealing a complete disregard for international law, a preference for a military solution over any negotiations at all, and a determination to seek unlimited objectives. In response, Britain issued an ultimatum to Germany, demanding that all troops be withdrawn from Belgium within less than one day. The demand was rejected and Britain declared war against Germany. With this, the great storm broke.

The leaders of the Great Powers thus failed to adhere to any of the principles of crisis management and thereby allowed a secondary conflict to escalate completely out of control. As a result of their failure, a local dispute in the Balkans led to the invasion of Belgium and the dispatch of British troops on the other side of Europe with a war everywhere between—and one that eventually drew in the United States, China, and Japan. Their monumental mismanagement resulted not only in the unanticipated horrors of the First World War, but the destruction of several of their own governments and the entire international system they had known.

Terrorism and the Mumbai Crisis, 2008

One of the most volatile and dangerous relationships in the world is that between India and Pakistan. Indeed, despite diplomatic efforts to improve their relations, it is not uncommon to hear people on either side of the border that separates them refer to the other as "mortal enemies." Ever since they were first created with the partition of British India in 1947, these two countries have fought three major wars and confronted each other over frightening border incidents, military standoffs, and an unending state of war preparedness. They have battled over the disputed Himalayan region of Kashmir, engaged in struggles between Muslims and Hindus, and vehemently contested cross-border terrorism. India and Pakistan also have compounded their rivalry by conducting a fierce and unrelenting nuclear arms race. All of these factors of bitter tension and six decades of poisonous mistrust established the context for the serious crisis that broke out in 2008.

Late in the evening of November 26, 2008 (a date often described as "India's 9/11"), a team of ten well-trained terrorists attacked Mumbai, India's largest city and financial center. They came ashore on two small inflatable boats and set out on an audacious, ambitious, and precisely planned attack against multiple and predetermined soft targets. These included civilians minding their own business at a train station, two luxury hotels, a café frequented by foreigners, a Jewish cultural center, two hospitals, and a theater. Over the course of a three-day rampage, they wreaked havoc, leaving a trail of destruction and bloodshed. More than 160 people were killed and hundreds more wounded. For sixty hours, the terrorists brought a city of 20,000,000 to a standstill as the world watched in horror. This might have remained yet another case of domestic extremism except for one fact: Indian authorities quickly determined that these attackers had come from neighboring Pakistan.

The suicide gunmen who launched this terrorist attack were all members of Lashkar-e Taiba, a powerful and deadly Pakistani-based jihadist organization. Its followers embraced radical Islam, calling themselves the "Army of the Pure" and seeing India as a part of what they described as the "Crusader, Zionist, Hindu" alliance. Struggles against Indians and the West served their ideology and their purpose. Observers believed that the organization maintained close ties to al-Qaeda and the Taliban. Authorities knew that, like other terrorist organizations, Lashkar-e Taiba received strong support from certain elements sympathetic to Islamic militants within the Pakistani Inter-Services Intelligence (ISI) (a point confirmed a few years later when Osama bin Laden was discovered, despite consistent official denials, to be living safely in Pakistan within walking distance of a military base). Moreover, it was known that this violent group had been used in the past by Pakistan as an instrument of state policy in an ongoing proxy war against India, as revealed in the dramatic and brazen 2001 terrorist attack against the Indian Parliament itself.

Visceral outrage in the wake of the Mumbai carnage thus ran at a fever pitch. Tens of thousands of Indian citizens took to the streets, shouting, "Long Live Mother India!" Many wore T-shirts emblazoned with a bloodstain-like design and the words "Turn Anger Into Action!" Others screamed over and over again: "Death to Pakistan! Death to Pakistan!" Public pressure mounted on Indian officials, and many of them joined in the popular hard-line cries for revenge. Indian Prime Minister Manmohan Singh described Pakistan as "the epicenter of terrorism" and vowed to respond "with all the means at our disposal." The crisis escalated further when the government of Pakistan adamantly denied any involvement at all in the attack. India placed its armed forces on high alert, and Pakistan responded in kind. A security official in Islamabad declared that his country would react to any Indian military mobilization by moving "all troops" from its border with Afghanistan and redeploying them along the frontier with India. Watching all of this at close hand, U.S. Ambassador to India David Mulford reported starkly: "There is war fever here. I don't know if the prime minister can hold out." At this stage, Indian Minister for External Affairs Pranab Mukherjee made a personal and threatening telephone call to Pakistani Foreign Minister Shah Mehmood Qureshi. According to his own account, "I said they were leaving us no choice but to go to war."

It was at this precise point that the extreme dangers of unpredictable escalation—and thus the challenges for crisis management—emerged. The prospect of war between nuclear-armed India and Pakistan, caused by misjudgment or sabotage, presented a terrifying possibility for them, for the region, and for the world. All parties knew perfectly well that militant terrorists could start long and punishing wars between nations, as revealed in the response of the United States to the 9/11 attack. If this crisis exploded similarly into a war, especially if it caused the nuclear threshold to be breached, perhaps by an accidental or unauthorized launch, the consequences would be disastrous. The reality of this began to dawn on the leaders of both sides, especially those in Islamabad who warned against "the blame game and knee-jerk reactions" as they listened to their F-16s flying overhead to counter a possible attack from India and watched the crisis start to career out of the control of their own already fragile and inexperienced government. One security official announced publicly, "We are expecting war." In growing fear, the prime minister, president, and foreign minister suddenly began contacting their counterparts in other countries, appealing for outside help to assist in managing the crisis.

Among the outsiders, the United States had much at stake in this crisis. It not only wanted to prevent war, but needed Pakistan as a critical ally in its battles against terrorism, especially against al-Qaeda and the Taliban; at the same time, the United States needed India to serve as what it described as a major "strategic partner" on a number of fronts. Its leaders knew full well that crisis management would not just happen on its own; it would require very specific and deliberate efforts. Toward this end—and recognizing the relationship between force and statecraft—the United States sent its highest ranking diplomat, Secretary of State Condoleezza Rice, and its highest ranking military officer, Chairman of the Joint Chiefs of Staff Admiral Mike Mullen, halfway around the world. They went first to New Delhi and then to Islamabad. The purpose was to use face-to-face meetings to persuade both countries to back away from the brink and to ramp down their confrontation in order to avoid war. To do this, they began by offering sympathy for the victims of the Mumbai attacks and then assistance to do whatever they could to help defuse the situation. They urged both sides to adhere to the principles of crisis management by exercising patience and self-restraint, avoiding actions that would trigger unwanted escalation, developing strategies appropriate to the situation at hand, and limiting the objectives and the means employed. They also employed coercive diplomacy by exerting pressure in a forcing function, trying to avoid either leaning on Indian and Pakistani leaders too hard or not leaning on them hard enough. They warned India not to mobilize its forces or to retaliate with an armed attack that surely would lead to war, and they simultaneously demanded that Pakistan take serious action against extremists in its own country. When Pakistani Prime Minister Yusuf Raza Gillani told Rice that the terrorists who attacked Mumbai "had nothing to do with Pakistan," she bluntly responded: "Either you are lying to me or your people are lying to you."

Rice importantly told both sides that U.S. intelligence agencies believed that the terrorist attack on Mumbai had originated from within Pakistan—but not from the Pakistani government. Evidence from highly sophisticated technological means indicated that the attackers likely had received assistance from rogue elements within the notoriously unreliable security services as well as from the nonstate organization of Lashkar-e Taiba. In other words, the attack had not been state sponsored and the gunmen had not been acting as agents of the government. This confirmed what the leaders in Islamabad had been saying from the beginning. Indeed, they argued that they, too, suffered as victims of terrorism at the hands of the militant extremists within Pakistan. President Asif Ali Zardari pointed out with personal poignancy that his own wife and former prime minister, Benazir Bhutto, had been assassinated only the previous year as a result of a suicide bomb attack.

Other outside actors became involved as well. The offers of assistance as well as the warnings from the Americans received increased credibility and potency when they were reinforced several days later during a visit to both India and Pakistan by British Prime Minister Gordon Brown. The United Nations Security Council not only urged all parties to do whatever they could to avoid war but was willing to take measures to impose sanctions on the leaders of Lashkar-e Taiba and its charitable organization that served as a financial front. In doing so, its members (including China, a long-time ally of Pakistan) sought to limit the ability of known terrorists to raise funds, acquire weapons, plan, or carry out attacks, while at the same time giving India a way out of the crisis that was compatible with its fundamental interests. Such efforts and intervention by outsiders certainly assisted in managing the crisis, but in the end it depended on the leaders in India and Pakistan themselves.

In this regard, the decisions to be made in New Delhi were not easy. There would be very heavy costs to be paid if India went to war. Even a limited use of armed force could quickly escalate out of control and strengthen the hands of the anti-Indian extremists. At the same time, there would be costs to *not* taking some form of military action. If nothing were done, not only would emotional public opinion erupt at home, but Pakistan would know that terrorist attacks launched from its own soil against India could continue with little repercussion.

A different, but extremely serious, problem also existed for Pakistan. One of the central requirements for any crisis manager is that of maintaining top-level civilian control of military institutions and actions. Only in this way can armed force be used as an instrument of policy and can diplomatic-military strategies of force and statecraft be developed and effectively coordinated. Yet, in Islamabad, Zardari—a civilian—headed a country going through a fragile transition to democracy after more than eight years of military rule under a four-star general who possessed the backing of the armed forces. Having been in office less than three months, he was completely untested and now faced the extremely difficult task of avoiding war with India while at the same time keeping Pakistan's powerful military and intelligence services in check. If he cracked down on the jihadists (especially if it was perceived as a result of external pressure from India, the United States, and certain other countries), he risked a serious backlash among those in these services and in the country who already intensely opposed his cooperation with the U.S.-led "global war on terror" and its attacks against Taliban forces and their own people in western Pakistan and Afghanistan. He hung on a precipice. Inflammable instability and violence could explode in an instant. Indeed, the magnitude of difficulty and danger prompted the news magazine *Der Spiegel* to run a headline reading: "Pakistan's President Zardari Attempts the Impossible." It ominously concluded that his efforts were "doomed."

Believing that the costs of failure would be overwhelmingly unacceptable, however, Zardari and other decision makers in both Pakistan and India resisted being pulled into this trap of throwing up their hands in despair and falling prey to notions of impossibility and inevitability. Instead, they desperately worked to manage the crisis. Despite their seemly irreconcilable differences and intense rivalry, they realized that they needed each other to work together in some measure of partnership. Both sides came to realize that the crisis itself was the most dangerous adversary and needed to be resolved before it careened completely out of control. They thus tried to slow down the tempo and avoid moves and countermoves that might convey a desire to seek a military solution. Indian leaders, for example, chose not to mobilize their armed forces, to amass them on the border, to send out its warships, or to fire artillery into Pakistan—at least for the moment. They wanted to give Pakistan time for an opportunity to respond. In addition—and very importantly—they decided to focus their attention on the immediate and limited issue of the terrorists involved with the Mumbai attack, rather than using it as an excuse to take action on the much larger and more volatile problem of Kashmir. For his part, Zardari appealed for everyone "to pause and take a breath." He also reiterated that he had proposed a nuclear "no first strike" pact with India several days before the carnage in Mumbai, and stood ready to bring it to fruition during this trying time of crisis.

After several agonizing days of trying to balance between domestic and international pressures, Zardari announced that his government would catch and punish anyone involved in the Mumbai attack. He therefore launched a number of highly public arrests of known terrorist leaders. When Indian air force fighter jets violated Pakistani airspace by briefly crossing the border, he deliberately—and significantly—chose to describe the event as only a "technical incursion" and "mistake" rather than an act of war. A government spokesperson in Islamabad reiterated, "We have confirmed it. We contacted the Indian air force and they said the violation was inadvertent." They concluded, in revealing words, "We don't want to escalate the situation." Leaders in New Delhi responded accordingly. Shortly thereafter, India's Minister of Defense A. K. Antony explicitly stated what many wanted to hear: that although relations between the two countries would never be normal until Islamabad took serious action against terrorists within its borders, his country was "not planning any military action" against Pakistan. The immediate Mumbai crisis had been managed.

ANALYSIS

By exploring these three cases in light of the principles discussed at the beginning of this chapter, we now can understand the nature of crisis management more clearly, see why some efforts succeed and others fail, consider what lessons might be drawn, and have a greater appreciation for the impact of historical context or, more specifically, the way in which the diplomatic revolution has affected crisis management in our own time.

There can be little doubt, for example, that an appropriate political-military strategy for crisis management cannot possibly succeed unless there is skilled, top-level civilian control over military institutions and actions. In this regard, modern policy makers enjoy many technological advantages over their predecessors. Improvements in communications and transportation allow leaders to exert much more personal control over military forces than ever before. One has only to compare the relative inaccessibility of the Balkans from major capitals at the time of Bismarck with the ability of Rice and Mullen in 2008 to fly to the crisis area in a matter of hours, or the capabilities of the present-day U.S. Department of State's Crisis Management Support team and the Department of Defense's National Military Command Center for rapid worldwide communications, which enable policy makers to be in instant contact with their military forces, even though they may be on the other side of the globe.

Having observed the need for civilian control, however, it is also important to acknowledge that the mere existence of civilian leaders is no guarantee that the requisite skills will be present or that successful management will result. The 1914 case certainly confirms this. At the beginning of both the American war in Vietnam and the 2003 invasion of Iraq, strong-willed and hawkish civilians, who thought they knew best, deliberately rejected the more prudent—and accurate—advice provided by professional military commanders.

With regard to the need to slow down the tempo of military actions, crisis managers in the contemporary world are likely to encounter greater difficulties than did statesmen in previous centuries. With events driven at an ever faster pace by sophisticated improvements in communication, transportation, and weapons technology, political leaders are under extraordinary pressure to make critical decisions in shorter and shorter periods of time. The crisis surrounding the Congress of Berlin, for example, dragged on for months. The crisis leading up to the outbreak of First World War was of several weeks in duration, and leaders frequently expressed their fears that "time was running out." The critical period in the 2008 Mumbai crisis lasted only about two weeks, and those leaders forced to make decisions understood that if missiles were launched, a single hour of delay could make all the difference in the world. It is extraordinarily difficult to create pauses when the momentum of events is so pressing.

Moreover, the increasing impact of public opinion and pressure groups on decision making has complicated the management task of slowing down or "freezing" a crisis. Those who met at the Congress of Berlin experienced the impact of some domestic politics and the press on their deliberations, but it was minimal. This is why Disraeli could boast about the delegates issuing a few statements for public consumption, and then going behind closed doors and doing what needed to be done. By 1914, public opinion could easily be whipped up by super-heated nationalists and a sensational press, and this greatly influenced European capitals in the last days before war broke out. In attempting to manage the Mumbai crisis, leaders in India and Pakistan had to contend with public opinion heated to a fever pitch, often feeding on itself through Internet social networking tools such as Twitter and Flickr. In addition, the leaders faced political rivals and extremists seeking to use the crisis for their own agendas, who stridently pushed popular hawkish and chauvinistic emotions that portrayed any moderation or compromise as weak and cowardly.

The requirement for coordinating diplomatic and military moves in a crisis also encounters both advantages and disadvantages under the impact of the diplomatic revolution. Successful coordination requires accurate and timely information and effective communication. In this regard, today's sophisticated technology for collecting and analyzing intelligence, such as satellite detection and electronic intercepts from space and computer-generated imaging and analyses of vast amounts of information, can (if used properly) give contemporary policy makers in times of crises many advantages in command and control that were completely unknown to their predecessors. In the Mumbai crisis, the United States possessed specialized technology that could trace calls and detect the global position and satellite phone systems used by the attackers. But, by the same token, the terrorists themselves had used Global Positioning System (GPS) handsets and high-resolution maps from Google Earth to plan their routes and targets, as well as Voice over Internet Protocol (VoIP) phone service, Blackberries, and Skype to communicate with their Lashkar-e Taiba handlers in Pakistan.

Given the potential scale and level of destructiveness made possible by technology in contemporary warfare, the decisions that shape the capabilities and doctrines of modern military forces do not always take into sufficient account the task of using these same forces as instruments of management in times of crises. This is the problem created when armed forces are viewed only in terms of "gross military capabilities" to fight large-scale warfare, thereby severely restricting the ability of leaders to find "usable options" and to fine-tune and coordinate military and diplomatic moves. In the case of the First World War, for example, the opposing sides possessed mass armies, weapons produced by an unprecedented arms race, and inflexible war plans that contained no options other than full-scale military conflict. Thus, the attempts of Germany and Russia at coercive diplomacy became de facto declarations of war once they ordered mobilization. In the Mumbai crisis, both India and Pakistan came to realize that, although they each possessed enormous military capabilities, none of these could be used as a carefully calibrated instrument to convey limited objectives or means. When confronted with the possibility of a nuclear threat, the only choices appeared to be doing almost nothing or risking total destruction.

This challenge will repeatedly confront modern policy makers who struggle with force and statecraft.

Paradoxically, the very destructiveness of modern weaponry, with its capacity to annihilate not only military forces but civilization as well, has strengthened strategic deterrence and the incentives to choose diplomatic-military options that will signal a desire to negotiate rather than to seek military solutions. Here, fear plays a critical role. In today's world of weapons of mass destruction, leaders are acutely aware of the horrors of modern war. For this reason, most rational policy makers are much more eager to explore avenues of compromise rather than employ force and are less likely to indulge in belligerent nationalism or fatalistically believe in the "inevitability" of war, as so many did in 1914. This explains why India and Pakistan invested so much effort to carefully signal each other during the 2008 crisis, for neither one wanted to place the other in a position similar to that of the German kaiser and thus risk a nuclear exchange that might follow. Nevertheless, any international system— including our own—must struggle with the problem of how to deal with those who do not share this fear and who are willing to recklessly resort to armed force to accomplish their goals.

Further complications arise for crisis management with the substantial increase in the number of individuals and departments that impact a modern government's foreign policy, as well as the existence of new and powerful nonstate actors. Bismarck's role as a successful "honest broker" was made considerably easier by the fact that he only had to deal with like-minded official representatives of the five Great Powers. It was not nearly as simple in 1914 when, for example, no one knew who spoke for Germany or which branch of government pursued which policy. The contrast becomes even greater when one compares the 2008 crisis in which Singh and Zardari shared few common values, had to contend with their own strong-willed bureaucracies and constituencies, and in the case of Pakistan actually faced dangerous rogue elements within its own army and intelligence services as well as nonstate terrorist organizations subject to no direction other than their own fanaticism.

The emergence of such extremism points to the increase in the ideological nature of many international disputes and crises. This has made it more difficult to exercise self-restraint, carefully establish limited objectives and means, select diplomatic-military options that leave a way out of the crisis, and avoid military moves that give the opponent the impression that large-scale warfare is about to be initiated. The key factor here is "impression," for as recent studies of human crisis behavior reveal, actions are not always perceived as they are actually intended, and this can lead to mistaken images with unintended consequences. This places a particular premium on the ability *to see the situation from the perspective of the adversary and to consider how its leaders might view one's own behavior*. Misperceptions can be a source of serious miscalculations, and these can lead to major errors in policy, missed opportunities, and avoidable catastrophes. The crisis of 1878 centered around classic power politics among participants who shared many common values and thus could be managed relatively quickly as long as the major actors received reciprocal compensation. By 1914, however, intense nationalism and imperialism had combined forces to add a more complicated dimension to the international situation, contributing heavily to the mismanagement of the crisis. At the time of the Mumbai crisis in 2008, volatile ideology and suicidal extremism created the crisis in the first place. This trend appears likely to continue. Consequently, separating an opponent's fundamental interests from the rhetoric—whether it rings with slogans about "the Axis of Evil," "the Great Satan," "holy war," "crusade," "infidels," or "*jihad*"—is one of the truly difficult challenges for those seeking to practice crisis management today.

Beyond the theoretical and operational principles demonstrated by the three specific cases treated above, our analysis of these and many other historical and contemporary cases of crisis management and mismanagement also indicates that not all crises lend themselves equally to manageability. In fact, some crises are peculiarly resistant to management because of the structure and dynamics of the international system, balance-of-power or alliance considerations, domestic pressures on the parties to the dispute, the unpredictable behavior and decisions of others, or because the interests or ideologies of the two sides are so fundamentally antagonistic that they cannot be sufficiently reconciled. The parties may see few opportunities for constructive engagement or few incentives to avoid war. One side or the other side may reach the conclusion during the crisis that no other alternatives exist to secure its objectives or to avoid an unacceptable outcome, or because one or the other side decides to embrace more ambitious objectives than it entertained at the outset of the crisis and is willing to accept the risk of war by resorting to armed force for this purpose.

One lesson of history remains clear from all cases: crisis management does not passively happen on its own but depends on the skill and the capabilities of individual people. Indeed, the entire concept of management itself is significant only as it is interpreted and implemented by men and women within their own particular context of time and place. Incentives and opportunities will not suffice to avoid war if individual leaders lack the intelligence to understand the nature of crisis management and diplomacy or the ability to function under great stress, to exercise self-restraint, to adhere to the operational principles of crisis management and apply them, to see the situation from the perspective of others, or to have some ethical sense of responsibility for the larger international system as a whole. This applies to policy makers on all sides during a crisis, for management requires partnership in the midst of intense rivalry, in which the behavior of one dramatically influences the other in a dynamic interaction. As political scientist Phil Williams observes, success requires "the traditional qualities of statesmanship—wisdom, diplomatic skills, and incisive judgment—[which] can prove decisive, either through their presence or through their absence." When, in the words of Winston Churchill, "the balance quivers," the stakes are high, and leaders stand poised at critical paths diverging before them, the lack of ability, the failure to reflect or empathize, poor judgment, or even one moment of carelessness on the part of a single individual can easily transform a crisis into an inadvertent war.

SUGGESTIONS FOR FURTHER EXPLORATION

For a detailed analysis of the principles of crisis management and its requirements, modalities, and challenges, see Alexander L. George (ed.), *Avoiding War: Problems of Crisis Management* (Boulder, CO, 1991). Other important analyses also can be found in Uzi Rabi (ed.), *International Intervention in Local Conflicts: Conflict Management and Conflict Resolution Since the Cold War* (London, 2010); Chester Crocker et al. (eds.), *Leashing the Dogs of War* (Washington, DC, 2007); Arien Boin et al., *The Politics of Crisis Management* (Cambridge, UK, 2005); Joseph Bouchard, *Command in Crisis* (New York, 1991); Sean Lynn-Jones et al. (eds.), *Nuclear Diplomacy and Crisis Management* (Cambridge, MA, 1990); Gilbert R. Winham (ed.), *New Issues in International Crisis Management* (Boulder, CO, 1988); Richard Ned Lebow, *Nuclear Crisis Management* (Ithaca, NY, 1987); Scott D. Sagan, "Nuclear Alerts and Crisis Management," *International Security*, 4 (Spring 1985): 99–139; Richard Smoke and William Ury, *Beyond the Hotline* (Cambridge, MA, 1984); Alexander L. George, "Crisis Management: The Interaction of Political and Military Considerations," *Survival*, 26 (September–October 1984): 323–334; Arthur N. Gilbert and Paul Gordon Lauren, "Crisis Management: An Assessment and Critique," *Journal of Conflict Resolution*, 24 (December 1980): 641–664; Paul Gordon Lauren, "Crisis Management: History and Theory," *International History Review*, 1 (October 1979): 542–556; Richard Smoke, *War: Controlling Escalation* (Cambridge, MA, 1977); Phil Williams, *Crisis Management* (New York, 1976); Ole Holsti, *Crisis, Escalation, War* (London, 1972); and Coral Bell, *The Conventions of Crisis: A Study in Diplomatic Management* (London, 1971). The Cuban Missile Crisis stimulated much thinking about crisis management.

Discussion of the Congress of Berlin in 1878 can be found in Norman Rich, *Great Power Diplomacy, 1814–1914* (New York, 1992); Paul Gordon Lauren, "Crisis Prevention in Nineteenth-Century Diplomacy," in Alexander L. George (ed.), *Managing U.S.-Soviet Rivalry* (Boulder, CO, 1983); Edward Crankshaw, *Bismarck* (New York, 1981); Immanuel Geiss, *Der Berliner Kongreß 1878* (Boppard am Rhein, 1978); William L. Langer, *European Alliances and Alignments, 1871–1890* (New York, 1964 ed.); W. N. Medlicott, *The Congress of Berlin and After* (London, 1963 ed.); B. H. Sumner, *Russia and the Balkans, 1870–1880* (Hamden, CT., 1962 ed.); and Edward Hertslet (ed.), *The Map of Europe by Treaty*, Vol. 4 (London, 1891).

Probably no crisis has been studied more extensively than that of 1914. Stimulating further reading can be found in David Stevenson, *Cataclysm* (New York, 2005); Richard Ned Lebow, "Contingency, Catalysts, and International System Change," *Political Science Quarterly*, 115 (Winter, 2000–2001): 591–616; James Joll, *The Origins of the First World War* (London, 1992 ed.); Jack Levy, "The Role of Crisis Management in the Outbreak of World War I," in Alexander L. George (ed.), *Avoiding War* (Boulder, CO, 1991); Ole Holsti, "Theories of Crisis Decision Making," and Samuel R. Williamson, Jr., "Theories of Organizational Process and Foreign Policy Outcomes," both in Paul Gordon Lauren (ed.), *Diplomacy: New Approaches in History, Theory, and Policy* (New York, 1979); Paul Kennedy (ed.), *The War Plans of the Great Powers* (Boston, 1979); Barbara Tuchman, *The Guns of August* (New York, 1962); Sydney Fay, *The Origins of the World War* (New York, 1930 ed.); and "London Times Sees War Inevitable," *New York Times*, August 3, 1914.

For the Mumbai crisis, see Condoleezza Rice, *No Higher Honor* (New York, 2011); B. Raman, *Mumbai 26/11* (New Delhi, 2009); Angel Rabasa et al., "The Lessons of Mumbai," RAND Occasional Paper (Santa Monica, CA, 2009); and K. Alan Kronstadt, "Terrorist Attacks in Mumbai, India, and Implications for U.S. Interests," Congressional Research Service Report (Washington, DC, 2008); "Pakistan's President Zardari Attempts the Impossible," *Der Spiegel*, December 17, 2008; and "UN Security Council Sanctions Lashkar Members," *Wall Street Journal*, December 10, 2008.

Many fascinating historical cases exist for further exploration of crisis management and mismanagement. These include, among others, the crises of Spain (1822–1823), Belgium (1830), the Near East (1852–1854), Fashoda (1898), Bosnia (1908–1909), Agadir (1911), Ethiopia-Italy (1935–1936), Rhineland (1936), Munich (1938), Iran (1946), Berlin (1948–1949 and 1958), Korea (1950), Suez (1956), Quemoy and Matsu (1958), Congo (1960), the Cuban Missile Crisis (1962), the Middle East (1967), Sino-Soviet border crisis (1969), management during the Arab-Israeli War (1973), the American hostage crisis in Iran (1979–1980), Able Archer (1983), Persian Gulf Crisis (1990–1991), Kosovo (1998–1999), and India-Pakistan (2001–2002). See also the International Crisis Behavior Project at www.cidcm.umd.edu/icb/dataviewer.

PART THREE

RESTRAINTS AND REFLECTIONS

——12——

Ethics and Other Restraints on Force and Statecraft

F or centuries of time and in a world where competition and violence seemed to be always present, thoughtful and frightened men and women have wrestled with the extremely difficult challenge of how to restrain their worst excesses. They have understood that at times their very survival depended on their ability to control their rivalries and passions and to contain the brutal destruction and loss of human life caused by the use of armed force. It is for this reason that the search to find some kind of restraints often has preoccupied the thoughts of those as divergent as political and religious leaders, diplomats, philosophers, generals, strategic theorists, theologians, international lawyers, investors, scholars, students, human rights activists, and pacifists, among many others vitally concerned about force and statecraft.

PRACTICAL, STRUCTURAL, AND POLITICAL RESTRAINTS

Diplomacy, it has been said, is "the art of the possible." This insightful description comes from lessons learned from long and sometimes painful historical experience and serves to remind us that statesmen rarely can do exactly what they would like to do. Instead, they generally must settle for the least harmful of a number of unpleasant alternatives because they are confronted with any number of constraints or restraints that limit their freedom of choice and action.

Very practical restraints, for example, are presented by geographical distance and terrain, limited information or time to make decisions, inertia, the crops, momentary state of health, the condition of the roads, and even the weather. In addition, every state has a finite resource base. Each possesses only a certain amount of territory and assets for their bases or port facilities, only so much population to provide soldiers for their armies or sailors for their navies, and only so many weapons for their arsenals. The amount of funding for military expenditures (even for those who engage in deficit spending) is ultimately limited by their natural resources, economic strength, and industrial capacity. Each faces limitations on the level of education of its inhabitants, the degree of technological sophistication, the effectiveness of its transportation and communications systems, and the cohesiveness and morale of its people. Some states—like the Great Powers during the classical system of diplomacy or the United States, Russia, and China today—obviously possess more of these resources than others, but none has an unlimited supply on which they can draw without end.

Restraints also are imposed by the power, capabilities, and interests of other states, each claiming its own prerogatives of national sovereignty. The extent to which one country can pursue its objectives is based in large part on the relative strength of other countries at any given time. The power and capabilities of others, including allies and adversaries alike, in other words, can place severe restrictions on any state's freedom of action by creating a fear of unacceptable consequences, thereby making it refrain from doing something that it wants to do or making it do something that it otherwise would not choose to do. Indeed, this is the feature that undergirds the strategies of both deterrence and coercive diplomacy, as we saw in Chapters 9 and 10. The traditional balance of power helped to keep the peace in part because it restrained leaders who feared that aggression on their part would result in unacceptable costs from a coalition of countervailing forces against them. It is thus in any state's prudent self-interest to make some level of accommodation with others and thereby to accept certain restraints.

In this regard, it is essential to remember that capabilities are measured in people as well as things. States, as observed in Chapter 7, do not make and implement decisions in international relations—people do. This is why de Callières and others who followed spent so much time stressing the importance of developing a knowledge of history and the professional skills necessary for the conduct of statecraft. Negotiation, deterrence, coercive diplomacy, and crisis management, as seen in Part Two, cannot possibly succeed unless leaders possess the requisite wisdom and skill to make them work.

The sheer complexity of international relations itself imposes restraints. At any given point in time, many issues and problems are competing for attention, and some of these may be inextricably linked and intertwined in complicated ways. This explains why the expressions of "complex interdependence" and the "indivisibility of security" have come into such prominence. Violations of human rights in one country may have serious implications for peace and security for neighboring governments, an economic meltdown or a conflict in one part of the world may have dangerous consequences for another crisis elsewhere, or a major commitment of armed forces in one region may limit the ability to deploy them quickly to another area should the need arise. As a consequence, those responsible for statecraft are restrained from devoting their full energies or resources to a single crisis that may involve the threat or the use of armed force.

Practical restraints also are presented by the unknown and the unpredictable. Those men and women who confront the challenges of force and statecraft never fully know all that they need to know. They operate in partial darkness because of the complexities of the world, the uncertainties and sometimes the irrationality of human behavior, ignorance and the capacity for self-delusion, deception, and the incomplete and often ambiguous nature of intelligence information and analysis. There can be unforeseen and unintended consequences, and sometimes things go wrong even in the best of plans. These are the factors insightfully described by Machiavelli as the "blind chance" of life, by Bismarck as the "imponderabilia" of diplomacy, and by Clausewitz as the "fog" and "friction" of war.

Limitations likewise are presented by the creation of structures or systems. During the classical system of diplomacy, as we explored in Chapter 2, the structure of the balance between the five Great Powers operating as the Concert of Europe placed significant limits on what states could and could not do. Its purpose, in the words of one nineteenth-century statesman, was to "neutralize and fetter the selfish aims of each." The founders of the United Nations, as seen in Chapter 4, hoped that they might create an organization with a system of collective security that would impose restraints on how states behaved toward each other and thereby severely restrict the use of armed force in the world. The International Atomic Energy Agency, the World Trade Organization, and other multilateral bodies are all structured as they are in order to provide some limitations on sovereignty and thereby restrain any single member state from acting unilaterally in pursuit of its interests alone. Systems of international law, treaties, and legal conventions also are specifically designed to provide checks on unrestrained behavior by states.

Domestic structures also create restraints on making and implementing decisions involving force and statecraft. Any large modern state possesses complex government bureaucracies organized to conduct its widely diverse business and composed of thousands of civil servants and those who lead them. These many individuals rarely, if ever, act in a monolithic way or speak with a common voice. Indeed, where they stand on a given issue often depends on where they sit. The vested interests, personalities, perspectives, and cultures of their particular departments or units or missions easily can determine what policy options they generate, what positions they take, how they protect their autonomy and use their capabilities, and how they engage in what is often described as "turf battles" or "bureaucratic politics." Particularly when dealing with issues of force and statecraft, it is not at all uncommon to see acute disputes and even severe competition between "hawks" and "doves," or between foreign ministries and military establishments, and thereby to appreciate, as discussed in Chapter 11, why successful crisis management requires the ability to keep them under control. Bismarck and his immediate successors constantly found themselves caught in contests between civilians in the German Foreign Office and military commanders in the General Staff insisting that they should be a "state within the state." More recently, the impassioned, acrimonious, and highly public fights between Secretary of State Colin Powell and Secretary of Defense Donald Rumsfeld manifested themselves over the inspection of suspected weapons of mass destruction purportedly held by Saddam Hussein, whether or not to seek United Nations authorization for military action, the American invasion of Iraq in 2003, and the use of torture. Indeed, one official describes the battles in these words: "State and Defense were at war—don't let anyone tell you different. Within policy circles, it was knee-jerk venom, on both sides."

Such structural and political divisions occur particularly in democratic regimes characterized by free elections, the rule of law, constitutions, and the division of power among different branches of government authority. The founders of the United States, for example, believed that lessons of history had taught them to be wary of authoritarian governments where, in the absence of genuine checks and balances, a king and his immediate advisors alone and in secret could make the major decisions of war and peace. For this reason, they deliberately created a structure of divided government, designed to provide restraints on the use of force. The U.S. Constitution thus entrusts the president with the principal authority to conduct the nation's foreign affairs and to serve as commander-in-chief of the armed forces, but, at the same time, gives to the Senate the power to ratify treaties and appoint ambassadors and to Congress the sole power to raise and support armies, to provide and maintain a navy, to call forth the militia, and to declare war. One scholar describes this arrangement as "an invitation to struggle." The Japanese Constitution provides even greater restrictions by explicitly stating: "Aspiring to an international peace based on justice and order, the Japanese people forever renounce war as a sovereign right of the nation and the threat or the use of force as a means of settling international disputes."

The extent to which these constitutional provisions actually restrain, of course, is a matter of politics and political will. In this arena, domestic rivals, opposition parties, contentious pressure groups, challenging nonstate actors, and determined constituencies all can impose powerful limits on policy makers. Even ideological beliefs can present restraints. That is, although ideology can instill purpose and mobilize energies, if it is rigidly conceived it can restrict thoughtful discourse, warp rational judgments about interests, lead to erroneous assumptions and misperceptions, dismiss other ways of viewing the world, accentuate fears, and foreclose opportunities, thereby holding leaders hostage. During their arms control negotiations in Reykjavik that could have resulted in monumental changes in eliminating strategic weapons, to illustrate, both Ronald Reagan and Mikhail Gorbachev came to realize that pressure from their respective hard-liners at home was strong enough to kill any agreement they might reach.

Domestic politics also impact force and statecraft in other ways. Facing unilateral presidential decisions to commit troops to Korea and Vietnam and to invade Cambodia in the clear absence of any serious consultation or declarations of war, for example, the U.S. Congress determined to pass, over the veto of Richard Nixon, the War Powers Act of 1973. The stated purpose of this legislation, in the words of its authors, was

> to fulfill the intent of the framers of the Constitution...and insure that the collective judgment of both the Congress and the President will apply to

the introduction of United States Armed Forces into hostilities, or into situations where imminent involvement in hostilities is clearly indicated by the circumstances, and to the continued use of such forces in hostilities or in such situations.

Toward this end, the act requires the president to consult with Congress "in every possible instance" where armed force might be employed abroad, to provide written notification within forty-eight hours of any military action in a hostile area, and to explain its "estimated scope and duration of the hostilities or involvement." If Congress does not approve of the action through either a declaration of war or specific statutory authorization, the armed forces must be removed within sixty to ninety days. Every president from the time of Gerald Ford to the present has chafed under these imposed restraints, however, and the controversies raised by the War Powers Act are renewed whenever American forces are sent into combat overseas. This could be vividly seen in the decisions to use military force in Panama in 1989, Kuwait and Iraq during the Persian Gulf War in 1991, Haiti in 1994, Bosnia in 1995, Kosovo in 1999, Iraq in 2003, and in a variety of other countries as a part of the "global war on terror." When Barack Obama ordered air attacks in a 2011 NATO-led military mission against Libya without Congressional approval, critics accused him of "trashing the law" and "ripping the War Powers Act into little pieces."

In each of these cases, politics determined whether constitutional, legislative, or legal restraints would be imposed on the use of armed force or not. But political will is ever changing and is subject to a wide variety of factors, including the media, vested interests, financial contributors, those with access to power, and election cycles. There certainly are times when clashing partisan interests of political parties play a heavy role. When Democrats controlled Congress, for example, they passed the 1984 Boland Amendment to prohibit Republican Ronald Reagan from providing military support to the Contra rebels in Nicaragua. When the Republicans gained the majority, they in turn were eager to restrain Democratic Bill Clinton when he thought it necessary to send forces to Bosnia. Especially during a time of the diplomatic revolution, political will can be affected dramatically by public opinion, whose level of support for military action can range (and sometimes quickly change) from passionate enthusiasm with flag-waving rallies to intense opposition with accompanying peace protests, and from those who would give their leaders utterly unrestrained *carte blanche* to do whatever they wanted in waging war to those who would impose severe restraints whenever armed force is used. Such contested opinions among voters also can be found among government officials, diplomats, and military personnel themselves, as they struggle to determine what kinds of restraints they are willing—and unwilling—to observe. These individual and collective opinions are influenced by perceived interests, fears, aspirations, and values. Among the latter, perhaps the most complex and enduring challenges are presented by the moral values of ethics.

ETHICS AND INTERNATIONAL POLITICS

Living life requires that we make choices among alternatives about what we will and will not do. Such choices are unavoidable. Normally these decisions involve matters of daily life, but for those bearing heavy responsibilities for force and statecraft, they can require momentous decisions about war and peace. Regardless of their scope, however, when these choices have an impact on other people, they involve ethics. This is due to the fact that ethical reasoning centers on *judgments about the relationship between human conduct and the well-being of others, made on the basis of normative standards.* These standards, in turn, usually comprise three elements:

1. Limit. The first of these is the essential and distinctive feature of ethical *limit*, or restraint. It maintains that there exists a limitation, or restriction, or a boundary drawn around our behavior that provides a restraint on how we should conduct ourselves in relation to other people. Not everything, in other words, is permissible. Certain behavior is acceptable and certain behavior is unacceptable—hence, the moral values of right and wrong, good and bad, legitimate and illegitimate, just and unjust.

2. Consequences. There also is a recognition that there are *consequences* of our behavior on the well-being of others. Good intentions are not sufficient, for what we do—and do not do—affects other people. They may be protected and their value as living human beings affirmed, or they may be harmed or even killed because of our conduct. Ethics thus prescribe that we take the interests and rights of others beyond ourselves into account.

3. Responsibility. Finally, ethical standards maintain that we bear *responsibility* for our conduct. We have an obligation or duty to honor the established limits. Thus, in one way or another, sooner or later, we are held accountable for our actions and inactions.

These elements apply to all ethical standards, but herein lies a serious challenge. There is not one standard of ethics on which every person can agree. Instead, there are many. This plurality results in part from the fact that what we regard as right or wrong is shaped by a multiplicity of different sources or foundations. Parents, teachers and schools, peers, religion, states, society, customs and tradition, institutions, prevailing culture, various groups or organizations, law, philosophy, exemplars whose qualities and behavior we admire, the standards of particular professions, personal experiences, and intuition all play roles in developing normative values that shape our "moral compass" or conscience.

Sometimes these different standards reach agreement at a point of overlapping consensus that reinforces the same or similar ethical values. Many times they do not. The customs, norms, and perceptions of different countries vary. The values promoted by a state are often determined by a particular leader or a majority of voters in democratic societies, and these can be contested and changed through time within particular historical contexts. Sharp differences occur between a sense of responsibility to broad-based humanity as compared to one's own country, or to the good of the world community as a whole rather than to its separate parts. Religious traditions vary greatly and at times can produce intense disagreements between liberal and conservative believers about core ethical values. Even within the field of moral philosophy itself, there are different schools of thought, ranging from the ethics of Aristotle grounded on personal character and virtue, to those of Immanuel Kant founded on universal principles, or of John Stuart Mill based on utilitarian calculations of the greatest good for the greatest number. There thus are times when these different approaches actually compete with each other in their efforts to nurture, to persuade, or to impose certain ethical values.

In the realm of force and statecraft, the most intense and serious competition between values most often occurs between those of religion and those of the state. Faith-based religious values tend to center on beliefs in enduring and universal principles, ultimate responsibilities to the divine, and ways in which these beliefs are faithfully held and expressed in how we live our lives and conduct ourselves toward the well-being of humankind. For this reason—and when at their best—they simultaneously look at the world and beyond the world, seeing it and its people in transcendent spiritual terms as they *should be*. State values, on the other hand, normally focus on ascribing moral worth to a particular nation or government, emphasizing responsibilities and loyalty to it alone, and placing priority on behavior that will best serve its own interests. They thus look at the here and now and the exercise of earthly power over discernable stakes, seeing the world and its people in secular terms as they *are*. As a consequence, religions and states can provide quite different—and sometimes fiercely contesting—answers to questions about appropriate limits, whose well-being should benefit from our conduct, and the ultimate point of reference for our allegiance and responsibilities.

The existence of these deep contrasts, the powerful impact and decidedly mixed record of both religions and states in the world, and the fact that some people hold their beliefs about ethics so intensely help to explain why so many individuals have wrestled so long and so hard with the challenge of ethical restraints in international politics and why they have reached such extremely different conclusions throughout history and into our own time.

Some observers, for example, have decided that because the distance between the spiritual soul and the secular state is so far apart that it can never be bridged, it is necessary for leaders to cast their lot unequivocally with the state and its emphasis on *raison d'état*, absolute sovereignty, and *Realpolitik*, insisting that ethical values based on religious belief have little or no place at all in international politics. Machiavelli reached this conclusion when he wrote in *The Prince* that "the gulf between how one should live and how one does live is so wide that a man who neglects what is actually done for what should be done learns the way to self-destruction." He contended that religious restraints may be applicable to the conduct of individuals as they live their personal lives—but rarely to states whose interests always must take precedence over any moral scruples. When possible, leaders should act "good"; but, when necessary, their responsibility to the state requires that they "know how to do evil" and be prepared to behave "contrary to good faith, charity, humanity, and religion." Toward this end, he sought to elevate the interests of one's own country to the status of a supreme ethical norm of its own, declaring in his *Discourses* that in conducting state policy, "no considerations of justice or injustice, humanity or cruelty, nor glory or shame, should be allowed to prevail."

Others carried this argument even further, arguing that in international politics, only "might makes right" and virtually *any means* can be used to secure *any ends* that benefit the state. This explains why Thucydides wrote about the militarily powerful Athenians contemptuously scoffing at the weak appeal of the Melians for what was "fair and right" and why Thomas Hobbes maintained that in a world of vicious struggle, self-imposed moral restraints are either simplistically naive at best or dangerous at worst. Political scientist Hans Morgenthau emphasized these arguments as well, contending in *Politics Among Nations*:

> a world society and … a universal morality do not exist. … The nation fills the minds and hearts of men everywhere with particular experiences and, derived from them, with particular concepts of political philosophy, particular standards of political morality, and particular goals of political action. Inevitably, then, the members of the human race live and act politically, not as members of one world society applying standards of universal ethics, but as members of their respective national societies, guided by their national standards of morality. In politics the nation and not humanity is the ultimate fact.

Statements such as these most certainly do not go unchallenged, for there are those who do see humanity and not the nation as the ultimate fact. Many strongly object to the proposition that ethics somehow stop at national borders. Instead, they argue strongly that ethical principles focused on humanity must serve as standards for judging the ends, the means, and the likely consequences of policy. Nation-states themselves are human constructs, "national interests" are heavily dependent on the broader values upheld by an international system, and the "necessities" of world politics, rather than being beyond the realm of ethical choices and moral judgment, ultimately rest upon them. As scholar Stanley Hoffmann maintains in his thoughtful book, *Duties Beyond Borders: On the Limits and Possibilities of Ethical International Politics*, ethical choices are inherent in virtually all major decisions of statecraft, for individual people do not cease to be responsible as moral agents just because they act as public officials in the name of collective groups or wear a military uniform. "We must remember," he writes, "that states are led by human beings whose actions affect human beings within and outside: considerations of good and evil, right or wrong, are therefore both inevitable and legitimate." This opinion is shared by many experienced policy makers as well, including those who concluded in the report of the Commission on the Organization of Government for the Conduct of Foreign Policy: "Virtually all major foreign policy issues contain some ethical component."

But even among those who believe that ethical restraints do and should play a role in international politics, there still are vast differences of opinion as to how this might be accomplished. There have been times in history when individuals have insisted that the values of their religion and the values of their state were not different at all, but rather one and the same. It is not at all difficult to find cases of political or military leaders who have built support for their own agendas by manipulating the language and fervor of religion, or theocratic leaders who have placed a higher priority on secular rather than spiritual objectives and used the power of a state to advance their own interests. Their words of explanation may be genuine expressions of sincere personal belief, or they may be nothing more than calculating statements of religiosity, designed to deceive others into thinking that the exercise of power is somehow ethically justified or divinely ordained. It is difficult to know precisely the motives of Bismarck, the very epitome of *Realpolitik*, for example, when he received his first diplomatic appointment as an ambassador and wrote: "I am God's soldier, and where he sends me there I must go." "I believe that I am obeying God," he said on another occasion, "when I serve my King." Similar statements can be found among those in Tel Aviv who equate Judaism with the state of Israel, or those in Tehran who equate Islam with the state of Iran. Former U.S. Deputy Undersecretary of Defense for Intelligence General William Boykin provided further evidence of this pattern when he asserted that since America was "a Christian nation," its terrorist enemies "will only be defeated if we come against them in the name of Jesus." He further declared: "We in the army of God, in the house of God, kingdom of God, have been raised for such a time as this."

Such a deliberate melding of the values of religion with the values of the state, however, leaves many other observers and practitioners deeply worried. To them, the idea that one is a chosen instrument of God can be, and often has been, a dangerous concept that can all too easily lead to moralistic self-righteousness, hubris, and megalomania. They view the simultaneous embrace of two often conflicting normative standards that pull in different directions as too seductively simplistic, too much like trying to square a circle, and too self-serving. As one of Bismarck's critics once bitingly observed, the chancellor conveniently "believes firmly and deeply in a God who has the remarkable faculty of always agreeing with him." They fear that such a mixture all too easily can cloak reprehensible actions with the mantle of virtue, to convince citizens that they can remain true to their religious beliefs while being loyal and patriotic to their state, or to arouse fanaticism about battles between "good" and "evil." This, they argue, encourages confrontational and uncompromising crusades and "holy wars" against "heathens" and "heretics," *jihads* against "infidels," or intolerant extremism that completely destroys any sense of limit or self-restraint at all.

For these reasons, many have agonized over the question of how they should apply ethics and act when faced with a genuine dilemma or crisis of conscience: when their religious and moral convictions clash with actions in the service of their government that they find to be deeply repugnant. Thus, sincere Buddhists sometimes have asked how they can possibly seek things of the spirit or follow the teachings of nonviolence while working on behalf of a state engaged in extending its power by military means. Dedicated Muslims similarly have inquired on occasion how Islam, which teaches compassion and mercy toward others, can be used to justify the expansion of a state by the sword or terrorist attacks against innocent civilians. In the same way, there have been times when earnest Christians have questioned how they could faithfully follow the commands of Jesus to "love your enemies and pray for those who persecute you," to "turn the other cheek if someone strikes you," and to honestly acknowledge that "no one can serve two masters...you cannot serve God and mammon," and yet at the same time support the deliberate launching of wars of choice, torture, or the use of "shock-and-awe" violence.

The incompatibility of these positions has led some devout religious believers to conclude that they must answer to a "higher law" whereby their responsibilities to their religious faith must transcend whatever obligations they might have to any human government. They therefore believe that, when necessary, they should reject the values of the state and completely remove themselves from any kind of action that might assist its quest for power. They reach a point where they determine that *the ends never justify the means*. Some individuals in this situation have resigned from office, for example Lord John Morley, who immediately submitted his resignation from the British Cabinet when his country announced that it would go to war in 1914; U.S. Deputy Secretary of Defense Cyrus Vance, who did the same in protest over the Vietnam War; and American Foreign Service Officer Matthew Hoh, who in 2009 resigned over the Afghanistan War, in his words, "based not upon how we are pursuing the war, but why and to what end." Others have become conscientious objectors. As Franz Jägerstätter, an Austrian who refused to perform military service in the German army during Second World War, expressed it:

> For what purpose, then, did God endow all men with reason and free will if, despite this, we have to render blind obedience [to the state]...? What purpose is served by the ability to distinguish between good and evil?...Now anyone who is able to fight for both kingdoms and stay in good standing in both communities (that is, the community of the saints and the Nazi folk community) and who is able to obey every command of the Third Reich—such a man, in my opinion, would have to be a great magician. I for one cannot do so. And I definitely prefer to relinquish my rights under the Third Reich and thus make sure of deserving the rights granted under the Kingdom of God.

In this case, the consequences of such faith-based ethical restraints presented too great a threat to the state. After writing these words, Jägerstätter was taken to another room and beheaded.

Most people have no desire to suffer this kind of punishment for their beliefs or to take one absolutist position or another in the tension between religious values and those of the state or between individual and group behavior. Instead, they find themselves in real world situations that impose real consequences, struggling to avoid having to choose between being described as either a secular amoralist or so-called crude political "realist," on the one hand, or a spiritual idealist or so-called "perfectionist," on the other. They therefore seek some way to navigate through the thicket of competing demands that confront them in a complicated world of imperfect human beings in which they exercise limited control, trying to reconcile the desirable of what *should* be done with the possible of what *can* be done. It is for this reason that theologian Reinhold Niebuhr concluded in his book *Moral Man and Immoral Society: A Study in Ethics and Politics*: "Politics will, to the end of history, be an area where conscience and power meet, where the ethical and coercive factors of human life will interpenetrate and work out their tentative and uneasy compromises." After reflecting on this thought-provoking statement, historian and veteran diplomat E. H. Carr felt compelled to add: "The compromises, like solutions to other human problems, will remain uneasy and tentative. But it is an essential part of any compromise that both factors [conscience and power] shall be taken into account."

The challenges of actually making these compromises and applying ethics to international politics are often profound. There is not always a simple and comfortable black-or-white distinction, for example, between conscience and power. Conscience, as we have seen, can be pulled in different directions, and general ethical principles do not provide clear-cut rules or policy directives that tell decision makers exactly what they should do. Similarly, as we shall explore in the Conclusion, it is essential to recognize that power is not confined to military force alone, but is composed of many different elements that also include skillful diplomacy, knowledge, technology, economic strength, reputation, culture, and what is widely described as the "moral force" of ethical values themselves. These factors are further complicated by the fact that there are a multiplicity of philosophical and religious traditions, that an overzealous commitment to a particular ethical principle may be inappropriate or even dangerous in certain circumstances, and that leaders in a world of complexity and ambiguity, where decisions are made with incomplete information, can never fully know all the consequences of their actions or inactions. All this helps to explain why it is so agonizing for those who seek to avoid absolutist extremes and abstractions and instead genuinely attempt to make reasonable ethical judgments about *what ends* and *what means* are justified in *what situations*.

But in this endeavor those concerned with international politics are not completely alone and not without guidelines to help them find their way through the dilemmas of making ethical choices. In fact, as a result of many historical experiences and individual and collective efforts, there has emerged a substantial body of consensual, normative standards developed to help regulate behavior in the international system by establishing ethical restraints for statecraft in general and, more specifically, ethical restraints for threats and uses of armed force.

ETHICAL RESTRAINTS FOR STATECRAFT

Even the earliest practitioners of statecraft came to understand that, for reasons of both necessity and conviction, they could avoid international anarchy only if they kept their conflicts and competition within bounds by developing certain normative restraints. They came to see that it was in their interest to respect diplomatic immunity, to protect foreign embassies and their staffs, to honor treaty obligations, and to establish and then follow rules that distinguished between acceptable and unacceptable behavior. As we saw in Chapter 1, the path-breaking writings of archbishop Bernard du Rosier, soldier-diplomat Philippe de Commynes, law professors Francisco de Vitoria and Alberto Gentili, and theologian Cornelius Jansenius all concluded that effective foreign policy can never be effective if governed by practical, state self-interest alone. Success, they insisted, ultimately depended on including more transcendent ethical values as well. After witnessing the horrors of the Thirty Years' War, the jurist and diplomat Hugo Grotius also stressed that those responsible for statecraft simply had no choice but to be governed by rules and laws based on larger moral principles. Seasoned diplomats such as Juan Antonio de Vera in the seventeenth century similarly stressed the critical importance of establishing ethical restraints in the conduct of foreign policy. After years of personal and hard-earned practical experience, François de Callières in the eighteenth century concluded that diplomats must be honest and of good character, practice "plain and fair dealing," be "good Christians" and persons "of peace," and be faithful to their states while recognizing that "such obedience cannot be held to cover any action against the laws of God or of justice."

Many of the successes of the classical system of diplomacy, as we explored in Chapter 2, can be attributed to the restraints and rules of accommodation that derived from a common set of diplomatic norms and the fact that statesmen of the time placed value on their reputation for honoring them. Metternich demonstrated particular skill in establishing the foundation for an international system by inducing other countries to submit their disagreements to this larger sense of shared values. Even Talleyrand, who certainly was no stranger to political manipulation, admitted the necessity of having ethical restraints for foreign policy, declaring that in the end any balance of power could "only last so long as certain large States are animated by a spirit of moderation and justice." The case of William Gladstone, who served four times as British prime minister during the nineteenth century, is particularly well-known as an example of a leader with strong religious convictions who believed that he had a larger duty to frame his statecraft in terms of the call from the Sermon on the Mount for compassion, humility, and peacemaking. Still others proposed that only morally praiseworthy objectives should be pursued in foreign policy, that statesmen should choose a course of action least likely to cause damage to things of value, and that the means selected should be proportional to the ends pursued.

These principles and general guidelines, among others, served to contribute to a slow but nevertheless progressive evolution of international ethical norms designed to provide restraints on the behavior of states with one another. They were handed down from one generation to another and further developed with various degrees of compromise and changes through time. Sometimes they clearly were honored more in the breach than in the observance. But on other occasions, they were taken very seriously. In fact, sometimes they moved beyond constraining action and actually helped to empower action, especially in efforts to alleviate suffering by promoting justice, peacemaking, conflict prevention and resolution, human rights, reconciliation, and humanitarian relief. Indeed, as political scientist Robert McElroy argues in his book *Morality and American Foreign Policy: The Role of Ethics in International Affairs*, such norms often enter the consciences of state decision makers, members of the domestic public, and those comprising global opinion, thereby influencing their perceptions of issues and their actions. For this reason, he maintains that it is not hard to find times when ethical principles based on the broader sense of responsibility to the well-being of humanity appear to have taken precedence over narrowly defined state interests.

One of his most interesting historical cases explores the choice faced by the U.S. government when confronting an event inside the Soviet Union. From the very beginning, American leaders viewed the Soviet Union as a major threat to American interests due to its repudiation of prewar debts, its confiscation of foreign property, and its propaganda against capitalism. Consequently, the United States tried to diplomatically isolate the Soviets from the world and economically cut off all trade with them in the hope that such actions would seriously weaken their government and lead to its eventual collapse. Suddenly, in the spring of 1921, the Soviet government faced the very type of threat to its existence that the Americans had desired: the outbreak of massive famine. The situation became so desperate that even Lenin concluded that if no way could be found to feed the peasants, the Soviet regime and its experiment with Communism would perish. Yet, within days of a Soviet appeal for help, Secretary of Commerce Herbert Hoover, a man strongly committed to his Quaker religious beliefs, began to mobilize a massive American relief effort to avert starvation in Russia. He, President Warren G. Harding, and members of Congress, according to McElroy's analysis, internalized the international norm that held nations responsible for helping other countries devastated by disaster, regardless of their political orientation. In conscience, they could not sit by and watch tens of millions of Russians starve to death, even if providing famine relief meant thwarting their own political, strategic, and economic interests by stabilizing the detested Soviet regime.

The strength of the perceived need for the creation and maintenance of such international ethical norms and restraints can be seen in the fact that so many of them have emerged precisely at a time when values themselves were—and are—seriously contested during the diplomatic revolution. The rise of highly ideological regimes in Communist Russia, Fascist Italy, and Nazi Germany, with their extraordinary demands in the name of the state, as we saw in Chapter 3, seriously challenged many previously accepted ethical standards and norms from the classical system of diplomacy. The expansion of the international community with actors from around the entire globe, as explored in Chapter 4, brought the values of many cultures and religious faiths to the fore. The escalation of the Cold War, as discussed in Chapter 5, exacerbated this breakdown of shared values even further when the superpowers framed their relations in terms of the "running dog lackeys of capitalistic imperialism" versus "Godless Communism" and "the Evil Empire." This trend has continued more recently, as observed in Chapter 6, with those who view international relations as nothing short of "the clash of civilizations," with those Americans who detest certain countries as "the Axis of Evil" or those who hate the United States as "the Great Satan," and with the intense arguments among different denominations of Christianity and different sects of Islam as to how their respective believers should behave in the world. The sheer magnitude of these challenges and contests of values makes the achievements in purposefully creating consensual, international ethical norms all the more remarkable.

In fact, it is precisely the existence of these normative standards that establishes the entire concept of legitimacy within any international system. Actions and the exercise of power are regarded as legitimate only insofar as they are consistent with general agreement on norms, or what they regard as acceptable—and unacceptable, or illegitimate—behavior. States find it in their interest to establish this kind of authority in an effort to provide restraints for ends and means, to shape expectations, to increase stability, and in the process to reduce uncertainty and insecurity in international politics. These standards, of course, are not static but evolve through time based on historical circumstances. This can be seen by the progressive changes in ethical values toward such international issues as the slave trade, human rights, social justice, the "Responsibility to Protect," humanitarian intervention, and democracy increasingly being regarded as the only legitimate form of government. Sometimes these norms may be sharply contested, or they may be breached rather than practiced. Nevertheless, with their limits, recognition of consequences, and acknowledgment of responsibility, they serve as a basis on which behavior in statecraft can be judged. Indeed, there are times when states are severely punished if it is perceived that they have violated the norms of the system.

Some of the most notable examples of these ethical norms and the restraints that they create can be seen in international law. In fact, the very rule of law itself is specifically designed to restrain arbitrary, abusive, or destructive behavior. States agree to accept certain restraints on themselves in the expectation that others within the international system will do the same and that some form of sanction will result in the event of deviation or noncompliance. These legal restraints can take a variety of forms. Sometimes they appear as *jus cogens*, or compelling law, based on what are described as peremptory norms that emerge not from any authoritative body or well-defined process but out of changing political and social attitudes. Today these include generally accepted prohibitions against genocide, crimes against humanity, maritime piracy, slavery, torture, and state-sponsored terrorism. At other times, normative restraints are reflected in *customary international law* derived from custom and practice. Although not always clearly codified, these rules reflect the actual conduct of states acting out of a sense of obligation that the law required them to act in that way. On still other occasions, the norms are precisely identified and articulated in the corpus of positive *international public law* comprised of treaties, conventions, and agreements regarded as binding and enforced through sanctions or punishment. As parties to these formal instruments, government leaders explicitly agree by mutual consent to accept certain norms, rights, and responsibilities designed to regulate and restrain their relations with one another. These, in turn, provide rules of law and standards of legitimacy against which state behavior is judged.

Such normative standards and the ambition to advance them are particularly striking in the area of international human rights. Indeed, it is here that the consequences of action without limit or restraint—and of inaction—on the well-being of others becomes so evident and so shocking. For centuries, the leaders of states understood that they could treat those under their control however they wished, as matters of exclusive domestic jurisdiction, without outside scrutiny, criticism, or intervention. They could engage in all manner of abuse, including discrimination, exploitation, segregation, enslavement, persecution, and even genocide in the knowledge that they could hide safely behind the cloak of national sovereignty. Victims had nowhere to run and nowhere to hide, and they could not look beyond their own borders for any assistance or protection.

Early efforts to change this traditional practice from impunity toward accountability for abusers and from vulnerability toward protection for victims began in the late eighteenth and early nineteenth centuries, but resistance remained determined and strong. The lessons of history taught that the greater the human suffering, the greater the pressure for establishing restraints. The consequences of horrendous unrestrained abuse drives people from indifference or toleration to judgments that certain behavior is wrong, illegitimate, and will no longer be accepted. This is exactly what happened once the horrors of the Second World War, the "Rape of Nanking," and the Holocaust became widely known and shocked the world as nothing else ever had before. Many concluded, with a particularly revealing choice of words, that these barbarous events had "violated the conscience of humanity" and "outraged the conscience of mankind." In response, as we saw in Chapter 4, the influential Commission to Study the Organization of Peace argued in its hard-hitting report, entitled *International Safeguard of Human Rights,* that an important relationship needed to be recognized: namely, that there could be no security without peace, no peace without justice, and no justice without respect for human rights. Their argument struck a powerful chord. A wide array of government leaders, activists, nongovernmental organizations (including those representing many religious faiths), returning veterans, survivors, and citizens alike thus became convinced that they had a responsibility to do what they could to protect those who suffered from abuse, irrespective of nationality, race, gender, or religion. To do this, they announced their determination to challenge the heretofore sacrosanct claims of absolute national sovereignty by states when necessary and to establish meaningful and viable international human rights norms.

This new attitude manifested itself immediately at the 1945 San Francisco Conference and its resulting landmark United Nations Charter. Here, all member states pledged to hold themselves responsible for promoting and encouraging respect for human rights and fundamental freedoms. The path-breaking and standard-setting 1948 Universal Declaration of Human Rights soon followed, with its language that the enumerated ethical norms applied to "all members of the human family." Through time, the vast majority of governments in the world, along with their peoples and emerging NGOs such as Amnesty International and Human Rights Watch, then worked to create a whole series of formally recognized declarations of normative values, followed by very specific and binding restraints in human rights treaties. These address many different issues, including racism, apartheid, civil and political rights, social and economic rights, discrimination against women, rights of the child, human trafficking, the rights of refugees and indigenous peoples, and the prohibition of torture. Together, these treaties, along with their treaty-monitoring mechanisms and special procedures, have placed restraints on state sovereignty and thereby contributed to the significant process of transforming individual victims of human rights abuses from mere objects of international pity into actual subjects of international law.

Further developments have occurred with the growing acceptance among practitioners of statecraft of the concept of "human security" and the "indivisibility of security." That is, that *international* security, *national* security, and *individual* security are not mutually exclusive, but rather mutually reinforcing and actually dependent on each other. A significant confirmation of this, among many, is evident in the decisions reached at the 2005 World Summit. Despite their differences of political structure, stages of development, and cultural settings, they unanimously agreed on the "values and principles" of human rights. They affirmed "the universality, indivisibility, interdependence, and interrelatedness of all human rights" and acknowledged their responsibility to enforce international law and provide protection to victims. Since then, the concept of the "Responsibility to Protect" (now increasingly known as R2P) has continued to evolve, calling upon members of the international community to take concrete action—including the use of force and statecraft in intervention—when it becomes necessary to provide practical protection to ordinary people whose lives are at risk because their own states are unable or unwilling to protect them. Even at an early stage, Eleanor Roosevelt, who served as the American representative on the United Nations Human Rights Commission, described this process of progressively seeing the relationship between security, peace, justice, and human rights as "the measure of mankind's evolving ethical sense."

Some indication of the degree to which these norms have been accepted and internalized can be seen in the reaction produced when it is perceived that they have been egregiously violated. Widespread moral outrage ensued, for example, over revelations about the cruelty against dissidents in psychiatric wards and the gulag of the Soviet Union, the murder of black activist Stephen Biko and the imprisonment of Nelson Mandela by the white minority regime of South Africa, the brutality of the dictatorships of Augusto Pinochet in Chile and Pol Pot in Cambodia, and the 1989 violent attack against students in Tiananmen Square and suppression of political and religious freedom in

China. Today the same kind of reaction is seen whenever egregious violations of human rights occur.

These same kinds of ethical values, focused on the well-being of others, can be seen in the growing international sense of responsibility for the consequences of unrestrained economic competition and the resulting disparity between the rich and the poor in the world. Many thoughtful observers regard this as one of the most serious challenges of our time. They see the enormous gap between affluence and poverty as a glaring case of economic and social injustice whose chronic deprivation not only causes untold suffering, but also serves as a breeding ground for discontent that easily can manifest itself in war and terrorism. In this way, destitution threatens both the human person as well as peace and security. It is not surprising, therefore, that a number of nation-states and NGOs have worked to create normative restraints on economic behavior and to coordinate policies that address matters of what is known as distributive justice. The results of their efforts can be found in the United Nations Development Program, World Health Organization, Food and Agricultural Organization, and World Bank and International Monetary Fund, among many others, as they seek to establish an international Multidimensional Poverty Index (MPI), to develop the Norms on the Responsibilities of Transnational Corporations and Other Business Enterprises with Regard to Human Rights, and to conduct programs focused on famine and disaster relief, foreign aid, debt and investment policies, health care, working conditions, and development assistance.

Ethics also play an important role in the development of international normative restraints designed to address the sufferings and the dangers that result from environmental degradation. It has become evident that the continued misuse and overuse of scarce and shared resources creates severe consequences for life throughout the planet. Observers as diverse as military strategists in the Pentagon to activists in Greenpeace increasingly see pollution, soil erosion, deforestation and desertification, water depletion, rising sea levels, and climate change as vital components in the security of the international system, the security of nation-states, and the security of individual humans. As a consequence, serious questions of ethical responsibility arise. Are we responsible for the health and well-being of those people within our particular nation, or to others beyond our borders who might suffer as a result of our action or inaction? Are we only responsible to ourselves and those currently alive, or, given the finite nature of many resources, to future generations as well? Do we have any responsibilities to other forms of life? It is exactly these kinds of questions that have prompted significant efforts to establish ethical norms that create restraints to protect the well-being of the planet as a whole. The 1992 United Nations Conference on Environment and Development, widely known as the "Earth Summit," proved to be the largest international conference ever held in history. It brought together more than 25,000 participants, including 172 official governmental delegations and the representatives of 2,400 environmental NGOs. Together they negotiated the Convention on Biological Diversity and the UN Framework Convention on Climate Change, which in turn led to the 1997 Kyoto Accord calling for a reduction of greenhouse gas emissions.

Several United Nations Climate Change Conferences have been held since, each revealing a high measure of cooperation on some issues and great resistance on others. When it became clear on one occasion that certain nations refused to meaningfully participate, the prime minister of Canada Paul Martin publicly called upon them to recognize the need for ethical restraints in statecraft and to heed "the conscience of the world."

Not all endeavors to establish restraints based on ethics, of course, have such a broad global perspective or result from international consensus. Sometimes states deliberately impose limits upon themselves alone. That is, they make choices from within about what they are willing and unwilling to do. One of the most striking examples of this occurred when the United States began to seriously investigate the Central Intelligence Agency in the wake of the Watergate scandal. Although fully aware of the necessity of having an effective intelligence service, Congressional committees discovered shocking accounts of unrestrained "tradecraft" and covert action conducted in the name of national security that entailed destabilization campaigns, the overthrow of democratically elected governments, plots to assassinate foreign leaders, use of illegal drugs on unsuspecting victims, insurgency, and counterinsurgency, along with many accompanying violations of human rights. The revelations prompted widespread public outrage and led Senator Frank Church to describe the CIA as a "rogue elephant out of control." Congress responded by establishing select committees to oversee and restrain operations, while presidents Ford, Carter, and Reagan issued executive orders explicitly prohibiting political assassinations by any agent of the United States under their administrations, declaring that such deliberately targeted murder was completely contrary to "basic ethical values."

ETHICAL RESTRAINTS FOR ARMED FORCE

The challenges that exist in creating ethical restraints in statecraft are rendered even more difficult when dealing with armed force. It is here that choices about whether, under what circumstance, and how to use force as an instrument of policy have perhaps the most severe consequences on the well-being of others, including intense suffering and death. It is here that questions of legitimacy arise most passionately. It also is here that universal values about the sanctity of all life and prohibitions against doing harm to others often come into such direct conflict with those values of the state when violence is deliberately employed or killing is specifically ordered. As Stanley Hoffmann observes, war is where people are most obviously torn between humanity and country—between their conscience as moral beings, whose thoughts and feelings about responsibilities transcend borders, and their loyalties as citizens of a particular nation-state. History demonstrates that wars provide the greatest opportunities for national self-righteousness, for political leaders and military commanders to plead "expediency" or "necessity" or "emergency" and to argue that they really have no choice but to respond to the wartime imperatives forced upon them, and for discarding standards, in the words of the *Oxford Manual of the Laws of War*, with "the unchaining of passion and sav-age instincts." It is therefore important to appreciate that in these particular matters of force and statecraft, the stakes are high, the consequences severe, and the arguments intense.

At one end of the spectrum, for example, are pacifists, who argue that any threat or use of military force at all is intrinsically evil. They believe that vio-lence only begets more violence and seek strength in moral force rather than physical force. They argue that killing—for any reason—is wrong and can never be justified. For this reason, dedicated pacifists unambiguously embrace nonviolence, oppose the possession of weapons as instruments of war, and reject war itself, even in self-defense. This position has a tradition extending over many centuries, often finding inspiration from Buddhism, the teachings of Jesus and practices of the early Christian church, Bertha von Suttner's book *Lay Down Your Arms!*, the examples of Mohandas Gandhi and Martin Luther King, Jr., and the Peace Testimony of the Quakers from 1660, declaring: "We utterly deny all outward wars and strife, and fightings with outward weap-ons, for any end, or under any pretense whatever; this is our testimony to the whole world."

In sharp contrast to this argument is that of militarists, who glorify the state and its naked use of power without reservation and who view violence and war not only as necessities but as morally good. The philosopher G. W. F. Hegel expressed this position, contending that war transcends the medioc-rity of everyday life, enhances domestic cohesion and unity, creates fear and respect abroad, and provides the ultimate test for the virtue of citizens and states. The Bolsheviks also embraced violence rather than turning away from it, for as Leon Trotsky bluntly explained:

> We were never concerned with the Kantian-priestly and vegetarian-Quaker prattle about the "sacredness of human life." To make the human life sacred we must destroy the social order which crucifies him...and this problem can be solved only by blood and iron.

This idea that war and violence are ennobling and that the end justifies what-ever means are necessary is echoed by others, including historian Heinrich von Treitschke in *Politics*, naval officer and strategist Alfred Thayer Mahan in "The Moral Aspect of War," front-line soldier Ernest Jünger in *Battle as an Inner Experience*, Adolf Hitler in *Mein Kampf*, any number of extreme nationalists, and those terrorists who seek glory by taking the lives of others in order to achieve their own martyrdom.

But most statesmen throughout history and in our own day, it is probably safe to say, have tried to avoid being pushed into either the pure pacifist or the rabid "anything goes" militarist positions. Instead, they have attempted to navigate their way through conflicting demands and responsibilities, com-peting ethical values, the pressures of domestic and foreign politics, and the various practical, structural, and political restraints of their own time and place. They have reached the conclusion that armed force has its defensive and peacekeeping as well as aggressive uses and that when leaders fail to avail themselves of the former, they are likely to find themselves at the mercy of those skilled in the latter. This has led many of them to keep armed force as a necessary instrument of statecraft, but at the same time recognizing its dangers and seeking ways of keeping it within certain limits. In such a process, they have tended to be nonperfectionist practitioners rather than dogmatic theoreticians, making many compromises along the way in their choices among all the variations of conscience and power and of what they should do and what they could do.

The results, as one would expect, thus often appear to be inconsistent, incomplete, and a peculiar mixture of self-interests and ethical values. Nevertheless, in their own incremental ways, they have led to serious moral discourse and deliberation, resulting in a variety of normative restraints regarding *if, when, how,* and under *what circumstances* armed force can be legitimately and most effectively used as an instrument of policy. These can be found in the progressively tighter limits on the legitimate purposes of war, uses of violence, targets, kinds of threats, limitations on the numbers and types of weapons, arms control, restrictions on weapons testing, demilitarized zones, disarmament, and codes of conduct for arms sales.

Some of these ethical norms can be seen in the persistent efforts over time to develop international treaty law establishing restraints or prohibitions on certain kinds of weapons considered to cause excruciating pain or traumatic suffering to others. Religious leaders of the twelfth century, for example, worked to place restrictions on the use of crossbows, which they described as "barbaric" and "unchristian." In the Hague Convention of 1899, statesmen from all of the major countries in Europe and Asia banned the use of soft-nosed dumdum bullets, which tore savage wounds in the human body, on the grounds that they were "uncivilized," "inhumane," and "against the laws of humanity." The widely ratified 1925 Geneva Protocol prohibiting asphyxiating or poisonous gasses openly declared such weapons to be "justly condemned by the general opinion of the civilized world" and explicitly stated its determination to bind alike "the conscience and the practice of nations."

Similar values influenced subsequent negotiations, as discussed in Chapter 8, producing a variety of restraints in other arms control agreements. A particularly notable example is provided by pressure brought to bear on the United States to conform with prohibitions on chemical and biological weapons. Widespread domestic opinion at home and global opinion abroad viewed these ghastly tools of war as morally "abhorrent," and on this basis, as McElroy observes, sufficient political pressure was mounted to eventually compel the Nixon administration to reverse course and make substantive changes in American military doctrine and force structure. Over the strong objections of the Joint Chiefs of Staff, the president announced in 1969 that the United States would destroy its stockpiles of biological weapons, formally renounce the first use of all lethal chemical weapons, and begin the process of ratifying the legal restraints of the Geneva Protocol. Ethical values similarly drive much of the effort to establish restraints and prohibitions on antipersonnel land mines and weapons of mass destruction today, including preparations for the 2015 review conference of the Nuclear Non-Proliferation Treaty, which remains the most widely observed arms control treaty in history.

Ethical norms also play a role in how threats of armed force are perceived. Because of its defensive nature designed to prevent aggression, as seen in Chapter 9, deterrence normally does not produce ethical problems as serious as those of other strategies. The one notable exception, of course, is the threat of nuclear annihilation. Some critics of nuclear deterrence, for example, argue that because it threatens to do what is morally reprehensible (namely, to inflict staggering mass destruction), it cannot possibly be justified. Others contend that such catastrophic damage can be threatened as long as it is never actually carried out if deterrence fails. Coercive diplomacy in its offensive variant, which seeks to extend control through intimidation and fear, as explored in Chapter 10, also raises significant ethical questions that challenge internationally established norms. This explains why the texts of the United Nations Charter and the Helsinki Final Act provide explicit restraints on coercive threats of force.

But history reveals that armed force all too frequently moves beyond the *possibility* of violence in threats to the *actuality* of violence and death in warfare. Since it is in war that the greatest harm is inflicted upon people, it is in war that the greatest ethical challenges arise. From the time of the ancients to the present and in virtually all cultures for which we have written records, there have been individuals who have been deeply concerned about this aspect of force and statecraft and have argued that because war is a human activity that involves human choices, it cannot escape moral argument and judgment. They thus have given much thought to creating ethical standards for judging the legitimacy of recourse to violence: how wars might be both permitted and restrained in when and how they are fought. In this process, they have sought to avoid the two extremes of believing either that *nothing* is justified in war—or that *everything* is. The various principles, conventions, and tacit and explicit rules resulting from their efforts over a long period of time are collectively and broadly known as the just war tradition (JWT).

Whether the use of armed force is ethically justified or not, according to the theory of just war, depends on compliance with particular restraints in both ends and means and is composed of several parts. The first of these is *jus ad bellum*, or **justice of war**. Traditionally, the norms for restraining any choice of going to war have included the following criteria:

1. Just Cause. The only ethical justification for going to war is to stop aggression and to defend against armed attack. This is the first and necessary condition, but it is not sufficient in and of itself. That is, even if a state has received an injury constituting a just cause, it cannot go to war unless the other requirements are met as well.

2. Right Intention or Purpose. A war is just only if it seeks to provide self-defense or to protect others and their human rights from grievous harm if they are attacked and then to create a more secure and just peace. Wars of aggrandizement or conquest designed to acquire territory or resources, subjugate, or annihilate thus do not qualify, nor do preventive wars based on conjecture.

3. Legitimate Authority. The use of force is ethically permissible only when it is sanctioned by a legitimate, responsible, and duly constituted authority. Violence initiated by dissident groups, terrorist cells, or private individuals therefore is not justified.

4. Public Declaration. There must be a formal, public declaration of war in order to open to public debate the judgment of whether the injury received warrants a resort to arms and to provide the offending state the opportunity to offer redress in lieu of violence.

5. Limited Objectives and Proportionality. A war is ethically warranted only if its objectives are limited to a specific political end and if the good toward which the war is aimed is proportional to the original offense and to the harm that the war will cause.

6. Reasonable Chance of Success. Given the destruction, pain, and death that it will cause, the use of force in war is ethically justified only if it is likely that it will succeed in achieving the limited objectives for which it is fought. This condition, like the one that precedes it, is designed to prevent futile causes, grandiose plans, or a crusading or "holy war" mentality and thereby protect against the pointless use of military forces by leaders who would recklessly steer a nation into armed conflict.

7. Last Resort. A state can resort to war only if all of these other conditions have been met and it has exhausted every effort to resolve the dispute first by nonviolent means (such as diplomatic negotiation, arbitration, or various forms of persuasion).

The second component of just war theory is that of *jus in bello*, or **justice in war**. This emerged to deliberately counter any argument that a noble end justifies whatever means are necessary. The decision to go to war in a particular case might be just, but this does not mean that once unleashed it can be fought in unjust ways. As a result of the deep concern over this issue, two principal criteria have been designed to restrain the actual conduct of war:

1. Protection of Innocents. Armed force can only be justified if it is used against an adversary's political leadership and military forces. Every effort, consequently, must be made to distinguish between combatants and innocent civilians or noncombatants who must be immune from attack or reprisals. Indiscriminate destruction of populations, unrestrained slaughter, violence and sieges against civilian targets, rape as an instrument of war, seizing of hostages, or the forced conscription of child soldiers thus is ethically impermissible. Indeed, it is exactly in this area that norms create international humanitarian law to protect human rights in armed conflict and establish the meaning of genocide, war crimes, and crimes against humanity.

2. Proportionality. The means used in the prosecution of a war must be proportionate to the ends for which the war is being fought. In order to restrain the devastation of warfare, leaders must avoid any excessive use of force in overkill that will inflict more loss of life and more damage than is necessary or congruent with what is at stake. Military actions, in other words, must use only the minimum level of force necessary to achieve the limited objectives of the war.

In recent years, some theorists and practitioners have proposed adding a third category to the theory of just war called *jus post bellum*, or **justice after war**. If ethical responsibilities are applied to the beginning and the middle of wars, they argue, then why not the end? Here, attention is focused on normative restraints addressing such matters as conditions for surrender and war termination, a just settlement rather than a "victor's justice" of draconian vengeance, legitimate punishment and restitution, war crimes trials, and postwar rehabilitation and reconstruction.

It is important to acknowledge that these normative values of the just war tradition do not come without difficulties. In fact, they can be fraught with theoretical, practical, and political challenges when being operationalized or applied within specific contexts. Who decides, for example, if there are serious disputes in determining what is a "right intention," the "legitimate authority," or what is truly "the last resort" in a given situation? Or, given the fact that modern WMD could annihilate a significant part of any state's population, can one engage in anticipatory self-defense instead of waiting until actually attacked? Or, under what circumstances is it justified to use force against a state in the name of humanitarian intervention to protect human rights abuses, even if that state has not launched an attack against another state? Or, what norms should apply in employing force against nonstate actors such as insurgents or terrorists with different values, who might deliberately prey on innocent civilians?

Despite the difficulties, however, these norms have an impact on force and statecraft by creating ever-tighter limits on what is regarded as legitimate justifications for the use of armed force. They now are regularly taught at most military and naval academies, including West Point and Annapolis. They establish the criteria for any implementation of the "Responsibility to Protect" when involving military intervention. Of particular significance, they have been highly influential in establishing many legal limitations such as the U.S. Uniform Code of Military Justice, the embedding of judge advocates within military command structures, formal international "laws of war" and "rules of engagement," and the expansion in the number and scope of international courts and tribunals to enforce restraints on the use of violence. One thinks of the Geneva Conventions, signed by almost every nation in the world, accepting responsibility for the humane treatment of prisoners of war, the protection of civilians, and the care of the sick and the wounded, and explicitly doing so in the name of "the laws of humanity and the dictates of the public conscience." As Justice Sandra Day O'Connor memorably wrote in *Hamdi v. Rumsfeld*, "a state of war is not a blank check for the President."

Moreover, the extent to which these norms and ethical restraints have been widely accepted and internalized is evident by the sense of moral outrage elicited when it is perceived that flagrant violations occur. That is, certain acts—regardless of the justice of the cause, the interests of the state, the claims of military exigency, or the confusion of battle—are regarded as atrocities. One can see this by the widespread public condemnation resulting from the My Lai massacre in Vietnam, Saddam Hussein's use of chemical weapons against the Kurds, "ethnic cleansing" in Bosnia and Croatia under orders from Slobodan Milosevic, and terrorist attacks whose victims indiscriminately (and sometimes deliberately) include women and children in order to increase the extent of fear. It is also evident by the nearly universal condemnation of preventive war, the extraordinary rendition of "enemy combatants" to clandestine "black sites" for interrogation outside the rule of law, the documented and graphically photographed abuse and torture by Americans of detainees at the naval base of Guantanamo Bay in Cuba and at Abu Ghraib prison in Iraq, the actions of rogue soldiers in Afghanistan deliberately killing civilian families and desecrating bodies, and the bloody assaults by Muammar Gaddafi in Libya in 2011 and Bashar al-Assad in Syria between 2011 and 2013 against their own people.

These ethical norms and their broader sense of limits and responsibilities on occasion become so powerful that they influence the consciences of military personnel to the extent that they refuse to obey direct orders from their state. German Field Marshal Erwin Rommel, for example, chose to burn rather than follow Hitler's written command that all Allied soldiers found behind German lines immediately be killed. More recently, one thinks of the more than 600 Israeli soldiers who have joined the "Courage to Refuse" movement, along with a number of elite commandos and fighter pilots, who have refused to participate in missions in populated areas of the West Bank and Gaza. "In the past we fought for a just cause," they declared in a written statement, "[but today] we have reached the boundary of oppressing other people." Moreover, they argue, attacks in these occupied territories must be regarded as "illegal and immoral" because they inflict death upon innocent civilians.

It is exactly these kinds of ethical judgments and normative values that have motivated so many statesmen and citizens in recent years to work toward the development of international criminal law. They have believed that the lessons of history are sufficiently convincing when it comes to atrocities perpetrated by unscrupulous leaders who are allowed to hide in a culture of impunity behind the shield of national sovereignty. For this reason they have argued that peace and security can best be maintained by establishing a rule of law that holds those who violate widely accepted ethical restraints personally responsible for their actions. Decisions rendered at the International Military Tribunal at Nuremberg and again at the International Military Tribunal for the Far East in Tokyo following the Second World War set important legal precedents in this regard by declaring that "just following orders" would no longer serve as a sufficient or legitimate defense for ethically reprehensible actions that violated what the prosecution described as "the moral sense of mankind." The UN Security Council explicitly cited these principles when it established criminal tribunals for the former Yugoslavia in 1993 and then for Rwanda in 1994. As these norms became even more widely accepted, a larger and larger number of states and their leaders began to work seriously toward creating a permanent international tribunal. This explains the major motivation for those representatives of more than 150 nations who worked in partnership to negotiate the treaty creating the first permanent and independent International Criminal Court (ICC) to try those accused of gross violations of these normative standards in cases of war crimes, crimes against humanity, and genocide. These particular atrocities, they revealingly stated in the preamble to the text, "deeply shock the conscience of mankind."

This search for limits and prohibitions against crossing unacceptable thresholds emerges with particular starkness with the element of technology that forms such an important component of what we have called the diplomatic revolution. One of the reasons that modern weapons of mass destruction generate so much debate about ethical issues is the fact that they have lost their traditional capacity to remain limited instruments of policy by other means. Their horrifying capabilities starkly violate the restraints of protecting innocents and proportionality. Nuclear, biological, and chemical weapons simply cannot be controlled, cannot discriminate between combatants and noncombatants, and cannot maintain any rational relationship between massive annihilation and limited political objectives. Thus, concludes scholar Michael Walzer in his influential book *Just and Unjust Wars*: "Nuclear weapons explode the theory of just war. They are the first of mankind's technological innovations that are simply not encompassable within the familiar moral world." It is for this reason that there are individuals today who diligently work to go beyond the familiar and establish new norms for precisely these kinds of weapons.

The existence of the many ethical restraints that we have discussed, as well as those currently being developed, of course, most certainly provides no guarantee that they will be consistently honored or that decision makers will give them conscientious attention and adequate weight when determining their foreign policies and military actions. Historical experience indicates that fierce rivalries and violence are never easy to restrain, and international relations do not always lend themselves to simple moral verdicts. Adversaries exist, agreements can be violated, self-imposed restraints can be exploited, and some leaders have a very poorly developed sense of conscience or moral responsibility. Wars continue to be fought, ethical quandaries among competing values persist, complexities and ambiguities remain, and perhaps more questions of ethics are raised than are answered.

Nevertheless, the very fact that such standards have been created—and continue to be developed—in the face of these enormous challenges bears remarkable testimony to the long-standing and enduring human desire to find limits and to appreciate their value in restraining destructive competition and brutal violence. There are times, as we have seen, when they possess a power of their own and provide genuine restraints on the conduct of foreign affairs and war, as analyzed most recently by cognitive psychologist Steven Pinker in *The Better Angels of Our Nature: Why Violence Has Declined* and political scientist Joshua Goldstein in *Winning the War on War: The Decline of Armed Conflict Worldwide*. Yet, even when they do not, their very existence provides valuable reminders of how leaders should act and what kind of an international order might be created. They remind us of the legitimacy and of the necessity of asking serious questions about ends, means, and consequences of policy in the world and give us a basis of judgment that can serve as a safeguard against the tendency to engage in convenient rationalizations, narrow definitions of interests and security, hypocrisy, or moral self-deception. In this regard, and as we shall see in the Conclusion that follows, there are reasons to believe that ethical restraints on force and statecraft—particularly in an age of weapons of mass destruction and terrorism—may become even more important in the future than they ever have been in the past.

Suggestions for Further Exploration

The fascinating, but challenging, matter of ethics in statecraft is discussed in Gordon Graham, *Ethics and International Relations* (Oxford, 2008 ed.); Mark Amstutz, *International Ethics* (Lanham, MA, 2008 ed.); Cathal Nolan (ed.), *Ethics and Statecraft* (Westport, CT, 2004 ed.); Douglas Johnston (ed.), *Faith-Based Diplomacy: Trumping Realpolitik* (New York, 2003); the special issue of *Orbis*, 42 (Spring 1998) on "Faith and Statecraft"; Douglas Johnston and Cynthia Simpson (eds.), *Religion: The Missing Dimension of Statecraft* (New York, 1994); Robert W. McElroy, *Morality and American Foreign Policy* (Princeton, 1992); National Conference of Catholic Bishops, *The Challenge of Peace* (Washington, DC, 1983); and Stanley Hoffmann, *Duties Beyond Borders* (Syracuse, NY, 1981). Recent scholarship appears in the journal *Ethics and International Affairs* and on the Carnegie Council on Ethics and International Affairs's Web site at www.cceia.org.

Some earlier studies still remain highly relevant to contemporary problems, including Hans Morgenthau, *Politics Among Nations* (New York, 1978 ed.); Hedley Bull, *The Anarchical Society* (London, 1977); E. H. Carr, *The Twenty Years' Crisis* (New York, 1964 ed.); Arnold Wolfers, "Statesmanship and Moral Choice," in his *Discord and Collaboration* (Baltimore, 1962); Reinhold Niebuhr, *Moral Man and Immoral Society* (New York, 1932); and Niccolò Machiavelli, *The Prince* and *Discourses*, in various editions.

For particular aspects of ethics and statecraft, see the Human Development Reports at www.undp.org; the journal *Human Rights Quarterly*; Paul Gordon Lauren, *The Evolution of International Human Rights* (Philadelphia, 2011 ed.); Lyn Boyd-Judson, *Strategic Moral Diplomacy* (Sterling. VA, 2011); Andrew Hurrell, *On Global Order* (New York, 2008); Ian Clark, *International Legitimacy and World Society* (New York, 2007); Paul Gordon Lauren (ed.), *The China Hands' Legacy: Ethics and Diplomacy* (Boulder, CO, 1987); Paul Gordon Lauren, "Ethics and Intelligence," in Al Maurer et al. (eds.), *Intelligence* (Boulder, CO., 1985); Alexander L. George, "Domestic Constraints on Regime Change in U.S. Foreign Policy," in Ole Holsti (ed.), *Change in the International System* (Boulder, CO, 1980); and Gordon A. Craig, *From Bismarck to Adenauer* (New York, 1965 ed.).

Ethical restraints in war are treated in Steven Lee, *Ethics and War* (Cambridge, 2012); Frits Kalshoven and Liesbeth Zegveld, *Constraints on the Waging of War* (Cambridge, 2011 ed.); David Perry, *Partly Cloudy: Ethics in War, Espionage, Covert Action, and Interrogation* (Lanham, MD, 2009); Mary Ellen O'Connell, *International Law and the Use of Force* (New York, 2008 ed.); Ivo Daalder and Robert Kagan, "America and the Use of Force: Sources of Legitimacy," Stanley Foundation Paper (Muscatine, IA, 2007); Michael Walzer, *Just and Unjust Wars* (New York, 2006 ed.); Brian Orend, *The Morality of War* (New York, 2006); Larry May, Eric Rovie, and Steve Viner, *The Morality of War* (Upper Saddle River, NJ, 2006); Arthur Holmes (ed.), *War and Christian Ethics* (Grand Rapids, MI, 2005 ed.); the thought-provoking Jean Bethke Elshtain, *Just War Against Terror*

(New York, 2004); Paul Christopher, *The Ethics of War and Peace* (Upper Saddle River, NJ, 2004 ed.); Paul Gordon Lauren, "From Impunity to Accountability," in Ramesh Thakur and Peter Malcontent (eds.), *From Sovereign Impunity to International Accountability* (Tokyo, 2004); Ward Thomas, *The Ethics of Destruction: Norms and Force in International Relations* (Ithaca, NY, 2001); Terry Nardin (ed.), *The Ethics of War and Peace* (Princeton, 1998 ed.); Joseph S. Nye, Jr., *Nuclear Ethics* (New York, 1986); Gordon Zahn, *In Solitary Witness* (New York, 1965); and Kenneth Waltz, *Man, the State and War* (New York, 1954). See also "Laws of War" at the Avalon Project at www.avalon.law.yale.edu; the "Courage to Refuse" movement at www.seruv.org.il; and the American Society for International Law at www.asil.org.

Those exploring historical cases that demonstrate some of the challenges of ethical restraints in force and statecraft will find much in Lieber's Code of Military Conduct (1863), efforts to create the International Committee of the Red Cross and humanitarian law (1864), the Declaration of St. Petersburg (1868), the foreign policies of William Gladstone (1868–1894), Woodrow Wilson (1913–1921), Jimmy Carter (1977–1981), and Nelson Mandela (1994–1999); the diplomacy of U Thant as UN Secretary-General (1961–1971), and the negotiations surrounding the creation of the International Criminal Court (1994–1998). Some of the ethical dilemmas of humanitarian intervention can be seen in the United Nations–sanctioned military action in Somalia (1992–1995) and the NATO campaigns against Serbia on behalf of Kosovo (1999) and against Libya (2011). Those interested in rival moral claims will find intense arguments surrounding America's decisions to drop nuclear bombs on Hiroshima and Nagasaki (1945), to engage in the Vietnam War (1961–1973), how to pursue the "global war on terror" after 2001, and whether to go to war in Iraq in 2003 and then how to wage it.

Conclusion

Reflections on Force and Statecraft
and the Challenges of Our Time

Those responsible for the momentous decisions of statecraft, as discussed throughout this book, have struggled from the very beginning with finding ways to survive. In a world where war and violence are always possible or present, they have learned that peace and security are always at great risk and that the challenges facing them can be agonizingly difficult. There are times when efforts to deal with international conflicts and competition by peaceful means of rational persuasion succeed—and times when they do not. Sometimes armed force appears to be the only language that certain leaders seem to understand. In these circumstances, force becomes a necessary instrument of policy. But even then, there are times when threats or uses of violence have not only been ineffective but actually counterproductive by seriously aggravating rivalries and even triggering wars that might otherwise have been avoided.

The challenges of these dilemmas are visually portrayed with remarkable insight in the allegorical statue *Diplomacy*. It is well to look again at this perceptive visual image, appearing on the cover of this book, and now to consider its meaning more fully. The figure possesses an obvious depth of dignity and strength. Her facial expression and body posture reveal that she is somber and deep in thought. She seems to have an unusual understanding of the magnitude and the weight of the decisions she must make. Her right arm is uncovered and in her hand she holds an olive branch of peace, poised over treatises of thought and human reason, documents of law, treaties signed in partnership with others, and books on ethical precepts. At exactly the same time, her left arm is draped with her garment and her hand is clasped around the hilt of a sword, to be threatened or used should armed force become necessary. She appears to appreciate not only the fact that each of these instruments possesses *power*—but that each possesses *limitations* as well. As she weighs the appropriate balance between these instruments within the larger international balance between partnership and rivalry in the circumstances, she also seems to know that she will be scrutinized for whatever decision she reaches. To make it all the more poignant, she appears to be pregnant, and thus acutely aware that her choices on force and statecraft will have consequences not only for the immediate well-being of others, but for future generations as well.

The perceptiveness of this image, of course, comes from the fact that it portrays real life. Her challenges are ours. Throughout history, policy makers caught between necessity and danger have found themselves compelled to make decisions about that olive branch and that sword. Most came to the conclusion that the decision was not a simplistic choice between one or the other, but rather a much more complicated one of how these elements could be combined and used together in appropriate measure. Toward this end, they experimented over time in partnership in creating a wide variety of diplomatic means and international systems to keep their rivalries within certain bounds and to devise ways of restraining and controlling armed force. Their experiences, their successes, and their failures not only provide ways to understand the past, but instructive lessons as to what we might expect in the diplomatic challenges of force and statecraft that confront us in our time and in the future.

Leaders throughout history, for example, have been forced to learn—sometimes through painful personal experience—that diplomacy is indeed the art of the possible. What is possible is dependent on the particular conditions of the time, or historical context. That is, the skills and personalities of individuals, the relative power and interests of other states, the structure of the international system, the level of technology, attitudes toward partnership and rivalry, and prevailing ethical norms, among other factors at any given point in time, play absolutely critical roles in determining what can and cannot be done. This is one of the reasons why it is so important for those interested in and/or responsible for foreign affairs to carefully study history in such a way as to learn about continuities and changes and to develop the ability to analyze the role of people, process, possibilities, perspective, and proportion. There are valuable lessons to be gained thereby—some of which may be remarkably applicable to a situation or case that arises, and some of which may not, depending on the context.

This context-dependent feature of the lessons of history also applies to theories or conceptual models of statecraft. Theoretical principles generally are developed in order to explain and understand those behavioral characteristics demonstrating patterns, or continuities, that appear to be valid across cases. The delineation of these principles for such important subjects as negotiation, deterrence, coercive diplomacy, crisis management, and ethical restraints thus provides extremely useful tools of analysis and diagnosis. In fact, at times these may offer considerable assistance, insights, and policy-relevant guidance to decision makers. On other occasions, the usefulness of these principles may be less so. They cannot simply be taken off a shelf and superimposed upon each and every circumstance and somehow assumed to be policy. As we saw in our discussions of structured, focused comparisons, each case study possesses both similarities to and differences from the others. The task is to develop the skills necessary to make discerning judgments about continuity and change and to appreciate that the degree of relevance for theory in any given case is again dependent on context.

In this regard, there is no broad or sweeping context more critical to the challenges of our time than the diplomatic revolution. As we explored in some detail, at the very end of the nineteenth and the beginning of the twentieth centuries, certain forces began to transform features of the classical system of diplomacy. Through time, these became even more pronounced, creating some changes that made statecraft easier and others that made it infinitely more complicated. These dynamics continue to this day and, for this reason, will greatly shape the challenges ahead.

One of these changes appears with the number and nature of actors within the international system. At one time, only five states, known as the Great Powers of Europe, roughly equal in strength and arranged in a balance of power, made and enforced the decisions for all the rest. As a result of the upheaval of two world wars, the whole process of decolonization, and the breakup of the Soviet Union, that number increased tremendously. Today, there are nearly 200 nation-states, each with its own interests and perspectives, each claiming the prerogatives of national sovereignty, and each demanding to participate in global affairs. These are not at all equal and vary greatly in size, strength, and influence, ranging from the smallest of countries to the world's only superpower, the United States, with no peer competitors.

But the number of nation-states alone does not tell the whole story. During the seventeenth and eighteenth centuries there were no structural mechanisms designed to manage diplomatic relations, and during the nineteenth century the Concert of Europe existed with a mere five members. But today nation-states belong to a vast array of intergovernmental organizations, alliances, and associations that also play roles as actors in their own right in international relations. Every state, for example, is a member of the United Nations and its specialized agencies. Most hold membership in the World Trade Organization and are parties to the monitoring bodies created by human rights treaties. Many participate in elaborate alliance systems, stretching from the North Atlantic to Latin America and Southeast Asia. A total of fifty-six are members of the Organization for Security and Cooperation in Europe, the largest security-centered association in the world. Some participate in regional groups like the European Union, the Organization of American States, the Arab League, the Shanghai Cooperation Organization, the African Union, or partnerships like the G-8 and G-20. The collective interests of the members and participants of these various organizations and groupings enable them to leverage their power in partnership, with the result that the whole often becomes greater than the mere sum of its parts.

At the same time, challenges continue to be presented by the expansion in the number of nonstate actors. Ever since the Treaty of Westphalia in 1648, the only actors recognized within the international arena were nation-states. They alone possessed sufficient power to threaten the security of the others. This is no longer the case. Indeed, there are many actors today that are not states at all, but who actually disdain them, are capable of challenging claims of absolute national sovereignty, and have the ability to create an enormous impact on global affairs. There are transnational corporations and international crime syndicates, for example, that possess far greater financial resources than many national governments and are able to make their power felt in economics and in politics. Virtually thousands of nongovernmental organizations (NGOs) with worldwide objectives continue to expand in numbers, size, and influence, particularly in the areas of international human rights and environmental protection. Added to these are a growing number of largely unregulated privatized military firms (PMFs) that provide training, logistics, intelligence, and even combat support in war zones under contract to the highest bidder. Moreover, there are the particularly dangerous, transnational nonstate actors of terrorist networks like al-Qaeda and its affiliates, which, although possessing relatively minor material capabilities, can cause great damage, inflict pain, sow fear, and thereby seriously challenge even the most powerful of nation-states.

The impact of nonstate actors on international relations is also a reflection of yet another feature of the diplomatic revolution: the growing role of domestic political pressures and public opinion. Diplomacy in the time of the classical system was regarded as the exclusive domain of government officials and professional diplomats. According to their defenders, they acted in privacy and with discretion for flexibility that would advance their national interest. According to their critics, they acted in secrecy to promote their own self-interests or hide decisions that might lead their countries into armed conflict. The tension between these two positions reached an explosion point during the First World War with popular cries for "democratic control" and a more open "New Diplomacy." It continues with even greater force in our own day, especially with the expansion of well-organized pressure groups, transnational civil society, and democratic governments, as well as the technological means of influence available to them. This certainly challenges those responsible for statecraft to be ever mindful of opinion and explains why so much attention is now devoted to what is called "eDiplomacy," "cultural diplomacy," and "public diplomacy." Its impact is felt in the use of armed force as well, for as General Wesley Clark writes about the Kosovo campaign in *Waging Modern War*:

> The weight of public opinion was doing to us what the Serb air defense system had failed to do: limit our strikes. The impact of this hasn't been lost on military or political leaders. . . . [F]or sustained operations, public support will be essential. This, in turn, can only be gained by accepting the restraints of public opinion and sensibilities on future operations.

Other challenges are presented by changes in the geographical extent and scope of international relations itself. The focus of attention throughout the classical system of diplomacy was on the continent of Europe, and statesmen could enjoy the relative simplicity of a small number of culturally homogeneous actors. But powerful historical forces transformed this Eurocentric system into something different, bringing North America, Asia, the Middle East, Latin America, and Africa increasingly into global affairs and into a complex and heterogeneous system of truly global scale. One of the challenges of our time, therefore, is the necessity of developing an understanding of the resulting diversity of cultures, political and social systems, and perspectives in the world today.

This process of expansion and extension has been accompanied by growing interaction and integration, or by what is described as "complex interdependence" and "globalization." The world is becoming increasingly interconnected, and what affects the people of one state affects those of another, over many issues and at a variety of levels. Virtually no country can remain uninvolved or untouched and, in this age of mutual vulnerability and the "indivisibility of security," any search for the security of one's own country alone is a strategy that will fail. The results bring not only benefits, but also serious challenges—to the human security of individual people, the security of nation-states, and the security of the international system as a whole.

Indeed, this is precisely the reason why leaders gathered together for the much-anticipated 2005 World Summit convened at United Nations headquarters. They understood that a diverse and broad array of threats confronts us in our interdependent, contemporary world: interstate wars between countries, intrastate or civil wars within countries, the proliferation of weapons of mass destruction, terrorist networks, global financial meltdown, a single superpower pursuing unilateral policies, failed or collapsed states, cyber attacks, human rights abuses, arms sales, transnational organized crime, poverty and starvation, population growth and migration, HIV/AIDS and other deadly infectious diseases, resource depletion and climate change, and environmental degradation, among other dangers. "Depending upon wealth, geography, and power," observed Kofi Annan,

> we perceive different threats as the most pressing. But the truth is that we cannot afford to choose. Collective security today depends on accepting that the threats which each region of the world perceives as most urgent are in fact equally so for all. In our globalized world, the threats we face are interconnected. . . . [and] whatever threatens one threatens all.

Secretary-General Ban Ki Moon emphasized the same point more recently when he announced, "No country and no region, no matter how powerful, will be able to address these threats alone."

In order to find collective ways to address these challenges, with their potential for catastrophic consequences, it will be necessary first to understand their nature. Of essential importance in this regard—especially in a book with the title of *Force and Statecraft*—is to recognize that some of these threats clearly involve war and military might, and others do not. The international security agenda is increasingly being broadened and extended and defined in multiple ways. Moreover, power itself is composed of and measured by many different elements. There can be no question about the fact that the "hard power" of armed force is one of these. Economic strength, industrial capacity, control of strategic positions, natural resources, size of territory and population, and technological sophistication are others. But the ability to influence behavior in order to achieve desired outcomes is not confined exclusively to measured material capabilities. It also can be found in the "soft power" that attracts in partnership rather than coerces or imposes in rivalry. These elements include political ideas and institutions, civic action, development assistance, culture, knowledge, and quality of education, commitment to justice and the rule of law, sense of responsibility, prestige and reputation within the international community, conformity to the standards of legitimacy, and the "moral force" of normative beliefs and ethical values. Given this wide range, some of the ever widening and global problems ahead simply do not lend themselves to the utility of crude armed force as the sole or even primary instrument of policy at all. Stated more directly, not all of the diplomatic challenges of our time are military problems. Not all solutions, therefore, will be military solutions. As one leading, four-star, American general recently reflected on the difficulty of the most powerful military force the world has ever seen to achieve its goals by armed combat alone, "We will never realize our objectives unless we wisely utilize our 'soft power' as well."

These challenges certainly will continue to be impacted by technology. So many of the changes in the diplomatic revolution, as we have seen, are the result of modern technological transformations that decrease distances, shorten time, and expand opportunities for international communication and interaction. Advances in transportation alone enable a person from one part of the world unprecedented mobility and speed (some traveling faster than the speed of sound) to reach almost any other location within hours. They also enable political leaders to meet face-to-face with their counterparts or to completely bypass resident ambassadors and professional diplomats if they so desire. At the same time, highly sophisticated satellites in orbit around the planet, unmanned reconnaissance drones, hyper spectral sensors, computers and the World Wide Web, fiber optics, nanosensors, wireless environments, smartphones, cameras, social networking sites such as Facebook and Twitter, and file exchange and video sharing sites such as YouTube have created not only a "digital revolution" but an "information revolution" as well. The resulting capacity to collect, analyze, and share information, images, and sounds around the world transcends national borders, severely challenges claims of national sovereignty, and gives a voice to the voiceless. In the area of human rights alone, for example, it enables policy makers, treaty-monitoring bodies, and activist NGOs to expose flagrant abusers in the act: to know almost immediately when a terrified female student in India is gang raped on a bus, when a dissident in China is jailed for speaking out on behalf of freedom of conscience, when and where government forces in Sudan seek to hide hundreds of victims in mass graves, or when armed troops in any country launch attacks against innocent civilians.

The impact of technology is particularly evident when one examines the wide-ranging revolution in military affairs (RMA). It is the tiny microchip that makes possible today's sophisticated C^{5}ISR of command, control, communications, computers, combat systems, intelligence, surveillance, and reconnaissance. The ability to gather and process information and to use geospatial technology to identify precise locations and very specific targets, increase situational awareness (SA), and conduct operations with what is called "network-centric warfare" (NCW) that connects all assets on a given battlefield has never been greater in all of history. As one U.S. Air Force general recently boasted, with reference to the capabilities of a new generation surveillance drone capable of transmitting live images to soldiers on the ground or to analysts tracking movements thousands of miles away: "We can see everything."

While these technological developments present both opportunities and challenges, the most serious for force and statecraft are nowhere more evident than in modern weapons themselves. During the classical system of diplomacy, the capabilities of the tools of warfare were extremely limited. Statesmen viewed war as controllable and, therefore, usable. It was serious enough that leaders might try to prevent it, but mild enough to enable them to invoke the threat or resort to force when necessary. This is why they considered force to be a legitimate and useful instrument of foreign policy—or, in the words of Clausewitz, "policy by other means."

But it is no longer as simple as this. At Waterloo in 1815 an infantryman could fire two or three times a minute, looking into the eyes of an enemy standing only a few yards away. It is estimated that in Napoleon's time it took a ton of lead to inflict a single casualty. At the Somme in 1916 the machine gun fired six hundred rounds a minute. The "Battle of the Drawing Boards" during the Second World War and then the closer melding of scientific discovery with weaponry during the Cold War accelerated this process even further. The capabilities of today's weapons from the RMA on the ground, at sea, in the air, and from space against adversaries continents away are almost unbelievable. One analyst writes about the transformation in these words:

> Ever since soldiers have been shooting at each other, from slingshots to howitzers, most shots have missed. In the next war, most shots—at least those against important targets—will hit. . . . Anything that moves, fires, is made of iron, emits light, sound, heat, or electronic radiation, uses electricity, or can be accurately plotted on a map, can be "seen" and then hit by sensors and weapons to which darkness means nothing.

In some ways, technological advances actually are making armed force more usable. Precision-guided munitions (PGMs), Stealth aircraft whose profiles and materials render them virtually invisible to radar, the Global Positioning System (GPS), satellite links, and unmanned aerial vehicles (UAVs) or drones, for example, make it possible for weapons operated by remote control from thousands of miles away and relying on gigabytes of information to hit very specific targets with unprecedented accuracy. One result of this development is the possibility of significant reduction in the amount of collateral damage and loss of life by combatants and by innocent civilians trapped in war zones. Despite the obvious and tremendous advantage in sparing lives, however, there is growing concern that such new precision weapons—and the ability to deliver them electronically with minimal risks and near immunity—may appear to lower the costs of war and lead to an exaggerated overconfidence in high-tech armed force. In this way, the military option may become more tempting for policy makers to select—blinding them to the need for caution and use of armed force only as a "last resort," the possibilities of diplomacy and persuasion, the vulnerability to debilitating cyber-attacks, or the dangers of overextension in asymmetrical wars against ill-equipped but nevertheless determined terrorists or insurgents fighting in unconventional ways.

Even more challenging is the fact that certain kinds of weapons technology fulfill the ultimate irony and tragedy of the "the fate of Nemesis" in which man was punished by fulfilling his wishes too completely. If there are dangers in having *too little* power, there also are dangers in having *too much*. Weapons exist today whose destructive capabilities cannot be controlled, cannot be confined in time or space, and cannot even distinguish between friend or foe. As such, they bear little or no proportion to rational objectives. This feature, by its very nature, alters important dimensions in the calculus of the relationship between ends and means in statecraft.

Armed force remains, as it has been throughout history, an absolutely necessary instrument of policy in particular situations against certain kinds of adversaries, especially when other efforts prove to be inadequate or unsuccessful. It can be threatened and used by individual nation-states, by coalitions and alliances, or by the international community acting with United Nations authorization for a variety of purposes. It can increase credibility in defensive deterrence and coercive diplomacy designed to protect peace and security or enhance negotiation and crisis management. It can be used to defend vital interests, to protect allies and others under attack from aggressors, to provide collective security in such a way as to maintain the international system, to support normative values and enforce international law, to save lives by shielding innocents from genocide and other egregious human rights abuses, to police cease-fire agreements in peacekeeping missions, to furnish particular means for practical peacemaking and for preventive diplomacy, and to enforce international norms and rules.

But armed force, as extensive historical experience demonstrates, is best used to check certain kinds of threats rather than to solve fundamental problems, and it entails some of the most serious challenges in all of statecraft. It is a blunt, costly, and dangerous instrument of policy containing an inherent tension between the logic of war as a political act for limited objectives and the "logic of the instrument" of war itself, which stresses the use of ample force to destroy or render impotent an enemy's forces. The very existence of military force threatens others, creates great uncertainties, and increases the risks of escalation in any crisis. It can be treacherously seductive for those leaders who mistakenly believe that military might alone will enable them to act as they wish and get what they want in the world and, therefore, that they somehow can substitute force for diplomacy. Armed force cannot always be controlled, can endanger delicate negotiations or crisis management, and can threaten the existence of the international system when used offensively to coerce and intimidate opponents, to inflict pain, to launch wars of aggression, to conquer or exterminate, to overthrow legitimate governments, or to engage in terrorist acts against innocent civilians. For all of these reasons, military force often can be inappropriate, ineffective, and even dangerously counterproductive.

This explains why so many of those who have practiced statecraft in the past have reached the conclusion that armed force must be seen as *one* among *several* instruments of policy. The hands of the statue *Diplomacy* simultaneously hold multifaceted tools for a reason. The major challenge—as it always has been—is to avoid the idea that there is a simplistic, dichotomous choice between either "hard power" or "soft power" and instead to exercise "smart power" by intelligently and prudently knowing how to use all of the available assets and resources, how to harness and coordinate them in combination, how to appreciate their strengths and limitations, how to mobilize them as means to fit feasible objectives, and how to keep them in appropriate proportion as particular circumstances require. It is when there is an overreliance on only a single instrument and the balance gets out of proportion that thoughtful policy makers become deeply worried. This is what lies behind President (and former general) Dwight Eisenhower's admonishment about a "military-industrial complex" capable of distorting the requirements of policy and the warnings of others that the entire United Nations budget is but a minuscule fraction of the world's military expenditures. More recently, Secretary of Defense Robert Gates (and former CIA director) publicly declared that America's military costs are untenable and decried the Pentagon's "culture of endless money." To see these expenses in perspective, he joined with former Secretary of State Condoleezza Rice in pointing out that the United States strikingly spends more money for musicians in its military marching bands than it does for diplomats in its foreign service.

Policy makers can expect to be confronted with these challenges and the difficult choices that they entail in the future as they have in the past, but with the full knowledge that the dangers become even more acute when some of those instruments include weapons of mass destruction. Technology and scientific discovery have vastly increased the capacity to kill millions of people with relative ease and terrifying efficiency. Indeed, we now possess the capacity to destroy life as we know it from the face of the Earth. This fact raises profound questions about the proportionality of ends and means and whether any conceivable political objective can possibly justify their use. To make matters worse, even weak and economically collapsed states and nonstate actors like terrorists can acquire chemical and biological weapons. More resources are required to procure nuclear capabilities, yet they are still within reach of even impoverished and starving countries like North Korea. Moreover, not all of these weapons require sophisticated missiles for delivery. Some may be easily concealed and taken to targets with deadly accuracy by airplanes, cars, boats, or backpacks, thereby penetrating the defenses of even the strongest of states. The perils posed by these weapons of mass destruction, including their accidental or unauthorized use, of course, are not limited to their use by terrorists or rogue states—but by all who possess them.

Some measure of the magnitude of these dangers can be seen in the fear that they generate even among those who actually stockpiled and prepared to use them. Intensely fearful that the world is currently hanging on a precipitous "tipping point" of possible disaster, to illustrate, former Secretary of State

George Shultz, former Secretary of Defense William Perry, former Secretary of State and National Security Advisor Henry Kissinger, former Senator Sam Nunn (who chaired the Senate Armed Services Committee), former Secretary of State and Chairman of the Joint Chiefs of Staff Colin Powell, all of whom describe themselves as conservative realists, and over two-thirds of all living former secretaries of state and defense and national security advisors are heavily involved in a nonpartisan campaign known as the Nuclear Security Project. Its purpose is to galvanize support for and action on practical and urgent steps designed to create a world completely free of nuclear weapons. In 2012, more than forty former European leaders, including those who held positions as prime ministers, foreign ministers, defense ministers, generals, and admirals, signed a formal and highly public statement calling upon the participants of the NATO Chicago Summit to change course by "creating the conditions for a world without nuclear weapons." In doing so, these men and women with vast personal experience in force and statecraft have come to appreciate the insight of commentator Jonathan Schell in his thought-provoking book, *The Fate of the Earth*:

> As scientists and technicians we live in the nuclear world, in which whether we choose to acknowledge the fact or not, we possess the instruments of violence that make it possible for us to extinguish ourselves as a species. But as citizens and statesmen we go on living in a pre-nuclear world, as though extinction were not possible and sovereign nations could still employ the instruments of violence as instruments of policy. . . . In effect, we try to make do with a Newtonian politics in an Einsteinian world. The combination is the source of our immediate peril.

This statement is not just an observation about existing weapons capabilities and the potential for cataclysmic war; it is a vital reminder of the critical importance of attitudes and values.

There is much to consider here. Technologies are tools, and the ways in which they are used and the purposes for which they are employed are determined by people. As technology steadily minimizes many physical barriers and practical constraints, it thereby makes those limits that we are willing to place on ourselves all the more essential. As a consequence, we need to give the challenge of accepting self-imposed restraints particularly careful consideration.

The relative simplicity and manageability of the classical system of diplomacy at times seem far removed from the complexities of our own day. Some of its elements, of course, are gone forever: five European powers alone making decisions for everyone else, sovereign nation-states as the only actors in foreign affairs, minimal influence of domestic opinion or economic interests, and limited technological capabilities for communication, transportation, and armed force. But it is worthwhile to remember that one of the most critical features that enabled the classical system to be successful did not reside in things, but in ideas and values. That is, statesmen of that time realized that no nation, however powerful, possibly could protect itself by relying on its own resources alone. They understood that their own long-term self-interests would be best served when defined in terms of collective security and the common interests of the system as a whole. They thus came to recognize the necessity of working together to develop shared normative values and to accept certain self-imposed restraints.

Those responsible for force and statecraft during the classical system realized that they had to find some way to avoid complete anarchy by regulating the level of their rivalry before it destroyed them. Competition, they came to understand, could not be allowed to become fatal to the competitors. One conflict after another, the catastrophic revolutionary and Napoleonic wars, and the possibility of still other unregulated military confrontations convinced them of the absolute necessity of reaching agreement on shared values. Painful experience and the lessons of history taught them that no international system can possibly survive unless there is a consensus by all the major participants on fundamental goals and objectives, basic rules of accommodation, and ethical norms of conduct with limits on what is acceptable and unacceptable behavior. For this reason, they agreed to accept certain self-imposed restraints upon themselves. They recognized the legitimacy of the system, their mutual coexistence in a balance of power, the use of limited means in the pursuit of limited ends, the validity of existing treaties, and their shared responsibility to cooperate in the collective defense of these norms and to work as diplomatic partners, rather than only rivals, to maintain the system itself.

The acceptance of such norms and self-imposed restraints by the participants in any international system is, of course, a matter of political will. This will can change through time, depending again on context. One thinks, for example, of the development of system-wide normative values in the wake of the warfare and anarchy of the eighteenth century, the support for the norm of self-determination in the process of decolonization following the Second World War, or the willingness of states to impose restraints or rules upon themselves in order to protect the value of human rights and hold those who abuse them responsible for their actions. It is the presence—or absence—of these shared norm values that tells us much about the successes—or failures—of the classical system, the interwar years, the efforts of the United Nations, the Cold War, and the evolving international system of today. This explains why the 2011 annual meeting of the World Economic Forum focused on the theme of "Shared Norms for the New Reality."

The significance of shared values and self-imposed restraints in statecraft is nowhere more evident than in the threat and use of force. Leaders at the time of the classical system of diplomacy realized that armed force could be regarded as a legitimate instrument of policy as long as limited means were utilized for limited political ends. The technology of the time certainly restrained the capabilities of the means, but values restrained the objectives and determined *jus ad bellum*, or the justice of war, and *jus in bello*, or the justice in war. This is an essential point to bear in mind, especially in today's world, seeking to establish *jus post bellum*, or the justice after war, in such places as Kosovo, Iraq, and Afghanistan, and in an age of weapons of mass destruction possessed by either terrorists or nation-states demonstrably unwilling to abide by established international norms or to accept self-imposed restraints.

It is precisely for these reasons that the organizers of the World Summit—the largest gathering of national leaders ever assembled in history—devoted so much attention to the challenge of trying to build what they called "a new consensus" on norms that could provide restraints for the future. Indeed, the very first agenda item for the conference as a whole was entitled "Values and Principles." Time and time again, the participants stressed that the degree to which they could achieve peace and security would be a function of their ability to find "common ground," to recognize that what binds them together is much more important than what separates them, and to reach agreement on "objective interests" and "shared values" concerning "moral imperatives." In this regard, they came to realize that normative values not only can restraint certain behavior, but also can encourage, empower, and legitimize other kinds of action designed to maintain peace and security. They declared that these features applied to all aspects of statecraft, but particularly and most poignantly to armed force.

Here, they immediately found themselves struggling with the challenge of the wide disparity in attitudes toward normative restraints involving nuclear weapons. Under the terms of the landmark Nuclear Non-Proliferation Treaty, a remarkable 183 nations have agreed to impose upon themselves a total renunciation of these weapons of mass destruction, even as a means of deterrence. Of these, four once possessed such weapons but voluntarily decided to give them up. Together, these nations strongly encourage others to accept similar restraints. Nevertheless, under the same treaty, five nuclear powers (the United States, Britain, France, Russia, and China) promised to "pursue negotiations in good faith" leading to "general and complete disarmament," but none of them has been seriously willing to do so. Israel, India, Pakistan, and North Korea refuse to be bound by the treaty at all, and Iran currently appears to be developing a nuclear industry capable of producing weapons. These problems are compounded by the fact that more than forty countries currently possess the means to make fuel for peaceful nuclear power, and this easily can be modified to make material for nuclear weapons. It is not technology, but political will based on attitudes and values that keeps them from doing so. In sharp contrast, recently discovered attempts to smuggle highly enriched uranium across international borders indicate that terrorists actively are seeking to acquire precisely these kinds of weapons as well.

Those assembled at the World Summit also faced one of the most difficult of all challenges: namely, the urgency of developing normative guidelines for when, under whose authority, and how armed force should be legitimately used in the world today. This centuries-old and persistent problem was raised anew after the end of the Cold War over the issue of using force for humanitarian intervention in Somalia, Bosnia, and Kosovo. But it virtually exploded with the advent of global terrorism and counterterrorism. Terrorists before and after 9/11 argued that they followed their own set of values and thus did not have to observe the normal rules of war. Some of those fighting against them argued exactly the same way. American leaders at the time insisted that in an age of terrorism they no longer needed to follow the United Nations Charter's norms governing the use of force or the criteria of the just war tradition, that the restraints of the Geneva Convention were "quaint" and no longer needed to be honored, that "no rules" applied in this struggle, that they could use torture and assassination, that they were free to launch a preventive war against Iraq if they chose. As President George W. Bush himself said: "I don't care what the international lawyers say, we are going to kick some ass." Almost all other nations, in sharp contrast, argued that whenever any state or nonstate actor refuses to accept established restraints and the rule of law in treaties to which it is a party, claiming that it unilaterally can define if and when force should be used, irrespective of the norms or interests of the system as a whole, others will feel free to make the same claim for themselves and a recipe thereby will be created for international anarchy rather than international order.

When these kinds of difficult issues and sharp differences of opinion arise, it is particularly interesting to note how frequently reference is made, in one way or another, to history and to theory. Speakers at the World Summit frequently referred to the "lessons of history" as well as the "new historical realities." Those at the 2012 NATO Summit did the same, making constant reference to historical experience providing "lessons that must be learned" and the past serving as a guide to the future. They also observed that we live in the context of the dynamics of the diplomatic revolution that has produced a number of dramatic transformations in the world, some of which present serious challenges of a new order of magnitude. At the same time, summit participants also recognized that many of the challenges are not completely new: that continuities still coexist with changes; that human nature stays much the same; that the debate between partnership and rivalry continues; that despite the decline in the number of interstate wars between countries, the central dilemmas surrounding the necessities and the dangers of armed force still remain; that although weakened, states are still the most dominant actors in international affairs; and that diplomacy still seeks to find ways to regulate competition and resolve disputes.

It may be, therefore, that many of the diplomatic challenges of our time are enduring and similar to the diplomatic challenges of previous times. To survive by making discriminating judgments about what has changed and what is new in these vital matters, it is essential to draw on the impact of people, process, possibilities, perspective, and sense of proportion in the past, while at the same time seeking guidance from the principles of negotiation, deterrence, coercive diplomacy, crisis management, and ethical restraints. In so doing, and in an effort to find workable solutions to the challenges for peace and security ahead, there may be much to be gained from the lessons of history and the insights of theory as found in the study of force and statecraft.

SUGGESTIONS FOR FURTHER EXPLORATION

The challenges ahead can be monitored more closely today than at any other time in history. Daily news can be followed on those Web sites with international capabilities, such as the British Broadcasting Corporation at http://news.bbc.co.uk; CNN at www .cnn.com; *Le Monde* at www.lemonde.fr; *New York Times* at www.nytimes.com; *Die Zeit* at www.zeit.de; al-Jazeera at www.aljazeera.com; and the UN Wire Service at www .unwire.org. Thoughtful discussions, analyses, opinion, as well as reviews of newly published books appear in leading journals such as *Diplomacy and Statecraft, Ethics and International Affairs, Foreign Affairs, Foreign Policy, Human Rights Quarterly, International Affairs, International Conciliation, International Organization, International Security, International Studies Quarterly, Internationale Politik, Journal of International Affairs, Orbis, Review of International Studies, Whitehead Journal of Diplomacy and International Relations, World Affairs,* and *World Politics,* among others.

In addition, all major nation-states and regional and international organizations now use technology and the Internet to maintain active Web sites as a means of presenting their positions on contemporary challenges of force and statecraft. Among these, see the African Union at www.africa-union.org; the British Foreign Office at www.fco.gov .uk; the Chinese Foreign Ministry at www.fmprc.gov.cn; the European Union at http:// europa.eu.int; and French Foreign Ministry at www.france.diplomatie.fr; the German Foreign Ministry at www.auswaertigesamt.de; the Japanese Foreign Ministry at www .mofago.jp; NATO at www.nato.int; the Organization of American States at www.oas .org; the Organization for Security and Cooperation in Europe at www.osce.org; the Russian Foreign Ministry at www.mid.ru; the United Nations at www.un.org in several different languages; and those of the United States government, including the Central Intelligence Agency at www.cia.gov, Department of Defense at www.defenselink.mil, Department of Homeland Security at www.dhs.gov, Department of State at www.state .gov, and Office of the Director of National Intelligence at www.odni.gov.

Recent efforts by the international community to prepare for the challenges ahead can be found in the documentation for the 2005 World Summit at www.un.org; Secretary-General Kofi Annan's report, entitled *In Larger Freedom: Towards Development, Security, and Human Rights for All* (New York, 2005); the report from the High-Level Panel on Threats, Challenges, and Change under the title of *A More Secure World: Our Shared Responsibility* (New York, 2004); and the *United Nations Millennium Declaration* (New York, 2000). Other discussions about the future include Philip Taubman, *The Partnership* (New York, 2012) and the related www.nucleartippingpoint.org; Dan Caldwell and Robert Williams, Jr., *Seeking Security in an Insecure World* (Lanham, MD, 2012 ed.); Paul Gordon Lauren, *The Evolution of International Human Rights* (Philadelphia, 2011 ed.); Joseph Nye, Jr., *Soft Power* (Boulder, CO, 2005); Donald Snow, *National Security for a New Era: Globalization and Geopolitics* (New York, 2004); Peter Hough, *Understanding Global Security* (New York, 2004); U.S. National Security Intelligence Council, *Mapping the Global Future* (Washington, DC, 2004); Philip Bobbitt, *The Shield of Achilles* (New York, 2002); Thomas Ricks, "A New Way of War," *Washington Post National Weekly Edition,* December 10–16, 2001; Wesley Clark, *Waging Modern War* (New York, 2001); Martin van Creveld, *Nuclear Proliferation and the Future of Conflict* (New York, 1993); the still thought-provoking Jonathan Schell, *The Fate of the Earth* (New York, 1982); and Robert Heinl, Jr., "A Look at Future Wars," *Christian Science Monitor,* July 31, 1977.

CREDITS

p. 16.   François de Callières, *On the Manner of Negotiating with Princes* (British Library Board)
p. 66.   Photo by IstitutoNazionale Luce/Alinari via Getty Images
p. 93.   Photo by Keystone, MPI/Getty Images
p. 140.   UN Photo
p. 183.   JUNG YEON-JE/AFP/Getty Images
p. 224.   AP Photo/Iranian President's Office
p. 235.   Photo by Cecil Stoughton/Time Life Pictures/Getty Images

INDEX

War, 242–46; inter-war years (1919–1939), 49, 52–54, 56, 58–68, 74, 157, 194–97, 203–204, 215, 233; post-Second World War and Cold War, 74, 81–83, 93–94, 156, 163; in evolving international system, 134, 225, 249, 297, 299; and United Nations, 75, 78, 83–84, 86. *See also the names of individual British leaders*
Great Depression (1930s), 60, 64, 71–72
Great Northern War (1700–1721), 13
Great Powers: characteristics of, 8–11, 20, 38–43; emergence of, xii, 3; in seventeenth century, 7–13, 122; in eighteenth century, 13–21; in nineteenth century, 24–43, 47, 101, 168–70, 180–81, 193–96, 203–204, 207, 233, 239, 253, 260–61, 288, *see also* Balance of power (European); Classical system of diplomacy; in twentieth century, 47, 54, 71, 73–75, 96, 127, 138, 172, 246; and United Nations, 74–77, 80–85, 87–88, 90, 102, 108, 132–33, 136, 139. *See also* Austria; France; Germany; Great Britain; People's Republic of China; Prussia; Russia; Soviet Union; United States
"Great Satan, the," 126, 222, 254, 272
Greece: ancient, xv, 3–4, 98, 148, 188, 211, *see also* Melian dialogue, Thucydides; modern, 29, 35, 48, 82–83, 89, 94, 96, 130, 195, 233
Grenada, 110
Grey, Edward, 243
Gromyko, Andrei, 112
Grotius, Hugo, 10, 149, 270
Group of Eight (G-8), 136, 288
Group of Twenty (G-20), xiii, 125, 136, 140, 288
Guantanamo Bay, Cuba, 136, 282
Guatemala, 110
"Gunboat Diplomacy," 215–19, 226, 228–30. *See also* Naval forces
Gustavus Adolphus IV (king, Sweden), 9

H

Hague Conferences (1899, 1907), 28, 37, 186
Hague Convention (1899), 278
Haiti, 54, 110, 132, 231, 233, 263
Hammarskjöld, Dag, 83–84, 86–87, 89–90, 140
Hampson, Fen Osler, 182
Hapsburg dynasty, 8, 14
Hardenberg, Karl von, 169
Harding, Warren, 271

"Hard power," xii–xiii, 290, 294. *See* Force; Naval forces; Power
Hart, Michael, 182
Havel, Václav, 17
Health, 52, 88, 125, 163, 183, 259, 275
Heatley, D. P., 151
Hedlam-Morley, James, 53
Hegel, G. W. F., 277
Hegemony, 12, 39, 47, 61, 74, 121, 128, 134, 194
Helsinki Final Act (1975). *See* Conference on Security and Cooperation in Europe
Herzegovina, 35, 117, 242
Hierarchy, xviii, 39, 79, 88. *See also* Great Powers; International systems, composition of; Structure; Superpowers
Hinduism, 3, 54, 246–47
Hiroshima and Nagasaki, 81, 99, 285
Historical analogies, 147, 153, 155–58
Historical case studies, xii–xiii, xviii, 155, 157–60, 168–79, 184, 186, 192–202, 204, 206, 209, 213, 215–25, 233, 236, 239–50, 254, 256, 271, 285
Historical context, xii, xviii, 30, 80, 96, 108, 128, 147, 150–53, 157–58, 160, 168, 177, 188, 192, 202, 206–207, 215, 220, 229–31, 238–39, 242, 244, 246, 251, 264, 272, 281, 287–88, 296, 298
Historical experience, xv, xvii, 3, 5, 7, 14, 18, 21, 24, 26, 30, 32, 38, 43, 50, 55, 64–68, 71–73, 77, 90, 94, 98–100, 104, 106–107, 131, 138, 147, 149–51, 153–56, 158, 160, 165, 170, 172, 176, 178, 193–94, 202, 216, 220, 226, 234, 236, 239, 241, 248, 251, 259, 264, 266, 269–70, 277, 283, 287, 293, 295–96, 298. *See also* Historical case studies
History: as a discipline and subject, xii–xiii, xv, 3, 9, 13, 15, 20–21, 24, 30, 36, 42, 49, 53–54, 64, 96, 106, 117, 139, 147–50, 154–59, 203, 216, 234, 240, 243, 260, 269, 277, 287, 298; landmarks and points of comparison, 35, 51, 62, 71, 76, 79–80, 84–85, 87–88, 92, 94, 99, 103, 109–10, 116, 129, 133, 179, 234, 245, 275, 279, 292, 297; lessons of, *see* Lessons of history; scope of, xv–xviii, 3, 33, 42, 88, 90, 98, 100, 113, 127, 131, 148, 157–58, 164, 187, 215, 218, 226, 234–35, 265, 267, 269, 277, 287, 293; use of, 147–60, *see also* Lessons of history
Hitler, Adolf, 58, 60–61, 64–68, 156–57, 194–97, 203–205, 207, 215, 233, 277, 282
HIV/AIDs, 123, 290

Vattel, Emmerich de, 19

Velvet Revolution (1989), 112–13, 174

Venice, Republic of, 5–6, 16

Verona, Conference of (1822), 28

Versailles, Treaty of (1919), 50, 53, 60, 63, 65,
67–68, 206. *See also* Paris Peace
Conference

Vertzberger, Yaacov, 158

Vienna, Congress of (1814–1815), 24–32, 34,
37–38, 46–47, 50, 75–76, 150, 168–71,
179–82, 184, 193, 206–207, 241, 246

Vietnam War, 104–106, 108–109, 150, 152,
156, 184, 191, 199–200, 233, 251, 262,
268, 282, 285

Violence, xv–xviii, 3, 6, 10–11, 13, 15, 19, 24,
64, 72–73, 90, 117–19, 127, 136, 148,
164–65, 202, 212, 250, 259, 268, 276–81,
283, 286, 295. *See also* Use of armed
force; War

Vitoria, Francisco de, 6, 270

Voltaire (François Marie Arouet), 17

W

Waddington, William, 240

Waltz, Kenneth, 189

Walworth, Arthur, 216

Walzer, Michael, 283

War: acts of, 175, 219, 250; as a force for
change, 8, 32, 51–52, 55, 58, 71–73,
76–77, 90, 288, 296; costs of, xvi–xvii, 8,
13, 15, 20, 32, 46–48, 51, 58, 62, 71–72,
92, 129, 149, 191, 279, 292; deliberate,
xvii, 9–10, 12, 33, 43, 58, 65–68, 74, 91,
118, 127–29, 133, 194, 197, 203, 239,
243–46, 268, 279–80, 293, *see also*
Aggression; developments in, xii, 41,
43, 49, 119–20, 252, 289, 291–93, *see also*
Technology, impact on weapons; ethics
in, *see* Ethics, for armed force;
inadvertent, xvi, 103, 191, 220, 234,
236, 238, 240–42, 248, 254, 286; as an
instrument of policy, 13, 41, 188, 283,
295, *see also* Force, as an instrument of
statecraft, "Hard power"; intrastate
(civil) war, 13, 90, 94, 106, 109–10,
118–19, 209; just war, *see* Just war
tradition; limited war, 32, 41, 48, 94,
101, 278, 280–81, 292; methods of
avoiding, xvi, 3–4, 6, 19, 24, 29, 33, 35,
51, 79, 86, 98, 156, 177, 188, 206, 238,
248–49, 254, *see also* Appeasement,
Collective security, Conflict resolution,
Crisis management, Deterrence,
Diplomacy, Negotiation, Pacifism,

Peaceful settlement of disputes,
Peacemaking, Peacekeeping forces,
Preventive diplomacy, Restraints,
System building, System maintenance;
nature of, xv, 20, 30, 51–52, 74, 96,
148–50, 188, 211, 261, 276–77, 279, 293,
see also Violence; "network centric
warfare" (NCW), 291; preemptive war,
110, 128, 133, 202, 215, 235, 238;
prevalence of, xv, xvii, 6–21, 32, 46,
87–88, 117–18, 126–31, 133, 136, 170,
246, 263, 283, 286, 296–97, *see also the
names of specific battles and wars;*
preventive war, 133, 225, 235, 280, 282,
298; proxy wars, 92, 247; rules of, 5, 32,
35, 277, 280–81, 298, *see also* Laws of
war, War crimes; against terrorism, *see*
"Global war on terror"; thermonuclear
war, possibility of, 101–104, 109, 112,
163, 201, 219, 221, 227, 234, 295; "total"
war, 48, 51, 55, 76

War crimes, 124, 132, 280–81, 283. *See also*
International criminal law; Just war
tradition; Laws of war

War plans, 37, 45, 157, 242–43, 245, 252

War Powers Act (1973), 109, 262–63

Warsaw Treaty Organization, 98, 113, 119,
132, 171

Washington Naval Conference (1921–1922),
53, 65, 186

Watergate scandal, 109, 276

Waterloo, Battle of (1815), 21, 170, 192, 292

Watkins, Michael, 168

Weapons, xii, 4, 17, 32, 41, 46, 61, 68, 88, 92,
94, 98–103, 106–107, 109–10, 112, 114,
119–20, 123–24, 126, 129, 132, 175,
177–78, 181, 184–85, 187–88, 190–91,
200, 207, 210, 212, 214, 222, 228, 230,
237, 249, 251–52, 259, 282–83, 292–95;
abolishment of, xvii, 38, 277, 297, *see
also* Pacifism; "cultural weapons,"
95–96; "economic weapons," 59, 61;
"financial weapons," 59; impact of
technology on, *see* Technology, impact
on weapons; limited capabilities, 19,
30, 43, 93, 183, 187, 230, 278, 292;
"propaganda weapons," 96; restraints
on, xvii, 53, 124, 262, 278, 283, *see also*
Arms control, *and the names of specific
treaties*

Weapons of mass destruction (WMD),
xii–xiii, xv, 43, 71, 90, 99, 128, 142,
164, 175, 183, 187–88, 191, 207, 219,
235–36, 253, 261, 278, 281, 283–84, 290,
294, 297. *See also* Biological weapons;
Chemical weapons; Nuclear weapons